GREEK AND ROMAN SCULPTURE

A. W. LAWRENCE

JONATHAN CAPE

THIRTY BEDFORD SQUARE LONDON

FIRST PUBLISHED UNDER THE TITLE *Classical Sculpture* 1929
THIS REVISED EDITION FIRST PUBLISHED 1972
© 1972 BY A. W. LAWRENCE

JONATHAN CAPE LTD
30 BEDFORD SQUARE, LONDON WCI

ISBN 0 224 00709 2

PRINTED AND BOUND IN GREAT BRITAIN
BY W & J MACKAY LIMITED, CHATHAM

CONTENTS

PLATES

FIGURES

PREFACE

THIS book is a long-overdue replacement for my *Classical Sculpture*, which was published in 1929 and never re-issued after the blocks for the illustrations had been melted down to supply metal for wartime purposes; by the time a new edition would have become practicable I was too occupied with other concerns to bring the text up to date, although a comparatively small amount of alteration would then have sufficed. Many more sculptures have since come to light, while there has been a great increase in the output of international scholarship that must be taken into account; furthermore my own opinions changed to some extent in the course of teaching the subject for nearly twenty years at Cambridge (with the aid of the excellent cast collection) and, more recently, of repeated visits to museums in Greece and other countries. Hence approximately half of the present revised text consists of new material, while scarcely a page in the remainder has been left unaltered. Because a personal outlook is essential for presenting a coherent account, I have cited (and combated) only a selection of views that conflict with my own, limiting it to those which seem to me fairly plausible or would, if accepted, involve reconsideration of the general development. I have, incidentally, taken the opportunity to incorporate some data and illustrations from my *Later Greek Sculpture and its Influence on East and West* (1927)—a work of pioneer research, now inevitably obsolete as a whole—to which *Classical Sculpture* referred for supplement.

Classical Sculpture was the first English attempt at a large-scale consecutive history of Greek and Roman sculpture; it has remained the only such attempt, owing to the subsequent accumulation of knowledge. My data had been acquired during research on the linking Hellenistic phase, which derived something from every earlier Greek style and was itself imitated under the Romans; so ill-defined then was the course of development in those preceding and following periods that I gave a disproportionate amount of thought to them, whereas nowadays a student of Hellenistic could obtain such comparative material from authoritative books. Actually, facts and theories relating to the sculpture of a thousand years have now become so numerous that progress depends increasingly on specialization. I could not have ventured on this revision but for most generous aid from Professor R. M. Cook on the archaic period, Dr G. B. Waywell on the fifth and fourth centuries and Professor D. E. Strong on the Roman Republic and Empire; they have saved me from many errors and omissions, but are not responsible for others that will doubtless be perceived, nor do they agree with all the views expressed.

Classical Sculpture synthesized the thinking and knowledge derived from my studies of the subject between 1919 and 1929. At that time a number of elderly scholars could see merit only in the sculptors of about 460–300 B.C., whose work they studied more in Roman copies than in contemporary originals; they had, in fact, almost exhausted the possibilities then available for that line of research. The middle-aged already tended to admire and study originals of 550–460 B.C., while a few had begun to investigate the problems of Hellenistic and Roman sculpture. Subsequent finds have multiplied examples of early sculpture, particularly of 650–550 B.C., and also throw light on the preceding centuries, in which, although no stone or marble carvings were produced, Greek aesthetic ideas took shape. Hence the range of dubiety reflected in *Classical Sculpture* has so narrowed that practically everything said in this present book about works prior to 460 B.C. is newly written. The course of development under the Romans has, to a great extent, been elucidated quite recently, but Hellenistic sculpture retains its former mysteries unsolved; consequently the Hellenistic portion of *Classical Sculpture* has required comparatively little change, whereas approximately half of the Roman matter is different. A few new discoveries (but of exceptional import) and much speculation have entailed alterations concerning the 'classical' periods of the fifth and fourth centuries. The introductory chapters have been re-cast, and pruned of matter that is now superfluous. The bibliographical references are, of course, predominantly to recent publications.

London   A.W.L.
January 1972

ACKNOWLEDGMENTS

In addition to the general guidance I received from Professor R. M. Cook, Dr G. B. Waywell and Professor D. E. Strong, I have been advised on specific points by Mr J. N. Coldstream, Mr Brian F. Cook, Professor H. A. Harris, Mr D. E. L. Haynes and Dr R. A. Higgins.

For help in assembling photographic and other material I am indebted to Professor B. Ashmole, Professor R. M. Cook and the Museum of Classical Archaeology at Cambridge, the Hon. Mrs Henry Hankey, Mr D. E. L. Haynes, Dr R. A. Higgins, Mr F. H. Jenkins and the Institute of Classical Studies of London University, Dr D. Ohly and Dr K. Vierneisel of the Staatliche Antikensammlungen at Munich, Professor Sir Denys L. Page, Professor D. E. Strong, and both Dr and Mrs J. B. Ward-Perkins.

I was granted permission to reproduce photographs taken by Professor Ashmole (Plates 8*b*, 10*a*, 22*b*, 38*b*, 46*d*), Mr M. H. Braüde (62*a*), and Miss Alison Frantz (1*a*, 1*e*, 42); from negatives belonging to the Agora Excavations of the American Academy in Athens (35*a*), the American Academy in Rome (90*b*), the British School at Rome (34*d*, 91*b*), the German Archaeological Institute at Rome (88*a*, 94*c*), the Bildarchiv Foto Marburg (4*d*, 9*a*, 16*b*) and the Oriental Institute of Chicago (27*b*); also from *Antike Denkmäler* (48*d*, 49*b*). By courtesy of the Trustees of the British Museum, all objects in their care are illustrated from official photographs, some of which were taken specially through the kind provision of the Department of Greek and Roman Antiquities. Permission to use official photographs was granted also by the Directors, past or present, of the Berlin Museums, Boston Museum, Art Institute of Chicago, Ny Carlsberg Glyptotek (Copenhagen), Dresden Museum, Fogg Museum of Harvard University, Munich Glyptothek, Metropolitan Museum (New York), University of Pennsylvania Museum (Philadelphia) and Rhode Island School of Design (Providence). Photographs of which the copyrights belong to firms represented in London by the Mansell Collection are by: Alinari—Pls 6*a*, 6*c*, 11*b*, 15*a*, 17*a*, 22*a*, 24*b*, 40*b*, 43*a*, 46*c*, 51*b*, 66*a*, 66*b*, 70*c*, 73*a*, 77*a*, 78*a*, 83*b*, 89*b*, 90*a*; Anderson—24*a*, 25*a*, 28*c*, 37*b*, 56*b*, 57*a*, 59*b*, 60*d*, 61*b*, 63*b*, 64*a*, 65*b*, 69*c*, 73*c*, 75*b*, 82*c*, 93*b*, 96*a*; Brogi—35*d*, 36*c*, 62*c*, 74*a*, 76*a*, 76*c*; Giraudon—1*b*, 11*a*. Of the line illustrations, Fig. 1 is reproduced by courtesy of the Archaeological Institute of America; the others, apart from Fig. 20, are repeated from *Classical Sculpture*, although two (Figs 4 and 16) among those made from drawings by Miss Mary Parker have been slightly altered to take account of subsequent research.

The new matter was typed, and the wording improved in the process, by my wife, Mrs B. I. Lawrence. In the final revision at the publishers the book gained much in detail from the assiduity and good sense of Mr M. J. Petty.

To all those who contributed assistance I offer my sincere thanks.

May 1972   A.W.L.

I

Content and Functions of the Sculpture

THE continuity of Greek and Roman sculpture is in some respects superficial; it was due to the Roman employment of Greek artists, the persistence of certain stock subjects and the adaptation of others to specifically Roman purposes. The religious outlook of the two peoples was basically different, although the gap is concealed by the veneer of Hellenism that all upper-class Romans acquired. Since a very large proportion of sculptures had a religious significance (though it is no longer always conspicuous), the purposes they served in the Greek period and in the Roman will here be discussed separately, in that order.

The divergence between Greek art and any that preceded it was aided, rather than dictated, by the exceptionally anthropomorphic nature of the gods and the vivid personalities they displayed in a mythology that also included a host of lesser supernatural beings and merged with semi-historical legend, equally suitable to artistic exploitation. A more potent cause of the divergence was a unique element in Greek religion, worship by the medium of athletics; such physical activities as the religions of other peoples have demanded were either formalized (dances, for example) or else performed by teams, whereas the Greek athlete exerted the utmost effort in a competition of individuals. The human body as an entity—a young man's for choice—was inevitably accorded unprecedented respect, to which the conviction that 'Man is the measure of all things' gave further impetus. No other subject for sculpture could be so worthy; the early sculptors, however, were able to represent it only as an almost abstract mass composed of lines and planes. Such figures, imitated from those made by the Egyptians, could not satisfy the Greeks, who required the muscular action of the body to be revealed; hence development took a steady course towards naturalism. Female nudes started (if we ignore very early copying of Oriental prototypes) towards the middle of the fifth century, with studies of girls; figures of well developed women were introduced a hundred years later, on the triumph of naturalism.

Another difference from the arts of the Oriental peoples lies in the general absence of magical purpose in work of good quality. The Greeks were the first to add an intellectual motive to the preoccupation with natural phenomena common to all peoples; their interest was not merely religious or superstitious, relating to the consequences to themselves and their control by rites, but also rational, based on curiosity and expressed by unawed study. This rational outlook was, of course, restricted for centuries to a small proportion of the urban population, but the patronage of expensive sculpture obviously lay in the hands of this minority; the officials in charge of state funds must generally have been educated, as were, no doubt, many persons who ordered private memorials or offerings of good quality. The element of magical significance rapidly disappeared from the best sculpture, though it persisted in work of less aesthetic value. Only in the archaic period did an occasional temple bear a relief of a Gorgon's head, which was believed to avert evil, while only one famous sculpture took the primitive form of a herm (a pillar with a head of a god and a phallus); significantly, Alcamenes carved it in a pseudo-archaic style. It was installed at the entrance to the Acropolis within a few years of 415 B.C., when most of the herms that stood outside Athenian temples and houses were mutilated at night, supposedly by educated young men whom the populace assumed to have thereby declared an intention to overthrow democracy. The death-sentence imposed for this act of sacrilege, and the martyrdom of Socrates by the re-founded democracy of 399, testify to the power of orthodox religion in the most civilized of Greek cities but also to the menace that rationalism was already seen to present. In fact, a majority of Greeks everywhere continued to believe in the gods, though with diminishing fervour; devotion lapsed into superstition, but the mythology was still accepted as true centuries after the philosophers and their pupils had recognized it as fiction.

The earliest statues belonged to a category that persisted till the end of paganism; they originated in an age of simple faith, when deities were believed to frequent the temples dedicated to them. Worshippers required a symbol of divine occupancy, even if it were only a post or a lump of stone curiously shaped by nature, but a tree-trunk carved into a semblance of the human form gave a surer indication of the invisible anthropomorphic presence. If the temple were dedicated to more than one deity, each received veneration by proxy through a distinct idol, conventionally termed a cult-image. Any temple might, in the course of time, acquire other statues, diverse in subject, but these had no share in the cult of the divine household.

In very early times all cult-images seem to have been wooden, though they might be sheathed with bronze; in size they ranged from well below to several times human height. Gigantic dimensions continued ever after to be thought an appropriate means of doing honour to a deity, while they were also a source of pride to the local population and must, to some extent, have been chosen for that motive; emulation between city-states never ceased to be expressed in ostentatious showpieces. The adoption of new materials for statues—marble or limestone, and cast instead of sheet bronze —did not impose restrictions on size so long as unvarying simple poses kept every figure safely balanced. But the freedom of pose introduced after 480 B.C. entailed such problems in distributing the weight of stone that the largest figures were usually either cast in bronze or else built on a wooden framework to which was attached wooden drapery (sometimes covered with gold) and a head and arms of stone or ivory. A number of existing marble heads, one and a half times life-size or more, presumably belonged to cult-images with wooden bodies; a few all-marble examples of similar scale are known but the normal height is unlikely to have greatly exceeded two metres.

Cult-images can be distinguished from other statues of deities by their stiffer poses and generally more formal treatment; religious conservatism always laid some restraint on the sculptor, putting him at a disadvantage. Famous artists were employed but under strict control, and might be ordered to reproduce a decayed old image, however uncouth; Onatas of Aegina, about 500 B.C., even replaced the horse-headed Demeter of a sanctuary in the most backward part of Arcadia, though a dream which he claimed to have received from the goddess may have excused some modifications for aesthetic reasons. As late as the second century A.D., a visitor of religious inclination, like Pausanias, felt stronger emotions for the crude wooden objects of the remote past than for magnificent cult-images by later artists. These on the whole inspired admiration rather than reverence. The enormous Athena of gold and ivory in the Parthenon could not attain the religious importance of the much older wooden image, for which a garment was woven every four years. Many cult-images were so draped, and even the best was always loaded with attributes. It seems logical to assume that cult statues acted as a brake upon the trend towards naturalism.

Statues of deities were often dedicated for purposes other than cult, whether by a state, a group of persons or one individual; they might be set in or outside a temple or in some public place. By convention they were generally of superhuman size; since the Greeks were a short people a height of 1.90 m. was adequate for a god and 1.80 m. for a goddess, but a figure of peculiar significance might be given enormous dimensions if it were to stand in the open. (The Athena 'Promachus' on the Acropolis may have been the tallest of Greek statues till it was surpassed by the Colossus of Rhodes; both were war memorials erected out of patriotic pride as well as gratitude to the patron deity who had helped the state to victory.) The motive for each dedication more or less controlled the sculptor's design, but he escaped the restraint to which he would be subjected in the case of a cult-statue. He could represent the deity in a relaxed posture, with few attributes or none, and engaged in all sorts of occupations; eventually he acquired licence to ignore the divine side of the personality. Consequently it is not always possible to distinguish a statue of a deity from one of a demigod or a hero, who might either be a legendary character or have been sanctified after his comparatively recent death; nor was there much occasion to differentiate, because the circumstances of the dedications would be similar. The hazy borderland of the pantheon also permitted personifications. The first to appear in sculpture, Victory, regularly served to commemorate battles; in the fourth century were added many others, such as Peace and Wealth, Good Luck, Opportunity, Desire; from the third century onwards a new city would enshrine a statue to its own Fortune.

Since the family was a religious unit with its own particular cult, its dead members received veneration from their relatives to roughly the same extent as would be accorded to a 'hero' by the whole community. Accordingly the statues placed at tombs, mostly in the archaic period, might be of superhuman size even if they represented the deceased and not, as also was permissible, a deity. Sepulchral reliefs are more common in all periods; they illustrate a typical or noteworthy scene in the life of the deceased, most often a meal in the home. The term the Greeks applied to them, *stele* (latinized as 'stela'), was derived from the verb 'to stand' and literally meant an 'upright', so that it did not always connote a tombstone or cenotaph; archaeologists have adopted it in order to take advantage of that imprecision because votive reliefs are sometimes indistinguishable from sepulchral.

Votive statues and reliefs were dedicated at sanctuaries, usually in fulfilment of a vow or as thank-offerings, though sometimes out of pure devotion. Only in the archaic period was it customary to dedicate a statue of an adult, presumably in the guise of a servitor of the cult; the excellent *korai* of the Acropolis symbolize, no doubt, individual women who wished to pay tribute to Athena. Most of the later statues, which are generally of poor quality, represent either a deity of the sanctuary or else a child, for whose well-being we may suppose the deity to have been responsible.

Strictly, however, the innumerable honorific statues of athletes should also be classed as votive offerings. They impersonally commemorated outstanding service to a cult; the sculptors took care to differentiate between the physique of a runner or a boxer, but seldom, if ever, did they reproduce his own features in the face.

A slight element of portraiture can be discerned late in the fifth century when honorific statues still represented the ideal general or statesman but with some modification to resemble the individual. During the next hundred years the number of ostensible portraits increased rapidly while the features became more differentiated; at the end of this period the face could express a distinct personality though the basis might still be a type, even if the subject were living. The opposite procedure, whereby the sculptor took the individual as his basis, may already have been followed in some cases (e.g. portraits of Alexander) and was unquestionably prevalent not long after, when Lysistratus is alleged to have been the first to take a plaster mould from a man's face and make a wax cast for use in a bronze. An occasional portrait of later date was so idealized that it scarcely differed from a type; a Hellenistic king often required such emphasis on his forcefulness as obliterated his real features, but the general tendency was towards veracity. By the close of the second century, therefore, sculptors were trained to map a face in accurate detail. The Romans, who then first came to the Aegean in large numbers, found such work to their taste, so that a demand for it arose in Italy, setting the pattern for Roman portraiture.

Spirits of the woodland or the sea, who (except for centaurs) had rarely appeared in sculpture till the fourth century, were habitual subjects in Hellenistic art. Owing to the decline of the city-state system and of the orthodox religion bound up with it, statues of athletes were not often dedicated, but sculptors continued to display their ability to represent the body at its best by producing gay figures of satyrs. Fabulous marine beings, part human and part fish, offered scope for virtuosity; the giants of legend, who in earlier art had taken entirely human shape, were transformed on the same principle by substitution of writhing snakes for legs. By such means sculptors enhanced the extravagant vitality that was the quality most admired in the second century, at any rate east of the Aegean; eventually Romans rated it quite as highly. Meanwhile craftsmen in Athens found a ready sale in Italy for marble vases and panels carved with meaningless rows of figures, sometimes deities rendered in mock-archaic quaintness, sometimes prancing satyrs alternating with maenads too drunk to care how much of their elegant bodies was disclosed. A Roman decorative style was soon created in imitation but used mainly for terracotta friezes of little merit; they must, however, have educated public taste to appreciate clean, simple lines.

The technique of the one new art-form in Roman sculpture, historical relief, was borrowed from the architectural sculpture which the Greeks placed on temples, Treasuries and altars. Initially they required it on temples in order to counteract the geometrical rigidity of the building, and particularly to induce the eye to scan laterally as well as following the upward direction of the columns and the roof-slope. The thick columns of a Doric temple supported a tall superstructure, which needed diversification by sculpture to a greater extent than the low superstructure of an Ionic temple, wherein the same total height might be attained owing to the slim proportions of the columns. The Doric form originated on the mainland of Greece, Ionic in the eastern Aegean, where only one Doric temple was built in the early centuries, at Assos (Fig. 1). Here the indigenous tradition was strong enough to enforce the addition, absolutely contrary to Doric

1. Restoration of temple at Assos

practice, of a continuous frieze, the only sculptured feature an Ionic build-ing might carry between the columns and the roof. At Assos it ran perforce immediately above the columns, along the architrave. The overlying course was faced with the Doric equivalent of a frieze—a series of alternat-ing metopes (rectangular panels) and triglyphs (triple conjunctions of verti-cal blunted bars); in all Doric buildings they are placed at this level. On the peak and corners of the roof stood acroteria, which in Doric often took the form of human figures but in Ionic usually of floral ornament. The pedi-ment (the triangular space within the gable) was normally left empty in Ionic, though almost always filled with sculpture in Doric.

The subjects of architectural sculptures often bear no obvious relevance to the cult-deity. The designer seems to have been allowed to choose whatever topics would help him solve the aesthetic problem at each level of the building. The shape of a pediment called for a symmetrical composi-tion in which the central figures were tall and upright, those to either side smaller or crouching and those near the corners recumbent; continuity throughout the pediment was best obtained by making the arms and legs of the various figures overlap, and the resultant contrasts of light and shade furthered the general purpose of diversifying the façade. Metopes, being smaller and placed lower, needed less contrast; each was best filled with a group of two or three figures engaged in joint action—preferably combat. Similar groups were often distributed along an Ionic frieze, the continuity of which severely limited the choice of subjects (to, as a rule, battle-scenes or long sequences of figures, seated or in procession); a skilled designer would avoid monotony by interruptions to the even flow of the composi-tion.

Continuous friezes were put to new uses early in the second century, when the wall enclosing the great Altar at Pergamon was faced externally with one of unprecedented dimensions, and internally with another less abnormal in size but not in content, for it recounted the life-story of a mythological hero; both appear to have influenced the development of Roman sculpture. It remained customary to place a frieze on an Ionic temple till 100 B.C. or slightly later, but very few Doric temples after 300 were supplied with any sculpture (except perhaps acroteria), because the proportions of the buildings changed. By elongating the columns and reducing the height of the superstructure the Hellenistic architects elimi-nated the necessity for sculpture in the pediments, while the metopes became so small as to be not worth carving. By 300, however, practically every sanctuary and great city throughout Greece was already rich in temples.

The Romans plundered works of art wholesale when they sacked Corinth and Athens, and acquired a great many piecemeal, but did not appreciably reduce the accumulation of past centuries in Greece; there was nothing comparable in Italy, either in quantity and quality or in kind. The Greeks had first required objects of worship in which the aesthetic element was unimportant compared with the religious utility. Soon they also wished to please the deities with temples and sculptures in which the aesthetic element predominated. Powerful stimuli to artistic production existed in every period until the Roman annexation of Greece in 146 B.C. and of Asia Minor thirteen years later. Perhaps the greatest impulse was given by sanctuaries, venerated by every city-state in the Greek world, where Games were held in the service of the patron deity and success evoked patriotic as well as personal pride. Every gap between the buildings at Olympia was crammed with statues, mostly of victorious athletes, which at Delphi were outnumbered by groups commemorating battles. Statues of special import, together with offerings vulnerable to weather, were dedicated in the temple, or, when that was impracticable, in 'Treasuries', built by individual states for the purpose, which resembled miniature temples but never contained a cult-statue. An ornate Treasury formed the supreme advertisement for a city which had donated it.

Rivalry between states not only inspired their dedications at the international sanctuaries but also stimulated each city to possess work of an enviable standard and to exhibit it in a seemly manner. From Pausanias' description of southern Greece we learn that, even where the population had never exceeded that of a modern village, there was usually at least one statue of note to be seen; sculptured temples, however, were exceptional. The concentration of sculpture of all kinds at Athens seems to have more than equalled the total dispersed among the other cities. The rich Athenians of the sixth century must have covered half the Acropolis with sculptured shrines and votive statues, while they also dedicated colossi on their country estates and at neighbouring sanctuaries. After the repulse of the Persian invaders in 490 and again in 480-479, Athens became instinct with conscious glory. In the grandiose concept of Pericles the ideal of Panhellenism was linked to the aggrandizement of Athens; his aim was to make a worthy capital for a federation of all Greeks. Religion often cloaked motives of which the substance was patriotism or ambition, and did so in his scheme for the beautifying of the Acropolis. After the political collapse of Athens the leadership passed to Sparta and subsequently to Thebes, states indifferent to art, with the result that the output of civic monuments decreased; huge tombs built for non-Greek potentates in Asia Minor provided greater opportunity for sculptors of the fourth century. Alexander's brief patronage was followed by a hundred years when commissions rarely came and were of small scale, till the kingdom of Pergamon sumptuously commemorated its successive victories. Even in this late period (which began shortly before 200) convention decreed an ostensibly religious aspect; the battle of the gods and giants served as an allegory of recent success over less formidable enemies. After the Roman annexation of Pergamon in 133 portraiture alone retained unimpaired vitality.

The Romans of the Republic were concerned more with family ritual than with the worship of their remote impersonal deities; a sparse and prosaic mythology was borrowed from other peoples. Their temples, few in number compared with those in Greece, aroused no deep feelings; the structure was too flimsy to carry sculpture except in terracotta, and the cult-images seem to have been of that material. The sanctuaries contained no other statues and were of purely local import. Athletics were unknown. Portraits became numerous only after the annexation of Greece, decorative reliefs even later. Meanwhile the patricians started to collect original works of Greek art and copies from old masterpieces, putting them in their houses and gardens or in temples.

Specifically Roman sculpture—though mainly or entirely executed by Greeks—was a political as much as an artistic creation, its purpose being to give visual expression to Augustus' ideology of Empire, which was legalized by constitutional changes in 23 B.C. His theoretically superhuman status was demonstrated at Rome and throughout the empire by the dissemination of portraits idealized into embodiments of beneficent but dispassionate authority. These received worship in his lifetime and became cult-images in the temples dedicated to him after his posthumous deification; selected members of the imperial family were accorded similar honours. An unvarying style was obligatory in every official statue, and required only slight adaptation for use on the Ara Pacis, where the first historical reliefs illustrate Augustus' achievement of establishing world peace. A rural scene included is the earliest and most formal of a series so welcome to the Roman taste for country life that production continued for a century; attempts were made to correlate figures and buildings with natural surroundings, showing each on a scale that aided the composition, whether or not it were true to fact—human beings in the background might overtop a tree or building in front.

The new motives Augustus found for sculpture rescued it from stagnation and launched it on another cycle of development, which likewise ended with decline to the verge of extinction, three hundred years later.

The intervening emperors followed the precedents Augustus had set, with modifications that must have been due partly to their personal insistence, partly to the changing spirit of their times. The portraits stress different aspects of the responsibilities laid upon them; the historical reliefs are concerned with war rather more than peace—though the balance may have been redressed by lost monuments of such personages as Nero. The murder of an imperial reprobate habitually induced an enactment of *damnatio memoriae* whereupon all portraits of him were destroyed or, if they occurred on reliefs, hammered out of recognition. The peaceful succession of an heir continued to entail deification of his predecessor till the third century, when most emperors fought their way to power, and the populace must have ceased to revere their office. Deification may previously have come to be regarded as a sham among the devotees of emotional religions, which proliferated under the empire. The worship of Isis, Mithras and other Oriental gods caused a large but generally undistinguished output of statues and votive reliefs, novel in type. The sculptures on sarcophagi, which became numerous from the middle of the second century, bear vague witness to more or less inchoate beliefs (Bacchic and the like) in an afterlife, and to the rise of Christianity, which eventually put a stop to pagan art.

II

Materials and Methods

Marble and Other Stones

THE early sculptors of Greece carved in the marbles and limestones of many localities and occasionally in less suitable stone, but almost all good work after about 540 B.C. was executed in a few specific marbles which allowed of the finest detail and gave the most pleasing surface. These were quarried at first only on the islands of Paros, Naxos and Thasos; not till early in the fifth century did the Pentelic of Attica gain acceptance, shortly after it had been tried as a building material. These four varieties were exported throughout antiquity for the use of sculptors everywhere. The marble quarried at Dolianà, near Tegea, was scarcely used outside Arcadia because the cost of transport would have been excessive; moreover its dull white hue, which weathers to grey, may have been found unattractive. From the third century onwards Rhodian and Pergamene marble likewise met regional needs.

There might be various reasons why sculptors executing a commission far from their place of residence worked in one marble rather than another, but, if free to do so, they would choose the type that best suited their style, which could actually have been formed by habitual use of it. The type was of greater importance than the locality from which the marble came, because every quarry contains beds that differ in quality; for instance, the crystals in the finer beds on Naxos can be smaller than in the coarser beds on Paros, while the finer beds of Parian correspond with the coarser of Pentelic, and exceptional pieces of all three may look alike. There is no scientific means of distinguishing between the marbles of these three localities since all alike were metamorphosed from calcite limestone, whereas Thasian, being metamorphosed from dolomite, contains magnesium which can be detected by X-rays. An experienced eye, however, can perceive such points of resemblance and difference between one piece of marble and another as will enable a subjective judgment to be reached. Hundreds of fragments from four different sets of reliefs have been sorted

29

for the forthcoming publication of sculpture from the Mausoleum at Halicarnassus, and it has been found that all those with the finest grain, some of
which contain veins of mica while some have acquired a brown patina,
belong to one particular frieze. Further, on comparison with specimens
from the quarries on Mount Pentelicus and from the Parthenon, the marble
has been identified as Pentelic by the size of the grains, the occasional
streaks of mica, the colour when patinated or in breaks and the texture
when weathered. Details could be carved with greater precision in this
fine-grained type than in the average Parian or almost any Naxian. But
those marbles offered a compensating advantage to a sculptor who required brilliance of surface, because the individual crystals show distinctly,
bright or dull according to the direction in which each lies, producing a
lively glowing effect very pleasing at short range. In Pentelic, on the other
hand, the crystals are small and the surface less diversified, although
sparkling. A difference in the result of long exposure to the atmosphere
cannot have been important to the Greeks, but now aids greatly in distinguishing the source of a marble; Parian changes but little, its natural
creamy colour darkening to a pale smoky tint, whereas Pentelic contains a
sufficient percentage of iron for its dazzling whiteness to turn to that rusty
gold seen in the ruins of the Parthenon.

Much of the better sculpture in the Greek colonies of south Italy and
Sicily was necessarily in limestone owing to the lack of marble deposits and
the costliness of importation; a city as rich as Selinus compromised by
fitting a marble head and arms on a limestone metope. The inexhaustible
marble of the Carrara mountains was ignored till the middle of the first
century B.C., when quarries were opened near the port of Luna. Their
produce has minute crystals, so that the surface does not sparkle like
Pentelic but is dead white when newly cut and looks dirty when weathered.
The Ara Pacis of Augustus is the first great monument carved in Luna
marble, which was afterwards used mainly for inferior or purely decorative
work. In the second century began the export of sarcophagi from Proconnesus, an island in the Sea of Marmara, but its marble (white or greyish,
often with pale blue streaks) was barely suitable for statues. Quarrying of
sculptor's white marble at Aphrodisias and other places in Asia Minor
primarily supplied local demand; for some years around A.D. 200, however,
Aphrodisian sculptors were employed in Libya carving their own imported
blocks.

Hellenistic sculptors in regions devoid of good white stone occasionally
restored to the red marble of Laconia or to Egyptian granite, and are
alleged to have carved statues in topaz and even in emerald (presumably a

misnomer for the green quartz, known as plasma, in which nothing remains larger than a miniature portrait head of the first century A.D.). When the cult of Isis gained converts in Italy, some of the statues dedicated in her temples were carved in the hard volcanic stones the Egyptians had favoured—granite, diorite, basalt, and so on; in Egypt these were utilized for portrait heads that are Roman in style. The Aphrodisians may have originated, and certainly exploited, a vogue that developed at Rome, especially under the Antonine emperors, for decorative statues in coloured stone; the whole figure might be of red, grey or black marble, or the flesh parts might be of one colour (usually white, red or black) but the drapery of another or of a variegated stone; the commonest subjects for this polychrome treatment were barbarian slaves or captives, animals, or a conjunction of human and animal figures. Portrait heads were often fitted to variegated busts. There are even statuettes carved out of stalactite, vertically striped in russet and yellow.

The ancient sculptor chipped a block into shape with an assortment of tools similar to that now used; he finished by rubbing the surface smooth with emery and then polishing it with a piece of softer stone, just as a modern sculptor does. But some uncompleted works are preserved, while in many that were regarded as complete there are parts that were justifiably left unsmoothed, so that the marks remain visible of tools used at every stage of the process. As might be expected, the technique in the last stages varied at one period and another, or between one workshop and another, according to the requirements of the design. The extreme instance of change is given by the use of the drill, which has left only inconspicuous traces in Greek sculpture, but enabled slovenly craftsmen under the Roman empire to hollow the folds in drapery more quickly than by chiselling, and contributed overtly to the style of the late empire when hair was represented by holes bored close together over the entire scalp. The drill, as it happens, is the one traditional implement that has ceased to be needed by modern sculptors, though it was indispensable from the Renaissance to the eighteenth century, and for some purposes into the twentieth; less drastic fluctuations in style may account for the varying degrees of reliance the ancients placed on one tool or another.

Every sculptor whose output fetched high prices is likely to have employed assistants to do as much of the work as he could reasonably entrust to them, while his share in sets of architectural sculptures must normally have been restricted to providing either drawings or small perishable models for a team of craftsmen to reproduce in marble on a larger scale. This operation might entail awkward results, owing to the prevalent inefficiency in measurement; in the pediments of Olympia, for instance, parts of some completed figures were actually trimmed away in order to make enough space. Probably the reason why pedimental figures are often carved almost equally well all round is because they might need to be slewed at unexpected angles in order to fit in. On the other hand there are figures made for placing at a known angle, and consequently not finished at the back, but the Greeks cannot always have known the boundaries of that portion till the whole set of figures went into position. The designer, no doubt, had kept to scale, but enlargement to precise dimensions is not feasible without an elaborate system of mechanical 'pointing'. Whatever devices for the purpose may have existed, they were crude in comparison with those whereby artists of recent centuries have been able to produce marble sculpture without doing any carving themselves. When their clay or plaster model had been measured at all the important points, a hired technician would drill the block at the corresponding positions to the requisite depths and then chip away the superfluous marble. The accurate reproduction guaranteed by this method was unattainable with the few 'points' taken in antiquity; a patchy approximation to the artist's original work would have resulted had an assistant completed it. Probably there was nothing to be gained by 'pointing' until the Hellenistic Age, when, according to Pliny, no statue was carved without the aid of a clay model, apparently of the same size; this practice was introduced by Lysistratus, a brother of Lysippus. Pliny explicitly confirms the adherence to it more than two hundred years later of Pasiteles, to whom he attributes a saying that 'modelling is the mother of sculpture'. Arcesilaus, another sculptor of the first century B.C., is stated to have commanded a higher price for his clay models than contemporaries could charge for finished statues, and is even reported to have sold the plaster model for a vase; these stories, taken at their face value, can only imply that he habitually delegated all the labour of carving, from start to finish, to the staff of his workshop.

The Greeks of the archaic period, when practically all statues took one or another of certain canonical poses, had not the slightest need for 'pointing'. They adopted an Egyptian method of plotting a figure of standard proportions on a grid. To each principal landmark of the body was assigned its invariable position on a certain line or within a certain square; when these had been marked on the gridded front of the block the whole outline of the figure was drawn on. The profile on either side could then be cut straight back, and only the fallibility of the sculptor prevented a perfect match; he would next cut the front and back, and proceed to round the transitions. But in a quarry on Naxos lies a roughed-out colossus six times life-size, the back of which was never detached from the rock; the front and sides had already been shaped till little more than trimming would be required for completion. In this instance (apparently of about 490–460) the normal practice of shipping a squared block would not have been feasible, and the weight was being reduced as much as possible when, for some unknown reason, work stopped.

Although the grid system ceased to be fully applicable about 480, because rigidly upright poses were then abandoned, some vestiges of it must have been retained. A grid with a much smaller number of squares, incised on an unfinished Hellenistic work in Egypt, may conceivably have been due to imitation of the traditional native practice but more probably is representative of a late Greek method; there was no easier way of avoiding a mistake in the axis of some part than by sketching the whole figure over both horizontal and vertical lines. Because such drawings of relaxed or contorted poses involved foreshortening, they gave no help as regards the proportions, which sculptors long persisted in trying to standardize. In fact, proportion is the element that redeems naturalistic sculpture, preventing it from becoming merely representational; quite logically, therefore, the first Master after 480 to win renown especially for statues of athletes, Polycleitus, devoted much attention to analysing the proportions of the body and formulating conclusions for the guidance of himself and his colleagues. He embodied his ideal in a statue and explained it in a treatise; which came first is uncertain. The treatise, now lost, seems to have insisted that proportion was no matter of taste or chance but dependent upon mathematical laws which could only be broken at the expense of formal beauty. From the belief in proportion, and from observation of many atheletes rather than of one individual model, grew the so-called idealism of classical sculpture; it was, in fact, a discriminating and selective naturalism, with a theoretical basis that did not remain static. The 'canon' of Polycleitus was modified within a century both by Euphranor and by Lysippus; the latter reduced the size of the head from the Polycleitan one-seventh to one-eighth of the total height, and also shortened the torso. For a figure in a simple pose the sculptor could dispense with a model until the last stages of the work; indeed, at all times many figures were apparently carved entirely from memory, to judge from their conventional appearance. Familiarity with the human body, gained from observation of nude athletes, prevented obvious errors.

It is impossible to assert that all Greek and Roman sculptures were coloured, at least in parts, though the diversity of those that retain traces of paint leads to that belief. Surfaces of coarse limestone, sandstone or peperino were covered with plaster, which must always have been painted in its entirety; the many sixth-century examples found in pits on the Acropolis were pedimental sculptures and seem to have been coloured more brightly on tall buildings than low, sometimes in most unnatural hues, such as blue on a beard or bright red for flesh. The marble statues from the same pits are coloured sparingly and their flesh parts not at all—as seems to have been the rule ever after. Generally the hair, the lips and the iris of the eyes are red, contrasting with black pupils and eyebrows and black outlines of eyelids and iris. Any visible pieces of a woman's undergarments are washed over with red or green, but the outer garment is usually untinted apart from patterns on the borders or other decoration. Although the colouring was not applied until the marble had been sealed with some compound, the hues cannot have been startlingly vivid, though less subdued than they have since become.

The practice of colouring the background of a pediment, attested on the Acropolis only in the case of small buildings, must have been general during the sixth century in order to show up the figures, and doubtless it persisted at all times. A few gravestones of the fifth century are known to have had red or, less frequently, blue backgrounds, both of which were used in the reliefs of a Lycian tomb shortly after 400.

The importance of colour in the fourth century may be gauged by the fact that the most prized statues of Praxiteles were completed by a celebrated painter, Nicias. He probably chose unobtrusive shades like those of the 'Alexander' Sarcophagus, which displays a much wider range of colour than the Acropolis material. A typical figure, that of Alexander himself, has the eyes, lips, hair and boots painted reddish brown; his lion-skin is yellow with brown eyes, the tunic purplish blue, his mantle rose and wine colour; his saddle is yellow with a blue border, the horse's bridle, nostrils and eyelids are reddish brown, other portions of the harness are reddish brown or yellow. The colouring of the sarcophagus has faded since its removal from the darkness of the tomb. But even when new it was probably less bright than architectural sculptures, especially friezes, in which the figures were made clearer by colour on the hair and by flat washes over the drapery, against a background of blue or red paint, or black stone in the case of the Erechtheum.

The taste for naturalistic colouring grew with time: thus a head in the British Museum (No. 1597) has yellow hair, pink flesh and black eyebrows, eyelashes and pupils. The late Hellenistic statues of Delos show the same fashion, but the head in question belongs to the empire. At all periods gilt was applied to portions of marble statues, occasionally (especially in later times) to the whole figure; sometimes marble was painted to resemble bronze. In Greek and early Roman sculpture the eyes were normally painted on the marble. Sometimes, especially in the archaic period (perhaps under Egyptian influence), they were inset in other materials; valuable gems are said to have been so used in late cult-images. Instances of enamel fillings in Hellenistic and Roman heads conform with a practice habitual in bronze statues. Early in the second century A.D. it became common to carve the iris and pupil; the iris, being partly covered by the upper eyelid, forms a crescent, with the pupil indicated by a deep hollow between the horns. The first attempts at this method, inspired no doubt by the similar treatment of bronzes and terracottas, come from the House of the Vettii at Pompeii, and so cannot be later than the eruption of A.D. 79; after the reign of Hadrian it is exceptional not to find it. At the same period it becomes usual to carve the eyebrows, formerly added by paint, and these two conventions prevail into the Byzantine Age.

Sculptors did not hesitate to carve a statue in a number of separate pieces, the joints of which were concealed. The head and neck of draped statues usually form a separate piece that fits into a rounded socket, arms and other projecting parts are attached by clamps sunk into the smoothed surfaces. The incomplete state of so many ancient sculptures is largely due to these customs, which were very prevalent in archaic times, less so in the fifth and fourth centuries, after which they again become common. An economy found chiefly in Hellenistic Egypt is the use of plaster for the hair: the material was more easily worked than marble, and was indistinguishable under a covering of gilt or paint.

It frequently happens in marble that the unrelieved whiteness of the surface produces such a glare as to confuse the modelling of the muscles and other details, even when the work stands indoors. Dead whiteness was avoided in ancient sculpture by applying sealing matter to the surface and rubbing it in with a cloth. The latter process, called *ganosis*, needed constant renewal, so that the exact appearance of a statue so treated will never be known apart from ancient descriptions. But the buttery complexion of the Hermes of Praxiteles serves to suggest the smooth glow obtained by the process, which subdued the glare of the fresh-cut marble while retaining the play of light over the crystals. In the fourth century the custom of polishing the surface was carried to such a degree that the muscles lay merely suggested beneath the gloss. This convention of excessive smoothness, known by the Italian terms *sfumato* or *morbidezza*, developed from Praxitelean methods, and was especially popular at Alexandria. To the hardness characteristic of early imperial sculpture there remain few exceptions, but an era of high polish returned under the Antonines, reaching its zenith in the bust of Commodus (Pl. 89*b*), where the texture of the material has been so obscured that the surface looks more like ivory or porcelain than marble.

Metal

A very large proportion, probably more than half, of all Greek statues were composed of bronze, a metal so valuable in the Middle Ages that few objects made of it escaped the melting-pot. Roman statues of bronze seem to have been comparatively rare, but the literary evidence is sparse and they have come to light in numbers only thanks to concealment under the ash and lava ejected from Vesuvius in 79 A.D.; there remain so few of later periods as barely to prove that the technique of casting was never forgotten.

The Greeks may have been able to cast little statuettes as early as the eighth century but for large work they depended on sheet bronze till roughly the middle of the sixth century, when they learnt to cast hollow figures of life size. The process required specialized skill of a very high order; so far as we know this had not previously been acquired in any country except Mesopotamia, and no Greek craftsman is likely to have visited a foundry there. An Oriental craftsman with the requisite knowledge may conceivably have exercised it at a Greek city, but more probably the Greeks discovered the process independently. The two Samians, Rhoecus and Theodorus, whom Pliny credits with the invention of bronze-casting, may actually have been the first to succeed in large-scale hollow casting. Without guidance from Mesopotamian experience it would have been no sudden development but the result of very gradual progress. The problems that a life-size statue might involve, even to a sculptor who had already cast quite large works of simpler design, are flamboyantly described in Benvenuto Cellini's autobiography. He encountered horrifying difficulties with his Perseus and succeeded in casting it only by chance; even so, he failed to conduct the metal to the end of one foot. He had chosen a design more complex than had then (1553) been attempted in bronze for many centuries. With the straightforward archaic poses, on which the first two generations of Greeks gained experience, it should have been comparatively easy to conduct the metal wherever required, but the figures were habitually cast in several pieces, to be soldered or riveted together when cooled. A vase-painting of about 470 shows a foundry where artisans are busied with a nude bronze statue that has just been extracted from the casting-pit, complete except for the head which is lying on the ground. That a contemporary almost nude statue, of which the 'Chatsworth' head is the sole relic, consisted of no less than six main pieces was probably due to its Cypriot makers' inability to cast anything larger. Most later statues were cast entire. An exception, which likewise might be explained as the work of a backward region, was a Hellenistic draped statue of a goddess or queen, the head and torso of which have been recovered from the sea off Halicarnassus and show junctions for several other pieces.

Hollow casting is effected by pouring molten bronze into a narrow empty space, bounded on the outward side by a mould taken directly or indirectly from the sculptor's work; on the inward side is a solid core of non-combustible material. Several methods of taking the mould can result in a satisfactory cast. By the process likely to have been the first used, because it was most similar to that involving solid casting, the sculptor models a clay figure in full detail, then from it are taken moulds (in various pieces) of each half separately; these are lined internally with clay or wax, inserted piecemeal to the varying thicknesses that will be required in different areas of the bronze. The core can then be formed either by putting the two half-moulds together and pouring the cohesive material between them, or by pressing it into the half-moulds before joining them. When the closed mould is opened, the core is removed and its surface smoothed to obviate irregularity in the eventual thickness of the bronze; the lining is cleaned out of the mould, which can be re-assembled with an air-space between it and the core, ready to receive the molten metal. Alternatively the space is filled with wax and the mould discarded; instead, continuous coatings of clay are applied all over the wax, forming a one-piece mould, and when that has dried the wax is heated till it all runs out through a hole at the foot, leaving a space into which the metal will be poured. If a bronze has been cast by either this or the previous method, the interior is apt to retain marks due to the tools used for smoothing the core; such marks are visible inside the fifth-century 'Chatsworth' head, together with outlines of the compartments by means of which the lining of the mould had been gradually inserted. A further method can leave indications of compartments but the core is not smoothed with a tool, being in fact inaccessible; this is common practice for modern sculptors if they do not wish to preserve their original model. They arrange for it to be repeatedly coated all over with clay to make a one-piece mould, which is cut when dry into a set of piece-moulds; this will be assembled, lined with wax and filled with a core, after which the wax is run out and metal poured in. Unless or until someone observes traces of a lining alone on an otherwise hand-smoothed interior we shall not know whether the Greeks ever used this method. There can be no indications whatever of another method so simple that the Greeks are quite likely to have substituted it for any less direct means—only one of which is demonstrated (by the 'Chatsworth' head) to have unquestionably been practised. On this least complex of methods the sculptor's plaster figure itself forms the core and is overlaid with wax, modelled in greater detail so that nothing more is needed, except coating with clay to make a one-piece mould, before the wax is run out and the metal poured in. Whatever the method used, the core must have been held in place at the time of casting by strong nails or metal rods fixed into it and projecting across the air-space, so that their heads would make contact with the mould. The few scraps of moulds preserved consist of terracotta, for which the clay was applied gradually, beginning with a layer liquid enough to enter every depression or crevice in the figure. A mould, unless it were a final one-piece casing, was necessarily a composite assemblage in the manner of a jigsaw, because every undercut surface in the figure required a separate piece, which would make an exact join with the next, and so on till that half of the figure was enclosed. A number of wax bars were incorporated in the mould, to be converted into empty pipes when heat was applied; one such pipe led upwards from every projecting part of the figure to serve as a vent for the air and gases expelled when the molten bronze was poured down other pipes. Superfluous metal then filled the pipes (as can be seen in a fragment of the mould for an archaic statue); this was cut off flush with the surface of the statue after it had cooled. Unless the positions of all pipes had been chosen with consummate skill, defects caused by air bubbles would need to be made good by filing a larger area of the surface to a uniformly lower plane or by inserting a patch. The holes due to the nails were plugged. The core was usually raked out for lightness' sake.

The statue, when cast, still needed several days' labour to smooth the surface and sharpen the modelling where necessary. The light yellow shade of the fresh metal was changed to the required tone by a varnish or paint, whereby flushed or pale cheeks or sunburn could be indicated. Details were sometimes added in other metals (as in Mesopotamian art), the lips and ornaments being supplied in silver or gold, the nipples in copper. The eyes were usually inlaid in glass or enamel as a cheap substitute for the Oriental use of precious or semi-precious stones, to which the Greeks seldom aspired, though the Delphi charioteer has pupils of onyx. The close-lying hairs on the body were engraved. Curls of hair were sometimes, eyebrows often, eyelashes regularly, cast separately and attached.

Literary sources distinguish several varieties of bronze, largely obtained by alterations in the proportions of tin and copper and by the addition of other metals: Corinth was supposed to have made three kinds, in one of which the preponderance of tin and silver gave a light colour; Myron was supposed to have preferred the alloy of Aegina, while Polycleitus preferred that of Corinth. But although the incompetence of ancient metallurgists inevitably led to variations dependent upon the ingredients of the ore, a few analyses by chemists have not revealed further local peculiarities; a mixture of 10 per cent tin and 90 per cent copper has been found in two works of the classical period, but over 20 per cent of lead and a reduced proportion of tin in some of Hellenistic or Roman date.

To their greater dependence on bronze the Greek sculptors owed their emancipation from the stiffness of Oriental art, for a bronze statue could be made to stand in almost any pose without other support than the lead clamps at its base; if needed, lead or stone could be inserted into the interior to maintain the balance. The enormous cost of transport in antiquity made for the greater popularity of bronze: it cost as much as 400 drachmas (each a day's wage) to move the drum of a column from the Pentelic quarry to Eleusis, while limestone fetched to Delphi from the neighbourhood of Corinth cost ten times as much in transport as at the quarry (expenses of cutting the block, 61 dr.; transport by sea, 224 dr.; transport by land, 420 dr.—this for seven miles of steep gradient). Bronze was more easily moved, especially as the material could be assembled in small quantities; but it was of course expensive. In Hellenistic times a life-size statue of bronze cost 3,000 dr. A statue of twice the normal size was regularly estimated at eight times the normal price, for it required four times as much surface and twice the thickness. The Colossus of Rhodes, 105 feet high, is said to have cost 7,800,000 drs.—all paid to the sculptor, as was the custom.

A bronze head (Pl. 35a), found at Athens, retains traces of a silver sheathing, which had probably replaced an earlier covering of sheet gold. In general, though, gold in that form was fastened to wood or plaster, as described in the following section. Silver was commonly used for inlaying details on bronzes, and sometimes to contrast with gold. A few statuettes consist entirely of it but no large work has been preserved, though some scraps of thin sheeting at Delphi obviously belonged to an archaic statue of a lion, of natural size; they were fixed by bronze rivets to a bronze armature. Sculpture in iron or in copper must have been rare even in primitive times; lead was scarcely used, except at Sparta in the early period when hundreds of little figures, shaped to lie flat, were dedicated as offerings.

Wood and Adjuncts

Carving in wood is perhaps the most obvious means of artistic expression and was not neglected by the early Greeks, whose favourite varieties were cedar, pine, poplar, cypress, olive or ebony. But the climate of the country, with its stormy winters and rainless summers, does not preserve wood like the perpetually dry air of Egypt, and few examples of Greek carving in that medium have been discovered. It is only from the notices of authors that we learn of crude images shaped from tree-trunks, and these were often dressed in actual clothes. Sculpture in wood alone barely outlasted the sixth century as a distinct art. A combination of wood and stone never ceased to be employed, though as a rule only for very large statues, in which draped portions consisted of wood but the flesh extremities of stone (usually marble). This technique, known as acrolithic, was sometimes adopted merely for its cheapness, but more often for structural reasons, because no more than a light facing of wood was necessary and the hollow interior could contain a sturdy framework to support the weight of the head and arms.

Wood frequently formed a groundwork upon which to place more decorative materials, especially gold and ivory; when these were used in conjunction, the former was applied to the drapery and hair, the latter to the nude portions. The hammered plates which composed very early bronzes must have been nailed on to a wooden framework, and the chryselephantine (gold and ivory) technique might be considered a development from this principle, were it not known to have already flourished in the Oriental kingdoms. The tomb of Tutankhamun yielded several small instances of combination of the two materials, the most relevant being the figure of an Asiatic captive upon the handle of a ceremonial walking-stick, where the nude extremities are of ivory and the dress is formed of sheet gold inlaid with precious stones. In Mesopotamia, colossi of bronze and ivory are recorded, in addition to a statue of the sun-god in gold and lapis lazuli, and other statues of gold. The Greek adoption of such materials for cult-images was therefore no original idea.

The ivory itself came through Egypt or the coast of Lebanon and Syria. Small quantities were imported, to be carved into figurines, long before the construction of the earliest statues yet known in a primitive chryselephantine technique; remnants of eight of these, including three that were life-sized, have been found at Delphi. They vary in date from about 600 to shortly before 550, and so belong, according to ancient belief, to the initial period of chryselephantine work. The flesh parts consisted of ivory, which was fixed by means of *wooden* rivets (to prevent staining) to the wooden core of the whole figure; pure gold was used for the hair and some ornaments, but for the drapery, electrum (63 per cent gold, 37 per cent silver), stiffened by a backing of bronze sheets which were fastened to the core by iron rivets (over 400 in all; a few silver nails are more likely to have been used with the other materials).

Fifth-century sculptors followed different methods. Pausanias (i.40.3) describes an unfinished Zeus, on which Theocosmus of Megara was working at his native city when the outbreak of the Peloponnesian War (in 432) put an end to the project. (The date may be erroneous, since Theocosmus was still active after 405.) The ivory face and some adjoining gold (part of the hair, no doubt) had been completed but the rest was formed merely in clay and plaster. Behind the temple lay partly shaped blocks of wood which had been intended to bear the precious casing, in substitution for the preliminary clay and plaster; the necessary wooden backing is not described but presumably was built up of pieces of board. Internally, all such statues contained elaborate scaffolding; the warping of the beams caused constant trouble.

Unlike Theocosmus, Pheidias built a full-size mock-up for the chryselephantine Zeus at Olympia, in a workshop of the same dimensions as the temple chamber. Excavations under the floor have recovered waste pieces of iron, bronze and lead left over from the armature or backing, some tools of bronze or bone, including a little bronze hammer such as a goldsmith might use, and many terracotta moulds of pieces of drapery, obviously not intended for casting because it was a matter of indifference whether the rims were sunk below the level of the centre or rose above it. The moulds were taken from some uncertain material; the excavators have provisionally suggested it was wood, but thoughts of Theocosmus' clay and plaster inevitably spring to the mind. The sheet-gold of the drapery must have been beaten into shape, piece by piece, on the moulds (which surely would have been superfluous if wood had already been carved into the same shapes). The gold was presumably thick enough to be fastened on the statue without an overall stiffening of another material, but it must have been supported here and there by a bedding; Pausanias may rightly have assumed that the partly shaped wooden blocks he saw at Megara were destined for bedding.

Chryselephantine work was still executed, or it might be more correct to say, was revived, under Hadrian. An ivory face and arm in the Vatican belong to a statue which was either a poor work of the Pheidian Age or an imitation; from the circumstance that it was found at Monte Calvo, near

Rome, the latter is more plausible. An ivory fragment of an archaistic statue cannot be much earlier.

Terracotta

The modelling and baking of clay figures was no more than an occasional side-line of potters' activity until about 700 B.C., when specialists in terracotta appeared. Owing to the cheapness of the products and the gaiety of colours, necessarily applied over a coating of plaster, demand constantly increased till near the end of the Hellenistic Age, persisting to a minor extent for some centuries thereafter. In spite of the fragility of the material, places with exceptionally good clay exported figurines in vast numbers. Larger works, which could scarcely have travelled, mostly date from the sixth and fifth centuries; they were mainly used to ornament the upper portions of temples. Along the eaves stood rows of antefixes, mostly in the form of life-size heads or busts, individually modelled or cast from moulds; these were especially common in southern Italy and Sicily, regions devoid of marble. There are few instances of terracotta in pediments. It was less rare for acroteria; the best examples, which average about half life-size, are the Olympia group of Zeus abducting Ganymede, of about 470, and a later set of Victories found beside the Acropolis. A cult-image of Zeus at Paestum, datable shortly before 500, might have been occasioned by the lack of sculptor's stone in that part of Italy, but terracotta statues of the same period and later—some of them life-sized—have been found at Corinth. A Zeus by Theocosmus must have been one of the last statues in the material by an artist of distinction.

Archaic figurines can supply evidence on regional tendencies in sculpture if they resemble statues in miniature. The fifth-century plaques made at Locri, probably by several generations of the same family, are exceptional in quality as well as in form; they faithfully reflect the sculptural style of southern Italy. The relation of figurines to statues became steadily less close during the fifth and fourth centuries. Shortly before 300 the products of Tanagra, a small Boeotian town, developed into a distinct though minor art; the craftsmen freely modified types of figure used in contemporary sculpture with independent detail. In general, Hellenistic terracottas are as distantly related to sculpture as their eighteenth- and nineteenth-century equivalents, the china statuettes of Staffordshire or Dresden. In Asia Minor, however, famous statues of the past were occasionally reproduced on a small scale; there is even a parody of the prototype for the 'Spinario' (Pl. 72c), with the head of an imbecile substituted for the boy's.

The Etruscans utilized terracotta more than any other ancient people; as a consequence it had a greater vogue among the Romans, in many respects their heirs, than it ever had among the Greeks. A large collection of Roman statues in terracotta may be seen in the Naples Museum; they can claim very little aesthetic value. But a better class of work is offered in the 'Campana' reliefs produced in Rome, mainly under the early empire; the plaques were cast from moulds and joined together to form friezes. They treat mythological subjects in a purely decorative manner, which inspired Adam and Empire design.

Archaic architectural terracottas were baked when already tinted, with necessarily dull colours; no vitreous glaze is found. Mineral or vegetable pigments of contrasting (often vivid) colours were habitually applied to baked figures and reliefs over a thin coating of white slip; naturalistic colouring of the flesh parts did not begin until about 350 B.C. Contrary to modern practice, modelling entirely in plaster never became generally acceptable to either Greeks or Romans. In Roman Egypt, however, the mummies of rich natives or Levantines were often enveloped round the head or upper part with plaster modelled and painted in simulation of life. Cretan connections with Egypt may account for the discovery at Knossos in 1971 of a unique collection of large portrait busts in plaster, which await publication by the British School at Athens; they are provisionally ascribed to the third century A.D. In Italy, anyone requiring an inexpensive portrait preferred to have it made of terracotta, while there are surprisingly few instances of stucco relief even for the decoration of ceilings or walls.

IIII

Aids and Hindrances to Knowledge

ANCIENT authors supply much information on Greek sculpture but none whatever on Roman, though all those whose writings are extant lived under the Roman Empire; apparently they took no interest in recent work. On the other hand an avowed admiration for the Old Masters was as obligatory for men of culture then as it has been since the Renaissance; in particular, society required them to show a modicum of familiarity with sculpture, then recognizedly the predominant art as much as painting in recent centuries. Genuine appreciation may have been rare except in Rome and a few other cities where ancient statues abounded in temples and public places, but the distribution of copies gave the inhabitants of small towns opportunity to realize the variety of past achievement; travel also enabled some to widen their aesthetic experience. But we may suspect that even professed experts relied partly on copies for analysing the styles of individual sculptors. In any case, no one could acquire an understanding of the history of sculpture, except in vague outline, so hopelessly inadequate were the available chronological data.

There exists no treatise on an artistic subject written by a first-hand authority. The only large body of information is preserved in the *Natural History* of the elder Pliny, who died in A.D. 79 in the great eruption of Vesuvius. His encyclopedic work, a compilation of older sources cemented with a little original matter, treats of sculpture in marble and bronze separately, after a scientific discussion of stones and metals. Pliny's own knowledge would not have carried him far. He acknowledges the authors upon whom he drew; apart from Varro, a Roman encyclopedist of the time of Caesar, and Mucianus, who wrote an account of the province of Asia which he governed in Nero's reign, they were all Greeks of the Hellenistic period. The earliest of them, Menaechmus, was himself a sculptor, though of small repute: he wrote on artists and on sculpture, and may be identical with the 'Manaechmus' whom Suidas describes as 'a

Sicyonian historian, who lived under Alexander's successors'. Duris of Samos, quoted as the authority for an anecdote concerning Lysippus, was a member of the Aristotelian school early in the third century. Xenocrates, a sculptor trained by Euthycrates, son of Lysippus, or by his pupil Tisicrates, wrote about both sculpture and painting. A reference to a picture 'not cited by Xenocrates or even by Antigonus' proves that these authors included lists of artists' works; Antigonus, a sculptor, was employed upon the Pergamene dedications of the later third century. The traveller Heliodorus, whose account of the monuments of Athens was used by Pliny, was among the first to adopt this form of literature, of which many other instances existed in antiquity. Polemon of Troy described the sanctuaries of greatest artistic interest (the Acropolis at Athens, Delphi and possibly Olympia), paying special attention to inscriptions as a source of information; his *Exposure of Adaeus and Antigonus* no doubt attacked these two authors on the ground of inaccuracy. The most comprehensive of such books seem to have been the five volumes compiled by the sculptor Pasiteles in the first century B.C. entitled *Famous Works throughout the World* (*Nobilia Opera in Toto Orbe,* though actually the manuscripts read *Urbe*, which must be absurd).

Pliny constructed the artistic sections of his *Natural History* in the form of a list of artists and their works, adding occasional criticisms from the aesthetic standpoint, usually to show how far each had progressed towards naturalism. The exact meaning of these passages is hard to define, especially since most of them were translated from Greek when Latin possessed too meagre a vocabulary to express the ideas. An occasional misleading statement, the true significance of which is now uncertain, can be traced to Pliny's misinterpretations of his authorities. The names of certain statues and various terms appear in Greek because no Latin equivalent existed; some of these words have been misspelled and rendered unrecognizable by the ignorant clerks who copied and recopied the manuscripts through many centuries. Further, the absence of any thread of thought hindered each copyist from correcting the ordinary slips of the pen introduced by his predecessor, and the text has accordingly become corrupt in many passages. But even at the time of publication this enormous book must have contained a large number of slips which had escaped the notice of the author himself. The inclusion among the works of Praxiteles (who flourished in 364–360 according to Pliny's own statement) of a group of Tyrannicides taken to Persia in 480, is most easily explained as the result of a secretary placing this particular note in the wrong context during the composition of the book.

In Pliny's chronological table of artists their names are listed in groups, each of which is stated to have flourished (*floruit*) in a particular olympiad, the four-year interval between one Olympic Games and the next. The correlations appear to have been obtained by the method of assigning a plausible though more or less arbitrary olympiad to some sculptor associated with a historical personage or a firmly dated event, and then adding the names of other sculptors believed to have worked at any time during his active life. Seven sculptors are grouped with Lysippus, whose employment by Alexander the Great accounts for the olympiad chosen for them all, 328–324, i.e. the last in the reign. For Praxiteles, who heads another group, the olympiad 364–360 may have been chosen with reference to Euphranor's celebrated painting of the battle of Mantinea, fought in 362; his name follows immediately. The value to be attached to the dates must vary in every case according to the ground upon which they were chosen or the reliability of the sources; some are undoubtedly erroneous. The names have in certain cases been misspelled.

The chronological table ends at the equivalent of 296–292 B.C. with the blunt statement: 'Then art ceased, but revived again in the 156th olympiad', i.e. 156–152 B.C. That Pliny was quoting without comprehension is the more obvious because in other contexts he names with praise sculptors who worked during the alleged gap. His source may conceivably have referred exclusively to Greece proper, where there had been no prominent artist in that period, the centre of activity having moved to Asia Minor. Alternatively, if *ars* can be taken in the then unusual sense of 'Fine Art' instead of 'craftsmanship', the sentence may be read as a total condemnation of the style prevalent in the third and early second centuries; Pasiteles, the latest of Pliny's Greek sources, almost certainly abhorred it. He was the nearest ancient equivalent to the English Pre-Raphaelite painters, whose list of notable pictures in the Louvre branded any of Raphael's time as 'slosh' and those that were later as 'filthy slosh'.

Little value can be attached to accounts of 'inventions', which Pliny gives lavishly, in common with the other authors of antiquity. Thus Daedalus was the first to separate the legs of statues and to open their eyes; Dibutades of Sicyon invented the bas-relief, the first specimen of which was kept in a sanctuary at Corinth; Glaucus of Chios discovered how to weld metals, Rhoecus and Theodorus of Samos how to cast; Pythagoras of Rhegium was the first to represent the veins, Cimon of Cleonae to represent the folds of drapery, Polygnotus to paint transparent drapery.

Stories of inventions are even found in Pausanias, the most important of all ancient authors to the historian of art. A Greek of Asia Minor, his lengthy *Description of Greece* was written towards the middle of the second century A.D.; the book has survived in its entirety and contains a vast amount of useful information, best appreciated in the monumental edition by Sir James G. Frazer (6 vols., 1898), where a translation is accompanied by a very detailed commentary drawn from all available sources. The numerous extracts (usually in Frazer's version) which have been strewn throughout this book will convey a fair idea of the merits of Pausanias. Belief in his good faith remains unshaken in spite of questioning by some modern seekers of notoriety. In the few instances in which Pausanias can be proved in error his mistake appears to be an honourable slip; he had obviously visited the places which he describes, as well as reading what previous authors had written about them. A large proportion of his statements were derived from the stories of local guides, and here he was, of course, peculiarly liable to error.

Pausanias had preferences but he does not often indulge in criticisms of style. When such occur in Pliny or in the Roman essayists, Cicero and Quintilian, they seldom venture beyond superficial generalities, concerned especially with proportions and naturalism, which have been abstracted from some earlier author. These judgments are quoted in their context, if worth it. The one critic whose remarks show any true appreciation of style is Lucian, a Syrian Greek, contemporary with Pausanias, who devoted an essay, *The Images*, to the selection of features from various female statues to form an ideal beauty, while his other writings contain frequent allusions to works of art. He had indeed begun life by a brief apprenticeship to a sculptor, if we may believe his story in another essay, *The Dream*, which, whether truth or fiction, contains much that is interesting. It shows the low social status of sculptors and the hereditary nature of their trade; even in the age of Pericles the first condition held good, and in Roman times sculpture was a mean trade. Heredity dominated at every period of antiquity—the family of Canachus were artists for six generations, and the Attic family of Polycles worked during most of the Hellenistic Age. To the Greeks and Romans, art was a handicraft practised by a multitude of hacks from whom a genius occasionally emerged.

Lucian says, in *The Dream*,

After I had given over going to school, and was grown to be a stripling of some good stature, my father advised with his friends, what it were best for him to breed me to, and the opinion of most was that to make me a scholar the labour would be long, the charge great, and would require a plentiful purse; whereas our means were poor, and would soon stand in need of speedy supply; but if he would set me to learn some manual art or other, I should quickly get by my trade enough to serve my own turn, and never be troublesome for my diet at home ... This being concluded upon, we began to consult again what trade was soonest learned and most befitting a freeman ... With that some began to recommend one trade, some another, as every man's fancy or experience led him, but my father casting his eyes upon my uncle (for my uncle by my mother's side was there, an excellent workman in stone, and held to be one of the best statuaries in all the country). By no means, he said, can I endure that any other art should take place as long as you are in presence; take him therefore to you and teach him to be a skilful workman in stones, how to join them together neatly and to fashion his statues cunningly.

Lucian was not successful as an aspirant in the trade of sculptor, and broke a slab of marble, for which he was beaten by his uncle. That night he had a dream in which there appeared to him

a sturdy dame, with her hair ill-favouredly dressed up, and her hands overgrown with a hard skin, her garment was tucked up about her, all full of lime and mortar, for all the world such a one as my uncle when he was about his work ... and that sturdy drudge began with me in this manner: I, sweet boy, am that art of carving to which you professed yourself an apprentice yesterday, a trade familiar to you and tied to you by succession ... Disdain not my apparel, for such beginnings had Pheidias that carved Zeus, and Polycleitus who made the image of Hera, and the renowned Myron and the admired Praxiteles, who are now honoured as if they were gods.

The gulf between the respect paid to the long-dead sculptors and the degradation of their successors turned Lucian to a literary career.

Inscriptions

Inscriptions have long continued to supply the greatest aid to the classical archaeologist in his task of confirming the accuracy, or supplementing the information, of his literary authorities. Of all classes of inscriptions, sculptors' signatures prove most useful; they range with few exceptions between 550 B.C. and the time of Christ. The signature may still be read upon the base of many a statue that has long since found its way to the lime-kiln or the foundry; often, too, the dedicator's words provide some clue to the date. At the worst the shape of the letters forms a rough guide to their age, while comparatively precise datings are possible in the wealth of material at Athens. Local variations in the alphabet and in dialect grow steadily less with time, but often betray the period and nationality of an archaic writer.

A small proportion of extant inscriptions was subjected to recutting, to sharpen the lettering worn by a few centuries of exposure, and the work-man naturally modernized the form of the letters: conversely a new in-scription was sometimes written in old-fashioned lettering, especially in Roman times. In rare cases false signatures were placed upon copies to show the name of the sculptor responsible for the original, sometimes without reference to fact; such is the simplest explanation of the OPUS FIDIAE and OPUS PRAXITELIS cut upon two colossal statues on the Capitol. A forged dedication in lettering imitated from archaic inscrip-tions was presumably added by a dealer in order to sell, as an antique, a bronze Apollo of the first century B.C., when many sculptors imitated the archaic style; a tablet bearing the names of two sculptors, who worked in collaboration at that time, was found inside the statue when the staff of the Louvre examined it, soon after its recovery from the sea near Piombino.

The inscriptions of public bodies, such as the accounts of the Building Commission at Athens or Epidaurus, supply occasional items of informa-tion on the sculptures of temples, but these long texts have usually been pieced together from fragments, and their reconstructed forms are open to doubt.

Evidence from Other Arts

The coins of the Hellenic period had, as a rule, little connection with sculpture, though the figures thereon may sometimes have imitated the local statues; for instance, the head of Hera on the Argive issues may reflect the head of Polycleitus' statue, while the Helios of Rhodian de-signers must have resembled the famous colossus of the god. Demetrius Poliorcetes, at the commencement of the third century, struck coins that depict a Poseidon attributed to Lysippus. The reproduction of famous statues on coins grew vastly more frequent under the Roman Empire, when Greece was living on her reputation. But these are crude representa-tions on issues struck by the authorities of a small district and illustrate one of the local treasures, which can frequently be identified with the help of

Pausanias. In rarer cases a statue might be adopted as the coin-type of some distant city, in which case its identity remains unknown in the absence of other information.

Coinage maintained a high aesthetic level in the age of Greek independence, when each city insisted on supplying its requirements from its own mint. As evidence for the gradual development of art, coins of all periods have great value, being plentiful, intact, and usually dated within narrow limits. Heads of Roman emperors or members of their families, on issues generally of poor artistic quality, enable sculptured portraits to be identified and often assigned to a particular phase in a reign. Further, they reveal the changes of fashion in such points as hairdressing, by which means it has been possible to assign Roman portrait busts to their correct age. This criterion has, however, been treated as too definite, for allowance must always be made for personal taste which might cling to a mode already discarded in the most advanced circles: thus, the tall, curled wig of Flavian ladies may have survived for another half-century in North Africa, to judge from the reliefs from a mausoleum built of Hadrianic bricks. Moreover the simultaneous popularity of two distinct fashions cannot always be traced from coins: the tall wig, and the artificial waves flowing from a centre parting, flourished side by side under the Flavians.

Carved gems, though of finer detail than coins, have less historical value because they can seldom be closely dated. No trust should be placed in dogmatic assertions that architectural sculptures must be ascribed to a certain decade because of the style of the building; dating within a generation is not often feasible. On the other hand the development of vase-painting has now been studied to the point which admits a margin of error of no more than ten or at most twenty years; comparison with vases will sometimes determine the age of an archaic statue or relief. Statuettes of terracotta and bronze also have their uses, because of their multiplicity, especially in tracing the evolution of some particular type or to reveal peculiarities of local workmanship, which stray into larger sculpture but cannot be attributed to the correct district without the help of many examples.

Evidence from Excavation

The attempt to date objects by the position in which they were discovered is seldom justifiable on a classical site, even when the excavation has been carefully conducted—a rare occurrence till lately. The Acropolis at Athens provides a partial exception, because after the Persian destruction of its monuments in 480 the Greeks extended the area enclosed within walls and

levelled the surface with rubbish left by the sack; but this was not distinguished by the excavators from later material, and was even thought to
include a head of approximately 450 (Pl. 32*a*). On the other hand, the Wall
of Themistocles, built immediately after the Persian War, supplies a
definite limit of date for the objects incorporated in recognizably original
masonry, though not where there have been repairs.

When objects are unearthed beneath the foundations of a building, this
generally implies their priority but excavation is often a matter of guess-
work and the reports are not infallible.

Specialists on bricks can sometimes date the construction of a Roman
tomb to within a decade or two; the family portraits inside may, of course,
have accumulated over more than one lifetime. The enormous villa built
by Hadrian in the neighbourhood of Tivoli has proved of great importance
for the study of sculpture, for its ruins have yielded hundreds of statues,
chiefly copies of Greek works. Though most of these were produced in the
years 123–138, the period of construction and of Hadrian's own occupation, he probably collected older sculptures in addition to ordering new
ones; moreover the villa was inhabited after his death and some portraits
at any rate were placed in it by a later emperor.

In dealing with individual finds it must be remembered that propin-
quity does not unquestionably imply an original connection. Heavy
objects move from one end of a site to another for no apparent reason. At
Olympia some heads of griffins belonging to a tripod were found 200
yards apart, perhaps as the result of floods; and an extraordinary instance
of migration in recent times is given by an inscribed slab, two feet square,
which was seen by a traveller in a church at Athens, and by a later traveller
at a spot nine miles distant. When a statue was found in proximity to a base
upon which it might have stood, the relationship has often been accepted
at the moment but afterwards denied. The exploration of ancient sites
during the Middle Ages, in search of bronze to be re-used, or of marble to
be converted into lime, continued for centuries in a desultory way, not
only causing the loss of innumerable sculptures, but also disturbing the
soil. Even on a site hitherto untouched, an object has frequently been
moved from its original position; the writer once excavated a piece of
virgin soil in Macedonia which yielded a Roman coin at the depth of one
foot and a British Army button at three feet. Accordingly the presence of
coins or other datable material is not an infallible aid to the student, who is
misled, too, by the fact that fragments of several statues or of sculptures
from several buildings can be mixed together by natural agency.

It is customary to lament the carelessness of excavators in previous generations, but in few instances need their inexpensive, slap-dash methods be regretted by those whose concern lies only with sculpture.

Intrinsic Evidence

The surface of ancient sculptures never remains in its original condition unless they have been enclosed in a tomb impervious to air and moisture, or have escaped both by some other means. Most have been recovered after centuries of burial in the ground, but having first endured prolonged exposure to the atmosphere, which holds corrosive chemicals that result in patina. Contact with damp soil accelerates that process and has worse effects, at any rate on marble or limestone. Their constituents leach out and are deposited as an incrustation, while the roots of vegetation may embed themselves even into marble, particles of which are dissolved by the sap. In the recent past (especially before the nineteenth century) the incrustation was often hurriedly removed by chiselling, which might so impinge on the original surface that some re-carving was thought requisite; almost as injurious was the old dealers' practice of cleaning with acid, whereby detail became blurred. In the early days of collecting, only a small proportion of acquisitions escaped one or other of these treatments, while any missing parts were restored in a more or less arbitrary manner. Additions by peculiarly adept restorers are still being detected.

Many forgeries of complete sculptures, produced during and after the Renaissance, became recognizable owing to improved scholarship; others probably continue to be accepted as genuine, simply because no one has yet examined them with doubtful mind. Forgers have generally blundered in some respect, whether by using a technique incongruous with the ostensible period, by mispresenting details they did not understand or by infusing the sentiment of their own time; Italians of some three centuries ago imported a peculiar forcefulness into their portraits of notable (usually notorious) Romans. Antiquities, on the other hand, normally retain at least a remnant of the original surface, which may show patina or root-marks, neither of which have vendors been able to simulate by artificial means. Further tests are applicable in laboratories. During the exceptionally thorough investigation of the Boston 'Throne', ultra-violet light differentiated ancient from re-cut surfaces by the contrasting colours of the fluorescence; the incrustation was found to contain the broken shells of land snails, while a petrographic analysis proved beyond reasonable doubt that the marble originated in a particular island, Thasos. So ended, with an indisputable guarantee of authenticity, a controversy that had persisted for half a century, with no justification other than the unfamiliarity of the subject represented; no one with an eye for style had failed to realize, in the actual presence of the sculpture, that it could not be other than genuine.

Certain varieties of marble were considered appropriate to sculpture only in specific periods, characterized (as it happens) by styles so easily recognized as to be datable regardless of the material. A chronological criterion of great value seems likely to be obtainable from the composition of bronze, since the few analyses yet made reveal the use of different alloys at different times.

With the majority of ancient sculptures style forms the one remaining criterion of date, and where external evidence seems to exist the test of style enables the archaeologist to gauge its applicability. The conventions of artists were subject to frequent modifications, easily recognized by the practised eye, which judges the degree of stiffness in the pose, of smoothness in the surface, of naturalism in the treatment of the muscular system or drapery or such details as the eyes, hair and ears: even the distance between the breasts in female figures has been adduced as a criterion of age. The change in ideals from generation to generation extended, too, to the emotional content or 'feeling' of the work, and the composition of figures or groups. These criteria become more liable to failure when judging work dating from after the mid-fourth century, when personal taste and ability had more scope. Moreover it is rash to assume that a preference at any period for an expression of intense emotion, or for a well-knit or alternatively a loosely designed composition, implies that every work of the same period must comply with the prevailing trend: the hypothesis that denies the possibility of free will has proved unreliable when applied to the modern world (a notorious instance is the difference in composition between Correggio and other painters of the Renaissance). The principle has been adopted by certain scholars as a means of dating ancient sculpture even at its least hidebound periods, and their conclusions are doubtless correct in many cases, yet should never be regarded as final if they cannot be corroborated on other grounds. A dogma that art developed on the same lines in antiquity as at the Renaissance has also been used for dating Hellenistic and Roman sculptures, but is only generally true.

Stylistic dating is complicated by the fact that several schools could exist simultaneously, either at the same centre or in various districts. Local schools, consisting in most cases of artists of no great merit, had conservative habits and sometimes clung to mannerisms which had elsewhere been superseded by a previous generation. But even in the Athens of Pericles, where art progressed so rapidly, the sculptors employed side by side on public monuments differed in their work to an extent which might represent an interval of twenty years. Every date which rests purely on stylistic evidence should always be allowed a margin of error, varying from ten or twenty years in the case of a few of the best sculptures of the Hellenic period, to a century in the case of mediocre work of the Roman age, while thoroughly poor sculpture may range between Alexander and the Antonines (for example a head of Earth from Thessaly, which would be undatable without its Hellenistic inscription). Fortunately sculptors' technique altered most noticeably in late times. The Roman treatment of the eye supplies the most useful criterion, and the next is use of the drill in hair at the same period.

Attempts to assign plinths of certain types to certain periods cannot be described as convincing. Archaic statues were sunk into straight-sided blocks or masonry platforms, but the variety of form observed in the bases of small bronzes and terracottas preaches caution in assuming that this simple shape was invariably used in the fifth and fourth centuries, still less in Hellenistic times. Plinths with moulded sides were fairly common in the second century A.D.; the earliest dated example belongs to a Flavian statue.

The study of Roman official sculpture has been bedevilled by ancient alterations. A living emperor sometimes substituted his own head for that of a dead predecessor on a relief or a statue. Since the heads of draped or armoured statues had regularly been carved in a separate block, which merely rested in a socket, a new head of the reigning emperor could very easily be substituted; in fact, almost every figure wearing a cuirass, if it bears a head very late in style, originated as a statue of Hadrian. The shape of the bust forms a valuable aid to the chronology of Roman portraiture. The modelling of the oldest busts ceases at the base of the neck, but under the Empire the area grows steadily larger, finally reaching the waist.

Fashions in dress altered little in the ancient world: here it need only be said that the girdle of Greek women moves gradually up from the waist to just below the breasts at the middle of the fourth century B.C., and that Roman senators started to wear their togas in a different manner in the Constantinian age.

To the Roman hairdresser's rapid succession of new creations the Greek and Hellenistic periods can show no parallel. In the sixth century B.C. both sexes normally wore their hair long and unconfined (though several statues of short-haired youths date from the third quarter); subsequently men fastened it in a bandeau or tied it in plaits round the head, and, later still, cut it short, while women made up a bun at the back. From the early fourth century onwards, women's skulls are often corrugated by a series of strands pulled taut from the forehead to the bun (the so-called Melon-coiffure). Kings and emperors occasionally introduced new vogues for men—thus Alexander's inability to grow a beard ended the reign of the beard and moustache (only barbarians wore a moustache separately), and Hadrian popularized beards in Rome.

All points of this nature have their uses, but more often analysis of details and a general sense of style enables one to decide chronological problems without much external assistance. On the whole results are only open to serious question in sculpture later than the fourth century; by no means all Hellenistic and Roman sculptures can be dated with a margin of error of less than a generation, or even a century.

Attributions to individual artists are usually tested by comparison of their other supposed works in the pose and proportions, and in details, especially the shape of the skull and face, the eyes, ears and hair; where drapery exists it supplies a fair criterion. But since most attributions are carried out with the help of copies of doubtful reliability, unanimity is rarely found among those who attempt them.

Copies

It was not until the establishment of the empire that copying took place on a large scale; to this age belong almost exclusively the copies of celebrated statues, few of which have themselves been preserved. In the absence of the originals such copies acquire a value far exceeding their artistic merit; as it happens, there are remains, incomplete in every instance, of only six works which ancient authors ascribe to renowned sculptors. The present knowledge of the great masters is based almost exclusively upon copies—in the case of statues, copies executed under the empire; in the case of architectural sculptures, contemporary reproductions from their more or less cursory designs. Under these circumstances, a knowledge of the methods and limitations of the copyist becomes essential to the study of ancient art.

The problem is complicated at the outset by the fact that an artist himself sometimes carried out replicas of his own works, no doubt amending the first design where he felt capable of improving on it: probably the existence of two versions of some statues should be so explained, but there is always a faint chance that one was an imitation by another hand and does not accurately reproduce the style of the predecessor. When an artist's models or sketches for architectural sculpture were copied, usually on a larger scale, by a team of craftsmen, his own style might be traduced to varying degrees in one section or another. The discrepancies may even give the impression that the work was executed over a lengthy period, only because elderly craftsmen could not adjust themselves to the style of an innovator.

Portraits were sometimes set up in several places, even in Greek times, the duplicates being presumably made in the same workshop if erected simultaneously, but imitations of doubtful truthfulness if put up later. On an inscription in the Louvre, dated early in the second century B.C., the Ionian and Hellespontine Guild of Bacchic Artists (musicians and actors) decrees that three portraits of one of the officers shall be placed in his honour at Teos, Delos, and some other spot of his own selection. Under the empire, portraits of the ruler were needed by the hundred; most of the originals probably remained at Rome, copies being despatched to the provinces and there recopied again and again.

Contemporary copies were also required for religious purposes; an archaic instance is afforded by the duplicate Apollos by Canachus, venerated in Thebes and Branchidae. Moreover, as the appearance of each deity was determined by some famous statue, which sometimes fixed the type for centuries, the votive offerings representing the deity can almost be considered copies, although accuracy was not the workman's first aim. The influence of great secular statues can frequently be traced on gravestones, which sometimes coincide in the use of the same athletic figure or group.

The copying of statues purely from motives of aesthetic interest had commenced before the Hellenistic Age, but copyists have added touches of their own period, departing from their models with a lack of scruple customary before the Roman reverence for antiquity prevailed. In Hellenistic times there was a divergence between copies and originals both in style and composition, not only at Pergamon, where art possessed all the means and vigour that royal patronage could give, but also in smaller centres like Delos. Indeed, the Hellenistic copyist was inclined to bring his subject up to date, in the spirit in which a composer uses an old melody as the theme of his modern composition.

Several Hellenistic copies are illustrated in their context: indubitable examples are the Diadumenus (Pl. 36a) from a second-century house at Delos, which cannot be later than 88 B.C.; the Pericles (Pl. 35b), with its inscription of the second or first century; the Doryphorus herm (Pl. 36c) signed by Apollonius, son of Archias, member of a family of sculptors from Marathon.

The latest of Hellenistic copies, whether from Pergamon or from Delos, can scarcely be dated after the Mithradatic war of 85 B.C.; there follows a gap before the golden age of copyists opens with the establishment of the Roman empire. In this interim period, to which few extant copies can be assigned with certainty, fell the activity of Pasiteles, a Greek from southern Italy who received the Roman franchise in 89 B.C. His output was as varied as Cellini's, including plate as well as sculpture in all materials; and his interest in Old Masters was demonstrated by his great book on *Nobilia Opera*. There is no evidence that he himself is responsible for any copies, but a statue signed by his pupil Stephanus was taken from an athlete of the mid-fifth century; it is of poorer workmanship than some other extant replicas and cannot perhaps be taken as representative of this distinguished school. The group signed by Menelaus, pupil of Stephanus, is a more striking piece, of Orestes and Electra in an attitude rendered peculiarly unreal by the contrast between the overdressed sister and her almost naked brother; two originally separate Hellenistic figures appear to have been adapted arbitrarily to form a group, as in other instances of the same subject or of Orestes and Pylades. This custom may have started in the school of Pasiteles; it is significant that in these other groups a replica of Stephanus' athlete is used as Orestes while the remaining figures recall prototypes of a similar period. It appears that Stephanus and his asso- ciates—whether instigated by Pasiteles himself or not—sometimes found their inspiration in fifth-century paintings, for their themes are distinctly pictorial; they carved figures of their own devising in antique style, reducing, for example, the head of Polycleitus' Doryphorus to match a boy's body, constructed like that of the Idolino. Probably some member of the school is responsible for the 'Spinario' (Pl. 72c), a statue combining a fifth-century type of head with a fourth- or third-century type of body. Such work might almost be termed original.

Under the early emperors a great market for true copies grew up, especially in Italy. Wealthy Romans liked to surround themselves with reproductions from the Old Masters, the originals being unobtainable to the ordinary purse, if indeed they had not become national property. Such copies were required to be accurate, but the knowledge of the average purchaser did not extend so far as need have disquietened the careless copyist. The artistic quality sinks steadily from the first century A.D. on- wards, apart from a brief revival in the time of Hadrian. In the Antonine Age copies were produced in enormous numbers, and most are of an exceedingly low standard of work; after the second century the industry dwindled.

That some craftsmen of the Roman period were able to carve reproduc- tions with remarkable exactitude can be seen in the few instances when both an original and a copy of it survive. The elaborate folds of drapery in extant scraps of the colossal Nemesis at Rhamnus are immediately recognizable in figures on a reduced scale. In two instances, however, a meticulous full-sized copy is untrue to the spirit of the original that remains complete. The Antonine who copied the great fifth-century relief from Eleusis (showing the boy Triptolemus between two goddesses) imposed the aridity of his time on scrupulously accurate contouring. Detailed comparison of the bronze Athena from Piraeus with a marble version reveals a similar alteration in feeling, though less obvious owing to the difference in material. Such copyists must have taken a very large number of measurements with a 'pointing' mechanism as well as others by hand. The average copyist, working for a patron who probably did not know the original, took few 'points'; moreover, he could not work in the presence of the original, which usually stood in a sanctuary or public place. With casts made from piece-moulds, he could reproduce the figure in plaster in his studio, but often had only a cast of the face to assist him. Sometimes he was using a copy which was itself inaccurate, and thus he inevitably moved one stage further from the original. The greater liberty of the ancient copyist added value to his own personality and ability; even though a dull, unimaginative workman might attain more mechanical exactitude, a copyist with true artistic sense and less patience might catch more of the spirit of the original. Only by comparison of several copies of varying merit can their relative value as copies be estimated. Furthermore, in deciding whether one head or statue is a copy of another, it is impossible to insist on the 'lock for lock' dogma, which expects divergence in the expression but absolute agreement on details like the arrangement of the hair, for in the conditions under which copyists were obliged to work it is obvious that a complete correspondence of copy and original could never be effected, though two copies executed simultaneously in the workshop might so correspond to one another.

The material upon which these copyists and adapters drew consisted in part of works of art already in Italy (as spoils of war or by purchase), but to at least the same extent of originals still in Greek lands. In the latter case, piece-moulds had sometimes been taken and sent abroad; a collection of them, discovered in a copyist's studio at Baiae, includes one that had been made from a bronze statue recorded to have stood in the Agora at Athens. The process of moulding was apt to discolour marble, as is known from ancient accounts of statues that had been repeatedly subjected to it; some custodians, no doubt, refused to allow it, but copies made by local sculptors and exported were reproduced at second hand. In spite of the numer-

ous originals recorded to have been placed in Rome, most of the identifiable statues of which copies survive stood in Greece, generally at Athens.
The predominant use of Greek marbles in early imperial copies might
suggest that the industry flourished nowhere else to any significant extent,
but the copyists in Italy may have induced a large proportion of their
patrons to commission work in imported Greek marble rather than the
inferior though cheaper substitute quarried from the Carrara mountains.

The foundries from which bronze copies were issued have not been
located. The great number of such copies discovered at a villa outside
Herculaneum need not have been cast locally but may have been carried
by sea from the Aegean; bronzes formed a large portion of the cargo of two
ships sunk in the first century B.C., one off Anticythera, and the other near
Mahdia on the Tunisian coast. A single group of workmen may have
executed the Herculaneum collection, for they are mostly of one date,
probably within a century of the destruction of the villa in A.D. 79. Some
would no doubt be cast with the help in the more crucial portions, such
as the face, of moulds made from the original, to which the result would
then be almost equivalent, except that finishing touches had to be given to
the bronze by a different hand.

Bronze originals were frequently copied in marble, a cheaper material,
but in the process of translation certain difficulties inevitably presented
themselves. Eyes made to be shaded by a fringe of eyelashes would become
unduly prominent in stone, hence the lids were sometimes thickened or
the lashes painted on. Projecting pieces of hair, easily effected in metal,
were abandoned; whiskers, and the slight growth of hair on the chest and
armpits, which were engraved on the surface of the bronze, had to be
raised in relief in a marble copy. Such discrepancies reveal themselves in a
comparison between bronze and marble copies of Polycleitan heads. More
disconcerting than such details was the fact that many a statue which
could maintain its position in bronze would fall when carried out in
marble, while outstretched limbs were apt to break from their own weight.
Slight alterations in the pose may have been introduced, but more often
supports rose from the base or were stretched across to the outstanding
portions of the figure. The copyist endeavoured to render these additions
innocuous by disguising them as tree-trunks or clubs or other attributes
appropriate to the subject.

In reduced copies of large figures the detail of the original has inevitably been slurred. Large divergences from the original design can often be
explained by the necessity to fit a copy into the space for which it was
destined. In the copying of groups intended for architectural settings, great

liberties were taken; for a set of Muses (now in Madrid) only seated figures were required, so the copyist replaced upright members by duplicating two of the seated figures and adding two more which had no connection with the original composition. In other instances one or more statues were omitted, perhaps because the quota of figures had already been filled, or because the reproduction in marble of certain bronzes was impossible without the use of very unsightly supports, or simply because the remaining members of the group were less popular. For decorative purposes, moreover, duplicate statues were often arranged in pairs, and occasionally one is a mirror-image of the other.

Bronze and terracotta statuettes were often based on statues, but are more likely than not to differ intentionally from their originals. Far more drastic simplification was entailed when statues were represented in relief, especially on a relatively tiny scale; figures embossed on terracotta lamps must be peculiarly unreliable because of the modifications required to make a design attractive in its own right as well as reminiscent of the original. It is safer to place trust in coins of the Imperial epoch, when Greek cities illustrated their artistic treasures upon their coinage as accurately as the small scale permitted. The Hadrianic representation of the Zeus of Pheidias (Fig. 17) is a good example of the uses and limitations of such coins, in which alone does any record survive of the appearance of many of the acknowledged masterpieces of antiquity. Some, however, of these illustrations are not precise enough to establish the identity of their original with marble copies hesitantly connected with it; in general the workmanship of these coins is extremely poor. They have, in particular, a tendency to exaggerate the distance of the arms from the trunk.

IV

The Beginnings of Greek Sculpture

ARCHAEOLOGISTS in Greece have found no sign of any impulse towards large-scale sculpture during the four hundred years that followed the collapse of the Mycenean civilization in the twelfth century B.C., when almost all towns and villages seem to have been destroyed. Athens, exceptionally, survived intact with its population unchanged, but could not altogether escape sharing in the catastrophic fall of material and cultural standards throughout the Mycenean area—the southern mainland and islands of Greece, and the nearest fertile portions of the Asia Minor coast. Even among the Athenians handicrafts declined and the artistic instinct almost ceased to operate. Pottery, their only frequent product in this age of deprivation, was no longer well made, while the meagre decoration still occasionally applied to it soon lost every remnant of Mycenean tradition, becoming restricted to the simplest linear designs.

A general slow improvement in living conditions ensued, accompanied by an equally gradual recovery of technical skill and aesthetic expression. A Euboean terracotta centaur, 36 cm. high, is the earliest notable figure in Greek art, being dated shortly before 900. The pottery from which the Geometric period takes its name is painted with abstract designs, mainly composed of rectilinear patterns; a steady increase in their elaboration culminated in eighth-century Athens with groups of human figures, all stylized into abstract silhouettes. The most ambitious scenes occur on the huge vases the Athenians placed over graves in the Dipylon cemetery (Fig. 2). In the panel illustrated a dead man lies on a bed, surrounded by mourners; seemingly at his feet, but really in the background, a man who holds a child by the hand is depicted on a much smaller scale (merely because the space was cramped). The chief mourner sits on a chair with another child on his knee; his legs are drawn as though they did not reach the footstool. Two women (identifiable by their breasts) are seen beating their own heads—an immemorial gesture of lamentation, for which women are still hired at funerals in the Middle East. A dot in the centre of each head indicates the eye—never more than one, since the heads are shown in profile, as are the legs; the arms are stick-like; shoulders are drawn frontally, but the women's breasts appear close together at one side of the triangle that represents the torso, regardless of sex. Figures of goats and geese, under the bed, are comparatively lifelike. They were required to fill vacant spaces; smaller gaps contain rows of chevrons, circles and spots, while a mass of chequer pattern distracts from the imbalance between the heights at centre and sides of the composition.

2. Dipylon vase-painting

Other panels on the 'Dipylon Vases' represent the funeral procession; the corpse lies on a cart pulled by horses, which are drawn in the same manner as the goats. Bronze statuettes of horses, closely resembling them, first appear at roughly that time, about 750 B.C.; they were made in great numbers. Statuettes of men are comparatively rare, perhaps because they were less satisfactory—instead of 'Dipylon' conventions, they present an angular, often elongated approximation to human shape. There was some demand for Centaurs, which long continued to combine an entire human figure with the middle and rear of a horse; an exceptionally able 'Morgan' bronze (Fig. 3) of about 750 represents one grappling with a man or perhaps being stabbed by him. All the statuettes are solid; hollow-casting was, however, introduced for larger objects, notably the griffins' heads placed on the rims of cauldrons imitated from Oriental products. Evidently Greece, which had been isolated throughout the centuries of dire poverty, had already recovered sufficiently for overseas trade to develop. Renewed contact with Cyprus, where Greek colonies had survived from the Mycenean age, ensured ample supplies of copper. Beyond, on the present frontier between Turkey and Syria, a local ruler opened a port in about 825 at the site now called Al Mina, which immediately attracted a flow of shipping and, no doubt, of caravans from the interior; here the Greeks left so much pottery of the eighth century (mainly Euboean) that some of them must have been permanently resident. There is no evidence for voyages to Egypt, which did not yet grant such privileges to foreigners; though small objects of Egyptian origin are occasionally unearthed in Greece, they may all have come through intermediaries. But importation from Al Mina continued apace, especially of luxury goods, which displayed technical abilities that must have astonished the Greeks.

3. Bronze centaur and man,
Metropolitan Museum

Five ivory statuettes laid in a Dipylon grave of about 730 all represent a nude goddess stiffly posed, wearing a cap, in strict accordance with Oriental conventions and in a style reminiscent of Syria (or its neighbourhood) but not altogether characteristic. They may have been intended to please Greek taste, whether the order was placed through Al Mina, or executed in Greece by a craftsman who had learned his trade from an Oriental, whatever his own race may have been. Somewhat later an industry of ivory-carving arose at or near Corinth, and flourished for generations; another, centred at Sparta, apparently did not begin till well into the seventh century. Even at Sparta, however, the first works were fairly accurate reproductions of Oriental prototypes, but through gradual modification a Greek form was evolved. The raw ivory is likely to have been imported from Al Mina, where some tusks were found as though awaiting shipment; craftsmen, too, may have come from there to give the initial tuition. Knowledge of the prospects for skilled artisans must have been available also in the Phoenician cities of the Lebanon, which used their own ships to trade in the Aegean. Even towards the middle of the ninth century, a woman buried at Athens owned a variety of imported trinkets, all of which are likely to be Phoenician, and wore gold earrings of Phoenician technique but specially designed to please eyes accustomed to Geometric conventions. In Attic jewelry of the eighth century a change to designs which may be called Greek is so general as to imply that Phoenician goldsmiths had worked on the spot, with the result that Greeks learnt their methods and took over the craft.

Ancient historians accepted legends that the Phoenicians had actually maintained settlements among the Greeks; in Rhodes alone is there any semblance of archaeological corroboration. Unguents, sold in flasks made of local clay and Greek in style, captured the island market, replacing imports from Phoenicia, and surely would not have done so unless the ingredients had been very similar; a recipe could have been obtained by industrial espionage, but there is a greater likelihood that Phoenician workmen were employed. Their presence would account for some domestic pots of the same local clay that are Phoenician in shape and decoration; one, which is contemporary with the Dipylon ivory statuettes, bears a moulded head as similar as the different material could have permitted.

A large amount of ornamental work in bronze was imported from Urartu, a kingdom (equivalent in territory to Soviet Armenia and eastern Turkey) with an art of Mesopotamian character. Examples dedicated at Olympia show it in its pure form, but soon Greek elements were introduced, perhaps by Urartians who emigrated in search of employment; finally the Greeks, having learnt the technique, adapted the designs more freely. In Crete, a similar development is visible in votive shields from the Idaean Cave, the reputed birthplace of Zeus; they consist of thin bronze, which was hammered from the back into either high or low relief, after which details were incised from the front. The earliest (or so it is presumed) retain the style of Urartu, where the same practice of dedicating ceremonial shields prevailed. A peculiarly elaborate composition is unmistakably of Assyrian style (Fig. 4): a long-bearded god, carrying a lion above his head and bestriding a bull, is flanked by a pair of winged attendants, which, however, are clashing cymbals, an action never depicted in Assyrian art. The scene may allude to the Cretan myth of the Curetes, who danced around the infant Zeus clashing their swords against their shields so that his crying would not be heard by his cannibal father. Possibly an

4. Bronze shield from Crete, Iraklion Museum

alternative version is illustrated; however, if the craftsman was a foreigner he might have misunderstood part of his Cretan customer's specifications. The poor quality of his workmanship by Oriental standards might account for his emigration from, presumably, some borderland dominated by Assyrian influence. In any case, the sight of Orientals at work would explain how the technique came to be applied, seemingly without initial bungling, by Cretans who evidently continued to make such shields far into the seventh century. On the Greek mainland local craftsmen adopted this repoussé technique for ornamenting strips of bronze, at first with

Geometric patterns and subsequently with orientalizing animal or human figures. Potters in some areas ornamented large vases with compositions of flat figures raised a plane above the rest of the surface.

Long experience of working in clay resulted, as soon as terracotta figurines were imported, in local imitations or adaptations. Their rounded forms, in contrast to Geometric angularity, should have exerted an influence disproportionate to their negligible numbers and merits. It is conceivable, too, that potters may thereby have been stimulated to make large figures in terracotta. In any case the innovations in bronze statuettes and repoussé work must have created an environment in which sculpture could be appreciated. But the earliest statues are most likely to have been carved in wood, as, indeed, ancient writers intimate, though with such unreliable chronological data that none of the life-size or colossal wooden images they report can confidently be ascribed to the eighth century rather than to the seventh. Some were sheathed in bronze plates—an old Oriental practice, which the Greeks would not have borrowed till large wooden images had become fairly common. The Apollo of Amyclae, as described by Pausanias (iii. 19. 2), resembled a Geometric statue of the most primitive type, except for its height, which he estimated at forty feet: 'It has a face and hands but otherwise looks like a bronze pillar; on its head it wears a helmet, the hands hold a spear and a bow.' The lack of detail was, however, concealed by real clothing, at least on ceremonial occasions; every year Spartan women wove a new chiton for the god to wear.

Daedalic Sculpture

The Greeks made a new start in both architecture and sculpture about the middle of the seventh century. Till then they seem not to have put any dressed stone into any building, nor to have carved in stone, since the end of the Bronze Age some five hundred years earlier. The virtually simultaneous adoption of stone for architecture and for sculpture appears to have been inspired by contact with Egypt, a country which had hitherto not admitted Greeks. In 664, Psammetichus I gained the throne of Egypt with the aid of Greek mercenaries; thereafter he and his successors relied upon a corps of them to stiffen the native forces. Inevitably Egypt became open to Greek shipping; Herodotus alludes to a trading voyage of approximately 638 as though it were already a normal occurrence. The merchant crews must often have brought home a few curios including, we may suppose, figurines such as were mass-produced in Egypt for local customers; these casual imports would illustrate the returned travellers' descriptions of strange sights, among which none impressed Greeks more than the stone-built temples, each with a wealth of sculpture. If visitors to Al Mina were allowed to travel inland they might have seen reliefs but there were practically no statues in that region; Egyptian statues must therefore have inspired much excited talk. It can be no coincidence that the Greeks began to carve stone within a few years of Psammetichus' accession, and followed Egyptian precedents so far as such could be ascertained from easily portable objects.

Stone carvings of the earliest class, which may be regarded either as preliminary to archaic, or as the initial phase of archaic, are currently termed Daedalic, with reference to the ancient belief that Daedalus originated archaic sculpture. Some Greeks recognized the chronological absurdity of such an ascription to the legendary Athenian who built the Labyrinth of Cnossus (presumably the Minoan palace) and escaped from Crete on wings he had made. Probably the association was due to another of the many inventions attributed to him, that of statues which moved of their own accord. Praise of a living sculptor might therefore have taken the form of calling him a 'Daedalus'; Pausanias observes (ix. 3) that wooden images, generally known in his own time as *xoana*, were still made for a Boeotian cult and termed *daedala*, which could only mean 'wonders of craftsmanship'. Actually Daedalus was a fairly common name; a sculptor of fully historic times was so called, and there might have been another in the early period. Under the Roman empire, a large number of the most primitive statues still preserved in Greece—the majority in wood—were shown to tourists as works of Daedalus, but there was no means of investigating whether these claims rested on genuine tradition or were late inventions to assert great antiquity (just as many primitive Christian paintings have been popularly ascribed to St Luke). In general, though, Daedalus was reputed to have been responsible for the transition from the primitive *xoana*, which had few indications of the human form, to more recognizable figures; in the words of Diodorus, 'being the first to give them open eyes, and parted legs, and outstretched arms, he justly won the admiration of men; for before his time statues were made with closed eyes and hands hanging down and cleaving to their sides.'

Dipoenus and Scyllis, who are variously described as the sons or pupils of Daedalus, were settled at Sicyon, although reputedly of Cretan birth. Pliny's dating for them is equivalent to 580–577 B.C. They are stated to have been the first to gain fame by marble sculpture, but also worked in wood. Their two names invariably occur together as collaborators. Pausanias gives little information about their works; his only item of interest (ii. 22) concerns some cult-statues of the Dioscuri, their wives and two sons, supplied to a temple at Argos. These were carved in ivory, while the horses of the group had portions in ivory added to their ebony bodies. Other recorded works were to be found at Tiryns and Cleonae, in Aetolia and even at Ambracia.

Traditions of other Daedalids must often contain a kernel of fact. Four Spartans, Hegylus and his son Theocles, Medon and Dorycleidas, whose works remained at Olympia in the temple of Hera and in the Megarian Treasury, are accepted by Pausanias as pupils of Dipoenus and Scyllis (v. 17.1, and vi. 19); other pupils, Tectaeus and Angelion, the teachers of Callon (who was active around 500 B.C.) made the image of Apollo for the Delians, which is represented on coins of Athens. Yet another alleged pupil of Dipoenus and Scyllis, or of Daedalus himself, Clearchus of Rhegium, made the bronze image of Zeus for the Brazen House at Sparta; according to Pausanias (iii. 17) it was the oldest known bronze work and had been made in several pieces, which were riveted together. A second tradition, however, gives him a Spartan master, and makes him in his turn the teacher of Pythagoras of Rhegium, a sculptor of the early fifth century. Smilis of Aegina, whom Pausanias (vii. 4.4) believed to be a contemporary of Daedalus, made, for the temple at Samos, a cult-statue of Hera which is represented on coins. Cheirisophus, a Cretan, made the gilded image of Apollo in the temple at Tegea. As for Endoeus of Athens, whose own extant signatures place him late in the sixth century, Pausanias' statement (i. 26.5) that he was a pupil who accompanied Daedalus to Crete is explicable only if the tradition referred to another sculptor of the same name— perhaps an ancestor of the Endoeus whose statue of Athena Pausanias saw on the Acropolis (where it still remains).

Whatever the basis of fact that lies hidden in the traditions, they are chronologically worthless. They appear to associate Daedalids in general, if not Daedalus himself also, with the sixth rather than the seventh century, to which must be ascribed the earliest existing stone sculptures, now conventionally termed Daedalic. Some of these cannot be appreciably later than 650, and might be a decade or two earlier, according to the current 'token' dating, there being no basis for an absolute chronology. These works cannot be classified firmly in sequence, because they were found in places far apart, which did not necessarily keep pace each with the other's development. Terracottas demonstrate that local schools maintained stylistic differences; sculptors, however, must have travelled, with the result that any individual work may be unrelated to the local style, while one school should more readily have influenced another. In fact, Daedalic sculpture is relatively uniform in style whether found on the mainland, in the Cyclades, in Crete or on the eastern side of the Aegean.

Probably the earliest existing statue is one found at Delos, inscribed with a dedication to Artemis by a Naxian woman, Nicandra. That it is over life-size for a woman (1.75 m.) need evoke no surprise in view of the recorded precedents in wood. But it is also the first marble statue known to have been carved in Greece after 2000 B.C.; the deposits on Naxos and Paros, which the prehistoric inhabitants had quarried, now began to make these islands again centres of sculpture. The block used for Nicandra's offering was too thin for so tall a figure, which is almost flat on most parts of both front and back, so that in profile it looks not unlike a slab. The surface has corroded, especially in the upper part; little remains of the face, which was framed by long braids of hair, falling over the shoulders. The figure stands bolt upright, facing straight to the front; it is draped in a peplos from which the bare arms stretch down the sides, completing the military posture of 'Attention'.

Smaller female figures, in various materials, were given the same rigid pose with a similar flattening of the peplos. Nicandra's statue, when new, should be envisaged as resembling a statuette 40 cm. high (Pl. 1a), which was hammered out of bronze sheets over a wooden core and must have been supplied with inset eyes. It belongs to a group, of a god and two goddesses, which stood on a bench inside a temple at Dreros in Crete. The god (Pl. 1e), probably Apollo, was made disproportionately taller than either of his female companions, presumed to be his mother and sister; when intact, he cannot have been under half life-size. But for this larger scale, even the choice of tight-fitting clothing would not have allowed the artist to outline the forms of the body so definitely in sheet-bronze; he could, however, have indicated the goddesses' breasts more clearly. Comparison of these female statuettes with Nicandra's offering suggests that their style is more advanced, because there are folds in the garment between arm and side. But folds are lacking in a limestone statuette, 65 cm. high, which the Louvre acquired from Auxerre (Pl. 1b); its peplos is flat-surfaced as in the Nicandra figure, and the hair falls in the same number of braids to the same length, yet the modelling of face and bosom seems distinctly later than in that statue or in the bronzes (allowing for the restrictions imposed on hammered detail). Incised patterns on the drapery must have been distinguished by paint, which the grooves prevented from spreading; the coloured plaster-cast (Pl. 1c), in which a missing part of the face is restored, should be fairly true to the original appearance. On a life-size seated figure, of which the lower part alone has come to light at Gortyna in Crete, some brownish red paint can still be seen filling rosettes that were sunk into the flat of the peplos; this statue, too, would be rectangular in section both above and below the waist, but for rounding of the corners. The same rounding at the edges of flat surfaces is characteristic of the terracotta figurines that abound at Gortyna, a fact supporting the common belief that the 'Auxerre' goddess is also a Cretan work.

5. Horsemen from Prinia, Iraklion Museum

A number of limestone carvings in high relief came from some monument, perhaps a large altar, at Mycenae—which, it may conceivably be relevant to note, lay within a day's journey of Sicyon, the home of Dipoenus and Scyllis. One fragment shows the claw of some monster gripping a dead man; mythological scenes first occur in vase-painting near the middle of the century, whereas these reliefs can plausibly be dated about 630 or 620—perhaps twenty years after the 'Auxerre' statuette. The one remaining head in the Mycenae fragments belongs to a female figure, not quite life-size (Pl. 1d). The right hand grasps the end of drapery that

covers the head and overlies the peplos. The hair is as long as in the
Nicandra or 'Auxerre' figures but differently arranged; it forms curls as
regular as rosettes and falls to each shoulder in a striated mass, like the male
wig of Egyptian art (Fig. 8). The same fashion is displayed in profile on an
Attic terracotta plaque (Fig. 6), which gives a contemporary version of the
mourning scene that had originated long before on 'Dipylon Vases' (Fig.
2). The noses of the 'Auxerre' and Mycenae faces can be restored from the
women on the plaque or from the Dreros bronzes.

A pair of very high reliefs from Gortyna was carved in a soft stone
which has decayed particularly in the faces, where all details are blurred.
Each panel contained three upright figures of deities, practically life-size,
but in one case nothing remains of the central figure except its apparently
female head, wearing a tall hat of *polos* type and looking straight forward;
on the other the head and evidently male bust are likewise posed frontally,
though on the only lower fragment the shin of a leg is thrust sideways and
seems to be represented in profile (as are some legs in the Mycenae reliefs).
Each central deity stood between stiffly frontal goddesses, nude except for a
polos; all four are virtually complete. Their rounded forms must have been
imitated from Asiatic ivory or terracotta versions of Egyptian reliefs; as in
every subsequent Greek female sculpture no pubic hair is shown, but the
Asiatic convention was followed of marking the genital groove, which
later sculptors always omitted.

Daedalic low reliefs from Crete were inspired mainly by the compositions painted or raised in flat relief on contemporary vases, whether of
local make or imported from other Greek areas; the potters, now emancipated from the Geometric heritage, relied on human or animal figures,
often arranged in repetitive attitudes. A limestone frieze from the site at
Prinia represents a procession of cavalry, some 60 cm. high, above a band
of typical potters' ornament (Fig. 5). The five diminutive men preserved,
out of at least six, ride identical mounts and differ only in that one carries his
spear aslant instead of horizontally. The long-legged slim-barrelled horses,
and their proportions relative to the men, could be appropriate to the
middle of the seventh century, but the chronology of artistic development
is particularly obscure in the case of Crete. There can be scarcely any doubt,
however, that two little slabs from Prinia are the earliest of Greek sculptured tombstones, although they exemplify a technique of shallow carving
—almost comparable to drawing—which persisted in Crete till late in the
sixth century. Their subjects, a warrior and a woman spinning, afterwards
became habitual in the sepulchral repertoire of other regions. In a temple at
Prinia, twin limestone statuettes of goddesses, approximately half life-size,

seem to have been placed confronting one another in the fanlight over a doorway (Fig. 7), above a lintel which was carved with lions on the one side, stags on the other, and underneath with a pair of draped figures which may have been posed in the 'Auxerre' manner. Little remains of one statuette, while the other is partially restored. On her head the goddess wears a tall crown, beneath which the hair escapes in long twisted curls to lie upon her shoulders; her robes are embroidered with animal figures (a

6. Terracotta plaque, Metropolitan Museum

sphinx, a lion and a horse) as well as with patterns. The feet seem to be encased in thick boots. The work is too accomplished and the detail too elaborate for the statuettes to be very early; in spite of their rectangularity and other Daedalic characteristics they almost certainly date from the sixth rather than the seventh century. Had they been found in any other part of Greece the almond eyes would suggest a dating near the middle of the sixth century. No mouth is preserved, either in the statuettes or on the lintel, but from Cretan terracotta heads with comparable eyes we may assume that the lips conformed with the shape prevalent elsewhere towards the middle of the sixth century. Only on the hypothesis that Cretan sculpture kept in advance of Attic or Ionian can an appreciably earlier date be advocated.

The upper part of a draped male statue from Eleutherna is obviously another example of Cretan work in the lingering Daedalic tradition. The drapery, with patterns carved on its flat surfaces, looks as though it consisted of a close-fitting belted robe and a loose gown above, but the sculptor may have misrepresented the garments; perhaps he was influenced by painters' conventions such as were used about 570 on the Attic

7. Goddess from Prinia, Iraklion Museum

'François Vase'. Nearly all the surface of the head has perished but the features seem to be more strongly marked than was general before that period; in the only well-preserved portion wavy wrinkles diverge from the outer corner of an eye, and the hair above the temple ripples in much the same manner. In other Aegean areas that treatment of hair became common towards the middle of the sixth century but was more ably rendered (Pl. 11b). The Eleutherna statue may therefore be earlier, as its drapery appears to imply. If, however, Cretan sculptors had already lapsed into the provincial backwardness that is so manifest late in the century, the interval (if any) might have been quite brief.

Crete in fact was penalized by a lack of marble and even, in many localities, of good limestone. While it may have excelled the rest of seventh-century Greece in bronze work, there would be no reason to suppose it had ever taken the lead in carving but for the traditional association with the pioneer sculptors, Daedalus and his sons or pupils, Dipoenus and Scyllis. Since the traditions also assert that all three eventually pursued careers on the mainland, whatever importance Crete may have possessed for them would seem to have been transitory. Indeed, their connection with the island may be due solely to confusion of this semi-historic Daedalus with his legendary namesake, the aeronaut. Cretan sculpture should perhaps be regarded as a local variety of Daedalic, not unquestionably prior to any other school; it appears to have endured longer because the islanders could not keep abreast with the changes that occurred in areas where marble was readily obtainable.

Whether or not Crete was initially a centre of sculptural innovation, the lack of marble would soon have halted advance there in the field of most consequence to Greek sculptors, the male nude. On current dating nude male statues can be traced back to about 650 by marble fragments at Delos. The pose these presented is first seen complete in a somewhat later bronze statuette (19 cm. high) at Delphi, of a young man wearing a belt but otherwise naked; this may well be Cretan work—and the perfunctory treatment of the nude cannot be blamed entirely on the small scale. The pose, Egyptian by derivation, is already that which the *kouros* type retained throughout the archaic period; a few more or less intact examples could date from the seventh century but are not Daedalic in style and will therefore be considered in the next chapter. The middle portion of a belted *kouros* at Delos, apparently later than 600, requires mention here because of the likelihood that it was carved, though in marble, by a Cretan; it shows little or no appreciation of the body as a mechanism.

V

The Archaic Period

(620–480 B.C.)

Introductory

THE change from Daedalic to true archaic may seem to imply a difference
of purpose. It involved rejecting the vestigial Geometric tradition of turning natural forms into abstractions; henceforth the endeavour was to make
sculpture lifelike. Daedalic works may show that tendency in one feature
or another (in the bosom of the 'Auxerre' statuette, for instance); the
innovation lay in the consistency with which the tendency prevailed
throughout the figure, but may have resulted from a gradual process
instead of deliberate choice. It occurred first on the mainland, apparently at
Athens, in the last ten or twenty years of the seventh century. In Crete the
Daedalic style may have persisted to the middle of the sixth century;
sculpture then ceased to flourish in the island, which never regained any
artistic importance. On the eastern side of the Aegean, Daedalic was replaced about 600 by a style which became unlike that of the mainland
(with which can be classed the Cyclades). It was centred in the Ionic cities
of the Asia Minor coast—primarily, it would seem, at Miletus and offshore
at Samos, where likewise the Ionic dialect was used. Thasos, valuable as a
source of marble, belonged to this eastern sculptural zone. The Greek
colonies in southern Italy also became dependent on it but were artistically
backward; they would have been handicapped in any event by lack of
marble and in some places even of good limestone.

The general quality of sculpture is higher in the archaic period than
thereafter because aims were simple, so that experiment came within the
compass of the less able craftsmen; the gulf between them and any real
artist did not open until the fifth century, when the effect was to deaden
them.

The rapid advance of sculpture, both on the mainland and in the eastern
zone, coincided with the increase of wealth and, especially in Ionia, with
cultural progress. In mainland sculpture the pace quickened most as the
archaic period neared its close, which came with relative abruptness about

480, upon the defeat of the Persian invasions. A previous decline in the eastern Aegean must be connected with the waning fortunes of Ionia; there, prosperity diminished under the exactions imposed by foreign rule throughout the second half of the sixth century, with the result that sculptors must have found progressively less employment. An unsuccessful rebellion in 499 completed the ruin of Ionia.

Except for the Siphnian Treasury, which is known to have been built in 525 or shortly beforehand, archaic sculptures can be assigned only token dates on the basis of stylistic comparison. As a rule, these should be trustworthy within a decade or two.

The Mainland and Cyclades: Statues

The representation of the nude male body, a subject that evoked scarcely any interest east of the Aegean, formed the main preoccupation of archaic artists on the mainland and in the adjacent archipelago, where the best marble was quarried but less frequently carved. The earliest existing statues are new versions of a Daedalic introduction, the *kouros* type—so called by archaeological convention after the Greek word for 'a youth' in order to be non-committal because the subject can rarely be identified; in some cases a god is known to be represented, in others a mortal (for example an inscription declares the Anavysos *kouros* to be the monument of a man killed in battle, Croesus by name). A gigantic statue in the National Museum at Athens, restored from the fragments discovered at Sunium, was one of two there that stood some 3 m. high; it should come at the beginning of the Attic series, to judge from the remnants of Daedalic tradition shown by the almost flat-cut face and the lumpy body and limbs. The date almost certainly falls between, say, 620 and 590; many scholars put it near the earlier limit. Since, however, the work is dull, obviously uninspired, this may be an instance of a second-rate sculptor having failed to keep up with more gifted contemporaries. On that assumption, the Sunium colossus might not be earlier than other marble statues that are only a trifle over life-size, such as the Attic masterpiece in New York (Pl. 2b–d), commonly dated about 610, or the Delphi identical twins (Pl. 2a), which are not Attic and therefore fit less readily into the sequence; they are often dated about 600. Their faces, though, must have resulted from a Daedalic training, while the hair is treated in a purely Daedalic manner. Probably the stylistic divergences between *kouroi* were then due to a conjunction of other factors—the age, ability and training of the sculptor— as much as to the date. Unless the twins at Delphi are indeed earlier, they must be the work of an elderly man, while the New York statue should be attributed to a much younger man, who may also be the sculptor of a colossal head from the Dipylon, now in the National Museum at Athens, so close is the similarity.

However much *kouroi* vary, the pose remains the same. The figure stands taut, absolutely frontal, with the head upraised, the arms stretched

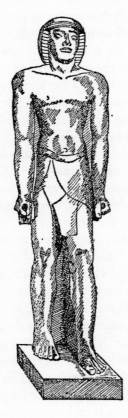

8. Egyptian male statue

close to the sides, the fists clenched; if a straight cut were sawn through the nose, navel and genitals, each half of head and trunk would form a mirror image of the other, but the left leg is always advanced. An impression of movement is conveyed by the slight bend of the elbows and the slightly uneven distribution of weight upon the legs. In all these respects the *kouros* type follows the precedent of innumerable Egyptian male statues (Fig. 8); these normally wear a brief skirt but very rarely are completely nude, as is almost every *kouros*—exceptionally a colossus at Delos was belted like the Daedalic bronze statuette at Delphi.

The type first appears almost as soon as sea-traffic with Egypt became practicable, probably owing to the importation of statuettes. The New York *kouros*, however, was designed with the knowledge of a method whereby Egyptian sculptors determined proportions. Their practice was to rule a grid of equidistant lines on the prepared surface of the block, and carve the figure with each of the main landmarks at an assigned position; trial pieces marked with the grid and the outline of the figure have been found in Egyptian workshops. (Although none are in the round, the conventions that governed Egyptian reliefs were readily adjustable to statues.) The figure sketched on a gridded block extends across seven squares horizontally at its maximum width (at the shoulders and upper arms) and twenty-one squares vertically from the soles of the feet up to a line drawn through the eyes. Thus the knee occupied the entire height of the seventh square upward, while the navel is cut by the thirteenth line. The same positions are obtained by gridding the height of the New York statue likewise into twenty-one squares with the eyes on the top line. In fact the sculptor of that *kouros* made all the principal landmarks of the body correspond with units of this grid. Six squares would extend from the soles of the feet to just below the knee-cap, which covers the seventh; three more end just below the genitals, which cover the eleventh; three more are needed to reach the navel and again to stretch from navel to nipples or from nipples to chin. The distance between the eyes and the top of the head exceeds that allotted by the Egyptians. The proportions of the face as a whole are also different, but seem to have been computed on the Egyptian principle that they should equal certain fractions of the length of the arm; the Greeks, however, chose another terminal point for their measurement of the arm, either through ignorance or deliberately. The width across the shoulders fills six squares compared with seven in Egyptian statues, and this difference must have been intentional. Its purpose can be surmised; the conventional relation of width to height, sanctioned to convey the majesty of Pharaohs or great officials, would have been inappropriate to an athletic stripling. The build of this statue befits that of a young runner; it is, in fact, abnormally slim for an early *kouros*, though similar proportions recur quite often in the mid-sixth century.

A grid modified to obtain the opposite extreme of width was used for the twin *kouroi* at Delphi (Pl. 2a). They stood together on a single inscribed base (now in fragments) on which is preserved the ending of the sculptor's signature, '... medes of Argos'; his name can be restored as either Polymedes or Agamedes. The statues, too, are named as representing Cleobis and Biton, young Argives who took upon themselves a duty reluctant oxen should have performed, of pulling the coach of their priestess mother to the temple of Hera, and there died; Herodotus has recorded the story. One figure (Pl. 2a) is intact except for the booted feet, now restored in accordance with the virtually identical brother's. The ponderous physique was intended, no doubt, to suggest the strength of an ox. That anomaly increases the uncertainty of date, which would in any case be even more problematical than in other statues of the period. Not only must the Daedalic tradition in the head be taken into account, but also incongruous treatments of parts of the body. Primitive conventions are seen in the incised lines of the rib-cage and knee-cap and the faulty junction of the trunk and legs, whereas observance of nature resulted in correct shaping of the shoulder-blades and muscles on the spine. The accentuation of the biceps and deltoids, the lift of the chest and the tension at the knees, all express the uncommon vigour appropriate to the individual subject.

The complete nudity of *kouroi* may have been dictated by that respect for the male body which differentiated Greeks from all other peoples; it was certainly in keeping with their obligatory nakedness in athletics, which must have directed attention to physique. The *kouros* type, which provided full opportunity for its display in an unvarying posture, involved enough problems to occupy sculptors till these were mastered, and then was abandoned. The course of development can be traced only broadly, though over two hundred statues are preserved either complete or in part. In the hundred and thirty or more years they span there is no means of dating except by style, which may be confused by local peculiarities or (as in the Delphi twins) by modification to suit the subject. Attempts to distinguish the products of local schools break down because in nearly every instance there is no signature, and usually no indication whether a statue was carved in the district; even when that fact has been ascertained (by the recognition of a local stone or by unfinished condition), there still exists uncertainty about a sculptor's place of origin, because artists moved freely from place to place. Only when a large number of statues have been discovered in one district can there arise any prospect of reasonable accuracy, and when this condition is fulfilled there are usually great divergences visible in their style. An unmistakable crudity brands as local products many of the limestone and some of the marble carvings found in Boeotia. At the outset, to judge from the semi-Daedalic aspect, must be placed a work executed in the highest possible relief, perhaps for fear that the limestone would prove unsound for a group in the round; the contiguous life-size figures of two youths stand like *kouroi*, except that the two inner legs are put forward and the inner arm of each encircles the neck of the other.

They are identified by an inscription as Dermys and Cittylus; their faces have been worn away, but a limestone head (Pl. 3a) represents the school at almost as primitive a stage. A figure of half life-size (Pl. 3b), in an unusual, perhaps Boeotian, marble, is obviously later; it can as plausibly be ascribed to about 580–570 as to the middle of the century, on different estimates of the allowance to be made for the backwardness of a provincial artist. The finest piece of that time, probably about 575–560, is a huge torso from Megara (Athens National Museum, No. 13), preserved from the shoulders almost to a knee, and measuring 2 metres; its superb mass cannot be appreciated from a photograph. The sleekly curving lad of Tenea (Pl. 3c), only 1.53 m. high, can scarcely be earlier than the middle of the century, but its place is not easily determined because the sculptor was obviously out of touch with Athens. An elongated streamlined colossus from Melos, 2.14 m. high, should be roughly contemporary. A more sophisticated and presumably later work, which departs from the *kouros* pose, compounds elements of both their styles (Pl. 4a, b); found at Piraeus, it is the oldest hollow-cast bronze statue yet known. But remnants of the Tenea hourglass outline are still found in good statues of about 530—the thickset but narrow-waisted Attic *kouros* from Anavysos, in the Athens National Museum (No. 3851) and another in Munich. A statue of the next generation, datable at about 500, has recently been discovered in Attica, standing on a base inscribed with the name Aristodicus. Its proportions were obviously calculated; for example, the height of the head equals one Greek foot (of 28 cm.) out of a total of seven such feet. In the 'Strangford' *kouros* (Pl. 4c), which cannot be placed appreciably before 500 and might be as late as 490, adherence to nature resulted in a comparatively regular outline.

The least inconstant factor in the development of the *kouros* type was a tendency to show an ever greater amount of anatomical detail with increasing fidelity. In the oldest statues, the original shape of the block can still be visualized; it has been trimmed as little as possible into a schematic approximation to the human form, and most of the surface is quite flat. The junctions between the planes are given a regular curve, for preference. Only a few of the most conspicuous surface-markings are indicated and those with less regard to their appearance in nature than to their effect on the whole design of the statue. All this is what might be expected from artists who had been acquainted in their childhood with the patterned shapes of the Geometric aftermath. Whereas the Egyptian prototype was a conventional simplification of the human form, a primitive *kouros* is almost an abstraction, an impressive mass with the essential constituents of a man. But the fact that artists had accepted the body as the basis for design obliged them to observe it carefully, with the result that they continuously found more detail worth including; their outlook and methods changed together by slow degrees. They progressed from observing only a few pronounced lines to seeing that these supposed lines were really bent surfaces, and perpetually discovered more bumps and hollows of interest. Surface features originally marked by incision on a flat surface, like the rib-cage in the Delphi statue, are soon represented by a bend joining flat surfaces above and below; later the trunk ceases to be flat anywhere. A similar transformation can be seen in the knee, the ankle, the ear and other complex parts, which were originally treated as patterns. In any individual statue, if the ear is patterned, so probably will be the knee or other parts; if the treatment of the ear approaches accuracy to some degree, just about that same degree may be expected in them also.

Before the middle of the sixth century, sculptors were concentrating so much attention on details that their statues frequently lack the dignity of the earliest work; they are composed rather as an assembly of parts, each carefully considered in itself but not in relation to the rest. The artists had become so concerned with the various surface-markings that they ceased to realize the shape as a mass. Whereas the Egyptians were concerned first with giving a good shape to the stone, and secondly with making it portray the human form, the Greeks reversed the priorities. But when they had gained more competence they redressed the balance. There may be well-proportioned *kouroi* of all stages in the sixth century but generally there was a steady improvement in that respect towards its end. Meanwhile such complex parts of the body as ears and knees were represented by simplified versions of their true form, while smoother areas were curved into an ever closer but still simplified approximation thereto. The process was very gradual. Only at the beginning of the fifth century was a satisfactory convention attained for the entire surface; the *kouros* type had then served its purpose as material for experiment and was abandoned.

Transition from rigidity to freedom of pose actually began before 480, as is demonstrated in the 'Critian Boy' (Pl. 4d), an Attic representation of a teenager on approximately two-thirds scale. The distribution of weight is definitely uneven, resting on one leg alone, and so involves departure from symmetry in the hips and belly. The slight turn of the head, a deliberate infringement of the 'Law of Frontality', may not have been so distinct an innovation, though the rare instances of somewhat earlier date seem due, as a rule, to errors during carving.

The changes that the archaic sculptors introduced in their treatment of the face were intended, no doubt, to make it conform with each successive advance in the anatomy of the body. In the early heads the eyelids are almost triangular, separated from the forehead and cheeks by grooves, and the eyes so protrude as to be almost aligned with the forehead; a depression separates the cheeks from the nose and the straight, thin-lipped mouth, which is undercut so that the chin is hollowed. A series of life-size marbles on the Acropolis of Athens illustrates the later stages, while in the limestone monster (Pl. 5a), assigned to about 570, both the upper and the lower eyelids already curve, and the corners of each eye are differentiated, but the mouths are straight. The eyes of the 'Moschophorus' (calf-bearer), probably not more than a decade later, were filled with pupils of other materials (Pl. 5b). The shape of the eyes is otherwise similar, but the mouth is arcuated and ends at a deep groove that stretches from beard to nostril. The beard and other hair must have been painted; the drapery—a chlamys alone—required colour to distinguish it from the flesh exposed all down the centre of the figure. The sculptor's signature is preserved only in part; his name should probably be restored as Rhonbus. One of his contemporaries, working in a very different style about 550, carved more old-fashioned eyes in the 'Rampin' head of the Louvre, actually part of an equestrian statue of which other fragments are preserved in the Acropolis Museum (Pl. 5c— from the historic photograph taken when Humfry Payne proved the conjunction in plaster casts). The cheeks are not as smooth as those of the 'Moschophorus'. When prominent cheekbones came to be combined with a mouth sharply demarcated at the corners and irregularly curved, the face assumed the 'archaic smile', which at first would be better described as a grin—and so remained in inferior work. It must originally have been an involuntary effect, produced by shaping the mouth and cheekbones to conform with nature while still allowing the eyes to protrude. Eye-sockets were not carved deeply till the close of the century, whereupon a severe expression became obtainable in conjunction with a naturalistic mouth and cheeks. Meanwhile sculptors could evade the smile only by flattening the cheeks as, for instance, in the 'Sabouroff' head in Berlin, ascribed to about 540; in this the hair is carved like a tight-fitting cap, with a rough surface which may have been covered with a metal wig. In general, however, the Greeks favoured the smile, no doubt because it imparted liveliness to a male face and charm to a female. But no more than a vestige of it is retained in the works of 500-480, such as the 'Critian Boy' (Pl. 4d) and the 'Blond Boy' (Pl. 6a), the hair of which was painted yellow; this head apparently belonged to a kouros which is represented by another fragment that comprises the pelvic region, in a pose like the other boy's. A very similar treatment of the hair and face is found in a female statue dedicated by

Euthydicus (Pl. 10b), which is surely by the sculptor of the 'Blond Boy'. The development in female and male faces had, in fact, kept parallel ever since the start of the archaic period.

Comparison with the Daedalic bust from Mycenae (Pl. 4d) shows that a new spirit already prevailed when a colossal female head (Pl. 6b) was carved for the temple of Hera at Olympia, a building dated by objects found underneath to roughly 590. Since the head is twice life-size and wears a crown, it should represent a goddess; the material is a soft lime-stone identical with that used in the temple for the base of the cult-statue, and the good preservation of work in such material proves that it has never been exposed to the air. From its size it must have belonged to a temple, and no temple except Hera's existed at Olympia at such an early date. That the head must be a relic of the cult-statue is confirmed by Pausanias' description (v. 17): 'In the temple of Hera is an image of Zeus; the image of Hera sits on a throne and he stands beside her, bearded and wearing a helmet on his head. The workmanship is crude.' The style of the head agrees with this criticism, for the formal waves of the hair, the large triangular eyes, the thin straight lips, the wide cheeks dimpled deeply at the corner of the mouth, all point to a remote antiquity, as do the out-standing ears and the general flatness of the face. At the time of discovery, traces of bright red paint remained on the hair and of dark red upon the encircling fillet.

Triangular eyes like the Hera's are found about 570 in the thinner and tapering face of a large sphinx (2.22 m. high), dedicated at Delphi by the state of Naxos (Pl. 6c); it sat more than ten metres above ground, on the top of a column. The sickle curve of the wings was habitual in the sphinxes painted on contemporary vases. The tapering of the body, from shoulders to haunches, is characteristic of the lions in similar marble that are arrayed along a terrace at Delos; they too were almost certainly dedicated by the Naxians.

It must be assumed that Attic sculptors were more advanced than the Naxian, because the little 'Hydrophore' from a pediment on the Acropolis (p. 102) seems roughly contemporary with the Delphi sphinx, though the eyelids are shaped as in nature and the mouth curves; the nose, which is intact, projects so far at the nostrils that the face appears beaked.*

* A marble statue of a goddess, not greatly over life-size (1.93 m. including the *polos*), was acquired by the Berlin Museum in the belief that it had been found in Attica. It is ascribed to about 580 or 570, a period from which nothing strictly comparable survives but some *kouroi*; however, the prominence of the cheek-bones seems incongruous with a dating before 550. The drapery is anomalous; a sleeved peplos falls to the ground in exactly parallel strips, simulating folds, and curves behind the shoulders in a series of overlapping strips from which two tails drop in front, ending in clumsy doubling. The

An ancient commentary on Aristophanes attributes the earliest winged figure of Nike (Victory) to Archermus of Chios, whose name occurs on an inscription found at Delos near such a statue (Pl. 8a); the lettering and the sculptural style alike should date from the middle of the century, but the conjunction is open to question. Similar outspread figures of Nike were often used as acroteria on the roof-peaks of temples. In bronze statuettes of the same type the drapery is allowed to reach the ground between the legs, so that the figure is supported by a wide mass of drapery in addition to the feet; the feet alone would certainly have been too slender a base for the Delos Victory and some such device must have been adopted. Two large wings with an upward curve should be restored, springing out from the middle of the back, two smaller wings from the shoulders and two small wings from the feet; the right arm was probably held level with the shoulders as far as the elbow, though the forearm was bent up; the left arm was bent to allow the hand to rest on the hip. Most of the drapery in front occupies one plane, the back another; the sides again are almost flat, merely rounded slightly at the corners. The bent knee indicates, by the convention familiar from archaic painting, that the figure is running.

Female figures are rare in the mainland and the western Aegean (though common in the eastern region) till shortly after the middle of the sixth century, when the Athenians began to dedicate figures of the *kore* type, probably in imitation of Ionian practice. The term (meaning 'girl') was not used in antiquity; it has been adopted, like *kouros*, to designate figures in a canonical pose, regardless of subject. Actually the type was sometimes utilized for sepulchral 'portraits' of women—a base with the feet of such a statue, signed by a sculptor named Phaedimus, has been found upon a tomb in Attica—but the extant figures were intended, probably without exception, as votive offerings. That some of these, too, stood in the open air is evident from the metal spike in the head to support a protection against birds. The Acropolis of Athens was crowded with *korai*, dedications to Athena of girl attendants, which were broken when the Persian

---

statue, coarse in treatment throughout and with a face of ugly inhumanity, compares most un-favourably with supposedly rather later sculptures on a much smaller scale in the Acropolis Museum, such as the equally beaky but smooth-cheeked 'Hydrophore' and a headless draped figure, No. 593. It could be a pretentious work by some rustic craftsman of that generation. A story (which should be verifiable by a chemical test) that it was found wrapped in lead has been adduced to explain its almost pristine condition, the supposition being that it was buried to keep it safe during the Persian invasion of 480–479; if so, the half-dozen or more Greeks who handled it must all have died that winter with-out disclosing their knowledge of the hiding-place. Charitably, we might imagine that the local community chose this means to get rid of their discreditable though hallowed cult-image.

troops sacked Athens in 480; the fragments were subsequently used to fill pits, where they lay till the last century without suffering further damage. Thus the surface preserved its original appearance, even to the paint, which was applied in contrasting tints to hair, eyes, nostrils, mouths and drapery, and simulated embroidered or woven patterns. They range from much under life-size to slightly over it, repeating the same type with variation in details of the drapery and extraordinary differences in the proportions. Each stands bolt upright, feet close together, one arm raised from the elbow holding a flower or some such object, the other hand gathering the folds of the chiton into a bunch on the hip. The dress is generally the ordinary Ionic costume, consisting of a chiton worn underneath a himation (see Appendix II); a shawl (*epiblema*) sometimes covers the head or the chest, or else hangs from the shoulders. Drapery clinging to the upper part of the body is distinguished by numerous close-lying wavering lines from parts of the same garment that fall free. One marked exception to the usual dress is supplied by a little statue (Acropolis Museum, No. 679) of two-thirds life-size (Pls. 7, 8*b*) where the Doric peplos is worn over the Ionic chiton, with no himation. Thereby it attains a touch of severity which enhances the delicacy of the head; other early members of the series, such as Nos. 682 and 674 (Pls. 9*a*, 10*a*), cloy from their unrelieved sweetness. Yet the insistence upon elegance of pose and beauty of part, which has ranked these statues among the daintiest known to man, never degenerated into mere prettiness. Such a lapse was prevented by the stiff vertical lines of the figure and the himation, the mathematical regularity of the folds, and the symmetry of the whole composition; these ensured a sober structure to the display of delightful form and texture in crisply carved marble. To modern eyes, however, a touch of the grotesque may be apparent, especially in No. 683, a short plump figure with swelling cheeks, dressed in a streaky chiton doubled over the concealed belt so as to bag round the hips, and wearing red shoes; in profile it is not sinuous but extraordinarily irregular. The markedly individual aspect would be consistent with an actual portrayal of the dedicator's own physique; variations in the build of other *korai* could imply that sculptors' predilections were discordant or again that the patrons imposed their own wishes. But the prospect of employment must have attracted sculptors from all the Greek regions to Athens, so that diversity is to be expected in their work. No. 683 has been attributed on no convincing grounds to a Peloponnesian; in fact, practically nothing is known about sculpture in the Peloponnese except that Ageladas (or Hageladas?) of Argos produced statues of Olympic victors of 520 and 516, and of an athlete put to death in 507.

The effort concentrated on decorative surface rather than on form tended to reduce the sculpture of *korai* to a minor art—the marble equivalent of the goldsmith's. The little 'Peplos Kore' escapes that taint, not merely owing to the character of the garment but because it is composed of such clearly defined planes (Pl. 7). An even more emphatic contrast to the average *kore* is seen in a statue one-third larger than life (Pl. 9*b*), which fits into an inscribed base that identifies the sculptor as Antenor; he was distinguished enough to execute a civic monument to the Tyrannicides. The exceptionally heavy build of his *kore* matches the wide and rounded face, the flesh of which hides the cheek-bones; the eyes, of inserted material, were large; the mouth must have been wide and probably did not curve into a smile. The drapery forms austere patterns, including an unnatural swirl of concentric circles between the left breast and the upper arm. The date indicated by the inscription, about 520, puts the statue slightly later than is stylistically plausible for the 'Peplos Kore', the head of which (Pl. 8*b*) is comparable to most of those dedicated on the Acropolis from that time (Pl. 9*a*) to the end of the sixth century (Pl. 10*a*), but totally different from Antenor's. In those statues the head is egg-shaped, the face broad above and narrowing sharply to the chin; the hair is waved and falls over the breasts in three zigzag locks, never far apart, and in a wide, solid mass at the back; the eyes are set aslant, which imparts a smiling effect, enhanced by the small curved mouths, prominent cheek-bones and pointed chins. All these mannerisms must have been adopted for the sake of attractiveness. But Antenor despised niceties and was, indeed, meticulous in avoiding them; furthermore, if he was really the designer of a very conservative pediment at Delphi after 510, he would seem by then to have become inflexibly opposed to change. Perhaps he represents an outmoded tradition of which there may conceivably be vestiges in other *korai*—an occasional sturdier body, wider face, level eyes or less curved mouth. The alternative explanation of his idiosyncrasy would attribute it to a conscious reaction against the fashionable prettiness; in that case no one immediately followed his example, though sculptors at the beginning of the fifth century obviously did so react. But the best example of their work, the *kore* dedicated in 490–480 by Euthydicus (Pl. 10*b*), appears to owe nothing specifically to Antenor; it merely expresses an inclination that then became prevalent, towards strength of form and line. The hypothesis that Antenor represents an outgoing tradition is therefore more likely. Since the very concept of dedicating a *kore* appears to have been introduced from the eastern Aegean, the style that embodied it may have accompanied the novelty, in which case Antenor, who belonged to an Athenian family of artists (his father Eumares, or some relative of that name, having won renown as a painter), might have refused to accept the foreign mannerisms. There is no means of proving that the style had not evolved in Athens, but it seems unrelated to work that preceded it there. It first appears, approximately when the Persian conquest of Ionia impelled much emigration, in the so-called 'Aphrodite of Lyons' (of which the head and torso went to France before 1719 while the legs were still buried on the Acropolis; the conjunction was proved by Humfry Payne). The drapery radiates downwards from the left hand in shallow folds, ultimately derived from Egyptian art, though commonly imitated in the Aegean, especially on the eastern side. At Athens the characteristic style of the Acropolis *korai* can thus be traced back to the middle of the sixth century. It cannot, therefore, be associated with the Cyclades if the carving of the Siphnian Treasury at Delphi, built in 525 or shortly beforehand, was entrusted to sculptors from the neighbouring islands, as might be expected; the *korai* (Pl. 16a) that served instead of columns in the porch are no less solid than Antenor's, their faces as heavy but crude, their hair partly corrugated and partly flowing downwards in a manner rare on the Acropolis.

Female statues, apart from *korai*, were still rare in Greece. A seated Athena on the Acropolis is presumably that seen by Pausanias, who says that an inscription declared it to be the work of Endoeus, whom he believed to have been an Athenian, a pupil of Daedalus. Several existing inscriptions prove that Endoeus worked as both sculptor and painter between 540 and 510, to which time the Athena evidently belongs. Though ruinous, the body retains a liveliness and latent vigour unequalled among archaic seated figures of either sex; the quality is best realized by comparison with a contemporary seated, draped Dionysus, also Attic. Ancient references to Endoeus attribute to him an ivory cult-statue of Athena at Tegea, a wooden Artemis at Ephesus and some marble Graces and Seasons in another sanctuary in that region, at Erythrae, where Pausanias saw a wooden Athena that looked to him as though it were by the same hand.

Another class of seated draped figures, known from fragments on the Acropolis, represented a man writing on materials spread over his knees; the subject, though not its treatment, may have been derived from Egyptian statues of scribes, but whether these Greek writers are correctly called 'scribes' is dubious.

A female type, which goes back to the supposed Victory of Archermus but was predominantly used for the acroteria of temples, is recognizable in the neck and torso, found on the Acropolis, of a winged figure—either Iris or Victory—which, as an inscription shows, was a monument to

Callimachus, the general killed at Marathon in 490. No other archaic work, except the Siphnian Treasury, can be dated so confidently.

The Eastern Aegean

Knowledge of archaic Ionian sculpture is almost entirely based, firstly on statues discovered in the sanctuary of Hera on Samos, on the territory of Miletus or in Rhodes, all of which are much alike in style but represent several different types, and secondly on the fragmentary high reliefs from a temple at Ephesus and another outside Miletus, which are obviously rather later than the generality of statues; low reliefs are practically restricted to peripheral areas—the Troad, Lycia, and eventually, towards the close of the sixth century, Thasos. From such disparate evidence the course of development cannot be traced as clearly as on the Greek Mainland, especially since the two regions held contrasting aims, at any rate during the earlier half of the sixth century. The Ionians were little concerned with anatomy; they preferred female figures to male, fleshiness to muscularity, rounded shapes to rectangular, smooth transitions to clear-cut divisions of parts. They were capable of constructing a finer mass than the western Greeks, and far surpassed them in delicacy of surface treatment until the emergence of the Acropolis korai, which may have originated under Ionian influence. Occasional movements of artists in both directions are attested by the ancient authors. Results of previous contact with the west may be discerned in the remnants of Daedalic sculpture at Samos, a semi-Daedalic ivory statuette from Ephesus, perhaps of a eunuch priest (Fig. 9), and the unfinished Thasian colossus (3.5 m. high), which differs from a kouros only in that the left arm bends at the elbow and clasps a ram against the chest. A number of later kouroi at Samos and a few in Rhodes are characterized by soft forms and paucity of detail but were clearly imitations of western prototypes; the Ionian pilgrims to Delos could see plenty of examples dedicated there. Most Ionian kouroi seem to date from the middle of the sixth century or soon after. At that time Polycrates, the Tyrant of Samos, maintained an alliance with Egypt; effects are visible in sculpture.

Extant authors tell us practically nothing about the archaic sculptors of Ionia, except for Diodorus' story of two Samians contemporary with Polycrates, Theodorus and Telecles; he says that one of them made half of a statue—a kouros, no doubt—in Ephesus while the other was working in Samos on the other half, yet the two pieces fitted exactly. He comments: 'This method of working was never practised by the Greeks, but was common among the Egyptians, and the statue, being made in accordance with the Egyptian system, is divided by a line which runs from the crown of the head through the centre of the figure.' Actually, of course, the archaic Greeks observed the 'Law of Frontality' no less rigidly than the Egyptians, whose grid system probably reached Samos through Attica or the Cyclades.

9. Ivory priest from Ephesus,   10. Ivory female from Ephesus,
        Istanbul Museum   Istanbul Museum

A heterogeneous assembly of east Greek statues has been found only at the Heraeum of Samos. The greatest masterpiece of the early sixth century (supposedly about 570 or 560) is a headless *kore*, still 1.92 m. high, inscribed with a dedication to Hera by one Cheramyes (Pl. 11*a*). Most of the lower part is almost as cylindrical in section as a somewhat later statuette from Ephesus (Fig. 10), but the drapery splays out around the feet. In this respect and in the general treatment of the drapery, the lower part is strikingly similar to the statue of an Elamite queen of about 1500 B.C.; the continuity of art in Western Asia is such that to assume a connection is not so unlikely as it sounds. The folds of the drapery are marked in both figures by parallel lines, except at the end of the garment, which is wrapped round the left side of the Samian statue; the upper part of its body has been modelled with greater care, although here too the sculptor's preoccupation lay with the drapery. On the Acropolis of Athens was found a torso of the same type, joined to a head (Pl. 11b) with shallow and stylized features, in which a trace of the Daedalic tradition might appear to linger, although it actually resembles the Naxian sphinx. The rippling of the hair accords with another old Mesopotamian convention. A surprisingly realistic detail in both statues, where two ends of the outer garment (a short Ionic himation) meet on the shoulder, is the pulling-away of the cloth from the brooches; but this too turns into patterns, composed of three diverging incised lines. At Chios the torsos of two *korai* are grooved, over both front and back, by wavering sets of three equidistant lines, a pattern for which no actual garment can have given justification. Another headless statue from the Heraeum, now in the Berlin Museum, bears an inscription, 'Cheramyes dedicated me, a lovely image, to the goddess.' Though of similar shape, it is less satisfactory because the folds of the himation are as narrow as those of the underlying chiton, so that the surface treatment in the upper and lower parts presents no contrast; the left hand supports a hare, the sacred animal of Aphrodite, to whom the Samians built a new temple about 560–555, and the statue is likely to have been dedicated then.

The same style recurs, apparently slightly later, in four life-size statues, also from the Heraeum, which were aligned (with a fifth, now missing) on a base inscribed with their names and that of the sculptor, Geneleus. The lower parts alone remain of a seated figure, which probably represents the mother, and of a reclining woman—perhaps her eldest daughter—but two standing girls are well preserved except for the loss of the heads; they are named Philippe and Ornithe. The right hand of each holds up a bunch of folds, pulling them upwards in a curve from the waist; the front of the chiton, between the hands and the feet, is thereby made to spread into broader folds, indicated by incised troughs, whereas those above form ridges as in Cheramyes' dedications. The chiton splays comparatively little around the feet, and unevenly, nor does it fall in cylindrical section; a rectangular instead of a square block was used, and much of the eventual surface is practically flat, though the shape of the body shows through the drapery.

Terracotta statuettes in the eastern islands of the Aegean often represent draped male figures in the *kouros* pose, and a life-size example in marble (Fig. 11) is in the Samos Museum; though the surface has perished, folds marked by curving lines can still be seen to diverge with the utmost regularity. This had long been a favourite system in Egypt (Fig. 12). The

11. Draped male statue, Samos Museum   12. Egyptian painting

heavy physique, round head and broad face are characteristic of Ionia. A comparable, though more developed head (Pl. 11*c*), larger than life, was brought to the Istanbul Museum allegedly from Rhodes; in fact, it belongs to a fragmentary statue at Samos, with which the break across the neck fits. The head is very round, the face is too narrow below in comparison with its width at the forehead, and when seen in profile the lower part recedes sharply; the eyes, which rest in extremely shallow cavities, are almond-shaped and set so that they point upwards at the outer corners; the eyeballs protrude beyond the level of the lids; the eyelashes curve in pronounced arches; depressions at the corners of the mouth produce a smiling effect; between the lower lip and the chin lies a deep indentation. In the details, though not in the general shape, the head is related to the Acropolis *korai*, in many of which the hair falls in similar crinkled locks.

Seated figures, which are exceedingly rare in the archaic sculpture of the Mainland or Cyclades, were common in Ionia. They are invariably draped and sit in thronelike chairs. A series of these statues lined the Sacred Way from Miletus as it approached the temple of Apollo at Didyma (also called Branchidae, after the family in possession); most of those extant are in the British Museum. One bears the inscription, I AM CHARES, SON OF CLEISIS, RULER OF TEICHIUSA—THE STATUE IS APOLLO'S. All, in fact, can be assumed to represent male votaries, though the sculptors took so little interest in anatomy that the sex is not always manifest; a similar figure, dedicated in the Heraeum of Samos by Aeaces (which was the name of Polycrates' father), has even been thought to be a Hera. Only one statue retains its head (Pl. 12*a*), which resembles that of the standing male figure at Samos (Fig. 11); the British Museum also possesses a fragment from Didyma—comprising only a head, neck and one shoulder—with a face that cannot have been very different. The arrangement of the drapery to swathe a vaguely outlined body in wide bands, marked by grooves and devoid of ornament (unless it were added in paint), distinguishes this statue from later members of the series, wherein the shape of the body becomes clear and the folds are represented by boldly overlapping planes, which gradually project further and are given individually uneven surfaces. They compose increasingly elaborate designs over bodies more accurately shaped, till eventually the drooping ends of garments divide into pairs of zigzag lines, as in Acropolis *korai* (Pls. 9, 10). The solidity of the mass, which no other pose could emulate, still confers some of the dignity inherent in the earlier statues. Indeed, the type was probably created for no other reason than to express dignity; it seems a greatly modified version of the Oriental formula for representing deities and kings. The Ionians had opportunity to see examples, at any rate in relief, for they now began to penetrate far into Asia.

Some of the finest Ionian sculpture, though preserved only in fragments, consists of figures in extremely high relief that were attached to the bases of columns, a practice limited to Asia Minor and probably not of Greek origin. The earlier examples come from the temple of Artemis at Ephesus, destroyed after two centuries and rebuilt so thoroughly that the details of the original plan are irrecoverable. An uncertain, but obviously quite large, proportion of the columns had been surrounded by figures, approximately life-sized, which must have been arranged to form circular processions, perhaps more regular than in the subsequent temple (Pl. 55). Since no one could view as much as half of each procession simultaneously, the composition required a row of self-sufficient figures, no more obviously related to one another than the statues of Geneleus' family group. The sculpture of the columns was thus designed on different principles from pediments, metopes or friezes, and cannot be classed with them as architectural.

The construction of the huge temple must have been already fairly advanced when Croesus of Lydia, late in his reign of 560–546, established a protectorate over Ephesus and made a handsome donation, from which (as inscriptions testify) the cost of some of the columns was defrayed; whether any existing piece of sculpture came from these is open to question. Since the two other great temples of the century remained unfinished into the Christian era, there is no reason to expect all the fragments to be contemporary; any stylistic differences might be explicable by intervals of time or alternatively by the employment of sculptors from more than one region—indeed, the cult-image is said to have been the work of an Athenian, Endoeus. The largest sure combination of fragments has resulted in the restoration of the lower half of a male figure (Pl. 12b), which is unmistakably Ionian; the drapery conforms with the Egyptian traditional pattern (Fig. 12), which was less closely imitated in the standing male figure at Samos (Fig. 11). A male face (Pl. 12c) is characteristically Ionian in that the planes of the surface melt one into another; the treatment of details, particularly the eyes, relate it to the damaged Samian head in Instanbul (Pl. 11c). A female head (Pl. 12d) is suggestive, at first sight, of the Acropolis *korai* but careful examination of the detail establishes that it is by no means so advanced; no other work can be as plausibly regarded as their prototype. The grounds for calling it Ionian are adequate, if not compelling; it is akin to another fragment, of a male head and bust wearing a leopard-skin over the shoulders, which can scarcely be other than Ionian. Because the superior quality of all the fragments is likely to make them appear later than the average contemporary work, a dating to the mid-sixth century may be as appropriate as any; it implies that they resulted uniformly from Croesus' benefaction, without which Ephesus might have been unable to afford these anomalous and expensive embellishments to columns.

Rivalry with Ephesus, where the population included an indigenous non-Greek element, may have induced the leading city of Ionia, Miletus, to incorporate some sculptured bases in the temple of Apollo at Didyma; it was built about the same time, and destroyed in 494. Fragments in the

Berlin Museum include a veiled female head from one of the columns, with a face resembling that from Ephesus, and another of much greater distinction, still joined to part of the body (Pl. 13a). The veil, formed by a wrap (*epiblema*) that hangs over the shoulder, is held by a thick double diadem, from beneath which escape curling locks of hair, concealing the ears. The face makes an undeniably later impression, but a sculptor of exceptional gifts might well have been in advance of all others at the time.

Historical considerations reinforce the arguments for placing the sculptures at both Ephesus and Didyma before or not long after 546, when Cyrus defeated Croesus and annexed his realm to the Persian empire. Whether Croesus' suzerainty had inflicted much or little hardship on the Ionians is a matter on which no ancient writer is explicit, but they seized the apparent opportunity to free the coast from dependence on the interior —a vain hope, as they found, but one that has arisen periodically ever since and caused unnumbered battles before the Greco-Turkish war of the present century. After this attempt the Persians subdued the coast, more humanely than was then customary; however, the population of two cities emigrated by sea rather than acquiesce in foreign domination, which involved the payment of a heavy annual tribute, aggravated by the extortions of tax-gatherers. Samos was not annexed till the next generation. Meanwhile the output of sculpture in Ionia must have dwindled.

A great Ionian work of the late sixth century, described by Pausanias (iii. 18), was the bronze throne prepared by Bathycles of Magnesia for the ancient Apollo at Amyclae, just outside Sparta. The excavations which have disclosed what seems to be the foundation of the throne leave its design problematical. It appears from Pausanias that around the image was constructed a huge bench, decorated all over with sculpture and supported by four caryatids, two Graces and two Seasons. The reliefs included the labours of Heracles and a swarm of other mythological subjects, some common and some abstruse.

Recognition of the fact that local sculptors were incompetent at the nude may account for the choice of a Peloponnesian to work in Ionia. This was Canachus of Sicyon, whose bronze statue of Apollo at Didyma was removed to the Persian court on the destruction of the temple but returned to its sanctuary after the fall of the Persian empire. A bronze statuette in the British Museum has been recognized, with the help of Milesian coins, as a copy on a reduced scale. The god is represented in the sturdy, upright carriage of a *kouros*, with legs close together, and the left foot slightly advanced. The right forearm is raised to the horizontal, with a fawn lying on the palm of the hand; the left arm is slightly bent and originally held a bow. Cicero's remark that 'Canachus' statues were too rigid to be true to nature' was certainly justified in this figure where the whole muscular system is stretched taut. An almost identical statue in cedarwood was supplied to Thebes.

Archaic Ionian influence has left traces in reliefs carved by the Lycians, a non-Greek people who inhabited the south-west corner of Asia Minor; they laid their dead in tombs of indigenous types, to which reliefs of semi-Greek character were applied. One of the oldest known Lycian works is the 'Lion Tomb' at Xanthus, now in the British Museum. It is carved on two sides with a lion in high relief and on another with a panel of a man fighting a lion (Fig. 13), inspired by Oriental prototypes such as had appeared on Assyrian gems (Fig. 14), but the clumsy proportions and the

13. 'Lion Tomb' from Xanthus, British Museum

14. Assyrian gem

striated hair demonstrate the predominance of a Greek element. Though the style suggests an earlier phase in the sixth century, the date may well be after 550. Another tomb, transported from Isinda to the Istanbul Museum, probably dates from roughly 530–520, because it must have been carved before the introduction of folds into Lycian drapery during the last quarter of the century. It bears upon one side the relief of Fig. 15. At either end walk armed men, in helmets and cuirasses, whose uplifted hands probably grasped spears, once painted on the stone. Between them a man, with striated hair and wearing a long robe, stretches out his arm to hold a rope, formerly represented in paint, attached to the horse's neck; beneath the horse walks a dog. The rectangular hole above the animals contained the 'false door' prescribed by custom as entrance to the house of the dead. The figures are slightly raised above the background but have a flat surface upon which details are worked by incised lines—one such line marks the leg where it is covered by the drapery. The knee-caps are marked by incision.

15. Tomb from Isinda, Istanbul Museum

A stela of somewhat better quality, roughly datable about 520, was found at Dorylaeum, in semi-hellenized Phrygia. One of the local gentry is shown on the back, in one scene riding a horse accompanied by his servant and dog, in another (immediately below) driving a two-horse chariot. On the front is a winged goddess wearing Ionian dress, which falls in long straight folds of slight projection.

Some reliefs set in the gateways of Thasos may be fairly representative of Ionian work at its best, even if they were carved by local sculptors. Two at least were installed not more than some ten or twenty years before 499, when the city-wall was made indefensible on Persian orders. The figures, of slight projection, are above life-size. The slab with a sturdy Heracles, crouched over his bow, is in the Istanbul Museum, but another gateway still retains an ithyphallic Silenus, shown as though striding into the city, with a huge cup of wine in his hand; early Christians battered away the details, so that little more than the outline has been preserved.

The output of sculpture in Ionia (the islands excepted) must have practically ceased for a decade or two after the revolt against Persia in 499 and its savage repression. A simultaneous improvement in the sculptural standards of Lycia can reasonably be attributed to an influx of Ionians in search of employment. To one such may well be due the pairs of supremely elegant sphinxes (Pl. 14a) which flank the 'false door' in each gable of a tomb from Xanthus; the date might be as late as 480. These figures are 63 cm. high; soft plumage on the upper part of the wings must have been indicated in colour alone. Reliefs from the 'Harpy Tomb', which also stood at Xanthus, look more archaic but an occasional detail seems appropriate to about 480. They decorated the four sides of a chamber placed upon a tall shaft of narrower dimensions. On one side (Pl. 13b) are enthroned two female figures, dressed in long robes which trail under the seats; the one on the right, who smells a flower, which she carries in the right hand, and holds a pomegranate in the left, is approached by a line of worshippers bringing similar offerings; the one at the left holds objects which can no longer be distinguished, but a cornucopia is possibly one of them. Behind is the doorway of a tomb, with a cow and calf above it. Enthroned male and female figures, attended by standing votaries, appear on the other sides of the tomb, and at the corners of these three sides are carved the so-called 'harpies', winged monsters with birds' tails and legs but like women from the waist upwards; they are flying away, carrying in their arms and claws tiny female figures, doubtless the souls of the dead. Like the mourning sirens on later Attic tombs, these 'harpies' must be spirits of death; beneath one of them reclines a woman in the attitude of mourning, which proves this contention. It is uncertain whether the enthroned figures are deities of the Underworld or deceased men and women heroized in their likeness—the latter alternative seems more tenable in view of the offering of a helmet, but in questions of Lycian religion no certainty is attainable. The relations of body and clothing proved too difficult for the sculptor: he either makes the drapery stiffly independent or shows the body practically nude, merely scratching folds upon its surface as a reminder that clothes are present. The plumpness of the figures connects them with the sixth-century Milesian and Samian school, which also carved drapery in the same superficial manner by means of parallel lines; these are still found about 490 on a doctor's tombstone (at Basle) which might well be Samian. Similar 'harpies' occur in fragments from the temple of Ephesus, apparently from the cornice.

Many of the ablest Ionian sculptors were induced or, more likely, conscripted to work in Persia from, at any rate, about 490 to shortly after 465. Throughout that period the official style for royal reliefs involved compositions of traditional Mesopotamian derivation but the details were treated in a predominantly Greek manner, which never advanced beyond the last archaic phase. This effective though lifeless amalgam had been invented during the sixth century—not later than 530 on the evidence of fragments at Pasargadae which bear the name of Cyrus inscribed on drapery resembling that of the Ephesus column-base (Pl. 12b). But the finest and most elaborate reliefs, the friezes at Persepolis, were carved during the last years of Darius and the reign of his successor, Xerxes (486–465); their designer has been hypothetically identified from a statement, cited by Pliny, that Telephanes ranked as a sculptor equal to Pheidias and the other Great Masters of the time but his works were 'unknown because he gave himself to the service of Xerxes and Darius' (Natural History, xxxiv. 68). He is described as a Phocian, which should, no doubt, be emended to 'Phocaean', making him an Ionian.

Indirect light on Ionian sculpture in the late archaic period is also obtainable from Etruscan imitations, though the influence visible in any particular figure could have been absorbed long beforehand; the life-size terracotta Apollo from Veii, for instance, was modelled about 500 with drapery that harks back to the Ephesus column-base. The Greek influence that transformed Cypriot sculpture must likewise have been mainly Ionian; in particular there is abundant evidence of trade with Samos (to which Cypriots constantly brought figures from their own island to dedicate in the temple of Hera). But native characteristics remained far more obvious than in Etruria, while close imitation of an entire Greek figure was rarely attempted till late in the fifth century.

The Mainland and Cyclades: Architectural Sculpture and Gravestones

A clear distinction persisted throughout the archaic period between the stiffly-posed statues (mainly kouroi or korai) that stood placed isolated on bases, and sculptures, whether in the round or in relief, that were attached to buildings, high above eye-level; in these as much freedom of posture was allowed as in contemporary paintings (known to us mainly on vases). Low reliefs, especially, were designed like paintings—indeed the craftsman may often have worked directly from a drawing supplied by the master; pictorial influence is also apparent in high reliefs and even figures in the round if they were affixed to a building. It is likewise perceptible in some gravestones, but their composition inevitably differed, because it involved either a single figure or a dominant figure, whereas an architectural panel was best filled with an evenly balanced group. The technique of gravestones is the same as that of architectural low reliefs, though finer detail was requisite, to be seen at close quarters. High relief, on the other hand, at first looked as if figures in the round had been intersected by the background, and the development of a satisfactory convention was not completed till quite late in the sixth century.

The early examples of low relief are generally small in scale; they consist more often of terracotta than of stone or bronze, and there is literary evidence for wood. Pausanias describes at length (v. 17. 5–19. 10) a chest of cedar, dedicated at Olympia by the descendants of Cypselus, who was reported to have escaped murder in his infancy by concealment within it. The elaborate decoration consisted of figures inlaid with gold or ivory as well as some merely carved in plain wood. It must have dated between 657, when Cypselus became Tyrant of Corinth, and 582 when his dynasty ended. The scenes included most of those dear to vase-painters, exemplifying the close relationship between relief work and painting at a time when statuary held quite a separate position. The chest, we learn, was divided into four fields covered with reliefs, and most of the figures had inscriptions attached, to allow spectators to identify the mythological subjects. Somewhat later, in all probability, was the bronze work at Sparta by Gitiadas, a local artist; Pausanias (iii. 17) saw it in the Brazen House, a famous shrine of Athena, the walls of which seem to have been sheathed with bronze plates. The reliefs included

many of the Labours of Heracles and exploits which he voluntarily performed; deeds, too, of the sons of Tyndareus, among others the rape of the daughters of Leucippus; and Hephaestus is seen loosening his mother's chains ... When Perseus starts for Libya to attack Medusa the nymphs present him with a cap and with the shoes which were to carry him through the air. Of the other reliefs those that represent the birth of Athena, also Amphitrite and Poseidon, are the largest and to my mind those most worth seeing.

While these scenes appear to have been very lively, the statue itself had a far more primitive character, if indeed it has been correctly recognized in a crude Athena seen on imperial coins of Sparta. She raises a lance in her right hand and holds a shield on the left arm, while the body from the waist downwards is surrounded by horizontal bands of relief.

We may presume that Gitiadas did not adhere to a peculiar local technique—for otherwise Pausanias would doubtless have commented on it—which distinguishes numerous small reliefs in stone that come from

Sparta or near it, and should be dated fairly early in the sixth century; they show remarkably angular figures by the simple means of outlines incised on a flat surface. Another technique for translating draughtsman-ship into stone produced low reliefs of overlapping planes. It must have originated long before its use in temples near Paestum, at the mouth of the river Sele; a sandstone metope of the earlier set, showing the giant Tityus abducting Lato (Pl. 14b), is as late as 570–560, so backward then were the Greeks of Italy. They remained backward half a century later, when another set (Pl. 14c) was carved, again with overlapping planes. The same method was followed at Assos, perhaps after 550, but the shallowness of the reliefs there may have been enforced by the difficulty of carving andesite, the hard but brittle local stone. The temple (Fig. 1), the only example of archaic Doric in Asia Minor, carries a frieze on its architrave (probably in imitation of temple-facings in terracotta), in addition to the alternating triglyphs and metopes, which take the place of the frieze in the true Doric order. The scenes represented cannot always be identified and are not clearly divided from one another: on the left section of the frieze Heracles is putting the centaurs to flight with an arrow from his bow, on the right he is wrestling with the Triton while Nereids hurry away in terror. The sphinxes at the centre should perhaps be situated at the corners; here, as elsewhere, the restoration is open to dispute and there is no likelihood that the true order of the sculptured slabs will ever be decided.

The style of Corinthian vases is reflected at the Aetolian site of Thermon in life-size terracotta heads used as antefixes and in pictures on terracotta metope-slabs, while its influence also appears in the pediment of a temple at Corfu—a Corinthian colony, which still kept up relations with the founder-city. The date must be approximately 580. Several figures are now lost or represented by insignificant fragments, but most can be almost completely restored (Fig. 16). A Gorgon, 3 m. high, occupies the centre of the composition; she is flying rapidly towards her left, with legs in profile, but otherwise frontally placed; the left knee is raised, the right near the ground. (The opposite pediment seems to have contained a similar figure in the centre.) The attitude invariably indicates flying or running in archaic Greek art. The Gorgon wears a couple of mating snakes as a girdle, and snakes issue from her hair, for in accordance with her function as an averter of evil beings, she must be depicted as fearsomely as possible; she displays formidable teeth and extends her tongue. To either side are placed her offspring, Pegasus and Chrysaor, and behind them her attendant animals—leopards, or lions spotted to suggest tufts of hair, such as are popular on Corinthian vases. Beyond the central, prophylactic group is the secondary subject, the battle of the gods and giants. On the extreme left lies a dead giant. The seated figure, whose chair is backed against a wall crowned with a parapet, probably represents Hera facing into Olympus rather than Priam at Troy; a spear in front is the sole relic of a combat in the next slab. The right corner of the pediment has perished except for a group of Zeus killing a giant; with one hand he seizes the victim by the neck, with the other he hurls a thunderbolt. In all the human figures there prevails a heavy rectangular structure, due to the flat, broad surfaces.

16. Remains of pediment, Corfu Museum

The material used for a series of early pedimental sculptures on the Acropolis of Athens, from buildings destroyed in 480, is a coarse limestone that goes by the name of *poros*; it was quarried in Piraeus. The stone was easily carved, being very soft, but the pitted surface needed plastering; as a cheap substitute for Island marble it could be tolerated where it could be

seen only at a distance, but ceased to be commonly used, even in such positions, after 540. The smallest and most primitive of the Acropolis pediments is a low relief of pictorial character, with a maximum projection of
only 3 cm. Its whole length, nearly 6 m., was devoted to Heracles' attack
on the Hydra. All the right side is filled with the coils of the Hydra (a
monster somewhat like an octopus); towards it strides Heracles, placed at
the highest part of the left side, while his charioteer stands behind him
holding the reins of the horses, which face the left corner. Comparison with
vase-paintings suggests a date about 570. The 'Olive-tree' pediment, so
called because the tree is carved in extremely low relief on part of the background, contains in high relief (17 cm.) a second feature common to vase-
painting, the representation of a fountain-house. The topless relief of a girl,
walking away from the doorway, was followed by the statuette in the
round of another girl emerging after filling her water-pot, which she
carried on her head. This standing figure, known as the 'Hydrophore'
(water-carrier), only a quarter life-size, is historically important as an Attic
predecessor of the Acropolis *korai*. The eyes, large and protruding, slope
downwards towards the nose; the mouth ends with a sharp downward
incision at each corner, like other *poros* sculptures, but is noticeably curved,
whereas the majority have nearly straight mouths. Waves run across the
hair from front to back, crinkling the edge above the forehead, while
three locks fall on the shoulders, maintaining the same distance between
one another instead of splaying out in the old fashion. A dark blue shawl
drops from both shoulders, exposing the front of a red peplos; both garments are smooth-surfaced but at the lower edges of the shawl several
overlaps of cloth are revealed. Smooth drapery occurs in the 'Introduction'
pediment on some of the deities assembled to welcome a newcomer to
Olympus, Heracles; a contrast is provided by the bold, if crude, folds of a
himation on a detached figure. The relief is so high that the figures are
almost in the round. The skill with which the bodily forms are rendered
under the drapery would be compatible with the middle of the century.

The dimensions of the 'Hydra', 'Olive-tree' and 'Introduction' pediments are appropriate to small shrines, but other works in *poros*, entirely
in the round, are of temple scale. The largest may have come from a
temple of Athena popularly called the *Hekatompedon* ('hundred-footer').
The centre at the less important west end could have held the fight between a lioness and a bull, while the coils of enormous snakes filled the
remainder. An attack by two lions on another bull might, if the fragments were suitably arranged, have spread across most of the east pediment,
leaving space at each side for a group that reached the corner. On the left,

Heracles' combat with a Triton, in extremely high relief (up to some 40 cm.) formed a composition like that of the silhouette of the same subject on the Assos frieze (Fig. 1); he lay on top of the monster, his legs and its tail becoming less bulky as they approached the gable-end. On the right, the plaited tails of a three-bodied winged monster dwindled back in the same manner, for he consists of triple snakes below the waist; above it he divides into three human bodies (Pl. 5a). His hands hold symbols of, perhaps, the elements—apparently a rippling stream, a tongue of flame and a bird; these, together with objects grasped in the missing hands, presumably enabled an ancient spectator to identify him with certainty, whereas now it is impossible to do more than make unverifiable guesses—at Typhon, Proteus, or the *Tritopateres* ('triple fathers') of Athenian legend, for example. Since the heads resemble that of the Heracles on the opposite side, they cannot have been intended to look grotesque; yet their faces were bright red and the beards a vivid blue. Acroteria from the temple roof are also recognizable; a Gorgon, which must have stood on the peak, seems to have been flanked by a pair of savage felines over the corners—as though these imaginary beings, which had been centred in the foreground at Corfu (Fig. 16), were now moved upwards to be adjuncts of the pediment.

The three-bodied 'Bluebeard' and the other supposed relics of the *Hekatompedon* are plausibly dated about 570–560, some ten years earlier than some limestone metopes which were incorporated in the foundations of the Sicyonian Treasury at Delphi. The structure to which these metopes belonged is likely to have been an earlier Treasury built for Sicyon; apparently this had taken the form of a roofed shelter, supported on all four sides by a colonnade, over which stood fourteen oblong metopes, 58 cm. high and none less than 84 cm. wide. To help spectators to identify the subjects, the names of characters were added in paint. The broadest and best-preserved metope (Pl. 15a) shows the Dioscuri together with Idas and Lynceus—the last-named is missing—driving off cattle during a raid; each man walks forward with his left foot advanced and carries two spears in each hand, one pair resting on his shoulder, the other swinging level with the bulls' heads. They wear the chlamys open down the front and swinging out against the bulls' ears and horns, for the animals in the two back rows hold their heads straight out in front of them like the lions below the Prinias goddess (Fig. 7), instead of turned at right angles as in the front row. The bulls in the back row are represented on a larger scale than those in front of them—an unnatural convention invented for the sake of distinctness. The use of paint also helped to remove any chance of confusion; the dark red cloaks worn by the raiders must, for instance, have contrasted sharply with their nude legs and with the animals. The repetition, an Oriental device seldom favoured by the Greeks, is broken by the position of the heads; in the case of the animals this has already been noted, and the third human figure turns his head round to full face, whilst the two before him look ahead in profile. Their long eyes, placed at a slight slant, are supplied with a tear-duct at each corner; the lips curve markedly. On another metope there is a horseman at either side, the horse pointing straight out of the field while the rider leans inward to listen to two musicians (one of whom has the name of Orpheus painted beside him) who stand upon the deck of a ship (presumably the *Argo*, in which Orpheus is said to have ventured). Large shields hang upon the bulwarks, and a bundle of pikes is tied at the prow; the ram at the prow slopes up towards its beak, now broken away. The stern of the ship was probably represented on a second metope, together with Jason and other heroes, for there remains a fragment of a ship's side that cannot be fitted into the Orpheus metope. The sideways movement of the rider is even less usual, in this period of stiff 'frontality', than is the bold foreshortening of the horses, and shows how deeply the influence of painting had affected sculptures of the kind. But no painter is likely to have been able to represent so many overlapping surfaces; some of the metopes consist of nine or even thirteen planes.

A Laconian school of sepulchral reliefs, possibly centred at Sparta, was clearly associated with Laconian vase-painting; the finest example (91 cm. high) discovered at Chrysapha is now in Berlin (Pl. 15*b*). Sculptural influence was derived from Ionia, at roughly the time of the Ephesus column-bases. A dating near the middle of the century is therefore plausible, though work of such markedly provincial character might be a great deal later than it appears. The relief is composed of a series of planes, flat apart from incised grooves. The scene was too complicated for the sculptor's ability, but he solved his problem by elongating both arms of the nearer seated figure. Either the deities of the underworld, or a man and woman who have been raised after death to the status of 'heroes', are seen enthroned in a chair, ornamented with animals' feet and a palmette at the back, over which rears the snake that represents the soul of a hero. In his right hand the man raises a drinking cup; the woman steadies one on her knee and pulls a garment away from her head with her left hand. His face is turned straight out of the field of the relief; the beard was presumably perfected with paint, while the upper lip is clean-shaven in accordance with an antiquated custom especially characteristic of the Spartans. Two tiny figures represent worshippers, bringing gifts of a hare, a flower, and fruit.

The temple called the *Hekatompedon* was reconstructed about 530 or 520, when marble figures in the round were placed in the new pediments. From many fragments it has been possible to restore a few of the statues, over life-size, that represented the battle of the gods and giants. One of the central figures, an Athena, looks as Antenor's *kore* might have done if she were in motion; she is swinging sideways to thrust a spear downwards. The heavy and reasonably proportioned bodies of the giants are smoothly rounded without surface markings; in the case of one who has slumped wounded to the ground, legs in profile merge quite well with the twisted belly but then an unconvincing transition leads to the completely frontal chest and arms. The attempt to present so difficult a posture, though bungled, deserves credit as a bold and healthy experiment.

Siphnos, one of the smaller Cyclades, was, so Herodotus states (iii. 57), 'the richest of all the islands because of its gold and silver mines. From a tithe of the proceeds was dedicated at Delphi a Treasury equal to the most sumptuous.' Pausanias says that the Oracle itself commanded the consecration of the tithe. The population, again according to Herodotus, used to share the profits of the mines, which were so large that when the Samians attacked the Island in 525 they exacted a sum equivalent to more than half a million days' wages from the few inhabitants; this occurred soon after the completion of the Treasury at Delphi. When excavated, the building was completely ruined, and was first restored to include portions of several other buildings, the identification of which remains doubtful. Investigation has since left to the Siphnian Treasury two caryatids, a pedimental group, and a lengthy frieze, all of marble. (These used to be attributed to a Cnidian Treasury, to which at present the fragments of two slightly more archaic caryatids are hesitatingly allowed.)

The caryatid forms a new subject for sculpture: the term is applied to female figures used instead of columns in a porch, though originally the town of Caryae had been famed only for its dancing women. The figures (Pl. 16a) are variants of the *kore* type so popular at Athens. With one hand each woman holds out a flower, with the other she raises the skirt of her ample chiton, a foolish motif in a statue intended to carry a heavy weight, since it narrows the base unduly. To ease the awkward change from architectural members to the human figure, a *polos* is inserted between the capital and the head; this circular basket-shaped hat bears scenes in low relief. The crinkly waves of hair, smiling faces, decorative costumes and studied poses have a pleasing air of delicate artificiality.

Unless the pediment of the Siphnian Treasury was left without sculpture, it presumably contained an unworthy composition which might, when

complete, have suited the width of the building, nearly 6 m. No clue is
obtainable from the subject—Heracles' attempt to seize the oracular tripod
of Delphi from Apollo, while Athena (in the centre) restrains them both.
The lower part of each body is attached to the background but the upper
stood free in the round. The carving is poor, showing no sensitivity to
form or line, no power to express depth; folds are marked by incision,
while the stretched portions of drapery are scarcely visible in the absence
of their formerly distinctive colouring. The designer, however, chose
appropriate attitudes to occupy the triangular field without resort to those
unnatural variations in size adopted in earlier pediments.

The frieze, 64–68 cm. high at one point and another, is a far more accomplished piece of carving as well as the earliest successful essay in continuous
composition; it was some 28 m. long. The subjects differed on the four
sides of the building, though one, the battle of the gods and giants, turned
a corner. The portion illustrated (Pl. 16b), from the north side, begins with
a giant attacked by one of the pair of lions harnessed to a chariot; next
come Apollo and Artemis drawing their bows (which must have been
supplied in metal), then a fleeing giant and three who are advancing past
the stripped corpse of a comrade—his name, Ephialtes, was added in paint.
On the east side, an episode in the Trojan War is watched by a row of
deities (Pl. 17a): Ares, whose elbow projects beyond the corner, Aphrodite, Artemis and Apollo all sit on stools, whereas Zeus occupies an ornate
throne. When excavated, the frieze retained many traces of the colouring
which had enhanced its clarity. The description in Frederik Poulsen's
Delphi (1921) no longer applies in the present faded state:

> The background was blue. The figures are treated in blue, green, and
> red, the last colour in two shades, light red and golden-red. The clothes
> are red with blue borders, while the colours are changed when two or
> more articles of clothes or armour are worn. The helmets are blue,
> with red ornamental stripes on the edges, to pick them out from the
> blue background; the last feature reminds one of the little red
> nimbus which in red-figured vases divides the dark hair of the figures
> from the dark ground. The outsides of the shields are alternately
> blue and red, their insides red, with a narrow colourless border
> along the edge, a colour scheme answering exactly to that of figures
> on the Aeginetan pediment. The bodies of Cybele's lions are colour-
> less, but the manes, harness and yoke are red. The tails and manes of
> the horses are red, or, where several are seen close together, alter-
> nately red and blue.

An instructive comparison can be made between the frieze of this Treasury and the earlier metopes of the Sicyonian Treasury, which, too, are in the Delphi Museum. In the later work the human body is slender; the taut muscles sharply rendered, in the legs sometimes by regularly curved lines, expressing the bulges produced in the great muscle (gastrocnemius) of the shin by violent action. The heads are more distinct in profile; crinkly, waved hair is common, whereas on the Sicyonian metopes only the head of one Dioscurus has waved hair; the mouths are more intelligently cut; the eyes, however, show little improvement, being sometimes excessively long when seen in profile, although otherwise they are usually round, but for a projecting tear-duct. Crinkly folds tend to oust the straight, parallel lines, but the wider arc-like folds of the riper Acropolis *korai* are still merely foreshadowed. As a further development in the Siphnian frieze, the pleats at the lower hem of the undergarment are graduated, descending in steps to a point instead of lying level with one another.

The designer (or designers) and the team of carvers employed on the Siphnian Treasury probably came from several widely separated localities, one of which is likely to have been Athens, while similarities to the Ephesus column-bases of the previous generation point to, at the least, influence from Ionia, in the design rather than in the execution. Siphnos might reasonably be expected to have recruited sculptors from the neighbouring islands, especially Paros where the marble itself seems to have been obtained, but the Cycladic style of the time is unidentifiable. In fact, local schools are distinguishable only if their work is manifestly provincial, in which case they may be presumed to ignore comparatively recent developments in Athens, or even in minor centres of art.

On the somewhat questionable assumption that time-lag increased with distance, its extreme should be found in the far west, and that is probably true. A set of metopes from the final Heraeum on the Sele, datable towards the end of the sixth century, is largely devoted to identical pairs of figures dancing along in a procession (Pl. 14c); the same agreeable but generally outmoded style is found on terracotta plaques from Locri and may have been typical of all southern Italy. Sicily appears to have been still more backward.

The crude metopes from 'Temple C' at Selinus were once thought to date from early in the sixth century but have since been ascribed with some plausibility to various times between 540 and 490. A metope that shows Perseus beheading the Gorgon in the presence of Athena, and another of Heracles carrying the two dwarf Cercopes slung upside down from a yoke, are carved in high relief, but in the chariot-group of a third metope the relief is even higher so as to accommodate both the foreshortened bodies of the horses and the three human figures behind them; two of those stand beside the chariot and one within it, yet their heads all reach the same level. The composition reveals a much later stage of development than the details suggest. The pediments in the same great temple are believed to have been left plain except at the centre, to which was attached a terracotta low relief of a Gorgon's head, nearly 3 m. high. A relatively trivial degree of provincialism appears in a Boeotian gravestone (Pl. 17*b*) of a young man who swings an *aryballos*—the oil-pot of an ath-lete—from his right hand while his left holds two pomegranates on their stalk. The formal treatment of the eye and hair is characteristic of Boeotia during the last decades of the sixth century, and cannot be due solely to the use of limestone, which would not take such fine detail as marble. His pose and the anatomical markings are likely to have been imitated from Attic gravestones, though incompetently, as the strange proportions below the waist demonstrate.

An Attic gravestone, more than half of which is preserved in New York and other scraps in Berlin and Athens, presumably commemorated a young man with his child sister; they stand side by side, the youth nude but the girl draped, her head reaching no higher than his waist. Most of both figures is either lost or badly damaged, but the heads are remarkably well preserved. The eye of the girl is narrower than that of the youth, in accordance with a well-established archaic convention for differentiating the sexes, and the eye in both is shown full-faced and projecting, although the head is in profile; the difficulty of transition between the corners of the mouth and the cheek is not yet overcome, but the full lips are not curved into the 'archaic smile'; the rendering of the hair is still schematic; the strong nose of the Attic school remains, and the small flat skull is anato-mically unsatisfactory. The contrast between the texture of the flesh and the background is skilfully brought out. Traces of paint linger on the eye of the youth, the hair and the background. The stela is customarily ascribed to about 540, but the treatment of the hair of both heads is paralleled in a pedimental group from Eretria (Pl, 17*c*), often said to have been carved only a few years before the destruction of that city in 490. It represents Theseus carrying off the Amazon queen Antiope. The faces on the gravestone look earlier, but considering the difficulty of carving features in such low relief they are remarkably alike. A dating about 520–510 is the most plausible for both works, which must surely be by the same Attic master. A less skilful contemporary at Athens failed in the delineation of features in the low relief of a helmeted man running (Pl.

18a), probably a monument to a hoplitodrome, the winner of a race in armour. That Attic arrangement of hair over the forehead and treatment of the heavy thighs is incompetently imitated in the Boeotian gravestone. Another Attic gravestone, of a bearded man with rather similar hair (Pl. 18b), in full armour, is inscribed with the name of the deceased, Aristion, and the signature 'Work of Aristocles'; it should be dated from about 510. The background was coloured red, as were the decorations on the blue cuirass; these comprised bands of maeander (Greek key) pattern under the breasts, at the waist and on the flaps around the hips, with a downward streak of uncertain import between the two upper bands, while the shoulder-piece bore a star and its extension over the right breast a lion's head. The plume of the helmet, the point of the beard and the genitals were made of separate pieces affixed to the stone. The cuirass differs from the 'anatomical' variety common in later times in that it is not moulded like the body it covers, but is left plain; the greaves, as always, imitate the muscular markings of the legs. The left hand grasps a lance, the right hangs down the side of the thigh in an unconstrained attitude; the clenched hand is by no means accurately drawn.

In many respects the Aristion stela invites comparison with contemporary vase-paintings, where such figures are often rendered in a style as nearly identical as the difference in medium would permit. Other low reliefs of about 510–500 decorated three sides of a square block of marble which was found in Athens together with two others; all three were pedestals of statues. A vermilion background survives on two of the sculptured sides; the exposed flesh of the figures seems to have been polished. The eyes, it should be noted, have almost an almond shape and stand out in relief, innocent of lids or other detail. Of the three sides, one (Pl. 19a) represents six young men divided into two teams, taking part in a ball-game, the ball itself being held by the youth on the extreme left; in another scene (Pl. 18c) two youths are inciting a cat and a dog to fight, while other young men stand by to watch; the third shows a pair of wrestlers in the centre, another youth holding a javelin and a fourth practising the start for a race—a less uniform composition. The sculptor throughout missed no opportunity to display the anatomical contortions of figures in attitudes which previous generations had been unable to represent. However, such poses were now habitual in vase-painting, the conventions of which he was, to a great extent, merely translating into relief. In the drapery, which was then less carefully observed, he conforms exactly with the vase-painter's conventions. He may have been a painter (though not of vases) as well as a sculptor. An earlier work of his in the round has been recognized—plausibly, in spite of the difference in scale—in the 'Rayet' male head at Copenhagen.

The fallibility of close stylistic dating is glaringly demonstrated by a set of architectural sculptures at Delphi in which neither the designer nor the executants gave the slightest intimation that they were aware of the changes taking place, although their work looks Athenian and was actually commissioned by Athenians. That fact is recorded by Herodotus; the temple of Apollo burned down in 547, and the new building had not grown much above its foundations in 513, when an exiled Athenian family, the Alcmaeonids, offered to complete it. They went beyond their contract, even to constructing the front of Parian marble, while the rest of the building was of limestone; this munificence may have been due to gratitude after the event or may itself have contributed to the advancement of their fortunes; in any case, the Delphic Oracle incited the Spartans to expel the Peisistratids from Athens, whereupon the Alcmaeonids at once took up a leading position in the republic. If the temple was finished towards 506 the pedimental sculptures and acroteria are probably a few years later than 510, for these would be among the last portions of the work to be undertaken. Many fragments of them have been unearthed, built into later foundations, for this temple also was destroyed and another erected on the site during the fourth century. One marble acroterion has survived in an almost complete condition; it is a Nike flying in the conventional attitude, supported on the drapery between the legs. Wings, curving upwards at the tips, sprouted from the shoulder-blades and ankles. The figure might be described as a *kore* in motion; the boldness of the folds connects it with Antenor's member of the Acropolis series. Two headless figures from the marble pediment resemble that statue so closely that the design is commonly attributed to Antenor. The composition of the whole pediment was no less old-fashioned than the inclusion of these rigidly posed *korai*—goddesses, no doubt. In the centre was a four-horse chariot, in which stood Apollo and perhaps another deity; standing gods and goddesses apparently came next on either side, while the corners were occupied by absolutely irrelevant groups, one of a lion killing a bull, the other of a lion killing a doe. The latter is better preserved; the lion has bitten into the doe's spine, causing her head to droop on to his mane in a pathetic manner, accentuated by her big eyes. The other pediment contained a battle of gods and giants, of which little remains; it was carved in local stone.

A small pediment at Olympia, from the Megarian Treasury, is ingeniously filled with a composition of advanced character but poor execution, so that it appears earlier than its actual date of about 500. Zeus stands in the centre, fighting a giant; Athena and Heracles follow on either side, attacking overthrown giants, then come Poseidon and Ares, each stooping to attack a fallen giant in the corner.

The Athenian Treasury at Delphi was built, so Pausanias declares (x.11.4), from the proceeds of spoils taken in 490 at the battle of Marathon, but he could have been led to that conclusion by reading the inscription (still extant) on a base along the side of the building, where stood some of the captured weapons and a row of ten statues which might possibly have constituted the whole thank-offering to Apollo. The base stands upon a little terrace built to match the Treasury, but while the foundation proves that the base cannot antedate the building, it neither proves nor disproves his belief that the two were contemporary. From the architectural standpoint the construction of the Treasury may be placed late in the sixth century as suitably as after 490, while its sculptures have been claimed for the sixth century because of their style. The sculptures of the pediments had apparently been removed in ancient times; there remain, however, fragments of the Amazons, dismounting from their horses, that formed the two acroteria, and large portions of many of the metopes, originally thirty in number, on which were illustrated the adventures of Theseus and of Heracles, or fights between Greeks and Amazons. Though all may have been designed by one artist, the metopes were obviously carved by a team, diverse in attainment; some are old-fashioned while others exploit the novel twisted anatomy. The subject of Theseus carrying off Antiope is represented in a more developed style than in the Eretria pediment, despite the much smaller size (which is uniformly 63 cm. in width and 67 cm. in height). The metope of Heracles killing Cycnus (Pl. 19b), which is unusually well preserved, displays a mastery of the new postures which does not quite vindicate Pausanias' statement but strongly suggests that the Treasury should not be dated appreciably before 490 and might well be somewhat later.

The face and torsion of the bodies in that metope justify an attribution to the same period as the 'Leonidas' at Sparta (Pl. 19c) which is evidently a relic of some combat group with at least two other figures, possibly from a pediment. Even if it were as late as 480, when Leonidas was killed, it could not represent him, because the statue erected in his honour was seen by Pausanias long after this fragment of an ideal warrior had been buried. The condition of all that remains is unusually good for that reason. The eyes must have been inlaid with realistic material; a row of pin-holes on the upper edge of the left socket may have been required for a subsequent

replacement of this eye alone. Each cheek-piece of the helmet is ornamented with a ram's head, so carved in the marble as to simulate embossing
in the bronze prototype. The neck is extremely thick, the torso massive.
The back is at least as well-finished as the front, and displays impressive up-
thrusts of muscles in violent exertion. A bronze sword must be envisaged
in the right hand, stabbing downwards, while the left arm, with a shield
strapped to it, was slightly raised; the figure was obviously placed askew,
with the back more visible than the front; the exterior of the shield may
have been almost aligned with the edge of a pediment.

The celebrated temple which stands half-ruined on the island of Aegina
was dedicated to an obscure goddess, Aphaea, but Athena is prominent on
its pediments. Most of the pedimental sculptures were recovered by an
expedition of 1811, after which the west pediment was restored with
undue thoroughness and some inaccuracy by the sculptor Thorvaldsen;
more careful excavations have since added numerous heads and other
fragments, preserved in the Athens Museum. The previous finds, in
Munich, have recently been stripped of restorations and rearranged with a
fair degree of assurance that the figures are now in their right order. In both
pediments, battles of the Heroic Age, probably of the Trojan War, are
shown watched by Athena, who stood erect in the centre (Pl. 20a); all
other figures are so posed as to reduce their height progressively the nearer
they were placed to the corners, each of which was filled with a wounded
warrior (Pl. 20b). Of the acroteria only scraps have been found, indicating
that on each peak of the gable stood a pair of *korai* separated by a palmette,
and on each corner a sphinx.

The west pediment, to which belonged the figures illustrated, appears
to have been of earlier style than the eastern, from which only five figures
remain out of a probable total of eleven or thirteen; a couple of fallen
warriors seem to have been put near each corner, as in the Megarian
Treasury. Spare figures in the style of both pediments have been recognized; a convincing explanation of their presence is not yet forthcoming.

The disparity in workmanship between the two ends of the temple
indicates a difference in date (though both lie in the first quarter of the
fifth century) rather than in workmen. On the west pediment the figures
are thinner, harder, more compressed, and an 'archaic smile' lingers: on the
east pediment the figures are more contoured, of greater fullness and softness of form, muscles and limbs contract with pain, the faces are grim and
expressive. Further, the reclining figure of the west pediment (Pl. 20b) is
still of conventional composition, with right leg in profile and trunk full-
face but no resultant twist in the body, while in a similar position on the

east pediment the contortion is represented, though very badly. But in both pediments the body is treated skilfully and surely, with greater concision of modelling than in Attica.

In the more developed style of the eastern pediment the veins are indicated—an innovation attributed by Pliny to Pythagoras of Rhegium. As to the heads, the hair is plaited round the back while wavy lines from back to front end in projecting spiral curls; the line of the eyelids is clear; the mouth is deeply cut and straighter than the Attic mouth. The figure of Athena herself is stiffer in each instance and shows either that the sculptor was less practised in the female figure than his Attic contemporaries or that convention demanded a representation of the goddess more rigid than of a human being.

The scanty knowledge of Aeginetan sculpture to be derived from literary sources bears out the assumption that the pediments are due to local talent. The famous sculptors of the island are supposed to have excelled in the representation of the nude male body, although the earliest of them, Callon, made an Athena for the acropolis at Troezen and a *kore* at Amyclae. Onatas, whose services were in request in many parts of Greece but especially in the Peloponnese, made a new image of the 'Black Demeter' of Phigaleia, a horse-headed monster which could not have contributed much to the advancement of his art; he executed a colossal Heracles for a Thasian dedication at Olympia, a chariot and charioteer for Hieron of Syracuse; many of the figures in a dedication by the Achaeans, of a group of heroes of the Trojan War, were attributed to him. Glaucias too was a famous Aeginetan, who made a chariot-group containing a figure of Gelon, Tyrant of Syracuse, after his victory at Olympia in 488, in addition to various statues of athletes. A fourth sculptor of repute from the island was Anaxagoras; a Zeus by him was dedicated at Olympia by the Greeks who had fought at Plataea in 479.

The heads from the Aegina pediments tend to be slick, smooth and dull. The style is exemplified at its best in a life-size bronze head (Pl. 21a) from the Acropolis at Athens; the face resembles especially that of the dying warrior in the corner of the east pediment, while bases signed by both Callon and Onatas have been found on the Acropolis. It is a finely finished piece of work; the mass formed by the hair of the head, beard and moustaches is cleanly outlined and the hairs themselves represented by tiny lines, except on the forehead where they form a frill of petal-like curls; the lips are full and deeply cleft; the eyelids project, giving the appearance of lashes over the sockets, in which the eyes were inlaid in some other material.

VI

The Early Classical Period
(480–430 B.C.)

The First Post-Archaic Generation

A N age of conscious glory opened with the defeat of the Persian invasions of 490 and 480–79, whereby the Greeks proved themselves individually as well as collectively superior to other peoples. A new spirit of unbounded self-confidence prevailed, to an even greater extent than in Elizabethan England after the defeat of Spain. The arts suddenly flowered in an outburst historically unparalleled. Sculptors, after the long probation of the archaic period, were able to express the new mood by creating a style aptly described in Georgian English as The Sublime. It was rooted in the satisfactory conventions attained between the two invasions for the faces and bodies of *kouroi*, and in the somewhat earlier successful representation of physical activity, which had been restricted to architectural filling or relief but was now introduced into free-standing statues. Liberty of pose was encouraged by the increasing use of bronze, with which scarcely any problems of equilibrium were encountered, while projections required no support. At Athens and in southern Greece development proceeded very quickly for thirty or forty years; elsewhere an aftermath of the archaic lingered—in peripheral regions even into the latter half of the century.

The murder in 514 of Hipparchus, the Tyrant of Athens, by Aristogeiton and Harmodius, was extolled by the Athenians of the republic as the act out of which their freedom grew. A bronze group by Antenor which commemorated these Tyrannicides was carried off to Susa in 480 as part of the spoil of Athens and recovered after the conquest of Persia by Alexander the Great; presumably it was executed about half a dozen years later than the assassination. A substitute, the work of Critius and Nesiotes, was dedicated in 477. A group which corresponds to descriptions of these statues is recorded on coins of Athens, as well as on a crude relief and minor works of art, whereby it has been possible to identify two statues at Naples as copies made in the Roman period, and to restore, by combining all the evidence, a fair semblance of the originals (Pl. 21*b*).

The evidence does not extend so far as to determine the precise angle at which the figures were placed one to another, but it appears that they were converging on their victim; the adult Aristogeiton stretches out the drapery on his right arm to shield the body of his young lover Harmodius, who is striking down the tyrant with his sword, which he holds above the head, pointing down his back. Aristogeiton held his scabbard in his left hand, while the pale streak across the chest of the Naples Harmodius proves that he had been equipped with a sword-belt of bronze, from which the scabbard may have hung. The order of the limbs in the two figures is carefully contrasted; the left foot of one corresponds to the right in the other, the left side in the one balancing the right in the other. Hereby a certain symmetry is attained when the statues are juxtaposed, giving a fine impression of vigorous and concerted action. When the bodies are closely examined they are seen to be covered with a confused mass of detail, adequately conveying the effect of strained muscles on lean and powerful frames, though anatomically inaccurate.

In the Naples copies, tree-trunks form a support necessary to marble statues though superfluous to bronze, of which material the original group was made; they are therefore an addition of the copyist. The right arm of Aristogeiton, the arms, right leg and lower left leg of Harmodius are restored; moreover, the head pinned on the statue of Aristogeiton is obviously incongruous, being in fact of a fourth-century style. A bearded head, the original of which must plainly be associated with the same school as the Harmodius, was found, like the group, in Hadrian's Villa near Tivoli and must be that of Aristogeiton. This head, now in Madrid, was wrongly mounted on a bust inscribed 'Pherecydes'; other copies exist. A plaster piece-mould of the face, discovered in an ancient copyist's store at Baiae, seems to have been taken from the original; a bar over the eyelid probably resulted from a protective covering to the eyelashes. A head of Harmodius in New York is an improvement on the Naples copy. The faces of both statues retain the stiff formality of the archaic, the drapery falls in rigid parallel folds, and the bodies must have conveyed an impression of metallic hardness.

Critius and Nesiotes (who appears to have been much the elder of the pair) habitually collaborated; how they divided the work between them is unknown. Their signatures, as equals, are preserved on the base of the Tyrannicides, and that of the lost statue of an armed runner, Epicharinus, which may be imitated in a bronze statuette at Tübingen. A similarity to the Tyrannicides, particularly to the youthful Harmodius, justifies the attribution to one or both of the two artists of the 'Critian Boy' (Pl. 4d), a marble original found in the wreckage on the Acropolis. This figure, of probably shortly before 480, illustrates the passing of the *kouros* stance; the weight is thrown chiefly on one leg, consequently the hip is raised and the median line no longer rigid.

The bronze torso of a comparably posed youth in the Archaeological Museum at Florence, though a dull work, may give a fair idea of the surface treatment on the Tyrannicides. It is of some interest, too, as a study of anatomy. The ligament from hip to groin is given due prominence, whereas in the 'Strangford' *kouros* (Pl. 4c) it had been shown only by incision, and comparatively naturalistic details take the place of anchor-like markings on the 'Strangford' epigastrium.

The ingenuity with which low relief could be carved about 480 is best demonstrated in a gravestone (Pl. 21c) discovered in Boeotia and made of the local stone, although the inscription proudly states in hexameters: ALXENOR OF NAXOS MADE [ME]: JUST LOOK. The man, wrapped in his himation, leans lazily on a knobbly stick wedged into his armpit, while in his right hand he holds a locust at which his dog leaps playfully. The position of the feet is unusual; only the toes of the left rest on the ground, leaving all the weight of the body to fall on the right foot, which is planted firmly at right angles to the other, pointing straight out of the field, and thus involves more foreshortening than could well be allowed in a relief of such slight depth. From a photograph the resulting awkwardness cannot be fully realized, although it is immediately appreciated in the original or in a cast. It may be thought that the artist was more accustomed to drawing or painting than to sculpture, otherwise he would not have attempted such a feat of illusion; but perhaps the sight of foreshortening in two dimensions stirred him to emulation. The smooth top of the head was at first interpreted as a skull-cap, to which it was objected that the double line below the hair resembles a fillet rather than the edge of a cap; moreover, there can be no possibility of a metal cap since there are no holes into which it could have been fitted. Perhaps the hair was painted over the crown, as happened later on in this generation in the Olympia pediments and had probably been the case with the early statue of the 'Moschophorus'.

To tie the composition together, the dog rests his forepaws on the side of the niche in which the figure stands. The drapery is made to run in parallel folds almost as schematic as in the Ephesus column, but naturalistic touches won by observation do occur; the stick collects a bunch of cloth around its head, the side of the slim left leg is marked out by one of the regular folds while the thigh and right shin are bordered by special short folds of their own making. The larger muscles of the neck and arm are well displayed in spite of the lowness of relief.

On some gravestones occupied by a comparably posed male figure and a dog, the drapery is more simply represented, with grooved regular curvature at wider intervals. One such slab, found at Apollonia on the Black Sea, is in the Sofia Museum; another, at Naples, might have come from southern Italy. Both regions had been subjected to Ionian influence, which accounts for the similarity and the backwardness of the works.

Intentional backwardness appears at Athens on a votive relief, probably of about 480, on which Athena is shown with worshippers, in drapery made quaint by imitation of sixth-century mannerisms. This may be the earliest instance of deliberate archaism in sculpture. The vases given as prizes in the Panathenaic Games had long been painted with a figure of Athena, for which the archaic style remained obligatory after it became obsolete for all other purposes; since many of these amphorae exist, and each bears the date of the festival at which it was won, the process of change can be followed from contemporary archaic to slightly archaizing and on to thoroughly archaistic figures. In decorative sculpture an occasional slightly archaizing piece occurs from this time onwards to the second century, when a full-blown archaistic style was evolved.

A contemporary of Critius and Nesiotes must be responsible for the life-size bronze charioteer at Delphi (detail, pl. 22a), which was found at a spot where a wall was built in the fourth century to prevent rocks and earth of the mountain slope from tumbling into the temple terrace; the chariot group must have gone down in some landslide, perhaps that of 373 B.C., and become buried too deeply in rubbish for discovery during later building operations. Its position saved it from the melting-pot—the usual fate of ancient bronze statues during the Christian era. The lower half of the figure was found first, in 1896, and the upper part some days later; with it were recovered a piece of a stone base, bits of the chariot pole, two hind legs of horses, a tail and hoof, remnants of reins and a childish arm. The base was supplied in Delphi, of limestone quarried in the neighbourhood, and on the block preserved is the end of a metrical inscription assigning the dedication to Polyzalus, whose elder brother, Hiero, was Tyrant of Syracuse. Probably Polyzalus won the chariot-race in 474; the only other possible date would be 478.

The complete group would necessarily have involved four horses and a chariot containing the figures of the prince and the victorious charioteer; two grooms might hold the bridles of the outer horses of the team, standing or mounted, and perhaps the arm belongs to one of them or to a youthful Nike perched on the car. No doubt the group was placed on a high terrace. The charioteer seems to have been set up in three-quarters view, presenting the right side to the spectator; this is suggested by the lack of symmetry in the features, the right eye being longer than the left, and the left side of the face uplifted. The quiet stance of the charioteer implies that he was driving at walking pace after the race. Everywhere the figure is finished with exquisite care and the flesh modelled with unprecedented diversity. It is a work of the greatest discretion, so balanced between stylization and naturalism as to be artistically unified though factually most inconsistent, lively but not lifelike. The long Ionic chiton, the conventional dress of charioteers, falls easily from the constraining girdle, away from the figure, in deceptively simple-looking folds, more regular than the heavy woollen cloth could have formed, but individually shaped; they are deeper and more rounded than any archaic folds. The gathering of material under the arm and on the shoulder is skilfully patterned without being stiff. The hair too is stylized; it lies quietly at the confining band, which should actually have pressed it down, while the curls over the entire scalp are unnaturally regular though each is of natural shape. The body is long, the limbs slender, the neck strong but not heavy and the head small. The head is turned slightly to the right, while the right arm bends in the opposite direction, imparting a pleasant and gentle rhythm. The face is austere, hard of line, without a trace of the 'archaic smile'. The lips are parted, to show a line of teeth rendered in silver; the cheeks are narrow, the bones not prominent. The eyes are straight set, almost almond-shaped, with a filling of white enamel and onyx; eyelashes of inserted bronze spikes also remain. The crown of the head is high and dome-shaped, unlike the Attic flattish crown with prominent occiput. The biceps swell gently; skin-folds in the hands, the vein in the inner side of the elbow, the tendons and veins of the ankles and feet, are kept within the bounds of a stylized naturalism.

It remains to discuss the sculptor, although it must be confessed that no certainty can be reached as to his identity. The Sicilian princes employed for chariot-groups in Olympia the Athenian Calamis, and the Aeginetan Onatas, and in other groups Onatas collaborates with his compatriot Glaucias, while a golden Nike at Delphi was by Bion the Milesian. The other great artists of the time were Pythagoras of Rhegium, author of a four-horse chariot at Olympia, and (if still active) Ageladas of Argos, who worked mainly before 500; he would surely have been incapable of so revolutionary a statue. Calamis of Athens and Pythagoras are the two most likely names, the Aeginetans being practically out of the question because of a lack of any resemblance to the pedimental sculptures from Aegina.

Neither original nor assured copy exists to witness the style of Calamis, the Athenian. He made many statues of gods, including especially a chryselephantine Asclepius at Sicyon, the Hermes carrying a ram at Tanagra and the Apollo *Alexikakos* (Averter of Evil) at Athens: the two latter were dedicated after plagues, the Apollo being traditionally connected with the great epidemic of 429, an impossible date unless the sculptor was another Calamis, who is known to have existed. The elder supplied statues of boys mounted on racehorses for the Sicilian dedication at Olympia in 467. He was peculiarly famous for his horses; Pliny has a tale that Praxiteles 'placed a charioteer of his own on a four-horse chariot by Calamis, in order that an artist better at representing horses should not be accused of failure in the case of human beings'. The poses of Calamis were considered less rigid than those of Canachus, less supple than those of Myron. Another general comment, by Dio of Halicarnassus, compares the oratory of Lysias with the sculpture of Calamis, 'for grace and delicacy', while he parallels the oratory of Isocrates with the art of Polycleitus and Myron, for strength and grandeur.

Pythagoras, a Samian by birth but naturalized at Rhegium (Reggio) in south Italy, presumably took part in the emigration of the 490s, when Samian refugees settled at Messina and fell under the domination of Anaxilas, Tyrant of Rhegium. On the base of his statue of the boxer Euthymus (erected after a third victory at Olympia in 472), he signs himself as a Samian. His figure of 'the lame man, the pain of whose wound seems to be felt by those who look on him' (Pliny) testifies to unusual powers for an early sculptor. All works of his which are described were of bronze and, with the exception of a Europa on the bull, male figures, mostly of victors in the Games. That he was skilful in representing details like muscles, veins and hair is proved by Pliny's remark that he was the first to 'work out' the subject carefully (xxxiv. 58); veins had been marked in the frieze of the Siphnian Treasury and in the pediments of Aegina, but Pliny may be correct in the sense that he was the first to treat the subject scientifically. According to Diogenes Laertius (viii. 46) Pythagoras was thought 'to have been the first to aim at rhythm and proportion'. Such characteristics and virtues would suit the sculptor of the Charioteer. But Pythagoras can be considered eligible only if it displays the influences to which he himself was subjected, first as an Ionian (assuming that he had entered upon his career before he left Samos), secondly as a resident in south Italy. A difficulty immediately arises, because the Ionian style at the time in question is practically unknown, except by inference from monuments of the past or from derivative work, especially in Lycia and the northern Aegean area.

Nor do many Greek sculptures survive that were unquestionably produced in Italy during Pythagoras' working life; they tend to be backward in relation to the standards of Greece.

A colossal statue of a seated goddess, now in Berlin, was found in the ancient cemetery at Taranto, where other monuments were concerned with the Underworld; the youthful face (Pl. 22b) is appropriate to Persephone. The figure and the chair are carved from a single block of Aegean marble, which must have weighed considerably over a ton when shipped. A row of small holes along the diadem carried a metal ornament, while metal earrings were also supplied; gold or gilt bronze would normally be used for such purposes. In the face can be traced a remnant of the 'archaic smile', the popularity of which was on the wane. The date may be about 470 because the artist was out of touch with the tendencies of the day. His skill shows to greatest advantage in the disclosure of the body beneath the drapery, in the formal design of the folds and in their distribution over the figure at regular intervals; seen in profile, the lines of the drapery, of the bust, of the plaits of hair, and of the nude forearms, all diverge from the same point like the petals of a flower.

The Taranto goddess must have been carved in Italy, so fragile are the fragments of the chair, but the marble head of Apollo could have been imported ready made for the cult-image at Crimisa (Cirò in Calabria); it seems to have been fitted to a wooden body. Metal hair was set on the bald pate. The face in general looks as though it might date from 480 but is probably much later. A possible relic of another such cult-image in Italy is the enormous 'Ludovisi' head (83 cm. high) of a goddess, in the Terme Museum; the blank countenance must likewise be considerably later than the Taranto statue. Four large metopes from Selinus consist of limestone with marble adjuncts to represent female flesh; the style suggests a date near 480, but the temple (known as 'E') to which they belong, dedicated to Hera, seems to have been built as a thank-offering to her for the aqueducts Empedocles constructed in 466, so that the time-lag implied amounts to some fifteen years—during which sculpture in Greece changed radically.

Comparison with terracotta plaques from Locri indicates that some existing low reliefs were almost certainly carved in southern Italy, though the marble came from the Aegean. The finest, beyond question, is the 'Esquiline' stela (Pl. 22c), on which the figure is life-size; it must have been taken to Rome as a collector's piece some two thousand years ago. Originally it stood on a woman's grave; the bird she holds could be an offering to the deities of the Underworld. The drapery is skilfully treated to recede on seven planes, beginning in the foreground with a twisting edge that hangs off the right arm and ending with a straight drop from the bunch held by the left hand. The system of parallel folds is clearly of Ionian derivation, harking back to the statues dedicated by Cheramyes (Pl. 11a), in which a thin cloth is shown as forming a set of identical ridges. In the relief, however, the folds are differentiated in width and also in shape, some being hollowed in front, others creased as they retreat. The archaic aspect of the work is, in fact, misleading, due simply to the backwardness of local tradition. Making allowance for the difficulty involved by the technique, the head might be contemporary with the Taranto goddess, which cannot be appreciably (if at all) earlier than the Delphi Charioteer. The same principle of design, though emancipated from the archaic formula, is applied to the thicker garment worn by the Charioteer where it drops in parallel folds; these likewise are hollowed in front and creased as they retreat. But the treatment of drapery on the upper part of the Charioteer, though in no way comparable with that on the 'Esquiline' stela, might easily have been evolved by a greater compatriot of the man who carved the 'Leucothea' gravestone (Pl. 23a, from a photograph on which some patches of restoration had been obscured). This too must be ascribed to southern Italy and is Ionian by inspiration; it belongs roughly to the next stage of development after the Lycian 'Harpy Tomb' (Pl. 13b), and follows a precedent known in archaic Laconia (Pl. 15b). The deceased, seated in the armchair, with a child on her lap, is receiving a woollen fillet from her maid. Two little figures, one holding a couple of birds, are identified by their immature forms as daughters of the seated woman, and the difference in their heights may relate to their respective ages. Under the chair is a basket, woven of rushes, though its surface was left plain for the details to be added in paint. That the maid's head should appear only on the same level as that of her seated mistress is owing both to her lower status and to a convention whereby seated or standing figures and animals were required to reach approximately to the same height, to avoid the introduction of irregular lines in a composition. It is questionable whether the three upright figures are to be visualized as standing in a row in front of the chair, or as dispersed along the side of it in less formal arrangement; in any case the graduation of the girls' figures is not to be thought of as an essay in perspective, in which the most distant appears as the smallest, for such an attempt would have no parallel. The chair and footstool were probably painted with palmettes or scroll ornaments of conventionalized foliage, such as occur on extant bronze specimens of ancient furniture, thus presenting a richness of surface in keeping with the elaborateness of the drapery.

A relief from Thasos (Pl. 23*b*) may serve as a reminder that sculptors of the northern Aegean also kept to the Ionian style. This scene of family life is an early instance of the 'Funeral Banquet' motif that recurs on tombs into the Roman empire. An attenuate youth is drawing a jug of wine from a huge mixing-bowl; the man upon a couch holds out his empty cup impatiently, while behind him sits his wife, busy with her distaff. The man's helmet and shield are hung upon the wall, a dog noses around under the table and a bird sits beneath the housewife's chair.

An extraordinarily good sculptor in the Ionian tradition can be assumed to have carved, between 470 and 450, the 'Ludovisi Throne' in Rome and its counterpart in Boston, which likewise was found on the Ludovisi estate inside Rome, though not till many years later. Analysis has shown that they consist of dolomitic marble, which must have been quarried on Thasos. Each 'Throne' was hollowed out of an oblong block into a shape vaguely suggestive of the arms and back of a chair, for the ends slope downwards from the long side, which must have been the front; it measures 1.40 m. by approximately 1 m. in height. The pair must originally have been intended to stand with the reliefs facing outwards, as a screen to some rectangular space within a sacred building; a temple at Locri contains a pit which could have been so enclosed, had the ends been placed in contact, but if a gap had been left between the ends there might have been an altar in the enclosure. At all events the correspondence in shape between the two blocks is sufficient to establish their original connection, whatever their purpose. Interpretation of the subjects of the reliefs has varied considerably, and none of the suggestions quite meets the requirements. On the 'Ludovisi Throne' the front (Pl. 24*b*) is occupied by two female figures stooping to lift a third, who rises from a hole in the pebbly ground between their feet while the lower part of her body is concealed by a cloth upheld for that purpose; on the ends are a nude girl playing the double-flute (Pl. 24*a*) and a veiled woman burning incense (Pl. 25*a*), both life-sized. The central relief presumably represents a goddess rising at birth from the earth or sea—Persephone in the first case, Aphrodite in the second—or else being raised from a ritual bath and drawing on a ceremonial robe, rites common to many goddesses; the figures on the ends should be votaries of the goddess. Similarly the ends of the Boston counterpart represent votaries, a young man playing the lyre and an old woman holding an object of uncertain nature, but the front (Pl. 25*c*) shows a winged youth, from whose hands once hung a metal balance; in each scale is a small figure of a youth, and by the heavier sits a rejoicing woman, by the lighter a mourner. This group may illustrate Death holding souls of men in the balance or Eros weighing out the chance of offspring to two wives, but there are other possible interpretations. The proportions of the 'souls' standing on the scales are attenuate, like the youth on the Thasian relief (Pl. 23b), while the closest analogy to the head of the old woman on the end (Pl. 25b) is to be found in a Lycian relief of an aged married couple; it filled the gable of a tomb at Xanthus, but is now in the British Museum.

The Ludovisi estate, on which the 'Thrones' were found, occupies the site of the Gardens of Sallust, which afterwards belonged to the Roman emperors; the heterogeneous collection of sculpture since recovered from the ground must have been acquired largely by Sallust himself about 40 B.C. The 'Thrones' were probably carved in Italy for some Greek city from rough blocks of imported Thasian marble; although the reliefs were shallow enough to travel ready-carved without injury, the hazards of a voyage made it more prudent to ship the marble to be worked on the spot and thus evade a possible loss of sculptor's wages. This artist evidently specialized in reliefs. His mastery of the third dimension (even more adept than his Italian predecessor's in the 'Esquiline stela') cannot fully be appreciated without handling the slight variations in the surface-levels; he used a depth of less than 6 cm. for the flute-playing girl—incidentally the earliest successful female nude in Greek sculpture. He made drapery appear as soft as cloth by relaxing the definition of folds till they become mere suggestions; the transparency he gave it on the ascending goddess anticipated a development of the next generation. The fact that he shows no trace of provincialism does not rule out the possibility of an Italian citizenship, as the example of Pythagoras demonstrates, but in that case we must assume that he had seen contemporary work in other countries, including the homeland of his style. Alternatively he could have been one of those Ionians who did not emigrate but fulfilled an occasional commission overseas.

The Temple of Zeus at Olympia was probably begun after 470 and was sufficiently complete in 457 for the Spartans to offer a golden shield to be placed on the roof. Statues of one and a half times life-size filled the pediments, and twelve metopes were sculptured. Pausanias (v. 10.8) attributes the western pediment to Alcamenes, the eastern to Paeonius, but this information is highly questionable. The ascription to Paeonius has not found many defenders, for the Victory signed by this artist (Pl. 43b) is a work of forty or fifty years later, and few profess to see any points of similarity. The Nike's inscription records the acroteria—likewise Victories—as the work of Paeonius, and it has been conjectured that Pausanias was somehow misled into a belief that the pediment also was included.

The chronological discrepancy is still greater in the case of Alcamenes, whom Pausanias himself records to have signed a relief dedicated to commemorate an event of 403. But in some of his works Alcamenes imitated styles of the past; in particular, the head of his Hermes Propylaeus followed broadly the manner of about 480 or 470, though careful examination puts it a generation later.

Looking at them without prejudice, the metopes and both pediments appear to have been designed by one artist but at various times. This 'Master of Olympia' remains anonymous; since his identity was not remembered at Olympia he probably died too young to achieve lasting fame. From certain indications he seems to have originated neither in Athens nor in the Peloponnese, but to have come under the influence of both those centres, gaining power especially from a study of the great mural paintings in progress at Athens. The carving must have been executed by a team of craftsmen, probably gathered from more than one city; their total work would have occupied one man's full time for at least 135 years, and is likely to have been completed within a decade, so that the number continuously employed may be guessed as between a dozen and twenty. Even had the Master supplied them with plaster models of the figures, his style would necessarily have been transmuted to some extent in the process of carving on an enlarged scale. But perhaps he did no more than supply drawings; it has even been suggested that he was a painter by profession. The hypothesis that he was a native of the eastern Aegean should be regarded as non-proven, but he was certainly familiar with the work of that region or of its western dependencies. The fact that some of the subordinate craftsmen achieved better female than male forms could imply that they too belonged to an Ionian school.

The Master's style is visible in its earliest form in the twelve metopes, six at either end of the building, which were placed within the colonnade over the entrance to the temple chambers. Portions of all survive, distributed between the Olympia Museum and the Louvre, for a French expedition in 1829 found and removed some large fragments, while many others were recovered during the German excavations later in the century. The metopes represent the twelve Labours of Heracles, in every case introducing Athena, the friend and patron of the hero; the figures are life-size. The slabs were brightly coloured, the backgrounds contrasting with the figures. The subject of the cleansing of the Augean stables, after which achievement Heracles was said to have founded the Olympic Games, naturally took pride of place (at the beginning of the front end of the temple) because of its local connection (Pl. 26a): Heracles is diverting a river into the stables while Athena seems to direct his effort with her spear. In some cases the Labour itself is not represented but its ending, as when Heracles stands exhausted upon the dead body of the Nemean lion, watched sympathetically by Athena, or when he hands the Stymphalian birds to her as she sits upon a rock (Pl. 26b).

In these metopes there is a beauty of part that is lacking in the more splendid pediments; the rendering of details is superior because the position was nearer to the spectator and required a finer finish, not because the carving was entrusted to a different group of artisans. The metopes display round heads with protruding occiputs, thick eyelids, pouting mouths, elaborate but naturalistic hair, muscular bodies, and leathery drapery.

Of the west pediment, which he ascribed to Alcamenes, Pausanias writes:

> His work in the gable represents the battle of the Lapiths and Centaurs at the wedding of Peirithous. At the middle of the gable is Peirithous: beside him on the one hand are Eurytion, who has snatched up the wife of Peirithous, and Caeneus, who is succouring Peirithous; on the other hand is Theseus repelling the Centaurs with an axe; one Centaur has caught up a maiden, another a blooming youth. Alcamenes, it seems to me, has represented this scene because he learned from Homer that Peirithous was a son of Zeus and because he knew that Theseus was a great-grandson of Pelops.

The arrangement of the figures, recovered in fragments, would in any case have caused difficulty, since all except the horses had been placed freestanding in a space nearly a metre deep, so that the directions they faced are not always evident—and may originally have not been determined with exactitude before installation on the temple. Furthermore, the Master took pains to balance each figure or group on one side of the pediment with an equivalent figure or group on the other side, and it is sometimes difficult to decide which should stand on the right and which on the left. But the sculptors were by no means eager to waste labour on portions invisible from below, so that except when a figure was intended to be placed facing straight to the front, the unfinished condition of its inner side usually establishes its original angle, and hence its position on the left or right of the gable; sometimes, too, the omission of some part of a figure to make room for the next discloses the arrangement.

The interpretation by Pausanias of the central figure in the west pediment as that of Peirithous is surely false, for the hero would not stand serenely apart from the fray, leaving a drunken Centaur to abduct his bride. It is undoubtedly a deity, standing here as an arbiter of the brawl, and from the youthfulness of the figure and the socket for a bow he must be Apollo, the ancestor of the Lapiths: the figure of Peirithous should be sought in one of the two men nearest to the god, his friend Theseus being the other. Occasional roughness of finish in figures aids in placing them correctly, although it is of course impossible to say which on either side of Apollo is Peirithous. Both attack Centaurs, whose tails are turned towards the centre and each of whom carries a woman in his forelegs (Pl. 26c); next come, on either side, balancing groups of a Lapith struggling with a Centaur, followed by groups of three, composed of a woman (Pl. 26d), a Lapith and a Centaur (Pausanias mistook one of these women for a youth); finally in each angle lie an old and a young woman watching the fight.

Three of these corner figures and an arm of a fourth are carved in Pentelic instead of Island marble; moreover their style stamps them as later replacements. The three figures are so like the fourth, where the arm only is restored, that they must be exact copies of destroyed originals.

The east pediment illustrates a local legend of King Oenomaus, who was unwilling to give his daughter Hippodameia in marriage because of a prophecy that he himself would be killed by his son-in-law. Any suitor that presented himself was made to run a chariot race from the River Cladeus at Olympia to the altar of Poseidon on the Isthmus of Corinth: he was allowed the first start, carrying with him the princess, and Oenomaus, after sacrificing a ram to Zeus, set off with his charioteer in pursuit, to kill the suitor if he overtook him. Thirteen perished in this manner, but finally Pelops bribed the charioteer, Myrtilus, to remove the pins from the wheels of Oenomaus' chariot, so causing the king to fall to the ground. Pausanias' description gives a better idea of the action than do the fragments themselves:

> ... there is represented the chariot race between Pelops and Oenomaus about to begin; both are preparing for the race. An image of Zeus stands just at the middle of the gable: on the right of Zeus is Oenomaus with a helmet on his head, and beside him is his wife Sterope, one of the daughters of Atlas. Myrtilus, who drove the chariot of Oenomaus, is seated in front of the horses: his horses are four in number. After him there are two men: they have no names but they were also ordered by Oenomaus to look after the horses. At the very extremity Cladeus is lying down; with the exception of the Alpheus, the Cladeus is the river most honoured by the Eleans. On the left of Zeus are Pelops and Hippodameia, and the charioteer of Pelops, and

the horses and two men supposed to be grooms of Pelops. Where the gable again narrows down, the Alpheus is represented.

Although Pausanias describes this pediment in greater detail than the western, its composition remains more problematical. Zeus, represented on a larger scale than the mortals, is easily placed between the two rivals, as the arbiter of the contest. But the other figures are so posed as to lack obvious relationship; incidentally Pausanias mistook the sex in the case of a seated woman. A gradual reduction in height ended at the corners with reclining figures which Pausanias took for river-gods; the 'Cladeus' (Pl. 27a) is anatomically remarkable.

In some respects these pediments stand at the highest point of Greek achievement. The carving has little detail, firstly because figures destined to be placed 16 m. above ground required bold treatment like stage scenery, and secondly because the addition of paint once made finish in certain parts superfluous. Greatness is displayed in the magnificent action of the bodies, the beauty of the limbs, the range of expression from the serenity of the gods through the vigour of the heroes to the bestiality of the Centaurs (representatives of untamed nature, which the civilized must combat). The faces are differentiated, as never before, by such means as the set of the eyes, the lines of the nostrils or a stiffening of the lips. The texture of hair differs in men, women and Centaurs. The solidity of the bodies is accompanied by differentiation of bone and muscle, while tense muscles are distinguished from slackened. Drapery, treated according to the weight of the material, responds to the movement of the figures.

An Ionian connection is assured by comparison of the Olympia pediments with the peplos *korai* from Xanthus, now in the British Museum, and with a statue found at Persepolis (Pl. 27b), which must have been sent to the Persian king to commemorate the reconquest of a city that owned it. When Alexander burnt Persepolis in 331 B.C. the main part of the figure escaped destruction and was buried under the refuse from which it has recently been excavated. But an almost identical statue remained visible somewhere in Greek territory, for it was copied repeatedly during the Roman period. The most familiar example is the Vatican 'Penelope', which has been much restored as well as incongruously completed with a male head; the type is better represented on a headless relief found in Rome. If any copy of the head exists it cannot be identified, but in every other respect the original appearance of the Persepolis statue is known. The subject is probably a mythological character, though such a figure might have been placed on the tomb of a woman. She sat on a stool, above a basket (carved contiguously to give support); she leant her cheek on her right hand while her left lay on the edge of the stool. Her dress combined the Ionic chiton and Doric himation, the latter being pulled over the head as a veil. The statue thus unites the motifs of the two seated figures on the front of the Boston 'Throne' (Pl. 25*b*), but the drapery is deeper cut and the folds are less symmetrical; the crinkled surface which archaic sculptors used to render the full linen chiton is still retained.

Another presumably Ionian work, the 'Chatsworth' bronze head (Pl. 27*c*), is unlikely to be much earlier than 450, though the great breadth of the face recalls the winged youth of the Boston 'Throne'. The Cypriot peasants who discovered it in 1836 asserted that it then formed part of a statue, which fell apart while being dragged from the spot, because the head, arms and legs had been attached only by solder. From their description the figure must have been posed much like a *kouros* and was nude except for something round the waist that resembled their own cartridge-belts. This non-Greek feature—probably the traditional Cypriot loin-cloth—is explicable on the assumption that the conservatism of the local cult required it, but it also masked the joint with the separately cast legs. The head must be due to a sculptor of Greek training, whether or not he was a native of Cyprus; the subject is certainly Apollo. The incised representation of the hair on the scalp evidently resulted from scratching with a pointed tool on the original clay model; the curling locks beside the face were cast separately and soldered into place.

The 'Chatsworth' head does not fit into the main stream of development, which was then directed by a number of acknowledged Masters at Athens and in the nearer part of the Peloponnese. Many statues of theirs are known from copies but the sculptors cannot be identified with certainty except in the instance of Myron. Some ancient criticisms of the works of Calamis can be taken as sound evidence, but absolutely nothing can be said of the style of many contemporaries whose names are preserved with short lists or notices of their work—the Athenian Hegias (a name misspelled by many ancient writers as Hegesias), perhaps the teacher of Pheidias; Micon, more celebrated as a painter, Glaucus and Dionysius of Argos; an Elean Callon; Menaechmus and Soidas of Naupactus; the Aeginetans Simon, Callon, Onatas, Glaucias, Anaxagoras. Yet if the extant remains can be taken as truly representative, it would appear that the work of all these masters differed but little; certainly no peculiar and distinct personality can be felt, except in the Olympia sculptures, until the appearance of Myron at the middle of the century.

Nor is the general similarity surprising, because sculptors of the generation after 480 established the classical types, whereby figures scarcely varied in proportions one from another and all faces and all bodies looked much alike. That this crystallization of Greek ideals did not take place in accordance with a precise imitation of nature is made especially clear by the adoption of such an abnormality as the 'classic profile', in which the nose and forehead run practically in one straight line; the convention did not come into use before the fifth century.

In male figures of about 480–450, variants of the *kouros* motive predominate, in most instances applying to Apollo, not to athletes. The most archaic is the type represented in copies by, among others, the 'Choiseul-Gouffier' statue in the British Museum (Pl. 28a) and an almost complete statue found in the Theatre at Athens close to an omphalus, and hence often miscalled 'Apollo on the Omphalus'. (Thongs such as boxers wore are carved on the tree-stump added by the 'Choiseul-Gouffier' copyist, while a quiver appears on two other copies as an attribute of Apollo.) The original, no doubt, stood at Athens, but its identity is unknown. Another Attic original of great popularity is best seen in the Apollo at Cassel. This type has a more dignified carriage and a nobler expression than the 'Choiseul-Gouffier'; some scholars believe it to be a youthful work of Pheidias. Another type, sometimes associated with the young Pheidias, sometimes with Calamis, survives in a copy found in the Tiber, now in the Terme Museum, and another at Cherchel in Algeria. In these the right knee is allowed to sag forward so far as to weaken the composition. Yet another Apollo is known from a marble copy at Mantua and a bronze from Pompeii. The originals of all these statues were presumably bronze; hence the tree-trunks necessary for supporting the marble projections differ in each copy.

A bronze of over life-size, the 'Zeus of Artemisium' (Pl. 28b), can be dated midway in the period; it was recovered in poor condition from the wreck of a ship which foundered in approximately 100 B.C. The figure stands aslant, the feet well apart, the left arm outstretched horizontally to the side, the right almost aligned with it but slightly bent at the elbow. The same pose occurs on coins which represent Zeus throwing a thunderbolt, but in this instance the position of the fingers suggests that they were holding a thong from which to project a javelin or spear; if so, the subject is not Zeus, nor probably would Poseidon cast his trident in that manner, though a heroized mortal might do so. The treatment of hair, face and body alike is so closely paralleled in the 'Choiseul-Gouffier' or 'Omphalus' type of Apollo that its original is likely to have been a work by the same good, though not great, sculptor.

Marble copies exist of several bronze female statues, all completely draped as was then the rule; among them must be the famous Aphrodite and Aspasia of Calamis, one or other of which (if they were not the same figure) was known as the 'Sosandra' (Saviour of Men). Lucian, in order to compose an ideal beauty, borrows for his imaginary conception its 'dignity, and the noble unconscious smile and the decorative neatness of the dress—but the head shall not be covered'. Copies of the statue may be identifiable in Berlin, but translation into marble ruined the effect of the swaddling drapery which in polished bronze would compose broad bands of light and shade; the Doric himation, passed over the head and around the body, allows the contrasting narrow folds of an undergarment to show only at the feet. Other statues wear a peplos; the heaviness of that garment appealed to the severe taste of the age. A very celebrated original, to judge from the number of replicas, is best represented by a statue in the Terme, completed with the plaster cast of a head in the Vatican (Pl. 28c); the conjunction is guaranteed by a poor copy at Iraklion, where the separate piece comprising the head and neck fits perfectly on the body. The contoured folds should be compared with the semi-rectangles on the peplos figures at Olympia (Pl. 26). Copyists rendering them in marble must have hardened the lines of the drapery, but the folds were obviously not only more varied than in the Delphi Charioteer, but also more austere, owing to the abrupt bends of their contours. An original of approximately this time, probably 460–450, was copied in the 'Giustiniani Hestia', whose outstretched left arm held a long sceptre, and who is thereby identified as a goddess.

Myron stands out from his contemporaries as an artist of exceptional originality, though his work is known only from copies. He was an Athenian citizen (though his native village, Eleutherae, belonged for a while to Boeotia). Sound external evidence for dating his activity is obtainable from his recorded statues of athletes victorious in 456, 448 and 444, when his son Lycius was already a successful sculptor; a tradition that Myron had been a pupil of the Argive Ageladas would, if true, imply that he was born not long after 500. In Petronius' novel, *Satyricon*, a pretentious ignoramus asserts that Myron practically caught the breath of life in his bronze men and animals, a statement contrary to fact, as any educated reader would have known. Pliny, indeed, grumbles that Myron expressed no emotions and was concerned only with the body, yet failed to improve on the old (that is, archaic) manner of representing hair. Those criticisms seem inapplicable to his later statues and were probably based on the 'Discobolus', one of his earlier works which may be dated about 470.

The 'Discobolus' (discus-thrower) was famous in antiquity. The 'Lancelotti' copy alone retains the head in place, but a torso in the same museum, the Terme, is better and has been completed with a cast of the head (Pls. 28d, 29a); the tree-trunk, unnecessary in the bronze original, was an addition by the copyist. The attribution to Myron is unquestionable in view of Lucian's description: 'He is stooping to make the throw, turning round towards the hand that holds the discus and slightly bending over one knee to straighten himself after his throw.' The whole body was, in fact, about to swing violently towards the left, pivoting on the right leg, behind which the left leg trails in momentary idleness. The figure, placed aslant like the 'Zeus of Artemisium', was intended to be seen from only one position; the pose was such as only painters had attempted, and Myron translated it too literally into the round. A lack of anatomical coordination above and below the waist, and the almost archaic treatment of the head suggest that the original was not much later than the Tyrannicides.

Myron seems to have worked exclusively in bronze, and was probably the first artist to pose his figures with all the freedom that material allowed. He is recorded to have made statues of gods and goddesses, athletes of every description, and cows. He chose a particularly daring attitude for the statue of Ladas, who died after winning a race at Olympia; no copy exists but to judge from epigrams the figure stood on tiptoe, straining forward as though running. Equally unconventional was the group of Athena and Marsyas (Pl. 29b) as reconstructed, on the evidence of a relief, a coin and a vase-painting, from statues in Frankfurt and the Vatican respectively, after removal of their marble supports.

According to legend, Athena invented the double-flute but noticed that the effort of playing distended the cheeks in an unsightly manner; she therefore flung it away, whereupon Marsyas picked it up gleefully, to the annoyance of the goddess. Myron has illustrated the moment when the satyr, dancing forward on tiptoe with excitement, suddenly started back, surprised by an angry movement on the part of Athena, just as he was on the point of stooping to seize the marvellous novelty that lay at his feet. He has not given up his intention, for there is no visible danger; although repulsed for the moment by a reflex impulse of fear, he is still bent on obtaining the flute, from which he can scarcely raise his eyes to note that the inventor looks contemptuously antagonized.

The artist's gift of catching the fleeting, dramatic moment is as finely displayed here as in the 'Discobolus' whose strong, well-trained body anticipated the slender vigour of the Marsyas. The slightness of the young goddess contrasts with the heavy build of the slightly later Parthenos or the female figures of the Parthenon. A peculiarity which in antiquity was considered among the artist's faults, a summary treatment of the hair, can be detected in the 'Discobolus', but in the best replica of the Marsyas head (in the Barracco collection) a restless ebb and flow of lock upon lock of close-lying wavy hair outlines the skull and swells high over the lips and chin. Myron had now completely broken with the archaic tradition. Discarding the remnants of pattern, he made the drapery of his Athena compose a varied, naturalistic design, carefully balanced, but without obvious symmetry. In the pose he avoided any suggestion of archaic frontality: the young goddess has been walking away and turns to look behind her, so that her whole body is twisted for a moment, pivoting from the feet upwards; unlike the 'Discobolus', the statue looked well from several viewpoints. Tresses of hair swell into naturalistic waves as they escape from her helmet. In the faces we see the beginnings of psychological studies in art; hers is petulant. An expression of surprise, delight and alarm that flashes over the satyr's face, so that the eyebrows crinkle down over his snub nose, comes well within the border of burlesque, and perhaps another touch of the comic lies in the disgust felt by a composed young lady at the sight of his ridiculous eagerness. The contrast of vertical and oblique figures is such as had often been presented in metopes but never, perhaps, in a free-standing group.

The Marsyas group cannot be dated appreciably before 450. Nor could it be later if the 'Mourning Athena' relief (Pl. 29c) was actually—as seems to be the case—imitated from Myron's statue, so old-fashioned is the treatment of the face in this work by some unknown artisan. The goddess is represented in a similar attitude but leaning propped on a spear in her left hand and looking down at a stela to read whatever words were painted on it. Her drapery follows the sloping outline of the body instead of falling vertically as the law of gravity demands. A pleasing simplicity disguises the craftsman's inability to keep abreast with a great artist.

A head identified by its winged cap (petasus) as Perseus or Hermes resembles the Athena of the Marsyas group, and perhaps should be associated with the 'Rondanini' head of Medusa (though that could only be an adaptation, not a true copy), as reflections of a work seen by Pausanias on the Acropolis, 'Myron's Perseus who has wreaked his purpose upon Medusa'. No other sculptor is as likely to have been the author of the Minotaur, a convincing combination of a bull's head with a powerful human body; the group must have been completed by a figure of Theseus, which may, perhaps, be represented in copies. A head from Perinthus so closely resembles the 'Discobolus' that it used to be generally accepted as a copy from Myron, but a duplicate afterwards found at Cyrene is attached to a body with a distinctive manner of rendering the anatomy such as was already known from the head and torso on a herm copied from a discobolus of different type, which had been ascribed to Pythagoras. Since both the herm and the Cyrene/Perinthus athlete show affinities to the Olympia pediments, it would seem that several eminent sculptors were profoundly influenced by one another's work.

Pheidias

The life story of Pheidias can barely be disentangled from the contradictory legends which grew up in later times. He was an Athenian, the son of Charmides; his master is usually recorded as Ageladas of Argos, which is almost impossible on chronological grounds, but Dio Chrysostom gives the name of Hegias if a textual emendation be accepted (reading the genitive *Hegiou* instead of the manuscript forms, *Hepou* or *Hippou*). Pliny states that he began life as a painter and that a shield painted by him was preserved at Athens; no confirmation of this tradition exists. His earliest recorded works are said by Pausanias to have been paid for out of the spoils of Marathon, but were, in fact, some decades later. Since the Athenians had won that battle unaided, except by a few Plataeans, they continued to set up memorials over a whole lifetime, ignoring the greater Persian invasion that had been defeated by the Greek states in concert. At Delphi the latest Athenian monument to Marathon consisted of statues, all allegedly by Pheidias. They represented Athena, Apollo, Miltiades (the general in command), seven heroes whose names had been conferred on the 'tribes' of Athens, and three more—Theseus, Codrus, and Phyleus. In a temple at Plataea, said to have been built from the spoils of Marathon, Pausanias saw a large Athena ascribed to Pheidias; it was 'of gilt and wood, with face and hands and feet of Pentelic marble, not much smaller than the bronze statue on the Acropolis which the Athenians dedicated as first-fruits of their battle at Marathon' (ix. 4). That Athena, known as the 'Promachus' (Champion), stood on the Acropolis in the open air; the point of the spear and the crest of the helmet were visible out at sea. To judge from the size of the base, which still exists, the statue could have been up to ten times life-size. It seems to have been made after 465 and before 455 or at latest 450 B.C. An inscription is presumed to refer to the *Promachus* in recording expenditure on an unnamed statue that took nine years to complete and cost half a million drachmas—equivalent to as many days' wages for unskilled labour. The *Promachus* is represented on coins of Athens, but no copy survives except, perhaps, among bronze statuettes. Neither does a description exist, unless the statue be identical with a bronze Athena which was removed to the Forum of Constantinople, where it perished in a riot of 1203. A bishop, writing about A.D. 900, refers to a bronze Athena by Pheidias in that place; the historian Nicetas, who gives a lengthy account of the statue destroyed by the mob, states its height as a mere 'thirty feet' and does not mention either the artist's name or the spear, but a Byzantine drawing confirms that it held a spear.

A consensus of ancient opinion recognized Pheidias as the greatest of all artists, entirely because of his later statues. Two cult-images of enormous size, composed of ivory for the flesh parts and sheet-gold for the hair and drapery, were naturally the most celebrated; their dates are established with relative precision. In 438, eight or nine years after work started on the Parthenon, he completed its cult-image of Athena *Parthenos* ('The Virgin'), and he was commissioned soon after to supply the cult-image for the Temple of Zeus at Olympia, which had stood empty since about 457. A workshop, identical in size with the room (cella) inside the temple, was built for him and his assistants in or about 435; presumably the statue was completed by or shortly after 430, and apparently Pheidias did not long survive it. He had been brought to trial at Athens on the charge of embezzling the precious materials of the *Parthenos* statue, which had required, it is said, more than a ton of gold and a great quantity of ivory. The gold could be weighed since it was detachable, and in this respect the charge failed; he was convicted, however, of misappropriating public funds avowedly expended on ivory, and was further accused of sacrilege, it being alleged that he had represented himself and Pericles on the statue's shield. This accusation was especially aimed at Pericles, against whose prestige the whole proceeding was in reality directed. Pheidias died in prison, according to Plutarch.

The *Parthenos* is said to have been 40 feet high and was profusely ornamented wherever possible; no copy on a reduced scale could contain more than a few details. Even the face, which should have been easier to reproduce than the decorated parts, differs greatly in the various marble copies and the imitations on gems and medallions. The majesty that impressed eye-witnesses is lost in every instance. Although artistically a travesty, the 'Varvakeion' statuette (Pl. 30*a*), which was found at Athens in a house of the second century A.D., should be comparatively reliable; it is just over a metre high. The proportions of both face and body are surely falsified; the thick-set young woman of this vulgar statuette can correspond only in general lines with the original figure, which must have had the solidity essential for a colossus but was not so sturdy as to be out of keeping with a two-storeyed Doric colonnade that framed it. The side-aisles of the room formed a murky surround to the space, some 13 m. wide, wherein the glittering image stood facing the only source of light, a distant, though huge, doorway.

The ivory and the gold formed an overlay to a shape of cheap materials built around a wooden scaffold. An upright beam, socketed into the floor, acted as the spine of the scaffold, which must have been elaborately shaped but apparently could not be trusted to carry projections simply by canti-levering. Against the left shoulder leaned a spear, propping the left hand, which also rested on the shield; the latter was kept in place by the coils of the serpent, sacred to Athens. Upon the right hand stood a statue, alleged to have been six feet high, of Victory holding a wreath. That hand rests, in the 'Varvakeion' statuette, on a column which is also shown on a relief, as Ionic, and on a lead voting-ticket; no ancient writer mentions the column, and most copies omit it, but it would presumably have been indispensable to support the weight, however strongly the arm were attached internally.

The goddess wore her peplos open at the side, like a girl, but the edges overlapped to conceal the limbs; the overfall reached below the waist, and over it lay an extra girdle, a peculiarity of the 'Peplos of Athena'. On the chest lay the aegis, with serpents writhing in and out of the Gorgon's hair to either side; the tongue protruded from the mouth, following the archaic custom. Wavy locks of hair fell over the goddess's shoulder on to the aegis, while the space between them was diversified by an ornate neck-lace; bracelets, too, were worn on the arm. The weight of the body was evenly distributed, except that one knee was relaxed very slightly, not enough to upset the symmetry which was the predominant feature of the pose. The head, too, was turned very slightly to the right, presumably towards the Victory, although the gaze is not directed downwards in the statuette; the hair fell equally to either side and the knot of the aegis and belt lay precisely on the central line of the body; the arms formed the same angle with the shoulders and the mass of the shield balanced that of the pillar on the right. The folds of the overfall ran in evenly to the girdle, below which both layers of drapery fell vertically in a manner suggestive of the fluting in the surrounding Doric colonnade.

The ornaments of the helmet consisted of a sphinx in the centre and two winged horses, each supporting a plume; across the forehead ran a row of the foreparts of animals, while griffins were embossed upon the upturned cheek-pieces, scraps of which remain projecting above the ears in the

Berlin copy of the head. Elaborate rings also hung from the ears, the nature of which can be best realized by the gold earring in Boston, in the shape of a Victory driving a chariot, which must have been attached to a colossal cult-image of the same period.

The shield, which in the 'Varvakeion' copy bears only a Gorgon's head, originally carried battle-scenes between gods and giants on the inner side and between Greeks and Amazons on its outer side. Other statuettes at Athens and fragmentary copies of the shield alone, from the Strangford Collection and in the Vatican, give a rough idea of the Amazonomachy, a loose composition arranged in groups of two or three figures apiece. A legend recorded by Plutarch states that Pheidias represented himself on the shield as a bald old man raising a boulder in both hands, while Pericles also appeared, though scarcely recognizable because an arm stretched across his face in the act of thrusting with a spear. But this may be an anecdote of late invention to explain both the artist's fall and the surprising individuality of some of the combatant figures. In the 'Strangford' copy, traces of red paint remain on the snakes around the Gorgon's head, on various portions of the drapery and on the shield carried by one of the Greeks; painted figures are visible as well on the inner side.

A large number of rectangular panels exist that illustrate groups of figures adapted from the circular shield; the largest series of these reliefs was found in the wreck of a burned ship in Piraeus harbour. They are decorative work of the Neo-Attic class and their evidence for the style of Pheidias is unreliable, except in so far as the poses may have been accurately copied, in which case such drapery as actually adheres to the bodies must also conform with the original composition.

The Zeus of Olympia, though seated, reached approximately the same height as the *Parthenos*. It was displayed in the same manner; visitors went upstairs to see it at closer quarters from the galleries of a similar two-storeyed Doric colonnade. No definite copy has yet been found, but intimations of the general appearance are recorded in one medium or an-other—best in painting—and it is reproduced on late coins of Elis (Fig. 17). Pausanias gives a full, if dry description:

> The god is seated on a throne: he is made of gold and ivory: on his head is a wreath made in imitation of sprays of olive. In his right hand he carries a Victory, also of ivory and gold; she wears a ribbon, and on her head a wreath. In the left hand of the god is a sceptre, curi-ously wrought in all the metals: the bird perched on the sceptre is the eagle. The sandals of the god are of gold, and so is his robe. On

the robe are wrought figures of animals and lily flowers. The throne is adorned with gold and precious stones, also with ebony and ivory; and there are figures painted and images wrought on it. There are four Victories, in the attitude of dancing, on each leg of the throne, and two others at the foot of each leg. On each of the two front feet are Theban children carried off by sphinxes, and under the sphinxes Apollo and Artemis are shooting down the children of Niobe with arrows.

17. Coin showing Zeus of Olympia

Between the feet of the throne are four bars, each extending from foot to foot. On the bar which faces the entrance there are seven images: the eighth image has disappeared, they know not how. These may be representations of the ancient contests, for the contests for boys were not yet instituted in the time of Pheidias. They say that the boy binding his head with a ribbon is a likeness of Pantarces, an Elean youth said to have been a favourite of Pheidias ... On the other bars is the troop that fought on the side of Heracles against the Amazons. The total number of figures is twenty-nine. Theseus is arrayed amongst the allies of Heracles.

The throne is supported not by the feet only, but also by an equal number of pillars which stand between the feet. But it is not possible to pass under the throne in the way that we pass into the interior of the throne at Amyclae; for in Olympia people are kept off by barriers made like walls. Of these barriers, the one facing the door is painted blue simply: the rest exhibit paintings by Panaenus. Amongst these paintings is seen Atlas upholding heaven and earth, and beside him stands Heracles wishing to take the burden of Atlas on himself; also Theseus and Peirithous, and Greece and Salamis holding in her

hand the figurehead of a ship; and there is the struggle of Heracles
with the Nemean lion; and the outrage offered by Ajax to Cassan-
dra; and Hippodameia, daughter of Oenomaus, with her mother;
and Prometheus still in fetters, and Heracles is born aloft to him ...
the last paintings are Penthesileia giving up the ghost and Achilles
supporting her, and two Hesperids bearing the apples ...

On the uppermost parts of the throne, above the head of the
image, Pheidias has made, on one side the Graces, on the other side
the Seasons, three of each; for in poetry the Seasons are also described as the daughters of Zeus ... The footstool, or, as people in
Attica call it, the *thranion*, under the feet of Zeus has golden lions,
and the battle of Theseus with the Amazons is wrought in relief on
it. This battle was the first deed of valour done by the Athenians
against foreign foes. On the pedestal, which supports the throne and
the whole gorgeous image of Zeus, there are figures of gold, the
Sun mounted in a car, and Zeus and Hera ... and beside him one of
the Graces, and next to her Hermes, and next to Hermes Hestia; and
after Hestia there is Love receiving Aphrodite as she rises from the
sea, and Persuasion is crowning Aphrodite. Apollo, too, and
Artemis are wrought in relief on it, and Athena and Hercules; and at
the end of the pedestal Amphitrite and Poseidon, and the Moon
riding what seems to me a horse—some say, however, that the
goddess is riding a mule, not a horse.

The size, costliness and elaboration of the Zeus do not in themselves
account for its repute. Pheidias imparted a numinous quality, which was
responsible for the unique impression the statue made upon spectators.
'Its beauty seems to have added something to the received religion,'
writes Quintilian. Unlike most cult-images it appealed to the philosophic
rather than to the superstitious or the hysterical, so that Epictetus taught his
disciples that it was a misfortune to die without having seen it.

Excavation in the workshop where the Zeus was constructed has recovered scraps of subsidiary materials not mentioned by Pausanias—rock-
crystal, quartz, obsidian and glass—among other wastage (including a cup
on which 'of Pheidias' is scratched); so far as the finds throw light upon the
process used, reference has already been made to them in Chapter II. But
the terracotta piece-moulds, upon which the golden drapery had been
shaped, are of more than technical interest because they prove his style to
have been dominant in the pedimental sculptures of the Parthenon. They
confirm the ancient tradition that the buildings with which Pericles

embellished the Acropolis were supervised by Pheidias on his behalf. The earliest of these, dated between 447 and 432, was the Parthenon, a Doric temple of Athena the Virgin.

The Parthenon carried more sculptures than usual, for in addition to those of the pediments and metopes, a continuous frieze ran level with the metopes, on the outer wall of the internal chamber. In this position it was only visible from a distance in occasional glimpses between the columns, while to those who walked inside the colonnade only a distorted view was possible, and that by much craning of the neck. But in the Athens of Pericles this was a matter of indifference; the tribute paid by weaker allies was pressed into the service of the glorification of Athens, so that the city could lavish richness even on beauties which would remain almost invisible.

The graceful refinements which the architect Ictinus introduced into the building are no concern of this book: the sculptures comprise one of the most remarkable sets of architectural decoration ever known, yet they attracted little attention in ancient times, perhaps on account of their inaccessibility on the building; some diminutive copies of the pedimental groups at Eleusis (probably from a building of the second century A.D.), and Pausanias' brief note on the subjects of the pediments, alone bear witness to what interest they aroused. For almost two thousand years the Parthenon stood unharmed, except that the east end was transformed into an apse to meet the requirements of Christian worship, thus destroying the centre of the pediment, and some minor alterations were needed to convert the building from a church into a mosque. But in 1687, during a Venetian bombardment, a shell dropped into the powder magazine which the Turks had installed, and the explosion blew out the sides without injuring the pediments of the temple. The Venetians attempted to remove the west pediment with faulty tackle, and the central group fell, to be splintered on the rock at the foot of the building. Fortunately a draughtsman who visited Athens in 1674, in the suite of a French ambassador, had recorded a large proportion of the sculptures in rough sketches of fair accuracy, allowing for the conditions under which he was obliged to work. This artist was probably an unknown Fleming, though formerly identified as one Jacques Carrey, whose name remains attached to the drawings for the sake of convenience. Subsequent travellers deplored the constant destruction of the sculptures, which continued till 1801, when Lord Elgin, then British Ambassador to Turkey, gained permission to remove such portions as he desired. His anxiety not to injure the structure itself induced him to leave much of the frieze and metopes in position;

these pieces have since suffered much deterioration from atmospheric action. Elgin's collection passed to the British Museum; fragments brought to Europe by other travellers have chiefly been assembled there or in the Louvre, whilst the Greek excavations of the last century disclosed a large number of pieces of well-preserved surface, which are housed in the museum built on the Acropolis.

The metopes were the first sculptures undertaken and must have been started soon after the temple itself; they were incorporated some years before 438, when the roof was completed, possibly about 442, at which time the walls reached their full height, to judge by the building accounts preserved in inscriptions of the Treasury officials. They originally totalled ninety-two, of which thirty-two were on the north and south sides, and fourteen on either end. Each slab, well over a metre square, is carved in very high relief, some parts of the figures standing almost in the round. Metopes on the north side of the building, now defaced, illustrated the capture of Troy. Of the metopes on the south side fifteen are in the British Museum, one is in the Louvre, one in Athens, and one still in position; the remaining fourteen can be seen only in the 'Carrey' drawings. The subject of the extant slabs is the battle of the Lapiths and Centaurs, and it has been hazarded that nine of the missing slabs relate the story of Erichthonius. Except for Nos. 6 and 7, the fourteen metopes of the western front of the Parthenon are still in position, so defaced as to be almost unrecognizable, but representing a battle between Greeks and Amazons. A cast of the first metope is in the British Museum and contains a figure on horseback with a chlamys flying behind; the right hand is drawn back as if to hurl a weapon. A drawing by Pars makes out the figure to be male, although what remains of the waist and breast suggests an Amazon. As far as can be ascertained from the mutilated metopes of the east end, all of which are in position, a Gigantomachy was represented.

The style varies greatly, for some sculptors retained archaic qualities (Pl. 30b) which others had discarded (Pl. 31a). Obviously the director of the work specified his requirements and gave a general design, leaving the details to individuals. The two contrasting metopes illustrated, now in the British Museum, stood next to each other on the south side and the builders are likely to have put both in place in the course of the same day's work; there is no reason to doubt that they were carved simultaneously, No. 31 (Pl. 30b) by an elderly craftsman, No. 30 (Pl. 31a) by a younger man. The Centaur and Lapith of No. 31 are fighting on equal terms, whereas in No. 30 the Centaur has the advantage; having seized the hair of his opponent, he is pressing him downwards with the forelegs, while the Lapith attempts to protect himself by raising a stone in his left hand and may have held a sword with his right. Both heads in No. 30 are austerely treated (though the Lapith's reveals suffering) and the bodies are well modelled. Pictorial influence can be discerned in a number of other metopes for they contain landscape elements—usually rocks—to an extent unparalleled in sculpture before the second century; these features, now scarcely distinguishable, must have been emphasized by colour.

A single artist evidently supplied the designs for all the metopes, probably in the form of drawings. Although the Olympia moulds reveal the style of Pheidias only in drapery, the presumption that he was the designer is warranted by the Neo-Attic adaptations of figures from the *Parthenos* shield. The drawings for the metopes would seem to have been on quite a small scale, but to ensure a general correspondence in such matters as the shapes of heads and bodies, at least one larger-type model is likely to have been made in plaster or terracotta for the craftsmen to follow. A marble head (Pl. 32a) in the Acropolis Museum (No. 699), which scholars of the last century mistakenly believed to have been made by Pheidias as such a model, actually belonged to a lost statue of a youth. Paint still remains on the eyes, and close-lying hair must have been shown in paint alone. If this head is not the work of Pheidias himself, it must be by one of his most gifted subordinates.

The frieze of the Parthenon was carved later than the metopes, probably around 440, by a larger team of craftsmen who had learned to reproduce the Pheidian style with comparative uniformity. But, in case their individual handiwork should be distinguishable (as, in fact, it is), none of them was allowed to carve an entire slab, on which, instead, each successive figure was entrusted to a different craftsman; owing to this policy of dispersal, no obvious dissimilarity interrupted the flow of a composition designed to be stylistically consistent throughout. The frieze, which wound round the external wall of the temple rooms and across their porches, was nearly 160 m. long, but seems to have been designed in its entirety by one man, evidently Pheidias. He would seem to have provided the craftsmen with a drawing more detailed than that for the metopes; the height of the frieze is approximately a metre, and the detail would not have been adequately represented on much less than quarter-scale. This designer, or a trusted subordinate, must also have given precise instructions as to how far each portion of the carving should project from the background, a matter that involved more calculation than usual because the frieze is tilted forward to compensate for the skied position. The depth of relief is always greater at the top, where it averages nearly 4 cm. and in places approaches

6 cm., compared with a maximum of barely over 3 cm. at the bottom. An illusion of greater depth is due to the overlapping of figures and to their many frontal or semi-frontal postures; this technique has been described as pictorial, but surely Pheidias had developed it for even shallower relief in gold, an art of which he was the acknowledged master.

Nearly half the frieze is preserved in the British Museum, and one-third elsewhere (mainly on the building or in the Acropolis Museum); of the lost remainder, only a length of some 15 m. had not been recorded by draughtsmen. Unfortunately 'Carrey' drew only the west end of the frieze, which was almost perfect in his day but suffered considerably in the explosion. The subject is the four-yearly Panathenaic procession, held in honour of Athena Polias, whose worship was associated with that of Erechtheus on the Acropolis. Its central feature was the offering of the peplos, woven anew every four years to be hung on her ancient wooden image, after being carried through the city. The participants in the procession were the Athenian maidens carrying baskets of objects necessary for the sacrifice (Canephori), the stool-bearers (Diphrophori), men who bore trays of cakes and offerings (Scaphephori), elder citizens with olive-branches (Thallophori) and the maidens who had woven the peplos (Ergastinae). Each town containing Athenian settlers sent animals for sacrifice. The procession was completed by chariots, horsemen and an escort of infantry; it was marshalled by the Demarch, the Hipparch and a special order of heralds, the Eunidae.

The accompanying diagram (Fig. 18) will explain the arrangement of the frieze. The procession starts from the west side, with the group of knights, and advances along both north and south sides, on the one from right to left, on the other from left to right, to converge upon the east side. Beyond the first knights is another group, moving on their way, and before them are warriors and chariots; next come various bodies of men, behind the sacrificial animals. Finally, on the east end, the maidens advance with their implements towards the officials and the central group, of which the chief figure is the priest holding a garment—either the old peplos being folded away or the new peplos ready to take its place. The gods to either side should be imagined as grouped instead of lined up in a row, as they appear upon the actual relief, and instead of breaking the continuity of the procession they should be regarded as invisible spectators seated in the background. The slab from the east end (Pl. 31b) contains the figures of two seated gods and a seated goddess; the older, bearded god may be Poseidon, since his left hand probably grasped the shaft of a trident, shown only in paint, while the young unbearded god, in whose hair holes are left where

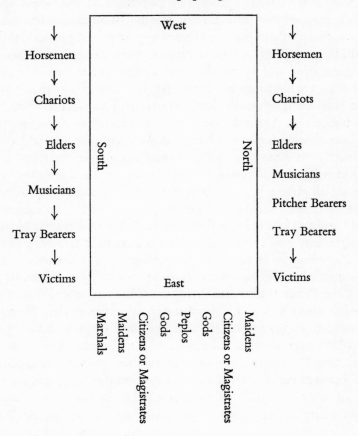

→ →

Horsemen preparing

West

↓ Horsemen	↓ Horsemen
↓ Chariots	↓ Chariots
↓ Elders	↓ Elders
↓ Musicians	Musicians
↓ Tray Bearers	Pitcher Bearers
↓ Victims	Tray Bearers
	↓ Victims

South North

East

Marshals Maidens Citizens or Magistrates Gods Peplos Gods Citizens or Magistrates Maidens

Perspective grouping of the East Frieze.

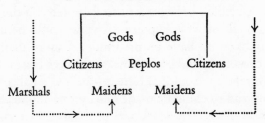

Gods   Gods

Citizens   Peplos   Citizens

Marshals   Maidens   Maidens

18. Diagram of the Parthenon frieze

a metal wreath was attached, must be Apollo, and the goddess has been named Artemis, although the Ionic chiton does not suit her habits. In spite of the very low relief the figures are well contoured, with the drapery and anatomy mapped out in a careful scheme of stylized naturalism. The horses on the west end give an illusory appearance of greater depth. On a slab still in place (Pl. 32*b*, from a cast), a youth stands at the horse's head, holding the reins, and by its side stands a taller man in an attitude of command, with a whip in his left hand (the rivet-holes show that it was prolonged in bronze); behind the horse an attendant waits with a thick chlamys over his shoulder. Again the same discretion is observed, and the delicacy of the composition is unspoilt by too violent action or unguarded naturalism. Exactly the same type of face is used throughout the frieze for every young man (Pl. 33*a*), likewise for every adult man and for every girl; the horses are all alike with one exception, when a filly is represented. The customary Greek reliance on types was thus carried to an extreme, deliberately and meticulously, perhaps for no other reason than to make the procession flow more smoothly. But Pheidias may also have decided to leave no opening for an accusation of sacrilege such as was actually brought against him when figures on the *Parthenos* shield were alleged to portray himself and Pericles. That risk would have been enhanced since the frieze avowedly illustrated a scene of contemporary Athenian life. Never before had a contemporary subject been treated on a religious building and no subsequent Greek instance is known, with the doubtful exception of the Erechtheum. The flagrant breach with tradition requires explanation. One can be found in Pericles' ambition to transform the Acropolis, the spiritual centre of Attica, to make it worthy of the empire then in process of creation under his guidance to become a rival to Persia. At Persepolis (which must have been known by repute since Greeks had carved there), friezes showed a procession in which representatives of the subject races brought gifts to the Persian king; on the Parthenon, a procession representative of the Athenians brought gifts to their deity. If the analogy was intentional, abnormally strict adherence to types would be inevitable.

The frieze is unlikely to have been completed more than a couple of years before the carving of the pedimental sculptures began. Except for a few pieces in high relief, the colossal figures (one and a half times life-size) were free-standing and so could be made one by one and kept till the time came to set them in place. The work was probably all executed between 438 and 432. Half-way through it Pheidias moved to Olympia, so that his supervision came to an end; even if the Zeus did not occupy all his time, he might not have dared pay visits to Athens in view of the hostility shown to him. But we may assume that he had supplied models for the pedimental figures before the completion of the frieze, because the clamps intended to hold them in position were built into the wall—a proof that rough models at least were prepared before 438. An inscription of 433 mentions the expenditure of 16,392 drachmas in 'sculptors' wages for the pediments'; despite the fragmentary condition of the passage the reading is almost certain, especially since the unusually large sum must have been expended on an important piece of work, amounting indeed to more than half of the year's expenditure on buildings. Stylistic divergences between the statues suggest that the models had not been carried out in full detail; the carvers had now had so much experience in the Pheidian style that they could be trusted not to produce incongruous details, and only required to know the main outlines.

Pausanias' note, that the birth of Athena was represented on the east pediment, is the only guide to the subject—probably the moment after the goddess had sprung in full armour from the skull of her father, Zeus, which was cleft by Hephaestus (or, following an Attic tradition, by Prometheus). Long before the time of 'Carrey' the central group, presumably consisting of the birth scene with Zeus and Athena as the chief figures, had been removed to make room for the apse of the Christian church. Near the left angle (Fig. 19) there remain now the neck and shoulders and outstretched arms of the sun-god Helios—designated by archaeological convention (A); the god, driving his four-horse chariot, is emerging from the sea, indicated by a mattress-like floor. Two of the horses in the British Museum (B, C) are carved out of one block of marble, the head of the outermost projecting from the pediment in a spirited manner; drill-holes mark the position of metal trappings. The two inner horses remain on the pediment. Next comes a reclining figure (D)—complete except for part of each forearm, the hands, part of each leg and the feet—which is commonly known as 'Theseus' (Pl. 33b). He is resting upon a rock, covered with a skin—probably that of the leopard appropriate to Dionysus rather than the lion of Heracles; traces of plaited hair lie on his neck, and drill-holes near the ankles held metal boots. Two female figures, seated upon chests, and a third in an attitude of running (E, F, G), complete the surviving members of the left side of the gable. All three are headless and handless, but are whole from the neck to the feet; the two figures on the chest, carved from one block of marble, are commonly accepted as Demeter and Persephone, while the running girl can scarcely be Iris, since she is not winged, but may be Hebe or, more likely, Artemis (if the small breasts are not a sign of immaturity). An exceptionally powerful torso, from neck to groin (H), is thought to belong to the central group, to the Hephaestus or Prometheus. On the right of the central gap is the unidentifiable group (Pl. 34a), known as the 'Fates' (K, L, M), of two seated women against the further of whom a third reclines; these are headless and armless. Finally, there comes Selene, the moon-goddess (N), driving her horses into the waves; the torso of Selene is not shown in 'Carrey's' drawings since it had already fallen down

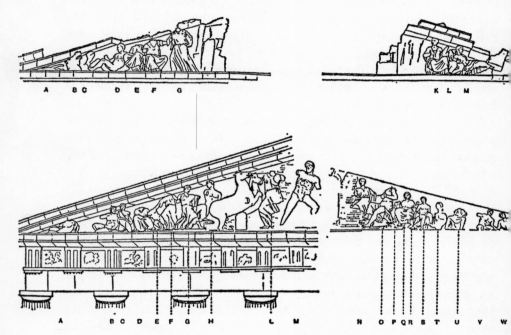

19. 'Carrey' drawings of the east (above) and west (below) pediments of the Parthenon

and was found only after Elgin's time, in excavations on the Acropolis. An excellent head of one of her horses (O) was removed by Elgin; two others remain in their original position.

Thus the birth takes place beneath the whole vault of heaven, with the rising sun on one side and the setting moon on the other side. A relief of the same subject on a puteal (well-head) in Madrid was adapted from the pediment. On the left stands Hephaestus with his axe, behind Zeus, who is enthroned and looks towards the right, to the armed Athena; a small Victory between them flies to place a wreath upon her head, and on the extreme right, behind Athena, are the three 'Fates'. By combining the evidence of the puteal and of 'Carrey' we can dimly visualize how the differences in the pose, axis and size of figures enlivened the tall middle of the pediment. The figures, skilfully graded to fit the slope of the roof, rise gradually from the head and shoulders of the sun-god with his horses to the reclining 'Theseus', the seated women and the slight young goddess, to the grand, upright figures of the centre, then fall again to seated figures, reclining figures, and finally to the Moon-goddess and her disappearing chariot.

For the subject of the west pediment, Pausanias is again the sole informant and he only mentions that 'the subjects at the rear of the temple are the contest of Poseidon with Athena for the land'. Tradition placed the scene of that mythical contest upon the Acropolis, on a spot covered by the joint temple of Erechtheus and Athena Polias; Athena showed her power by causing an olive tree to spring from the soil, while Poseidon produced a salt spring, or, according to some versions, a horse; Cecrops was judge or witness before a bench of deities.

The 'Carrey' drawing (Fig. 19) was taken before the explosion of 1687 and the attempted removal of the central group by Morosini, so that it gives a fair idea of the whole. In the left corner is a recumbent figure (A), interpreted, on the analogy of the temple of Zeus at Olympia, as one of the Attic rivers, Ilissus or Cephissus. The head, parts of the arms and the leg below the knee are missing, but from the attitude he must have rested his left hand upon the bottom of the pediment to support himself. A space, in which traces of another figure remain on the floor of the gable, intervenes between the river-god and the next two figures (B, C), which are interpreted as Cecrops and a woman of his house, perhaps his daughter, Pandrosus; his left thigh carries the main weight of the body, which leans towards the right, and his companion, also kneeling, has her arm about his shoulders; surprise is expressed in her attitude. Cecrops in literature is snake-legged, but here the snake lies near him. These two are still in position on the temple. Next comes in the drawing a group of two women, one seated, with a boy between them (D, E, F), of which nothing survives. The charioteer of Athena (G) survives only in fragments, of which one is possibly the 'Laborde' head. A male torso (now the sole remnant of the figure H, complete in the drawing) is perhaps Hermes, the friend of Athena and messenger of the gods, helping the charioteer with the horses.

Of the two central figures (L, M), the Athena's ruined head (discovered after 'Carrey's' time), neck and one shoulder and bust survive, together with the upper part of the torso of Poseidon. The goddess is identified by the aegis lying across her breast; holes show the place of the snake fringe and another hole marks the position of the head of Medusa. Among the fragments found on the Acropolis were parts of an olive tree which would fit into the pediment, but neither in the drawing nor among the fragments is there any sign of Poseidon's spring.

On the right the first remaining figure (N) is of a winged girl in flight (Pl. 34b)—Iris, the female messenger of the gods. The torso of the female charioteer of Poseidon (O) follows next and is shown by the dolphin in 'Carrey' to be that of Amphitrite, the wife of Poseidon, or of some Nereid. Close to her come the lower limbs of a seated woman, who held the torso of a boy (now lost) on her right knee (P, Q); she is possibly Leucothea (a sea-goddess) with her son Palaemon. The 'Carrey' figures, R, S and T, are missing; the unimpressive stump of U remains. A nude male (V) squatting upon his heels, probably a local personification, and the recumbent draped female figure, interpreted as the nymph of the spring Callirhoe, complete the gable: since the spring was closely connected with the Ilissus, the squatting youth (V) has been identified with the god of that river with greater probability than the figure A.

Apart from the 'Theseus' (Pl. 33b) no figure of either pediment retains a head. But the 'Laborde' head in the Louvre once belonged to a Venetian family, a member of which was serving as a secretary to Morosini when he tried to remove the central group of the west pediment to Venice; although the style and dimensions leave little doubt as to the source (and a groove at the back suggests that it fitted into the right side of a pediment), the features have so perished that it does not deserve illustration. Destruction of the nose, lips and chin—which a restorer replaced in plaster—leaves nothing of much interest. All faces, no doubt, were simplified into a set of broad sweeping curves, as in the frieze. The body of the Theseus is so massive that the statue was once thought to personify Mount Olympus, but it looks puny compared with the torso (H) from the same pediment (the fragments of which are unhappily divided between the British Museum and the Acropolis Museum). These figures exemplify the noblest convention ever attained for the male nude; the surface is designed in clearly defined areas, which actually bend everywhere but give the effect of planes. A similar compromise between pattern and fidelity to nature governs the treatment of drapery; the very texture is displayed but the arrangements of folds were all calculated to help build up the composition of the pediment. The drapery of figures in motion emphasizes the action in the manner usual since the archaic period, but even when the figures are seated and at rest their drapery moves restlessly in accordance with the surge and countersurge that prevailed throughout the pediment, contrasting with the severe geometry of its framing cornices.

One of Pheidias' later works, doubtless contemporary with the Parthenon, was an Athena on the Acropolis dedicated by the Athenian community resident in Lemnos. Pausanias and Lucian, the two ancient writers most worthy of trust, both considered the 'Lemnia' to be Pheidias' best statue. Lucian particularly remarks the beautiful outline of the face, the delicacy of the cheeks and the finely proportioned nose. It was presumably of normal size, since nothing is said on that point. Apart from these grains of certain information, there is a fair chance that the 'Lemnia' was the bareheaded Athena by Pheidias to which an orator refers, and the 'bronze Athena of extreme loveliness' noted by Pliny. Copies have been identified in two statues at Dresden, one of them headless and the other complete, and a head at Bologna; the complete figure (Pl. 34c) has no restoration of consequence apart from the nose and lips, and the Bologna head (Pl. 34d) is in perfect condition. The stylistic resemblance to the *Parthenos*, especially in the treatment of the drapery, is extraordinarily close, while the head bears out Lucian's comments. Since the original was evidently by Pheidias and almost certainly in bronze, the identification with the 'Lemnia' can be accepted. Far more tentative is the recognition in copies (Pl. 35c) of another recorded work by Pheidias among the various statues of Amazons that are discussed with reference to Cresilas and Polycleitus.

Resemblance to the Parthenon sculptures justifies the ascription to Pheidias or his school of many statues known only from marble copies; the originals seem to have been bronze. The subject of many is Athena, whose cult at this period acquired a political significance in cities allied to Athens. But the original of the armless and headless 'Medici' colossus in Paris is likely to have stood in Athens, since probably there only would so gigantic an Athena be wanted. It cannot be identified with the 'Promachus', the spear of which, as shown on coins, rested against the shoulder, where there is no depression on the 'Medici' drapery. Nor does the 'Medici' conform with the description of a large Athena at Elis, the work of Colotes, a pupil of Pheidias; the inward face of its shield bore a painting by Panaenus, who is said to have been either a brother or a nephew of Pheidias.

The 'Hope' type of Athena has been recognized as a late work by Pheidias, and the Naples variant as an imitation by one of his pupils, though both could have been by the same sculptor; neither can be identified with the Athena Hygieia by Pyrrhus, dedicated after a plague in 429, because the feet do not suit the indications on its base, which has been found upon the Acropolis. Another anonymous work is copied in the Zeus at Dresden, a standing figure in the style of the Parthenon frieze. A seated goddess at Athens was perhaps copied from a cult-statue by one of the Parthenon sculptors. A statue in the British Museum, the 'Farnese Diadumenus', of a boy binding a diadem round his head, is close in style to the Parthenon frieze and may reproduce the *Anadoumenos* dedicated by Pheidias at Olympia; but this is, of course, conjecture. In a headless statue of a goddess in Berlin the drapery is treated in the same way as in the east pediment; she probably rested one arm on a small image and one foot upon some object about 15 cm. high. This could be a copy of the ivory and gold cult-statue of Aphrodite Urania which Pheidias made at Elis, of which one foot rested on a tortoise, 'as an injunction to wives to keep silent'; but other extant types have been traced to this original and the conjecture carries little weight in each case. A statuette of Aphrodite which stands somewhat in the same pose, leaning on an archaic image, again resembles the frieze in its drapery.

Part of the head survives of the colossal Nemesis ascribed by tradition to Pheidias or to his pupil Agoracritus; it is discussed in the following chapter. The undistinguished 'Barberini Suppliant' in the Louvre has been claimed as an original by one of the sculptors employed on the Parthenon, since the drapery is in the manner of the pediments, but it seems to be merely the best of several Roman copies. The statue, of a woman crouched, apparently on an altar, may have belonged to either a pediment or a tomb.

Contemporaries of Pheidias

The influence of Pericles was by no means enough to put every Athenian state commission in the hands of Pheidias. A political intrigue may be suspected to account for the choice of a much inferior sculptor when metopes were required for the 'Theseum'—actually a temple of Hephaestus —the foundations of which were probably laid a couple of years before work started on the Parthenon. The metopes are badly preserved but the carving seems to have been as poor as their design is backward. A frieze of about the same date, or perhaps a trifle earlier, belonged to a very small temple on the Ilissus, outside Athens; it is interesting merely as an example of continuous composition. The two friezes over the porches of the 'Theseum' appear considerably later and have even been dated after 430. Their composition is based on a series of groups, more suitable for metopes; the figures are placed, for choice, either frontally or in profile, as though the designer were unaware that the three-quarters pose favoured on the Parthenon frieze would enhance the apparent depth.

In 433, after Pheidias left Athens, authorization was given for three 'golden' statues of Victory, half life-size, each to include gold to the weight of two talents (25 kg.). A bronze fragment in the Agora (Pl. 35*a*) seems to be the core to which the sheets of gold were fixed, joining at a groove between the forehead and the hair, at another that runs up the neck, and at the projection to which an additional topknot of hair must have been fastened. When found, however, the head retained traces of a silver sheathing which had doubtless been substituted for the gold stripped off to replenish the Treasury in the crisis of 406–4. The silver was gilded, at any rate over the hair and drapery; on the analogy of the statues of gold and ivory, one might expect the flesh to have been rendered in silver on both occasions.

Cresilas should not, perhaps, be included with the non-Attic artists of Pheidias' time, because, although born at Cydonia in Crete, he found employment especially in Athens, where there are still three of his signatures incised in lettering of about 450. He was even entrusted with the posthumous statue of Pericles dedicated on the Acropolis soon after 429. Although several portraits of Pericles existed, most of them (so Plutarch remarks) helmeted, none but Cresilas' was of such repute as would account for five remaining copies of its head; the finest, the inscribed bust in the British Museum (Pl. 35*b*), is known by the lettering to be late Hellenistic. The face resembles that of any elderly man on the Parthenon frieze, and probably Cresilas did not attempt to record the actual features of Pericles; a sculptor would not then have aimed at portraiture in the modern sense. The Pericles can scarcely be other than an ideal head of a statesman, helmeted as a reminder that he had also commanded an army in the field. There is a considerable chance that marble copies may exist of other works by Cresilas. A possible instance is a statue of Diomedes carrying the Palladium, while the head of a bearded man wearing a leather cap might belong to an Odysseus from the same group. A figure called 'Protesilaus' would suit the extant signed base of the 'bronze statue of Diitrephes shot with arrows', which Pausanias saw on the Acropolis; it must actually have represented an opponent of Diitrephes. Perhaps it was identical with 'the man dying of wounds' listed by Pliny, together with the Pericles and a wounded Amazon, as specimens of the artist's work.

The apportioning of the various types of Amazon among the sculptors of the time has not achieved much success. An improbable story of Pliny's must contain some grains of truth:

The most illustrious sculptors, both old and young, were led into rivalry, since they had made statues of Amazons for dedication in the Temple of Artemis at Ephesus; it was decided to choose the one most highly rated by the artists themselves, for they were there present. As it happened this was the one which each man placed second to his own work; this was Polycleitus', the second place was gained by Pheidias, the third by Cresilas, the fourth by Cydon, the fifth by Phradmon.

The name Cydon must be a mistake, explained by the fact that Cresilas came from Cydonia. Phradmon was an Argive, dated 420 by Pliny, but otherwise only known as the sculptor of a boy wrestler at Olympia and a group of twelve cows.

Of these Amazons, the Polycleitan statue is the only one recognized with any approach to certainty, in the 'Lansdowne' type, one of the two most often copied—but a somewhat different head is reproduced on a bronze bust that formed a pair with one bearing the head of Polycleitus' 'Doryphorus' (Pl. 36c), as though because these were the two most famous statues by that sculptor. A relief from Ephesus proves that the left fore-arm rested on a pillar, while the right arm was bent so that the hand rested on the head, that attitude being conventionally expressive of the pain caused by a wound in the right breast (but, in life, the stretching of the muscles by that action would increase the pain). The athletic body and the stern, set face expressed the concept of an Amazon, a vigorous girl trained to self-control and suffering. Another type, the 'Capitoline', bears some likeness to Polycleitus' 'Diadumenus' in the best copy of the head (Pl. 35c) but the concept is quite different. This Amazon has a rounded face and more voluptuous body, and wears a chlamys as well as the usual short peplos; she stands with her right hand above her head, resting on a spear; the ripe beauty of the side is disclosed to the waist, for the left hand draws the drapery away from the wounds, situated below the right breast. Neither this somewhat meretricious conceit nor the full development of the body would be expected to arise in the athletic school of Argos; the choice therefore lies between Cresilas and, preferably, Pheidias. In a third, unwounded type, best represented by the 'Mattei' statue in the Vatican, the right arm is bent across the top of the head to hold a spear, which rests on the ground close to the left foot; the left arm droops along the shaft. Furtwängler sought the fourth type in a torso of the Doria-Pamphili collection; it has been restored as Artemis, perhaps with justification, for when the attributes are broken off it is sometimes difficult to distinguish between the goddess and an Amazon, the dress being similar.

Polycleitus is said by Pliny to have been a Sicyonian, though according to his own signatures and other authorities he was an Argive; like other distinguished sculptors he is alleged to have been a pupil of Ageladas, in defiance of chronological impossibility. Little faith can be put in Plato's statement that his sons were adult in 433 or 432 or in Xenophon's testimony to his residence in Athens towards 430, because both passages occur in books of semi-fictitious intent written many years later. He must have lived till some years after 423, when the Argive Heraeum was burnt, because the gold and ivory cult-statue for the new temple was made by him; his statue of Cyniscus, whose victory at Olympia is dubiously placed in 460, need not have been executed immediately after the event, although his activity may well have begun at that period. His dating is complicated by the existence in the fourth century of a younger Polycleitus, to whom may have been due the Aphrodite of Amyclae, reputed to have commemorated the battle of Aegospotami in 405, and the marble Zeus at Argos, dedicated in expiation of a massacre which Pausanias dates in 418 but which may have been perpetrated as late as 370. If, however, the earlier dating be correct, this was the only marble statue attributed to the older Polycleitus.

He devoted most of his time to athletic statues in bronze, which were, according to Varro, 'squarely built and inclined to be all of one pattern'. Like many artists of progressive periods — Dürer and Leonardo are instances — he endeavoured to work out an ideal scheme of proportions for the human body and embodied his results, expressed in terms of so many fingers and palms (i.e. the breadth of the hand at the base of the fingers), in a book and a statue, both called his Canon. Thus the foot measured 3 palms, the lower leg 6, the thigh 6, the space from navel to ear 6; the foot was as long as one-sixth of the total height, the face one-tenth, the head one-seventh. The statue was more often known as the 'Doryphorus', or spear-holder (Pls. 35d, 36c); the subject may be a youth undergoing military service. Attempts to reconstruct the Canon from his proportions have not succeeded, though the figure may have set a new standard by the excellent interrelation of all its parts.

The 'Doryphorus' also exemplifies a new distribution of weight, by means of a walking attitude, introduced by Polycleitus himself or an immediate predecessor. In older statues, such as the 'Choiseul-Gouffier' Apollo (Pl. 28a), the weight rests on the rear foot, but the forward leg of the 'Doryphorus' carries it, so projecting the body forward as though advancing towards the spectator. The balanced distribution of tense and relaxed muscles, given on the one side by the stiffened right leg and hanging right arm, and on the other side by the loosened left leg supported on the toes, and by the stiffened left arm carrying the spear, was no novelty, for it is found in the 'Choiseul-Gouffier' and other statues. The veins are marked; the muscles of biceps, chest and abdomen all respond to the requirements of the movement of the body, but the sharp edge of the pectoral plane, caused by the working of powerful chest muscles, is unduly emphasized, and this is not the sole, though the most striking, instance of a love of well-defined planes, which gives the whole body, but especially the chest and abdomen, a formal aspect (not lost till the rounder, less broken surfaces of the fourth century take their place). On the whole, the complaints of ancient authors as to the 'squareness' of Polycleitan figures were justified. That quality may conceivably have been inherited from earlier Peloponnesian or specifically Argive sculpture of which almost nothing is known; it could be represented by an original bronze statuette of a youth from Ligourio (near the Sanctuary of Epidaurus) and a marble copy of a standing Zeus at Munich, but in neither case would the date, about 460, exclude the possibility of influence by the youthful Polycleitus. The 'Doryphorus' can be assigned to 450–440. A statue of Heracles has been recognized from copies as another work of his roughly contemporary with it.

The 'Diadumenus' (Pl. 36a), a youth binding the fillet of victory round his head, had a less severe aspect than the older statue: Pliny's epigrammatic judgment, borrowed doubtless from some earlier source, described the two as *molliter iuvenis* and *viriliter puer*. The difference can be explained on grounds of date, though Attic influence, resulting from the artist's dubious residence at Athens in 430, has been adduced to account for this softening of style; in reality a similar tendency prevailed everywhere. The difference between the statues lies in the treatment of the heads rather than of the bodies. Nose and lips are restored in the excellent Dresden head of this statue (Pl. 36b). The curls of the head are raised well above the skull, springing out from beneath the confining ribbon. The bend of the head is more appealing and the lines of the chin and mouth softer. The Delos copy (Pl. 36a) is of Hellenistic date, and although of greater artistic merit does not follow its original as closely as other replicas; the addition of a chlamys and quiver on a tree-stump characterizes it as Apollo.

The Canon, as we know it, applies only to adults, for several statues of boys, of much slimmer build, can be attributed to Polycleitus on stylistic evidence. Of one among them the best copy is the 'Westmacott Boy' in the British Museum. The feet match the base of the Cyniscus statue, but Polycleitus varied his poses so little that the identity of the two remains questionable. The boy stood upon his advanced left leg and with his right hand placed a wreath upon his bent head. Judging by the smooth features, it is not a work of the artist's early life, so that the proposed association with the Cyniscus is the more tentative. The 'Dresden Boy' also stands on one leg with head bent downwards towards the side, but both his hands were lowered, probably holding athlete's implements. Like the Amazon, the 'Narcissus' rests the left arm on a pillar, but leans the cheek against the hunched-up shoulder; again the weight is carried on one leg and the other drawn slightly back, but in addition the body is curved over the pillar. Other types and attitudes have been noted in copies, differing so slightly that they become monotonous, with their rather solid build and heavy faces. But the dullness may be the fault of the copyists, for it cannot be imputed to the fragmentary bronze head of a boy 'Diadumenus' at Oxford (Pl. 36d), the only surviving scrap of original work that might have been produced in the Polycleitan school during the Master's lifetime, if not by his own hands.

Polycleitus was inclined to plot his figures as mathematical exercises, yet technically he was excellent, and his very academic mind preserved him from attempting too much naturalism. Moreover his system of proportions had a great and steadying influence upon later sculptors; even though his Canon was soon modified in details, the principles of his book were generally accepted and it survived until the Roman empire, when it was read and approved by no less an authority than Galen, the physician.

The other schools of Greece claim small attention, being dependent on Athens or Argos for innovations in their style. In Boeotia a series of fine gravestones testifies to a considerable activity in this humbler industry; it centred at Thespiae, so far as is known, but its sphere extended over the neighbouring parts of Greece.

Some local school of Ionian derivation, probably in the north Aegean region though conceivably in southern Italy, produced the excellent sculptor of three statues found in Rome, on the site of the Gardens of Sallust (from which also came the 'Ludovisi' and Boston 'Thrones'). They evidently belonged, together with some lost figures, to a group that represented the slaughter of Niobe's children; probably it occupied a pediment, in view of the diversity in height of a youth and a girl, both in Copenhagen, and of another girl, in the Terme. The first (Pl. 37a) lies moribund, shot by an arrow that was affixed in bronze, the second is running for her life (in spite of which her face is serene), the third (Pl. 37b) has been struck in the back by an arrow, and the posture of the head conveys an impression of pain although the features remain calm. This statue is to many the most pleasing of its age, because of its mingling of naturalism, idealism and formalism, its singularly fine proportions and firm modelling. Yet it is by no means devoid of mistakes—the neck, for example, is too thick. In the brother too a courageous attempt has been made to grapple with anatomical problems, but in spite of such observations as the humping of the left shoulder, the flattening of the left armpit and the droop of the genitals (a point neglected in the pediments of Aegina and Olympia), there was still more to learn before such an attitude could be successfully rendered. (The 'Cephissus' or 'Ilissus' from the west pediment of the Parthenon has an easier pose, for the head and shoulders are raised, producing a single curve instead of two.) Judged especially by the close correspondence of the Terme girl's drapery with that of the Parthenon frieze, the date of these statues must fall between 450 and 435; their sculptor was in close touch with developments at Athens, but an Ionian element appears in the wide eyes and smooth rounded surfaces. The wind-blown independence of drapery around the Copenhagen girl presages the exploitation of that device in the Victory (Pl. 43b) by Paeonius of Mende, a Greek city in Macedonia. A theory that he was the designer or the actual sculptor of the Niobids is implausible because his Victory shows a different mentality; no artist would have utterly discarded the formality and elegance of the Niobids, even in a much longer interval than can have elapsed.

The 'Giustiniani' gravestone (Pl. 38a), once in a Venetian collection, seems a work of the central rather than the northern Aegean. The figure, 92 cm. high, of a girl wearing a Doric peplos with a short overfall, holds an open box such as was used for jewellery; she has put the lid on the floor by her feet and is removing from the box some object which must have been represented in paint; toying with jewellery is a motive frequent on gravestones, perhaps as a reminder of the enjoyment the dead woman drew from her ornaments. The simple, vertical lines of the drapery are bent below the arm, in sympathy with the angle at which the box is held; head and arm lie roughly at an angle of 45 degrees to the body, the line of the neck being continued by the cross-bands of the hair-ribbon, while the hair is collected at the back into a knot which prolongs the most marked line of the drapery. The figure is crushed against the edge of the stela to allow as much space as possible to the hands and box; lower down, to correspond with the arms, the feet and the lid of the box extend to the right side of the slab, while unity between the figure on the left and the less important right side of the composition is effected by the direction of the head and arms. Something of the stiffness and convention of archaic art lingers in the face, although the drapery is obviously dependent upon a Pheidian design of the peplos. The eyes are peculiarly unsuccessful, being carved almost as though seen full-face; the lowness of the relief offered great difficulty, since the surface was almost flat. The date may be later than 450 because provincial work is apt to be conservative, but must in any case fall within the time of Pheidias' activity; the stela illustrates the transition from stiffness to unconstrained calm that was effected largely through his influence.

The 'Sabouroff' stela from Euboea, which should be contemporary with the Parthenon, represents a man by means of similar shallow planes, again with the eye shown nearly frontal in the profile face. These characteristics also appear in Thessalian gravestones, obviously carved locally by craftsmen whose knowledge of the cosmopolitan work of the age was obtained only from portable objects. The earliest of the existing stelae may have been carved shortly before 450, the majority during the following twenty or so years, but a semi-archaic treatment of details persists throughout. The veiled head (Pl. 38b) of a girl, Polyxena, was half a century behind the times, while in her peplos an arrangement like that of the *Parthenos* is reduced to a few simple folds. Such reliefs exert the charm of the primitive. On the most elaborate of them, a slab in the Louvre known as '*L'exaltation de la fleur*', two women confront one another across a flower held between them. The workmanship is much better than the Polyxena's. The stela (in Athens) of a youth in hat and cloak, with a hare seated on his hand, seems due to yet another craftsman. But all three, and some who were less gifted, may well have belonged to a single family.

VII

The Middle Classical Period

(430–370 B.C.)

IN 431 opened that war between Athens and Sparta which was to end in 404 with the downfall of Athens; plagues in 430 and 429 and the death of Pericles in the latter year set the city on its decline. At the same time there came a change in sculpture; the grandeur and monumental character of the Periclean Age are replaced by charm and elaboration, strong lines change to delicate curves, and calm dreamy countenances are enlivened by emotion. The goal is a more interesting, if less inspiring, art than the Pheidian, but the technical equipment of sculptors still restrained their desires, and prevented an exuberant naturalism or emotional expression. It was not until after the experiments of the first quarter of the fourth century that sculptors gained the power to realize their new ideals. Politically all the period of transition was occupied with wars, the balance of power being maintained by a series of combinations, which changed whenever there seemed a chance that chaos would be terminated. No great programme of public works could be carried out by any of the Greek states; considering their poor financial position it is remarkable that they achieved so much.

Attic Sculpture, 430–390 B.C.

Athens remained dominant in art till at least the end of the fifth century. Although the civic monuments of this period involved less sculpture than in the time of Pericles, they continued to outnumber those of other states, while personal monuments became more abundant. Sculptured gravestones, which had been very rare in Athens earlier in the century, again became fashionable about 430, and provided employment for successive generations of carvers, including some of real merit. One of the first among them may have worked on the Parthenon, for he gave drapery like that of the Iris (Pl. 34b) to the young cavalryman, spearing a prostrate enemy, on the Villa Albani relief; this may be a fragment of a much larger stela, an official war memorial, but the motif persisted in individual grave-stones (Pl. 42).

The removal of Pheidias opened the way to innovation; Cresilas too is likely to have ceased work soon after making his statue of Pericles (Pl. 35b), probably in 428. But Myron's son, Lycius, survived to produce a statue of an athlete, Autolycus, victor in 421, which stood in the Prytaneum at Athens. No dates are known for his bronze statues of the Argonauts, of a boy holding a holy-water sprinkler, of a boy blowing up the embers of a fire and a boy offering incense, but his large monument at Olympia commemorated an event which probably took place about 431, the capture of Thronium by the inhabitants of Apollonia, a Greek colony in Albania. This consisted of a semi-circular pedestal of stone, on the middle of which stood the figures of Zeus, Thetis and Day, between several pairs of figures, Achilles and Memnon, Diomede and Aeneas, and other famous antagonists. Lycius' group of two horsemen at the entrance to the Propylaea at Athens was dedicated, as its base records, 'out of the spoil of their enemies, by cavalry commanded by Lacedaemonius, Xenophon and Pronapus', the occasion being, it seems, the conquest of Euboea in 446.

The two notable pupils of Pheidias, Alcamenes (an Athenian citizen from Lemnos) and Agoracritus, apparently were younger men, especially the last, to judge by his relations with Pheidias. Pheidias was, says Pliny (and his information is confirmed by other authorities),

> attracted by his pupil, Agoracritus of Paros, because of his youthful charms, and therefore allowed him to sign several of his [Pheidias'] works. However, both pupils competed against each other with figures of Venus, and Alcamenes won, not because his statue had greater merit but because the citizens voted in his favour against the foreigner. So they say that Agoracritus sold his statue on the condition that it should not stand in Athens, and called it Nemesis; it was placed at Rhamnus, a village in Attica. Varro preferred it to any other statue.

This Nemesis was commonly attributed to Pheidias, in spite of the signature of Agoracritus, which seems indeed to have been removed by Pausanias' time, no doubt to enable the local priesthood to proclaim their treasure as a work of Pheidias rather than of his less distinguished pupil; Pheidias was said to have carved the statue from a block of Parian marble which the presumptuous Persians brought to make into a trophy after their conquest of Athens. The figure stood on a pedestal covered with reliefs of legends connected with Nemesis. Of the statue itself Pausanias writes: 'On the head of the goddess is a crown ornamented with deer and small victories: in her left hand she carries an apple bough, in her right a bowl on which are worked figures of Ethiopians.'

Part of the head, twice life-size, survives in the British Museum; the lower eyelid, cheek and some of the hair on the right side are preserved, and resemble the 'Laborde' head, which is attributed to the Parthenon pediments. Among other fragments, taken from the site to Athens, is a piece of complicated drapery, by means of which headless copies of the Nemesis have been identified. Since they are only half as large as the Rhamnus statue, they may reproduce a prototype copy or else, conceivably, the model from which the cult-image was carved. The style is unmistakably Pheidian by derivation, approximating to that seen in pedimental figures of the Parthenon, but it lacks subtlety. The drapery over the torso is crumpled by unimaginative repetition of narrow folds, massed together as closely as possible; though the intervening hollows would, of course, have been doubled in width at Rhamnus, they would still have divided a monotonous series of uniformly bent projections. Admittedly cult-images were not intended to be exhilarating objects, but it is surprising that the name of Pheidias should have been associated with a work of such mechanical detail unless there were some factual ground for the belief; possibly he made a first little model, on which Agoracritus afterwards based a design of necessarily increased elaboration.

The statue should, from its style, be not later than 431, when the outbreak of the Peloponnesian War would have stopped work at Rhamnus, at least till the truce of 421–413; the temple itself seems to have been built just before 431. On the other hand, the small figures that surrounded the base are definitely of a more advanced style, which is shown consistently in the heads, in the nude parts of the body and in the drapery of no less than forty significant fragments exhibited in the National Museum at Athens. Moreover the subjects represented around the base are known from Pausanias to have involved Peloponnesian heroes, who would not have been given such prominence at the time of the Parthenon, when war with Sparta was imminent, nor during an uneasy truce. Their presence surely implies goodwill towards the Peloponnese, a condition fulfilled in 404–403 when a pro-Spartan government held power in Athens; no date could be more suitable for the sculptures on the base, which show the same uninspired ability as the Nemesis and may therefore be attributed to Agoracritus, though not with absolute confidence. He might simultaneously have completed the statue if it had been left unfinished in 431, or else have carved the whole of it after a model which had been kept since 431;

the ascription to Pheidias could thus have been partially correct. If the block of marble had been taken to Rhamnus before 431 and lay there un-carved till 404, remembrance of the fact might even have been distorted into the unquestionably fictitious story that the Persians had brought it, though the siting of the temple between Eretria and Marathon, the scenes of respectively their triumph and their disaster, might itself have seemed to warrant an association with those events.

A free copy of part of the base has been recognized at Stockholm: it contains four figures, all facing more or less towards the spectator's right and therefore derived from the left side of the relief. They are standing in a row, like independent statues put side by side, reflecting small credit on Agoracritus' powers of composition. The style of the copy can bear little resemblance to that of the original, but the correspondence of subjects with those of the extant fragments on the base can leave no doubt of its derivation; the copyist adopted in the drapery the style of his own day, the early Roman empire, rather than reproduce the hesitant lines of the close of the fifth century, which make the garment cling to the body and give an appearance of wetness.

The arrangement of drapery on some fragments from the Nemesis base is so closely paralleled on the 'Velletri' type of Athena, known from a number of copies, that it can be attributed to Agoracritus, though pro-bably at an earlier stage of his career, before the clinging texture had been developed. The head on the copy in Rome (Pl. 38c) should have been set looking slightly downwards; it is a plaster cast made from a poorer replica in the Louvre, which the restorer completed with arms in the wrong action. The right arm, in fact, bent sharply at the elbow so that the hand could rest on a spear; the left forearm emerged from the drapery almost horizontally, and the hand grasped a cup. A statue of Demeter or Hera in the Vatican, with 'wet' drapery and a head not unlike that of the Nemesis, may also reproduce a work by Agoracritus. The statue of Demeter at Eleusis is a poor original by one of his lesser contemporaries; figures in similar style occur on gravestones as far away as Rhodes and Cyprus.

The final stage in the development of 'wet' clinging drapery was achieved in a figure known as 'Venus Genetrix' because one like it appears on Roman coins with that legend, soon after Arcesilaus had made a statue so called for the forum of Julius Caesar, who claimed descent from the goddess through Aeneas. But this is not the only type that occurs on coins and the connection with Arcesilaus is disputable; if correct, he can only have adapted a well-known original of which several copies exist, the best being the headless example in the Terme (Pl. 39a). With one hand the goddess lifts the end of her drapery over her shoulder, like a figure on the Rhamnus base; in the other hand she holds the apple awarded by Paris to the most beautiful of goddesses. Furtwängler identified this statue as Alcamenes' 'Aphrodite in the Gardens' which stood outside Athens, but it might with greater likelihood be assigned to Agoracritus, because of its resemblance to the Nemesis base, or else to Callimachus.

The Aphrodite of Alcamenes was selected by Lucian to contribute to his ideal beauty 'the front parts of the face as well as the hands and well-proportioned wrists and slender flexible fingers'. Pliny remarks that Pheidias was said to have put the finishing touches to this statue, of which the pose is quite unknown. Alcamenes' other famous statue of Hephaestus, whose lameness was tactfully suggested, stood in the temple of the god at Athens, now popularly known as the 'Theseum'. An inscription of expenses on public works in 420–417 apparently refers to this statue and to its companion, which possessed a shield supported on foliage and may be presumed to have represented Athena. Now an Athena, whose shield rests upon an acanthus by her side, survives in copies, and appears conversing with Hephaestus on a relief from Epidaurus; probably this was one of the cult-statues in the 'Theseum'. The other has more questionably been recognized in a different Hephaestus represented on a lamp and in a marble copy of the head.

Other recorded works by Alcamenes included statues of Ares and Asclepius, one of Dionysus in gold and ivory, and a signed relief dedicated at Thebes by the Athenians who had started thence in 403 on the expedition that reinstated democracy in Attica. His activity, therefore, continued for at least thirty years after Pheidias left Athens (whereas Pliny and Tzetzes believed they had been rivals). A copy of his triple Hecate, which stood in the Propylaea, is plausibly recognized in a circular group of three figures, almost identical, standing backed together. A blend of pseudo-archaic and contemporary elements extends, in their case, to the drapery, whereas in the more celebrated Hermes Propylaeus the hair alone can be called archaistic; it is indicated on the scalp by parallel wavy lines and ends with three rows of tight curls over the forehead, as in the group from Eretria (Pl. 17c). The face and beard hark back to the period that immediately followed the archaic, but a Pheidian serenity is imposed. On that point the copies agree, while varying in detail; two (from Pergamon and Smyrna) are firmly identified by inscriptions. Alcamenes' adherence to old conventions was, in fact, obligatory because the head belonged to a herm (a pillar, unsculptured except for the head and a phallus); religious conservatism did not allow this primitive type of image to be brought up to date.

Sculptors often dedicated their own works at sanctuaries. A life-size group in the Acropolis Museum, of a woman with a young boy pressing against her side, must be identical with one seen by Pausanias—'A group representing Procne and Itys, at the moment when Procne has taken her resolution against the boy, was dedicated by Alcamenes'; by 'Alcamenes' he obviously meant the sculptor. The group offers a poor impression now, with the boy mutilated and half of the woman's face and her arms broken away, but at least it implies that to him is due the original of a headless female statue from Pergamon and the caryatids of the Erechtheum (Pl. 39b), for the drapery is treated in the same manner; moreover the wide face and strong neck are common to both Procne and the caryatids. The latter, rather more than life-size, are used as pillars to support the roof of a porch that projects from the main building; four scarcely differing from one another stand along the front, and one on each side wall. (The design is copied in St Pancras' Church in London.) One of the figures was removed by Lord Elgin and now rests in the British Museum, while all the others remain in their original position. The idea was no novelty, having been used in the Delphi Treasuries more than a century earlier, but the Erechtheum statues are better adapted to the purpose because the body retains the same thickness throughout instead of tapering to the feet; at both periods a thick mass of hair is used to strengthen the back of the neck. The construction of the caryatid porch is best placed, on the evidence of the inscribed accounts of the Building Committee, between the commencement of the temple (421?) and its temporary stoppage (413?); the statues were certainly in place before 409 and their likeness to some figures on the Parthenon frieze, of girls carrying water-pots on their heads, favours the earliest date permissible.

To Alcamenes or one of his associates can be attributed the originals of four reliefs known from copies. Their subjects are: Orpheus, Eurydice and Hermes in the Underworld; Medea and the daughters of Pelias standing beside the cauldron in which they boiled the dismembered body of their father; Heracles in the Garden of the Hesperides; Heracles with Theseus and Peirithous in the Underworld. These scenes might appropriately have been placed on or beside the Altar of Pity, which the Athenians at that date still officially called the Altar of the Twelve Gods. While technically derived from the Parthenon frieze, the panels express a later and enfeebled spirit, for they are merely pretty decoration; the theatrical posturing of the figures robs them of significance, so that the pathos of the subjects is not conveyed. On the gravestone of Hegeso (Pl. 40b), 95 cm. wide, which may have been carved only a few years later, a hint of pathos was introduced by the completely natural attitudes of the mistress and her maid, although looking at jewellery is a cheerful occupation. A fragment, in the Vatican, from a relief of draped horsemen, is unsatisfactory because the one rider preserved lacks strength and his garments flow too smoothly. The sculptor had probably been engaged twenty or thirty years earlier in carving the Parthenon frieze, of which, indeed, this relief was once thought to have formed part; but the material is a Boeotian limestone.

In the present state of knowledge the 'Borghese' type of Ares cannot be ascribed to any particular Attic master, though the Ares of Alcamenes naturally comes to mind. The god, wearing the helmet and sword-belt as his attributes, stands on the left leg, with the right leg advanced and to the side. The pose and anatomy recall the 'Doryphorus': in each the right leg is advanced and the left arm is bent upwards at the elbow, but in the 'Doryphorus' the weight rests on the forward foot in the attitude of walking and the right arm hangs slack by the side, while in the Ares the entire right side is relaxed, the entire left side tense, so that the symmetry of the earlier statue is lacking.

A quaint idea of the time was the bronze horse representing the Wooden Horse of Troy, with heroes climbing out of its back. Two statues of this subject are recorded. One, by Antiphanes of Argos at Delphi, commemorated an Argive victory in 414; the other, a work of Strongylion, was dedicated on the Acropolis at Athens slightly earlier, for in the Birds of Aristophanes, first acted in that year, there seems to be a topical allusion in the phrase 'horses as big as the Wooden Horse', while the extant base is inscribed in lettering of about 420. Its artist is also credited by Pliny with 'the Amazon called eucnemus [fine-legged] because of its admirable legs, for the sake of which it travelled around in Nero's retinue. He likewise made the boy of which Brutus (the hero of Philippi) was so fond that the glory of his own name has rested upon it.' Speaking of a group of Muses upon Mount Helicon, composed of three statues apiece by Strongylion, Cephisodotus and Olympiosthenes, Pausanias remarks that the first-named was excellent at representations of oxen and horses.

Of uncertain authorship is the frieze of the temple of Athena Nike—less accurately, Wingless Victory (Nike Apteros)—a small Ionic temple standing on a bastion at the entrance to the Acropolis of Athens, thereby preventing the expansion of the Propylaea to its natural limits; the fact that it obstructed Pericles' scheme explains why, though authorized in 449, it was not built till 427–424. The frieze surrounded the exterior and so was brightly lit; considering that the building was so low, one might expect the carving to be unusually delicate. But the site imposed unique problems. On the west the frieze was visible only from far below at a long distance; on the south, under the same conditions but also from just outside the temple; on the north, from just outside the temple or from a short distance on the steep approach to the Acropolis; on the east—the entrance side—from just outside or from no more than a few paces away on the same level. The designer made all four sides harmonious in spacing the figures widely, for the sake of clarity when seen from afar. He differentiated the entrance side, which alone was seen exclusively at close quarters, by putting an assembly of deities along it, whereas the other three sides received battle-scenes; here Greeks—Athenians, no doubt—are engaged not only with Persians (Pl. 39c) but also with other Greeks, dubiously identified as the Thebans who were allied to Persia in 479. Some of the slabs were collected by Elgin and acquired by the British Museum, others have been replaced (perhaps in wrong order) on the reconstructed temple; all are severely weathered and much damaged, but the details seem to have been coarsely treated, although the height of just under 45 cm. is almost half that of the Parthenon frieze. The contrast between the Greeks, naked except for a chlamys, and the Persians dressed in tunic and trousers must have been emphasized by colour, which also imparted variety to the drapery, itself of little interest, and showed up the uneven rocky landscape whereon the action takes place.

The depth of relief, the violent attitudes and a grouping of figures often in twos or threes instead of larger units, all recall the metopes rather than the frieze of the Parthenon; the tall lithe bodies, however, are a new departure, while the use of floating drapery to fill gaps in the composition is carried further. The ingeniously varied and forceful design was executed by inferior workmen; thus the bold foreshortening of the Persian on the extreme left gives him a leg of superhuman length, while the same exaggeration occurs in the figure of a Greek on the extreme right. The frieze constantly varies in style, so much so that Blümel, who made a detailed study of it, considered that the execution of its 26 m. took forty years, from about 450 to 410; this absurd conjecture met its proper fate when Praschniker noticed that two scraps assigned to the earliest and latest periods fitted together. The variation may be adequately explained by differences in the age of the carvers and in their personal conservatism or progressiveness; the whole is best placed about 425.

A temple of Apollo at Delos, built between 425 and 417 by the Athenians, had, for its central acroteria, groups of Boreas and Eos abducting two girls, as well as separate female figures on the corners. Most survive in fair condition; the style has less in common with the Parthenon than with the frieze of the Nike temple. To avoid the danger that weathering might cause each group to break apart, the drapery spreads sideways at the back, so consolidating the girl and the wind-god into one mass.

The bastion on which the Nike temple stands was surrounded (except opposite the entrance) by a parapet, which could have been added at any date after the completion of the temple and before Athens relinquished hope of winning the Peloponnesian War, possibly as late as 408. The slabs, over a metre high, stood with their sculptured faces outwards but, in contrast to the frieze of the temple, are most delicately carved. They compose a somewhat disjointed frieze in which winged Victories appear in various attitudes—two of them are leading a cow to the sacrifice, another kneels on a cow's back to kill it with a knife, another is fastening her sandal (Pl. 40a), while still others are constructing a trophy by placing a helmet on a pole. A seated Athena with a shield, at the end of the parapet, is the original of the Britannia on coinage. Half a dozen sculptors, ranging in quality from indifferent to excellent, seem to have been employed; the figures on the better slabs, especially the Victory fastening her sandal, are festooned with clinging 'wet' drapery, executed with the same perfection as in the 'Genetrix', presumably from a design by the same sculptor. If he was not Agoracritus he is likely to have been Callimachus, a perfectionist of whom Pliny writes: 'He was always criticizing his own work, and took endless pains over it, hence his nickname of *catatexitechnus* [he whose art dwindles away]—a noteworthy example that carefulness can be carried to excess. His Laconian dancing girls are of perfect workmanship but too much application has totally ruined their charm.' Pausanias and Vitruvius imply that his best asset was an extraordinary dexterity in carving marble; the former adds that he was the first sculptor to use the drill. He would seem to have been younger than either Agoracritus or Alcamenes, but the only means of dating him is the fact that he made a golden lamp for the Erechtheum, which was practically completed in 409; a bronze chimney in the form of a palm-tree brought the smoke up to a vent in the ceiling.

The 'Laconian dancers' of Callimachus may conceivably have been the low reliefs of which copies or adaptations remain, each slab bearing a single figure of a young girl wearing a hat of *polos* type and a short flared skirt. More in keeping with his reputation are the reliefs of Maenads dancing in Bacchic ecstasy, so that their drapery whirls round them in a manner already exploited by painters; the illusion of transparency had also been created in painting by the same method of marking fold-lines across the body. The series comprised at least four such figures; the most popular, showing a Maenad after she has sliced a kid in two (Pl. 41a), is known from twenty copies, some of which come from circular monuments.

The two friezes of the Erechtheum were unique in consisting of separate marble figures pegged to a background of dark limestone (quarried at Eleusis). The existing fragments, badly damaged by their fall to the ground, seem vaguely comparable in style to Alcamenes' Procne and Itys. There is, of course, no chance whatever of arranging them in their original order, and not much of apportioning them between the two friezes, so slight was the difference in size; one frieze, less than 62 cm. high and nearly 50 m. long, surrounded the whole temple except for the north porch, which carried a separate frieze 6½ cm. taller. An inscription of 407 records payments to sculptors employed on the main frieze, at the rate of 60 drachmas a figure (when unskilled labour earned a drachma a day). The sculptors included both Athenian citizens, who are named together with the demes (areas equivalent to parishes) to which they belonged, and aliens who are described as 'resident' in one deme or another. The preserved part of the inscription runs:

To Phyromachus of Cephisia for the youth beside the
   breastplate   60 dr.
To Praxias, resident at Melite, for the horse and the man
   seen behind it who is turning it   120 dr.
To Antiphanes of Cerameis, for the chariot and the youth
   and the pair of horses being yoked   240 dr.
To Phyromachus of Cephisia, for the man leading the horse   60 dr.
To Mynnion, resident at Argyle, for the horse and the man
   striking it. He afterwards added the pillar   127 dr.
To Socles, resident at Alopeke, for the man holding the
   bridle   60 dr.
To Phyromachus of Cephisia, for the man leaning upon his
   staff beside the altar   60 dr.
To Jason of Collytus, for the woman whom the child has
   embraced   80 dr.
    Total expenditure on sculpture   3,315 dr.
    Received, 4,302 dr. 1 obol.
    Disbursed, the same sum.
To ... for the young man writing and the man who is
   standing beside him   120 dr.
To ... resident at Collytus, for the ... and the chariot (but
   not the pair of mules)   80 dr.

To Agathanor, resident at Alopeke, for the woman beside
    the chariot and the pair of mules   180 dr.

Each individual seems, therefore, to have executed a very small share, but
only a third of the whole account has been preserved and the same names
may have recurred on other sections as constantly as that of Phyromachus
in this portion.

The stylistic revolution introduced by Pheidias' pupils seems to have
run its course before the end of the fifth century, and no change ensued
in the early years of the fourth. Such, at least, may be deduced from the
superb gravestone (75 m. high) of Dexileus (Pl. 42), who was killed in a
battle of 394. He is shown in a moment of victory, thrusting a spear into a
fallen enemy, in accordance with a convention already established in the
Villa Albani relief of some thirty years earlier.

Non-Attic Sculpture in Greece, 430–390 B.C.

Polycleitus, the only great sculptor of the Peloponnese, must have been
elderly in 423 when a fire destroyed the temple of Hera outside Argos, his
own city. A new temple was promptly built, to the design of an Argive
architect, and Polycleitus made the cult-image of the goddess, a seated
colossus of gold and ivory. Pausanias describes its accessories: 'On the head
is a crown upon which the Graces and Seasons are wrought in relief; in one
hand she carries a pomegranate, in the other a sceptre. The story about the
pomegranate I shall omit because of its mystic nature, but the cuckoo
perched on the sceptre is explained by a story that when Zeus was in love
with the girl Hera he changed himself into this bird and Hera caught it to
play with.' So Pausanias writes, and his account is substantiated by coins,
some of which even show the cuckoo.

The Heraeum has suffered almost total destruction; the marble sculptures are reduced to a cartload of shattered fragments. 'Of the sculptures
above the columns', says Pausanias, 'some represent the birth of Zeus and
the battle of the gods and giants, others scenes of the Trojan wars and the
capture of Troy.' Since the pediments required only two subjects (the first
and the last, no doubt), the other two were presumably restricted to
metopes, from which must have come the existing remains of figures less
than life-size. Among them is the greater part of a male figure with the
physical abnormality of a large lump on the groin (due probably to a
swollen gland), that must have been observed on an individual living
model; this is the first clear instance of carving from life, a practice that

may have obtained from the middle of the fifth century. Scraps of two figures of natural size, each a suppliant embracing a psuedo-archaic image, must belong to the pediment showing the capture of Troy. The influence of Pheidias can be seen in an intact female head (Pl. 41*b*) which may conceivably come from the other pediment, but the lobes of both ears are pierced to receive metal earrings (presumably of gilt-bronze) which at that height would have shown only as a gleam; the figure of which the head formed part may have stood on the ground, though it must, if so, have backed against a wall because the face was obviously designed to be seen from off-centre—the right profile is dull, the frontal view tolerable, the left profile appealing. Drapery from pediments and metopes alike is comparable with Attic work of the generation after Pheidias.

The style of Polycleitus must have been easily imitated by his pupils; in copies it cannot always be distinguished from theirs. But a basalt figure in the Terme, of a boy wearing the olive-wreath of an Olympic victor, was copied from a bronze that would have been too weakly pretty for his taste. Nor do his known works (which admittedly may include none of his latest) suggest that he wished to achieve such conscious grace as distinguishes a bronze statue in Florence, '*Il Idolino*' (Pl. 43*a*). Found at Pesaro, it was considered an indisputable original until a basalt copy of the head came to light in the Vatican cellars; the objection was then raised that a statue in so remote a town would not have been copied. Actually the surface of the bronze does not appear to have received much attention after it left the furnace, for the details are not sharp as in the fragmentary head at Oxford (Pl. 36*d*). Probably, therefore, the '*Idolino*' is a cast made from piece-moulds of a lost original. A bronze youth found at Pompeii may have been cast from another statue by the same master. Marble copies reproduce several more statues of vaguely Polycleitan inspiration, including one of a long-haired youth (or Apollo, perhaps); a bronze of this too has been discovered at Pompeii. In these statues an Attic influence appears, just as Argive influence can be traced at Athens, but the schools did not merge; the Argive head retains its elongated shape, its flat cheeks and sharp separation from the neck, and sometimes a bar of flesh over the nose is present. The sculptors of this class of work presumably included the large band of pupils of Polycleitus, many of whose names are recorded; some of them worked on a group of thirty-seven statues at Delphi, a memorial of the Spartan victory at Aegospotami in 405.

A statue of Victory, which Pausanias noted at Olympia, is identified beyond question by the inscription on the plinth: 'The Messenians and Naupactians dedicated to Olympian Zeus the tenth part of the spoil of their enemies. Paeonius of Mende made it; he also won the competition for making the temple's acroteria,' These acroteria were also statues of Victory. Messenian refugees settled at Naupactus in 456, and the combined forces won a success in 452 by taking a town in that district; this was the battle to which Pausanias referred the dedication of the statue, but the date is impossibly early, whereas a tradition he thought mistaken related it, quite plausibly, to the capture of Sphacteria in 424. The statue would in that case have been commissioned after the peace of 421. From the fragments discovered it has been possible to piece the figure together and make a restoration of its background drapery (Pl. 43b) without risk of error in any essential point, though whether the object grasped by the right hand was a crown or ribbon to place round the head of the victor, or a palm leaf or other emblem, it is impossible to state. A scrap of the back of the head is preserved, with the same arrangement of hair as in some heads which may be copied from an earlier work by Paeonius; in the reconstructions, however, a head from the pediments of the temple of Zeus was unfortunately utilized.

The goddess is represented flying down from Olympus to bring victory to the men of Naupactus, and to show that she was still hurrying through the air an eagle was placed beneath her feet; the bird was only in part carved out, being in part represented in paint, thus helping to conceal the block (coloured sky-blue, no doubt) that supported the statue. The pedestal was about 9 m. high, tapering sharply upwards, and triangular in form so that the spectator should not see more than one side at once: the solidity of a square mass of the same dimensions would have been much more apparent and would have utterly destroyed the illusion of flying through the air.

The design of the statue was a technical triumph. The goddess is leaning forwards; to counterbalance the forward and downward pull of gravity her cloak is blown far behind her. A happy expedient gives support to what would otherwise be dangerously thin sections of marble, for the overfall of drapery that covers the breast is also driven back by the wind. It was perhaps to strengthen the lower part of the statue that the peplos was made to open down both sides of the body—an unusual mode, although it was common for one side to be left open—so that the garment was held only by the belt and the brooch on the right shoulder, while the outstretched hands alone prevented the cloak from blowing away altogether. The wings that sprung from the shoulders gave direction to the flight, and their presence would remove that appearance of aimlessness which detracts from the statue; they also served as struts for the upper border of the cloak. But peplos and overfall, cloak, arms, wings, all fit so naturally into their places that the technical reasons for so placing them need to be thought out.

The stylistic difference between Paeonius' statue and the winged figure (N) from the Parthenon (Pl. 34*b*) might be thought to imply a much longer interval than the minimum of fifteen years assumed by relating the Olympia dedication to the peace of 421. The fact that he also supplied acroteria for the temple of Zeus, which had been practically complete by 457, can be dismissed as irrelevant, because they are likely to have been merely replacements of simpler acroteria (for the temple cannot have been left without any). However, there remains the possibility that Paeonius may have been a pioneer of the style adopted by Pheidias' pupils. If so, he cannot have learnt it at his Macedonian birthplace, where he would have been trained in the northern Aegean style, Ionian by derivation and backward by the standards of Greece (for instance, a large, badly defaced relief on a gateway at Thasos has been assigned to 411 though it looks considerably earlier than 450). Comparison of his drapery with fragments of the Nemesis base demonstrates close contact with Attica and hints, perhaps, that he followed where Athens had led the way, while there is no evidence to encourage belief in the contrary. A speculation already mentioned, attributing the Niobids of the 430s to Paeonius, is barely compatible with another that identifies him as the designer of the Bassae frieze, which is currently dated about 400 and could be even later.

The Doric temple at Bassae seems to have been founded in the middle of the fifth century. It was a thank-offering to Apollo *Epikourios* (the Helper) by the Arcadian town of Phigaleia, for preservation from a plague, but must have been under construction for a very long time, owing, no doubt, to the poverty of this highland district. The interior was eventually lined with a colonnade that combined an anomalous version of Ionic with Corinthian elements, which appear nowhere else before the fourth century. The frieze was placed above this colonnade. The extraordinary coarseness of its execution (Pl. 43*c*), on slabs 63 cm. high, cannot be blamed on incompetent carving but must have been deliberate, with the object of suiting the unique conditions in which it was displayed. Unless the room lay open to the sky (as is most unlikely), only subdued light could enter, and the sculpture would have been only dimly visible with the aid of reflection off the floor and again off the ceiling. Detail of the usual fineness would have been not merely wasted but confusing in the gloom, more than five metres above eye level, whereas the crude emphatic carving and presumably contrasting colours gave visitors a chance to follow the action represented, which was correspondingly violent. Moreover, since the frieze ran along all four sides of the room, the composition needed to be more uniform than in the case of an external frieze, of which never more than one side could be seen full-on from any viewpoint. This requirement was accentuated by the arrangement of the figures in self-contained groups, inevitable because the marble (quarried in central Arcadia) could be transported across the mountains by no other means than on pack-animals; each slab, no thicker than safety demanded, appears to have come ready-carved, and was then fastened to the wall with clamps and pins (the hole for a pin shows behind the centaur's neck on Pl. 43c, and another pierces a deep fold in the drapery behind the child's head; two pins were spaced across the middle of every slab). The junctions of the slabs were necessarily left bare; since no projecting foot or arm binds the composition together, the original order cannot be decided throughout.

More than half the blocks are occupied by a battle between Greeks and Amazons, the remainder with a battle between Greeks and Centaurs, while the gods, whose figures divide the two scenes, take part on the side of the Greeks. A soldier throws an Amazon off her horse by her shoulder and foot, a Centaur fixes his teeth in the neck of one adversary while kicking out with his hoofs at another, who protects himself behind his shield, and a Centaur seizes a woman before she can escape with her child (Pl. 43c); two other women take refuge at an archaic image, and a suppliant is dragged away from the altar. Wildly flying drapery fits the confusion of the scene, but the faces are as impassive as those of the sedate young men on the Parthenon frieze, for this was an age of transition. The thick proportions of the figures are reminiscent of Argive works, yet there is much evidence of Attic influence; one of the groups reproduces a motif from the frieze of the 'Theseum', while the composition is based on the same principles as that of the frieze of the temple of Athena Nike—close groups of single combats, diversified by longer stretches of narrative, in which the only touches of quiescence are given by the dead and wounded. The arrangement of drapery in parallel folds, an old Ionian method, could also have been derived from the Nike temple frieze, which might be an earlier work by the same designer. The eclecticism at Bassae is such as might be expected of Paeonius, who must have shed the provincialism of his northern upbringing when he moved to the great centres of sculpture, but would have retained some degree of regional peculiarity.

Sculpture in Asia, 430–360 B.C.

The style of the late fifth or early fourth centuries is represented by no work of distinction found east or north of the Aegean, and in Italy by nothing better than a pair of ridiculous acroteria from Locri—each of a nude Dioscurus sliding off a horse which is supported by a Triton, from whose draped human torso a long fishtail emerges. These are feeble decorative pieces. A great deal of better sculpture was commissioned by foreigners who appreciated Greek art, but this too is primarily decorative and often somewhat weak; the purpose was invariably sepulchral. The Lycians, a people who have left hundreds of rock-cut tombs (some on cliff-faces, others shaped from isolated boulders), also built a few of marble on which the reliefs are naturally finer in detail. The work was done chiefly by Lycians, who must now have been more practised than the Ionians, but an occasional designer may have been Greek; the style was of Ionian derivation. Sculptors of that school also provided marble sarcophagi for the royal family of Sidon. Other bodies in the same tomb were laid, according to older Phoenician custom, in stone or marble coffins of a type copied from the Egyptian wooden mummy-case, plain except for a human head; the style of the head became Greek instead of Egyptian at this period, when the rich took to ordering marble coffins (which may often have been shipped ready-carved, so their distribution as far as Cadiz seems to imply; however, the many votive statues of little boys at Sidon prove that Greeks worked there in the fifth century).

The 'Satrap' sarcophagus, the earliest from Sidon, consists of a rectangular box and a separate lid which vaguely resembles a temple roof, with upturned corners—a precaution against breakage—in imitation of acroteria; the shape is Greek (and can be traced back to archaic Ionian sarcophagi, of which the best known are in painted terracotta, mainly from Clazomenae). But the reliefs on both the long sides and one of the ends illustrate characteristic activities of an Oriental potentate—not specifically the king of Sidon but an ideal figure; the other end is occupied by a group of four young men standing, engaged in conversation. On one of the long sides a two-horse chariot and a led horse are brought to the enthroned potentate (Pl. 39d); on the other he is on horseback, has just killed a deer and is attacking a leopard with the aid of an attendant—one of three who are still mounted, a fourth having fallen from his bolting horse. The scene on the end, in which the potentate is feasting in the presence of his wife and courtiers, is an adaptation of the banquet motif common in Greek sepulchral reliefs (Pl. 23b): and the furniture is all purely Greek in type. In general the garments on all four sides are more Greek than Oriental, though the head-dresses and sleeved tunics are such as Persians might wear. Most of the drapery is closely furrowed by shallow parallel folds reminiscent of the 'Harpy' Tomb (Pl. 14b); a few wind-blown portions are divided by bolder though again parallel folds, not very different from some on the Bassae frieze (Pl. 43c).

The 'Lycian' sarcophagus in the Istanbul Museum was likewise found in the royal tomb at Sidon (actually a rock-cut catacomb). In shape this sarcophagus reproduces, on a smaller scale, a type of tomb peculiar to Lycia, rectangular beneath a tall convex lid, in simulation of a thatched building.* The carvings, disposed on the ends and sides of the lower piece and on the ends of the lid, seem all due to one sculptor who had probably worked in Greece. On one side young men in chariots are hunting a lion (Pl. 45b). On the other two separate groups of mounted young men gallop from left to right in pursuit of a huge boar which runs through the centre of the field; the sculptor could not represent the hunt coming straight forward towards the spectators and therefore adopted this unsatisfactory compromise. One end contains a fight between two Centaurs and a Lapith, below a pair of griffins in the gable; the other shows two Centaurs disputing possession of the body of a deer, while a pair of opulent sphinxes occupies the gable, their pointed wings stretching up to the peak. In many respects the reliefs of this sarcophagus are so reminiscent of the Parthenon metopes and frieze that conscious imitation would seem plausible, but the sculptor made no attempt at Pheidian grandeur; his work is purely decorative, slick and pretty. The date can scarcely be as early as 400.

Although Lycia produced an abundance of architectural sculpture clearly datable between the extreme limits of 425 and 350, the course of development has not yet been convincingly determined; scholars differ in their estimates for each monument by as much as a generation, and so invert one another's chronological order. On the assumption that the genuinely local sculptors were backward by Greek standards, none of these works need be earlier than about 400 or even 390, while in so far as it was native the style could have remained unchanged till its decadence, which seems to have been far advanced by 370. The occasional introduction of a Greek designer or carver could then account for the divergences in character and quality of either composition or execution—for they might not

* Two actual tombs of this sort, taken from Xanthus to the British Museum, stand some seven metres high: in the inscriptions can be read the names of their owners, Merehi and Payava. Neither can be much earlier than 350; a dating around 360 for Payava's tomb may be obtainable from the supposed reference in the inscription to 'Autophradates, the Persian satrap', though four letters in the middle of the name are lost. The reliefs on Merehi's tomb are severely weathered but the carving seems to have been incompetent; Payava obtained a rather better version of the same scheme. On each of the curving sides of both roofs is carved a four-horse chariot in full gallop; the sixteen bent equine legs are evenly spaced at a uniform level, producing the ludicrous effect of a pattern of suspended chevrons. Human figures occupy the upright lower part; some wear armour, standing absolutely frontal, probably because the craftsman could not make the cuirass distinguishable in any other pose.

always occur in both together; divergences so caused would have no clear chronological implications.

In the belief that the two greatest Lycian monuments in European museums are virtually contemporary, the one with the simpler detail but more accomplished composition may be considered first. It was removed almost in its entirety to Vienna from the remote site of Trysa, of which the modern Turkish name is generally printed in its German spelling, Gjölbaschi. The almost square enclosure contained a large sarcophagus and several subordinate graves. In the south wall is the gateway, consisting of a lintel carried by two upright posts, which are plain outside but carved on the inward side with a pair of male dancers; upon the outside of the lintel are the foreparts of four winged bulls with a Gorgon's head in the centre space and rosettes between the other monsters; below are seen the persons buried within, two men and two women attended by serving maids and pets. The inner face of the lintel bears a relief of dwarfs dancing and playing musical instruments, an un-Greek subject. The remainder of the tomb's sculptures decorated the courtyard wall, the two highest courses of masonry being occupied by reliefs along the whole of the interior and on the exterior of the south side. Each band of relief is 109 m. long and usually bears an independent design, the height of the upper varying around 40 cm. and of the lower around 45 cm.; where, exceptionally, the same scene covers both bands, their combined height is reduced to 58–9 cm. The relief is so shallow—often less than 3 cm. and nowhere over 4 cm.—that the treatment was necessarily pictorial. The dominant subject is the siege of a town; the others are the battle of the Seven against Thebes, the repulse of invaders landing from ships, Greeks fighting Amazons, Lapiths fighting Centaurs at the wedding of Peirithous, a four-horse chariot carrying a boy and his driver, Bellerophon slaying the Chimaera (a local myth), a warrior carrying a boy in his arms, a banquet and dance, Odysseus killing the suitors, the hunt of the Calydonian boar, a battle of Greeks and Amazons, the rape of the daughters of Leucippus, hunting scenes, and four of the exploits of Theseus.

To match the other subjects which were all taken from legend, the besieged town must surely be Troy, especially since a Lycian king was believed to have been killed in its defence; the details, however, illustrate the contemporary mode of warfare. For this scene alone a single composition (Pl. 44a) covers both strips of relief instead of one, to include a view of the interior of the town as well as of the walls where the attack is in progress. At the extreme left an upright bar in the upper field divides the siege from the battle illustrated on the next slab; a tree-trunk in the lower field fulfils the same purpose in addition to masking the junction of two slabs. The scene opens at a corner of the town, where a storming-party climbs up the rocks outside the wall; the defenders, manning the battlements and towers, are throwing down large stones or thrusting with their spears, but the shields of the attackers keep them safe; another group endeavours to force a passage through a postern gate, and around the next tower a third party is unopposed, because the defenders are hurrying to help repulse assailants who have won a second gateway (not illustrated. Further off to the right, the scene ends with a woman seated on a mule, a man in attendance, and a donkey loaded with their property; these are fugitives preparing to leave the doomed city at the point where the walls bend round to the right, away from the danger zone.) As the last resource (Pl. 44a) an officer stands upon the walls, with hands upraised in prayer, calling on the gods to help, while a boy by his side sacrifices a ram, his knees gripping its horned head as he lifts the knife to stab. Close by sits the aged king Priam, with a lion under his throne and a boy crouching by its side; Helen is seated under a parasol with one of her women by her; an attendant stands with raised hands resting on his spear.

Although a siege was a frequent subject in Assyrian relief it was rare in Greek relief, indeed its presence on this and the 'Nereid Monument' suggests a specific demand of the Lycian patrons; the merlons of the battlements are of Oriental form, rounded instead of rectangular as in Greece. The composition of the frieze as a whole must have been inspired by paintings, for its design has no parallel in Greek sculpture, whereas Polygnotus and other famous painters of the late fifth century seem, from the accounts of ancient authors and the testimony of vase-paintings which they influenced, to have composed great pictures of similar subjects, using similar means of perspective. An Attic draughtsman was perhaps responsible for drawings after which the frieze was cut. Whatever his nationality, he was accustomed to working on a flat surface, as his habit of design and use of perspective reveal; in the temple, for instance, two sides are displayed, whereas earlier artists of the fifth century, whether painters or sculptors, would have shown one side only. Moreover on a fifth-century Attic vase-painting, of Odysseus killing the suitors, occur several motifs used for that scene of the frieze; it has therefore been inferred that both have borrowed from Polygnotus' picture of the subject or from some similar masterpiece. Analogies to individual figures may often be seen on Attic gravestones. No traces of colour can be detected in the frieze, but the absence of details which can scarcely have been omitted intentionally can only be accounted for on the conjecture that paint gave its customary aid. The carving does not reach a particularly high level, and the junctions of the blocks are clumsily prominent. The present state of the surface is deplorable, for the local variety of white limestone used in the monument has become irregularly pitted and roughened by the weather, from which it had no protection for twenty-three centuries—an earthquake had overthrown the eastern wall but otherwise the ruins were still upright when they were discovered in 1842 by a German explorer.

The 'Nereid Monument' from Xanthus, now reconstructed in the British Museum, was actually a tomb in the form of an Ionic temple on a very tall base. There are no less than four friezes, all of different heights (ranging from 1 m. to 44 cm.); the two largest were placed on the upper courses of the base, a much smaller one on the architrave above the columns, and the smallest around the exterior of the cella behind them. The pediments were filled with sculpture, the roof supported acroteria (the best-preserved is composed of one figure carrying another), while between the columns stood statues of Nereids or Aurae (Breezes), all now headless. They must represent spirits flying above the surface of the sea, because under the feet of each was put a bird, a fish, a crab or a shell. Their wind-blown drapery is mostly of rather thick material, arranged in repetitive folds somewhat in the manner of the Bassae frieze. But one figure (Pl. 44b), which is far superior to the others and must be Greek work, wears extremely thin cloth crumpled across the body in a series of flat strips like tape. The same technique occurs in the largest frieze, on the drapery of Persians engaged in battle with naked Greeks. Here the designer—presumably the Greek who carved the best Nereid—took the utmost care to avoid monotony, by grouping combatants in twos or threes, and by such interruptions as a scene of an archer taking aim or of two Greeks helping a wounded comrade off his horse. Many of the heads are intact; their faces are sleek, with a stylized expression according to the action in which the figure is engaged. The standard of carving is undistinguished, though better than in the other friezes.

Definitely local subjects appear in some sculptures of the tomb. Though the western pediment was filled with a battle between infantry and cavalry, the eastern shows a Lycian ruler with his wife receiving homage. In the frieze on the architrave he appears hunting and in battle; a procession of men carrying meat must illustrate the bringing of tribute to him. The frieze on the cella includes a dinner-party, where the guests sit behind an immensely long table instead of reclining beside separate little tables in the Greek manner; musicians are in attendance. If the sacrifices shown preceded the meal, it had some ritual character; a hint that it was funerary may be given by the group of nine figures conversing beside one recumbent, though he may perhaps be merely waiting for the saddled horse that a man is leading. Interpretation of the scenes is the more difficult because the original order of the slabs cannot always be determined. The same difficulty occurs with the lesser (63 cm. high) of the two friezes from the base, an inept composition which can scarcely be ascribed to a Greek; it is concerned with warfare around three walled cities. On one slab the ruler stands under a parasol, the symbol of Oriental monarchy, to receive a deputation of elders offering surrender. His soldiers are climbing a ladder to storm a city built on a hill of such irregularity that the walls must needs form a series of salients and re-entrants (Fig. 20); only in Lycia are there

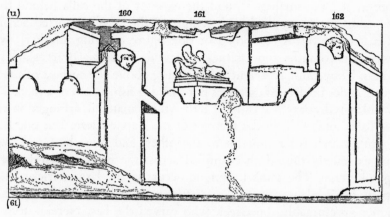

20. City on frieze of Nereid Monument, British Museum

even more venturesome groupings of buildings in landscapes, rock-cut in a tomb at Pinara. At the second city on the frieze there is no visible cause for alarm, but guards are gesticulating excitedly, on noticing (if the next slab is correctly placed) the approach of some civilians leading a mule. The defenders of the third city are fighting outside it, aided by their reserve troops on the battlements, who are throwing stones at the advancing enemy. In this instance the perimeter is rectangular and contains an inner fortress, seemingly not an acropolis such as often existed inside a Greek city, but a second defensive line parallel with and close behind the outer, in accordance with Oriental practice. In all three cities the walls are equipped with merlons of Oriental type, as at Gjölbaschi. The Xanthians may have encountered such fortifications in their wars, but the frieze cannot safely be assumed to represent historical episodes.

To the hereditary ruler of Limyra, Pericles, who conquered nearly all the rest of Lycia in 375–365, is ascribed a tomb comparable to the 'Nereid Monument' though much inferior in workmanship; it was discovered in 1966 at his birthplace and has subsequently been excavated on behalf of the German Archaeological Institute. The full publication is awaited of caryatids, acroteria and two friezes believed to represent funeral ceremonies; photographs of the caryatids show that their drapery is stylized in a pseudo-archaic repetitiveness, while the slabs of frieze already illustrated are poor in both design and execution.

Sculpture in Greece, 390–360 B.C.

A growing interest in portraiture is shown by the busts copied from statues of the orator Lysias, who died about 380, and the philosopher Antisthenes, who died in 365. Each, for all we know, may reveal the public concept of a personality with little regard to his actual features. But an Attic sculptor, Demetrius of Alopeke, was remarkable for his lack of idealism. He 'was fonder of accuracy than beauty', says Quintilian; 'a maker not of gods but of men,' says Lucian, who elsewhere observes that one of his statues 'looked as though it would run off its pedestal', and described his portrait of Pellichus as 'paunchy, bald, only half covered by his cloak; some hairs of his beard blowing in the wind and his veins protruding—an absolute likeness of the man'. Demetrius also made a statuette of the aged Lysimache, who held the office of priestess of Athena for sixty-four years; Pausanias saw it on the Acropolis and estimated its height at one cubit (under 50 cm.). Another lost statue portrayed Simon, the author of a treatise on horsemanship, whom Aristophanes mentioned in the Knights, performed in 424. But the surviving inscriptions of Demetrius belong to the early fourth century. No element of portraiture is found in the gravestones which were being produced at Athens in ever-increasing numbers. For the most part they have little artistic value and their similarity renders a large collection a monotonous sight. In general they repeat the motives of their predecessors, scenes of a family taking farewell of one of its members or of daily domestic life.

The temple of Asclepius in his great sanctuary near Epidaurus must have been built between 390 and 370, probably nearer the former date; an inscription states that its construction occupied four years, eight months and ten days. An almost contemporary relief may reproduce the cult-image, which is crudely illustrated on late coins and described by Pausanias:

The statue of Asclepius is only half the size of the Olympian Zeus
at Athens and is made of ivory and gold; an inscription records Thrasymedes, son of Arignotus of Paros, as its sculptor. The god sits upon a
throne, with a staff in one hand and holding the other above the head of
his serpent, while his dog is seen lying down by his side. Reliefs on the
throne show the exploits of Argive heroes, Bellerophon's adventure
with the Chimaera, and Perseus after the decapitation of Medusa.

The long inscription recording the expenditure on the temple, piece by
piece, would have left insoluble problems even if the text had survived
intact. Three or possibly four named sculptors, all presumably Athenians,
were employed on separate contracts; since two of them, Timotheus and
Hectoridas, are known to have survived into the later half of the century,
the work at Epidaurus can scarcely be earlier than 380. The contract bound
each to supply the marble—Pentelic brought from Athens—for the figures
he undertook, but he would clearly have been entitled to engage assistants to carve at his own charge; there can be no certainty that he designed
the figures himself. But the work was so apportioned that it did not require
overall coordination. Hectoridas was entrusted with the entire sculpture of
one pediment, by two successive contracts (for 1400 and 1610 drachmas),
while a single contract for the same amount of 3010 dr. was made with
Theo ... (the end of whose name is missing) for the other pediment.
Timotheus contracted to supply the acroteria of one gable for 2240 dr.;
those of the other gable, by a sculptor whose name is lost, probably cost
2320 dr., though the numerals cannot be read with certainty. Timotheus,
who in his old age had achieved enough celebrity to become one of the
sculptors of the Mausoleum, may already have stood out among his
colleagues, for he was allowed to undertake some carvings described by
the vague word *typos*; it could mean a model or a relief or even an image
in the round. The sum, 900 dr., is too large to have been earned from
models (for which, in any case, the inscription twice uses another word,
paradeigma, though not with reference to sculpture); obviously the cost of
the material accounted for all but a small fraction of the total. No vestige
has been recovered of any objects that might be relevant; a suggestion
that they were metopes in the porch does at least comply with the
amount of marble the sum should have involved.

Most of the sculptures found have been removed to the National
Museum in Athens, though some are housed near the Sanctuary. The many
fragments pieced together have resulted in no complete figures but give
ample evidence of their subjects and style. Fragments of slightly over

lifesize come from the pediments; the eastern was filled with a battle of Greeks and Centaurs, the western with a battle of Greeks and Amazons. Two Nereids or Aurae (Breezes), each mounted sideways with an arm round the horse's neck, must be corner acroteria, while a Victory, standing holding a bird (Pl. 45a), came from the peak of, perhaps, the same gable (supposedly the western because it was found built into a late wall away to the west). Generally the work of the several sculptors differed much less than might be expected on the assumption that each had been free to design his own figures, but the team as a whole may have been dominated by convention; Timotheus and Hectoridas were certainly too young to have reached their full powers. The influence of the Nike Parapet is most apparent but daintiness had ceased to be the primary consideration in drapery, which now tends to conglomerate into masses that outline the body, leaving it disclosed as though naked, except for an occasional thin fold. A novel and bolder treatment distinguishes the Victory with the bird, questionably ascribed to Timotheus; drapery which either lies blown smooth over the body or with a few sharp creases gathers in deeply furrowed masses. A mounted Amazon from the west pediment—probably by Hectoridas—reproduces the pose of the Dexileus relief, but the drapery is of thicker cloth. The faces either grimace or are blankly impassive, according to whether the figures are strained or relaxed. Drapery characteristic of the Epidaurus sculptures occurs in headless female statues found elsewhere, notably one in the Agora at Athens and an Aura (perhaps an acroterion, reputedly from Hermione) in Copenhagen, and in copies of a Leda caressing a swan, which closely resembled a statue of Hygieia from the sanctuary; attributions to Timotheus are of course hypothetical.

The Argive school of the early fourth century was dominated by the sons of a sculptor, Patrocles, who may have been a brother of Polycleitus; at any rate one of his sons was also named Polycleitus, the others were Naucydes and Daedalus, who established himself at Sicyon. Naucydes appears to have been the eldest, for he made two statues of Cheimon, a wrestler victorious in 448, and his Hebe beside the Hera of Argos may have been contemporary with the cult-image; moreover he had a pupil working in 405. Copies of the Discobolus of Naucydes have been recognized in the figures of a youth standing with a discus held loosely in his left hand, and an athlete in the Conservatori suggests a copy from an original by the same sculptor. The figures are livelier than any of those by the elder Polycleitus, the hair rougher, the eyelids narrower and the features coarser, but fundamentally the style is a development of his. Four boxers in Dresden may copy later works of the same school, perhaps after 370. An Aphrodite wearing a sword-belt, found at Epidaurus, and related to the temple sculptures from that site, has been thought to be a copy of the armed Aphrodite supporting a tripod, dedicated at Amyclae after the battle of Aegospotami (405). Pausanias gives the artist's name as Polycleitus, without specifying whether he means the elder or the younger sculptor of that name, but on chronological grounds the latter has the greater claim.

The influence of this Peloponnesian school can be traced in Attica. A Pan (?) from Eleusis in the Athens National Museum is almost a replica of the 'Westmacott Boy'; the weight lies entirely upon the left leg, the head is supported by the right hand, the upper arm continuing the line of the shoulder, while the left arm hangs down by the side. The body is superficially modelled and the sensual face wears a dreamy expression which points to an Attic sculptor of the fourth century. Another instance of the increasing adeptness in rendering expression is seen in a head belonging to the Fogg Museum of Harvard University (Pl. 46a). It has a forcefulness unknown in the fifth century, the result of minor innovations in the treatment of details; the lower part of the forehead bulges rather more, the inner corners of the eyes are more deeply set and the eyes themselves are narrower. It is, however, an unpleasant expression which results from the attempt to gain intensity of gaze by these means. A head of similar type in Athens and a related statue in Madrid, the 'Joven Orador', reveal Polycleitan elements so strong as to cast doubts upon the attributions to Cephisodotus of Athens, whose statues of 'an orator with uplifted arm' and of 'Hermes feeding the child Dionysus', noted by Pliny, have both been proposed for their originals.

Another work by this Cephisodotus was the Eirene and Plutus (Peace and Plenty), a group known from coins of Athens and from marble copies. The finest of these, though headless and armless, is in New York; one in Munich (Pl. 46b), of poorer quality, is complete except for the restored nose, both hands of the goddess, the child's head, arms and feet. Eirene rested her right hand on a long sceptre, the child held in his left hand a cornucopia, the symbol of abundance. The relation of this statue and the Erechtheum caryatids is so close that it might almost be thought to commemorate the end of the Peloponnesian War in 403, but the cult of Eirene was not officially recognized at Athens until 374. With this later date agree both Pliny's *floruit* of 372 and Plutarch's statement that Cephisodotus' sister was the first wife of Phocion, who lived from 402 to 317. Moreover the head bears less resemblance to the Erechtheum type than to the early works of Praxiteles, who is supposed to have been the son of Cephisodotus, probably rightly, since Praxiteles had a son of that name. Other heads which have been ascribed to the sculptor of the Eirene, because of their similarity to that statue, seem to be older, if anything, than it: but in dealing with sculptures known only by one or two copies, and those by indifferent workmen, it is rash to argue on such premises, for the delicate curves of eyelids and lips might easily be hardened into a Pheidian aspect by the copyist.

A case in point is the 'Hope' type of Hygieia, one of the masterpieces of this clear-cut style out of which developed the softness of Praxiteles. The Terme head (Pl. 46c), although itself a good copy, produces a later effect than the worse replicas. The original has been recognized in a fragment in the Acropolis Museum. The Terme copy is perhaps of the time of Augustus or a little later; in it the ends of the mouth are disfigured by drill-holes and a blunder in the parts behind the ear results in the presence of a mass, neither hair nor bandeau, that breaks without reason into the line of the latter. Further, as Ashmole remarked, the original was 'fresh, soft and incomparably delicate in all its transitions', whereas the copyist 'plotted out the Terme head, executed it with all the precision he could and produced a mathematical exercise, hard and almost cold'. The complete statue is known best from the 'Hope' copy (Pl. 46d) and a statuette from Epidaurus in the National Museum at Athens; the goddess held a box in her left hand, a saucer in her right, to feed the snake lying over her left shoulder.

Although the actual type of dress in the Eirene and the Hygieia is not the same (the one a Doric peplos with himation hanging behind, the other an Ionic chiton with himation wrapped round), the drapery of the two statues has much in common. As Ashmole has explained,

If one thinks away the difference of material and composes the actual scheme of drapery about the lower part of the legs, one finds that it amounts almost to a simple reversal. A group of three or four narrow vertical folds on the outside of the supporting leg; two, splitting into three, over the supporting leg itself, the toe of which projects; a heavy mass between the legs, composed in both of a broad fold and a narrow one slightly behind it; a heavy fold falling from the knee of the free leg, tapering and then expanding again to fall just inside the foot, to sweep up over it and to cling, a subsidiary fold or two between, to the outer side of the calf. Finally this outline of the leg framed at the upper part of the thigh by the himation, below this by the chiton, in both statues. This kind of drapery arrangement, an elaboration of the simple, explanatory scheme of the second half of the fifth century (contours of free leg shown by clinging drapery:

supporting leg covered by columnar folds), is common in the time of the youth of Praxiteles, but there is no closer parallel to the Hope Hygieia than the Eirene of Cephisodotus. With this scheme of drapery is intimately connected the ponderation of the figures, and this again, except for the arms, is virtually a reversal, as well in the body as in the head. Passing from the pose to the general conception we may remark a characteristic which is apparent in both. In the Eirene as in the Hygieia one has a feeling of the posing of the figure as well as of the material upon it.

After Ashmole wrote that comparison, a bronze statue of Athena was discovered at Piraeus, with drapery very similar to the Eirene's but a dull conventional face. In the face of the Hygieia we can detect a novel sensuality; with its deep-set, finely finished eye, less brooding than the Praxitelean eye, with its soft but not fleshy brow, it is peculiarly typical of the final stage of transition from the age of Pheidias to that of Praxiteles.

VIII

The Late Classical Period

(370–323 B.C.)

THE city-states, upon which sculptors depended for large commissions, recovered their freedom of action when Spartan domination was reduced by battles in 371 and 370 and abolished by a third in 362. But in 338 Philip of Macedon brought all Greece under his control; Athens, in particular, never regained other than cultural importance. Then followed Alexander, in whose reign of 336–323 Greece became economically as well as politically insignificant compared with the vast territories he conquered. The half-century before Alexander's death was the last age to produce a considerable number of renowned sculptors; several of them, moreover, were regarded in much later times as superior to any who worked in the following centuries. The most eminent of them was Praxiteles, at any rate till near the end of his life, when Lysippus arose; each, in his turn, did more to set the course of development than his contemporaries of the second rank—Scopas, Euphranor, Leochares, Bryaxis, Silanion and Timotheus.

Praxiteles

As we have seen, Praxiteles, an Athenian, was obviously a relative—in all probability a son—of the sculptor Cephisodotus, whose name he gave to one of his own sons. This advantage with which he started accounts, in part, for his success, which may not have been as great in his lifetime as posthumously. Under the Roman empire he seems to have been the most popular of the Old Masters; Pausanias, however, had the dislike of the religious for too much naturalism and preferred the work of an earlier age. Thanks to his brief notice of 'a marble Hermes carrying the child Dionysus, the work of Praxiteles', among the contents of the Heraeum, the excavators at Olympia were enabled to identify a statue they found (Pl. 47a): copies of his better known works have also been recognized, and it seems likely on stylistic grounds that at least one other original survives. But the Hermes must provide the chief basis of study.*

The statue had fallen off its pedestal face-downwards, and was covered over with mud from the disintegrating walls of the temple, which were composed of sun-dried bricks. Hence its surface was excellently preserved, though some of the projecting portions of the body had been broken away; the child's left arm, most of the right arm of Hermes, both his legs from below the knees and the left foot, are missing still, but restoration has offered no problems except in the case of the right arm. Dionysus is obviously gazing at some object held in this hand, while Hermes himself looks dreamily into the distance; on the analogy of some later figures of satyrs the object has been explained as a bunch of grapes, a suitable bait to excite the infant wine-god. Less appropriately, other theories propose cymbals or a rattle or a purse (an attribute of Hermes himself), though the apparent inattention of Hermes can then be described as an attitude of listening to the noise produced by shaking the object in his hand. His left arm rests upon a tree-trunk, over which falls his chlamys in rich folds that set off his smooth, naked body; the left hand seems to have held the herald's staff, the chief attribute of the god. A metal wreath must have been affixed to the hair, a deep groove for its support being visible at the back.

The statue was cut from a magnificent block of Parian marble, not white but cream-coloured; where polished, the surface glows with reflected light. The placing in the temple, at the mouth of a shallow recess, allowed only the front to be seen; the back therefore was not carved in detail but merely shaped enough to ensure that the front could be anatomically consistent; parts near the spine even bear marks of the chisel claws. The rendering of the anatomy of the front is more elaborate than in any earlier

---

* The authenticity of the Hermes has often been denied in the past fifty years. The claim that it is a copy of the Roman period rests on a variety of specious arguments. The pedestal is of a type presumed to be later than the fourth century – but the statue may originally have stood on another. The unfinished condition of the back is claimed to be anomalous for a work of the fourth century, though any sculptor might have saved labour if he knew his figure was destined to stand against a wall. The high polish of the front has been said to prove Roman date, ignoring the many instances in Hellenistic sculpture wherein the polish is essential to the style, which itself was ultimately derived from fourth-century masters. It is true that the technique of the carving is unparalleled in any assured work of the fourth century; on the other hand, ancient authors refer to Praxiteles in terms that imply exceptional virtuosity, so that he might well have invented methods of his own to gain effects no one else attempted. Whatever grounds have been or yet may be adduced against accepting the Hermes as an original by Praxiteles, they will be inconclusive so long as no unquestionable original of his time, equal in quality and as well preserved, is available for comparison. Meanwhile the point is worth considering that the subsequent development of sculpture implies the pre-existence of works like the Hermes. In any event, would or could a copyist of the Roman period have reproduced an old statue in such extraordinary detail and (apart from the back) complete consistency, and how much vitality might be expected to result? Even those of us who dislike the Hermes must admit that it has remarkable vitality.

work, though the transitions between one area and the next were so meticulously slurred that changes in level are almost imperceptible except to
the touch; the visual effect with the high polish is to make the surface
ripple with life. The texture of the flesh is differentiated from that of the
leather sandal (which was painted dark red as a foundation for gilt), of the
tree-trunk, of the woollen cloak and especially of the hair—a rough
jumbled mass in which curls are suggested instead of delineated as previous sculptors had laboriously done. The statue, in fact, marks the
logical conclusion of all the effort expended in past generations towards
more naturalistic representation. The means were now available to bring
Greek sculpture to its climax (and consequently to its downfall). The
Praxitelean face could express a fleeting mood, to which the body re-
sponded; at most the temperament, not the character, of the subject is
revealed, together with the physique appropriate to his manner of life.
The precedent set by Myron in his Marsyas group was thus refined. The
arrangement of drapery had already been brought nearly to perfection by
Pheidias and his successors, but Praxiteles improved the representation of
the texture. (Soon after the discovery of the Hermes, so the story goes, a
distinguished scholar complained that a photograph sent to him should
not have been taken when a piece of cloth hung over the child's legs.) Only
a lack of interest on his part kept him from exploring a new field, childhood, which some of his less gifted contemporaries had discovered, as is
shown by the lifelike heads of little girls at Brauron, commemorating their
service in the temple of Artemis. Praxiteles' child Dionysus is no better
than a doll; he might have told an assistant to copy it from the Plutus of
Cephisodotus (Pl. 46b).

The subject of the Olympia group recalls not so much the Eirene and
Plutus as another work of Cephisodotus mentioned by Pliny, 'Hermes
nursing the child Dionysus'; the word nutriens, 'nursing', should imply
actual feeding. But the statue at Olympia is too adept to be ascribed to
Praxiteles' youth. Probably, too, a political allusion was conveyed by the
fact that Hermes, the god of Arcadia, was shown holding Dionysus, the
god of Elis; symbolism of this order is familiar from its occurrence on
coins, and an alliance between the two states may well have been solem-
nized with the dedication of Praxiteles' work. Two suitable occasions have
been recorded, the first being the reconciliation arranged after the Arcadians and Eleans had come to blows at Olympia in 363, and the second a
more sincere alliance when in 343 the Arcadians assisted the aristocratic
party in Elis to win a decisive victory over the democrats. In all probability
the Hermes and Dionysus commemorate this event.

The collation of vague or dubious evidence leads to belief that Praxiteles' career extended from about 370 to not more than some ten years after 343. One of his early works, evidently, was the Apollo of which many copies exist, securely identified by Pliny's description: 'Apollo as a boy, waiting, with his arrow ready, for a lizard to crawl up to close-quarters; this is called "*Sauroctonus*" or the lizard-slayer.' The passage occurs among the list of the sculptor's works in bronze, and one bronze copy on half the normal scale survives in the Villa Albani. Apollo, represented as a boy in his teens, stands with an arrow poised in his right hand to strike the lizard that walks up the tree-trunk, unconscious of its danger, since he is hidden from it round the side of the tree: the curious theme may have had reference to the practices of divination, although it may with equal likelihood be interpreted as genre, for children often try to catch these quick-moving little animals, and a vase-painting shows a boy striking at one. As in the Hermes, the left arm rests on the tree, but higher up (the level varies in different copies); the right hip is thrust outwards in the same manner, thus producing sinuous curves throughout the body. The arrangement of the arms and head is simpler in the 'Sauroctonus' than in the Hermes; the left arm is raised, the right lowered, and the head bent downwards towards the left, giving an effect of weakness accentuated by the extreme slightness of the figure. The Hermes, a powerful man in his prime, avoids those willowy lines by a more erect carriage of the head, and by the reversal of the position of the arms— the uplifting of the right arm strengthens this curved side of the body. In this respect the Olympia figure has a more developed character, for the feeble pose of the 'Sauroctonus' detracts from its effect and can scarcely have been the choice of an experienced artist; indeed in the 'Sauroctonus' the flexion of Polycleitan boys is merely exaggerated, with no compensating adjustments. The body appears extremely weak and soft, in conformity with the indolent attitude, although the taste of the copyists may have corrupted the style. In the head, however, the copies seem to be trustworthy (the nose is restored in Pl. 47b); the original must have differed from Praxiteles' later works like the Hermes, being little more advanced than the Hygieia, although in profile the line is distinctly less rigid. A similarity to the Eirene and Plutus can be traced in many details, proving that Praxiteles was only beginning to depart from the teaching of Cephisodotus. Thus the lower eyelid is marked as distinctly as the upper, in both Apollo and Eirene, whereas in Hermes it is scarcely raised above the eye and sinks imperceptibly into the cheek. The eye itself loses its regular form and the forehead becomes fleshier, especially in male heads, so that the brow droops over the outer corner of the eye, and a thick bar above the nose casts the inner corner into deep shadow. The convention known as the 'Greek profile', introduced a century earlier, in which the nose almost continues the same straight line as the forehead, is thus modified.

The fact that the Apollo 'Sauroctonus' was in bronze accounts for the hardness of line in copies, which makes the face look earlier. The appearance of the original may be envisaged with the aid of a bronze head (Pl. 47c), which was probably cast from a mould taken from a contemporary statue. Of this there exists a marble copy in Madrid (Pl. 47d), a streamlined figure of an adolescent in the attitude of a long-distance runner. It is known from an epigram by Statius to represent Hypnos (Sleep), with his left arm stretched downward and an opium poppy in the hand, while the right arm came straight forward so that the god could pour his gift of sleep from a horn as he sped across the world. The sculptor must have been Praxiteles or someone profoundly influenced by him. Comparison with the Hermes avails little, because the technique was specifically intended for bronze; comparison with the little bronze 'Sauroctonus' would probably be misleading because the copyist's own technique may predominate in that work. The subtleties of the bronze Hypnos would not easily be copied. The face looked at horizontally expresses a passive sleepy contentment, but when seen from below—the correct position—the god is wholly intent on his purpose. The modelling is very shallow for the fourth century; the effect depends on the precise angles which various parts of the surface present to the light, rather than on the relations of one mass to another. The limits of the highlights are not sharply defined but merge gradually into shadow through half-lights; the surface is so nearly flat that a slight forward or backward tilt spoils the appearance by making the areas of light and shade change places.

The most popular statue of antiquity was Praxiteles' marble Aphrodite at Cnidus, the earliest female nude recorded (though anticipated in the fifth century by the relief on the 'Ludovisi Throne' and by a bronze statuette of a girl, and long before by high reliefs in Crete). The innumerable copies and adaptations of the Cnidian Aphrodite differ outrageously; few can bear any relation to the original, which would seldom have been reproduced on the spot (Cnidus being a small and remote town) but generally from some copy elsewhere. The goddess was about to take a bath, but a statue at Munich shows her picking up her garment after the bath, instead of dropping it beforehand. The other almost complete copy in the Vatican (Pl. 48a) is comparatively trustworthy, though of poor workmanship. The missing right hand covered the crotch, an action that was accepted as the automatic result of modesty; it is exaggerated into a self-conscious coyness in later Aphrodites. A firm treatment of the flesh contrasts with their opulence but may be partly due to the copyist's omission of detail. Even in the most satisfactory version (Pl. 48b) the head has obviously been simplified and hardened but retains a distinct similarity to the Hermes of Olympia.

The raptures of ancient literature read strangely in the light of the clumsy bodies and dull heads which now represent the Cnidian, yet Pliny voiced the general opinion of antiquity in saying that

> the finest statue, not only of Praxiteles but of the whole world, is the Aphrodite, for the sight of which many have sailed to Cnidus. He had carved two statues and sold them at the same time; the other, a draped figure, was preferred by the people of Cos, who had the chance to buy whichever they wished at the same price, because they considered it more dignified and modest. The statue which they refused was bought by the Cnidians and its reputation grew out of all proportion to that of the Coan choice. At a later date King Nicomedes [of Bithynia, 90–74 B.C.] desired to buy it from the Cnidians, offering to redeem the whole debt of state, which was enormous, but they preferred to put up with anything and not unwisely, because by that statue Praxiteles cast a glory on Cnidus. Its shrine is completely open to display every side of the statue, which is believed to have been made with the help of the goddess herself; it is equally admired from every position.

Lucian equips his ideal beauty with the head of the Cnidian Aphrodite, the rest being disqualified only because of its nudity; the hair and forehead and eyebrows are retained as unimprovable, as well as 'the melting, languishing eyes with their brightness and charm'. The lips were parted in a slight smile of disdain. Poetasters suggested that Praxiteles worked with the goddess herself as model, while sober authors mention Phryne or another courtesan. The extremely detailed, sensual treatment of the figure must have necessitated the use of a model; its voluptuous character was expressed in the common tale of a young man's passion for the statue. A similar story was told of another female statue by Praxiteles, the Good Fortune.

Phryne was a native of Thespiae, a Boeotian city; she is recorded to have been the mistress of Praxiteles, who made two statues of her, one of gilt bronze, dedicated at Delphi, and the other of marble, set up in a temple at Thespiae. Here too stood another Aphrodite by Praxiteles and his famous statue of Eros, the special deity of the place; Phryne is said to have dedicated these statues, which were presents to her from the sculptor. The Eros was removed to Rome in the first century A.D., and perished in a fire. From it is perhaps derived the frequent copies of a youthful Eros with large wings, best known in the replica from Centocelle in the Vatican. The god is represented as a full-grown boy standing in an easy attitude, holding the bow in the left hand; the head is sunk over the right shoulder, the eyes directed towards the right hand, which is shown empty in a Pompeian stucco, while in two other copies it holds a torch. These copies have no wings and may therefore be intended for some other deity, a genius of death; the original may have carried an arrow, for in some copies a quiver hangs on the support by the left leg. The pose has Polycleitan analogies, being indeed almost identical with that of the 'Dresden Boy', but the thin adolescent face beneath the shock of curling hair asserts such power as Polycleitus could not have expressed and as would probably have been abhorrent to his successors in the Argive school. The statue was surely a product of Attic eclecticism, like the somewhat earlier Pan from Eleusis.

A young satyr, leaning against a tree, comes fairly late in the career of Praxiteles; in it the pointed ears of Greek tradition are present while other animal traits of earlier times have been omitted. He rests his right arm upon a stump of a tree, holding a flute in the hand, while the left hand is laid upon the hip; the left foot carries the weight, the right being crossed behind it. A leopard-skin is thrown over the right shoulder and the left side, emphasizing the slope of the upper part of the figure. The face bears a cheerful, animal expression, very different from the ideally intellectual aspect of the gods by the same hand. Of the many copies in existence, the 'Capitoline Faun' is the best known, the Louvre torso the finest; in it the contrast between the flesh and the leopard-skin is so excellently shown that some critics formerly considered this to be a fragment of the original.

It is questionable whether this type should be identified with the celebrated satyr that stood in the Street of the Tripods at Athens. According to a legend of dubious authenticity, Praxiteles offered Phryne her choice of any statue in his possession, and in order to ascertain his own preference she instructed a slave to rush into her house, while the sculptor was present, to announce a fire in the studio. When he exclaimed that he was ruined if his Eros and Satyr had perished, she calmed his fears and chose the Eros, while the Satyr was dedicated in this spot. At the end of this anecdote Pausanias continues with the words, 'In the neighbouring temple to Dionysus is a satyr-boy acting as cup-bearer; Thymilus is the sculptor of an Eros standing with it and a Dionysus'; the text appears to be corrupt and it is uncertain whether this satyr is to be identified with the Praxitelean statue. Little assistance is given by Pliny's mention of the satyr, because this text is likewise untrustworthy and his meaning ambiguous where he lists among the bronze works of Praxiteles 'a Dionysus, Intoxication, together with the celebrated satyr, called by the Greeks the World-famed'; the opening words are generally emended to read 'a drunken Dionysus'. But the only statue of Dionysus which can be attributed to Praxiteles is the draped and bearded 'Sardanapalus' of extreme sobriety. A satyr answering to the description by Pausanias exists in almost as many copies as the 'Capitoline' type. The tall, youthful satyr stands gracefully on the left foot, raising a jug above his head with his right hand, and pouring the wine into a horn or cup held in the left hand at the level of the navel. A strong Polycleitan influence appears both in the pose and head, although the resemblance to the Eros suffices, if not to establish the authorship of Praxiteles, at least to give plausibility to the theory.

Another statue of Eros, which existed at Parium on the Sea of Marmora, had considerable fame. From the illustrations on local coins it has been proposed to identify it as the original of the 'Farnese' Eros of the Louvre and another replica at Parma; but the nondescript character of these headless figures leaves room for doubt as to whether they are true copies or merely sculptures inspired by the Praxitelean type. Still another work, the bronze Artemis Brauronia of the Acropolis, has been recognized in a Louvre statue, called the 'Diana of Gabies', and other copies, but the style is not unmistakably Praxitelean, and nothing is known of the Brauronia except that it was a standing figure. The Artemis on a relief found at Brauron has nothing in common with the Louvre statue.

A few more statues by Praxiteles are depicted on coins, while the names of many survive. They include a wide assortment of subjects—a Weeping Matron and a Rejoicing Harlot, Persuasion and Consolation, Good Fortune, as well as a large number of deities; a sepulchral group of a warrior standing beside a horse was the single portrait recorded until an inscription came to light in Boeotia belonging to the statue of one Thrasymachus.

In addition to all these, museums contain many a statue or head which from its style has been labelled as a copy from Praxiteles; there are also two original heads that could be his work. The 'Leconfield' head of Aphrodite (Pl. 48c), to which Lucian's appreciation of the Cnidian so well applies, is undoubtedly in his manner, and it is generally believed that its sculptor was Praxiteles himself, not a pupil; the surface, however, has been destroyed owing to drastic cleaning with acid. When compared to the Cnidian the hair is seen to be treated less formally, the face more individually; yet the resemblance is great enough to imply that Phryne was again his model, though now attaining middle age, for the features are less firm and the neck fuller. The date cannot be far removed from that of the Hermes of Olympia. Yet another original of this last period of the master's life seems to have survived in the 'Aberdeen' head in the British Museum (Pl. 48*d*). The contrast between this and the Hermes is superficial, expressing simply the different characteristics of Hermes and Heracles, and, when the details are examined, the relationship becomes clear; an alleged influence of Scopas is not really perceptible. The head reveals the weakness of Praxiteles—the lack of a sense of design or of form—more plainly than his strength. With his ambition to produce the illusion of life, he appears as a sculptor whose skill was unsurpassed, but to whom beauty meant little more than seductiveness. A base discovered at Mantinea is known from Pausanias to have supported the cult-images of Leto, Apollo and Artemis, which he ascribes to Praxiteles; three reliefs which sheathed the base remain, in Athens. On one slab are carved Marsyas playing the flutes (an imitation of Myron's statue), the slave holding the knife with which Marsyas was to be flayed, and Apollo seated on a rock with the lyre. The other two slabs contain six figures of Muses; the total of nine was completed in another slab which no longer exists. Pausanias speaks only of a 'Muse, and Marsyas playing the flutes', an interesting example of his methods of reporting, and of textual corruption, for the manuscript should certainly read 'Muses' instead of 'Muse'. The style of these poor reliefs bears no close relation to any known work of Praxiteles, but they might well be contemporary.

Scopas

An artistic individuality no less distinct than Praxiteles' may be claimed for Scopas of Paros. He may have been the son of Aristander of Paros, who worked on the memorials for the Battle of Aegospotami, because a sculptor named Aristander, son of Scopas, of Paros, was active at Delos towards 100 B.C. and the whole family of sculptors may have continued to use the same names for generations. Pliny assigns Scopas to 420, but as he was employed on the Mausoleum towards 350, this *floruit* cannot be correct. The upper limit for his active life cannot be determined. Many years may have elapsed between the burning of the temple of Athena Alea at Tegea in 394, and its reconstruction with Scopas as architect, for its great size must have entailed expenditure that outran the revenue of the state.

Pausanias in his account of Tegea, says:

I was informed that the architect was Scopas the Parian, who made images in many places of ancient Greece, including some in Ionia and Caria. On the front gable is the hunt of the Calydonian boar. The boar is set just in the middle. On one side are Atalanta, Meleager, Theseus, Telamon, Peleus, Pollux and Iolaus, the comrade of Heracles in most of his labours; and there are also Prothous and Cometes, sons of Thestius and brothers of Althaea. On the other side of the boar is Epochus supporting Ancaeus, who is wounded and has dropped his axe; beside him are Castor and Amphiaraus, son of Oicles, beyond them Hippothous ... and last of all is carved Peirithous. On the back gable is represented the fight of Telephus and Achilles in the plain of the Caicus.

In spite of the absence of any definite statement that the pedimental sculptures reproduced designs of Scopas, the assumption may pass unchallenged, because the singular individuality of the work postulates the employment of a great sculptor, and this would naturally be Scopas, who supplied marble statues of Asclepius and Hygieia to the interior, besides serving as architect. The cult-statue, an ivory work by Endoeus, had been rescued from the old temple and was finally carried off to Rome by the order of Augustus; these statues by Scopas stood in Pausanias' day on either side of an Athena transferred as a substitute from a neighbouring village.

Marble from a local quarry was used for the sculptures, which cannot be much earlier than 350 or even perhaps 340. Two draped female torsos (Pl. 49a), one of which retains sockets for wings to be attached, were presumably Victories, and therefore acroteria. Bunched folds in the overhang (partly missing) and at the split of the peplos contrast with the tightly strained drapery over the left leg, so accentuating vigour of movement; elegance is lacking. Of the pedimental figures there remain three damaged heads and numerous fragments of bodies in violent action, akin to the Epidaurus pedimental figures but more muscular; scraps of drapery are stylistically compatible with the acroteria. The heads and bodies were visibly integrated by the same impulse; the heroes (Pl. 49b) were totally absorbed in combat, and the purpose for which their limbs were straining could be read in their faces. Much of the effect was obtained by a deep setting of the eyes, under heavy brows rolled down across the outer corners; in strong sunlight this overshadowing must have imparted a startlingly dramatic quality to the faces, some fifteen metres above ground level. But restored casts of the heads show that they cannot have looked as unlike the Praxitelean type as their present condition might lead one to suppose. The chief difference was actually in the shape of the face, to which Scopas gave equal length and breadth whereas Praxiteles made it oval; since, in real life, a face can more easily appear determined if broad, intelligent if long, the distinction was really one of subject. The Tegea eyes are set only slightly deeper, but the narrower lids make them appear to open wider. The bodies are much less fleshy than a Praxitelean adult's, again as befits the subject.

With the help of the Tegea fragments a few copies have been traced to works of Scopas. A statuette in Dresden (Pl. 49c) reproduces or closely imitates his figure of a Maenad dancing in ecstasy, head thrown back, hair dishevelled and arms wildly brandishing the goat she has killed, while the short Doric peplos, flying open at the side, leaves the body partly nude; a long, rhetorical description by Callistratus identifies the type. The colossal seated Ares, which had been taken to Rome by Pliny's day, has been recognized in the 'Ludovisi' statue of a young god moodily clasping his knee. It is curious that all the copies are life-size (though perhaps they are copies at second hand from a reduction), and for this reason an alternative theory attributes the type to Lysippus, which is stylistically improbable. The *Pothos* (Desire) of Scopas has been sought in a figure which usually appears with wings in the minor arts, though copies in statue form are restored as Apollo; it is but distantly related to any known Scopaic type and the pose recalls the 'Sauroctonus'. A Heracles by this sculptor stood at Sicyon and may well be the original of the Heracles crowned with a wreath of poplar known from the 'Lansdowne' copy to have somewhat resembled the 'Doryphorus'; the god held his lion-skin at the full length of his right arm and shouldered his club with his left. A more interesting head, best seen in the 'Townley' bust (Pl. 49d), may have resulted simply from more skilful copying or could be derived from a different original; sculptors were often required to duplicate a statue and they must have introduced variations when they did so. In this instance the original material was bronze, no doubt, so that copyists may have worked with the aid of casts, not always taken at first hand. The face shows a touch of the mobility so emphatic in the Tegea heads, although Heracles was walking unconcernedly.

The Meleager, a frequently copied statue, is not mentioned by any ancient author, but the subject connects it with Tegea or Sicyon, and the original may have been taken thence to Rome, for the Villa Medici head could be an actual relic; it is really impossible to distinguish between an original and a copy when the marble has weathered to the extent that it has in this instance. The powerful body of other copies reveals the surface markings more clearly than Praxitelean statues and there is no languor in the pose; the stance is erect, the weight carried on the right leg, with the left hand holding a spear and the right resting idle on the buttock, while a dog sits by the feet. The original has been ascribed both to Scopas and to Lysippus, because of the wide discrepancies in the style of the copies.

An Apollo in long voluminous Ionic chiton may reproduce the statue by Scopas brought from Rhamnus to the Augustan temple on the Palatine, where it stood beside an Artemis by Timotheus and a Leto by the younger Cephisodotus: a base from Sorrento apparently illustrates these three statues, with which aid copies of the Apollo have been traced.

A more exciting work was the group, afterwards set up at Rome, said by Pliny to have included figures of 'Poseidon himself, Thetis and Achilles, Nereids sitting on dolphins, whales or sea-horses, together with Tritons' and many other sea-creatures. As yet, the only copy recognized is limited to the upper half (at Ostia) of a single figure, a Nereid or a female Triton, whose body is tossed like a wave in a stormy sea; fishes are caught in her spraying hair. The posture is certainly in keeping with the Dresden Maenad. Scopas would appear to have been the first sculptor who designed a statue to be viewed from every direction; neither the Maenad nor the Nereid can be appreciated without walking all round it, as the twist seen from any angle compels the spectator to do.

Lesser-known contemporaries of Praxiteles

In contrast to the purely mythological conceptions of Scopas, the work of Silanion of Athens (author of an essay on proportions) was confined, as far as our information extends, to portraits of prominent men and athletes or characterizations of historical personages, such as Achilles, Theseus, Sappho, Jocasta and the poetess Corinna. The last-named may be imitated in a statuette inscribed with her name in Greek characters, but discovered at Compiègne; its style would agree with the fourth-century dating but gives little indication of Silanion's powers. If Pliny is right in saying that he was self-taught, his style might be expected to have been more distinctive than the average sculptor's. He could have exhibited an unprecedented combination of emotional and physical suffering in his statue of the dying Jocasta (for she is said to have hanged herself on learning that she had married her son, Oedipus), but doubtless |he idealized, ignoring the hideous effects of strangulation and toning down the mental anguish. A statement cited by Plutarch that 'an infusion of silver imitated the hue of death in her face' is technically impossible—if an admixture of silver were put into molten bronze it could not be localized in one part of the figure; probably a pale colouring matter was applied after casting.

Silanion's portrait of Plato, commissioned by a Persian admirer named Mithradates, who died in 363, is presumably represented among the extant busts of the philosopher, which vary from a grim forceful expression in the Holkham head to a pensive melancholy more consonant both with the character of Plato and the usual conventions of portraiture in the early fourth century, as they are known from gravestones. The face, while it has more detail than the Pericles of Cresilas, yet presents no individual features. A bronze portrait of Apollodorus, who had known Socrates in his boyhood (in 416, if Plato may be trusted), must have resembled the livelier copies of the Plato, judging from Pliny's description: 'He was himself a sculptor more painstaking than his rivals and a harsh critic of his own work, so much so that he often smashed his finished statue because of inability to satisfy his ideals, and was therefore nicknamed "The Madman". The statue has expressed this trait; it is no mere bronze man but an embodiment of rage.' A copy has been dubiously recognized in a bust at Naples; the period may be correct but the rage is not apparent. A striking head at Bologna, the portrait of some unknown Greek, bears some relationship to the Plato. A bronze head at Olympia (Pl. 50a) may be an original by Silanion, broken from a statue (seen there by Pausanias) of the great boxer Satyrus, whose victories were spread over some thirty years; only one is dated, to 335–334, and the head could scarcely be earlier. The uncompromisingly faithful rendering of the flattened nose and sweat-matted hair might, indeed, be thought more appropriate to an early Hellenistic sculptor. On the other hand equal accuracy is found, seemingly about 340, in a portrayal of racial characteristics in an original bronze head which the British Museum obtained from Cyrene; it unmistakably represents a young Libyan with the high cheek-bones and drooping brows still frequent among Berbers.

The funerary stelae, of which many hundreds were carved at Athens in the mid-fourth century, usually bear heads of certain recognized types, young or old. One of the finest, that of Aristonautes charging the enemy, has as ideal a head as a Scopaic hero. There are, of course, other exceptions, but for the most part these memorials were executed by artisans of little originality, and since the name of the deceased could be inscribed the purchasers felt no need for any attempt at a likeness. An anthology of female sepulchral types is preserved in the sarcophagus of 'Les Pleureuses', found in the royal cemetery of Sidon (Pl. 50b). This probably Attic work of about 350 is decorated with eighteen of the mourning women from which it derives its name, in addition to hunting scenes around the base, a funeral procession on the longer side of the lid, and pediments and acroteria at its ends. Similar figures occur plentifully on stelae and occasionally in the round, when they were placed upon tombs: a relief at Athens, of one such woman standing between two who are seated in attitudes of mourning, seems to have been destined for a metope.

The Argive-Sicyonian school established by the pupils of Polycleitus still flourished through the second quarter of the fourth century. In honour of the campaign of 370–369, when the Thebans and their allies invaded Spartan territory, a group of nine statues was dedicated at Delphi by the Arcadians: Antiphanes of Argos, Daedalus of Sicyon and two other sculptors shared these figures of gods and heroes between them. The Argives placed a larger group at Delphi in memory of the same war, and here the signature of Antiphanes is cut upon two bases; on the six other inscribed bases no artist's name appears, so that Antiphanes may be responsible for the whole set of perhaps twenty statues, representing the legendary heroes of Argos. His equally distinguished contemporary, Daedalus, son of Patrocles, seems to have specialized in athletic sculpture, and one at least of the 'two boys scraping themselves', which Pliny attributes to him, is probably reproduced in a bronze statue from Ephesus and numerous marble copies, in which two slightly divergent types exist. A youth of somewhat heavy build is represented scraping the grease from his hand with a strigil; the weight rests firmly on the right leg, the head sinks forward for the eyes to follow the action of the hands, which are held in front of the groin. The head has a strong resemblance to the supposed Discobolus of Naucydes, another son of Patrocles, but the date must be slightly later, around 370–360. The third brother, Polycleitus the younger, may have lived long enough to collaborate with Lysippus, for both their signatures are cut on one block at Thebes, upon which two statues stood; the figure by Lysippus represented an athlete named Coreidas, whose success in the boys' pancration at Delphi cannot be dated before 342, but it is uncertain whether the other statue must be equally late, because the signatures seem to be renewals, added after the destruction of Thebes in 335. There is, in any case, no ground here for the hypothesis that a third Polycleitus practised sculpture towards the end of the century.

Euphranor, either an Athenian or a native of the Corinthian isthmus, flourished both as a painter and a sculptor of note, producing statues and reliefs in marble and bronze. His picture of the Battle of Mantinea (fought in 362), his chariot-groups of Philip and Alexander at Olympia (doubtless ordered about 336, the year of Alexander's accession), and the inscriptions of his son (roughly dated at 300), reveal him as an almost exact contemporary of Praxiteles. 'He was unusually impressionable and painstaking and in every class of work reached the same high standard. In his pictures', continues Pliny, 'he seems to have been the first to express all the majesty of heroes and to have mastered the problems of proportion, although his bodies were too slight and his head and limbs too large. He also wrote on the subject of proportions, and on colours.' Many of his works are reported by Pausanias, including one which has, in all probability, been discovered in the Agora at Athens, the cult-image of the temple of Apollo; the head and arms are missing. From the representations on late coins, the left arm clasped a lyre while the right was outstretched holding a patera (saucer). The god stands wearing a long Ionic chiton, in accordance with musicians' custom; the treatment of the drapery is perfunctory, by no means indicative of outstanding talent, but may have been deliberately conventional to suit the concept of a cult-statue. A celebrated statue by Euphranor revealed the whole character of Paris as the 'judge of the goddesses, lover of Helen, and destroyer of Achilles'. Several figures of Paris, Attis or Ganymede, recognizable by the Phrygian cap (imitated in the Cap of Liberty of the French Revolution), are now represented by copies; a seated draped statue in the Vatican, of which no other replica exists, has been acclaimed as Euphranor's Paris. Furtwängler, however, selected a nude standing type, extant in more than one variation, of a tall, slim youth leaning cross-legged upon a tree-trunk, with his head turned languidly to one side (the side varies in different statues); the type is noteworthy, whoever its author might be. A nude female torso at Naples in a similar attitude has almost a fifth-century air in its freedom from Praxitelean sensuality. The 'Eubouleus' bust (Pl. 51a), which ends with some sketchy drapery around the shoulders, and nine other copies from the same original seem to portray Alexander in adolescence, at which time both Euphranor and Leochares made celebrated statues of him; since Euphranor's stood on a chariot it would have been draped, and may for that reason be the more plausible original.

A ship, wrecked at the time of Christ off Anticythera (Cerigotto), was laden with sculpture, including a bronze statue of a youth (Pl. 51b), which has been pieced together from fragments. It is almost certainly an original of the Argive-Sicyonian school; though the face reveals the influence of Praxiteles, the heavy build of the trunk follows the Polycleitan tradition. The head is relatively very small; the arms and legs too are slighter than would really be appropriate. The right arm is raised to exhibit some small object that was clasped in the bent fingers. The subject might be Paris

holding the apple of discord or Perseus dangling the head of Medusa by th
hair (though the absence of a sword-belt weakens that explanation).

Apart from the temple of Tegea, the great sculptural monuments of thi
age stood in Persian territory: these were the Mausoleum at Halicarnassu
and a new temple of Artemis at Ephesus, built after its predecessor had been
burnt in 356 by a citizen anxious to perpetuate his name, but not completed
for more than twenty years. The tomb of Mausolus, who died in 353, wa
perhaps commenced in his own lifetime, following the usual custom o
Oriental rulers (he was a Carian dynast under Persian protection), thougl
tradition attributes the conception to his widow and states that the artist
finished the work, purely for the sake of their own credit, shortly after he
death in 351. The sculptures must therefore be earlier than those of Ephesus

In the absence of any account by an eye-witness the design of th
Mausoleum remains problematical, and no two restorations agree, but
basic similarity to the Nereid Monument attests the Asiatic idea of th
whole. It was an oblong building, somewhat like a temple, and was sur
rounded with a colonnade of the Ionic order. Above this, according t
the questionable account abstracted by Pliny from some older source, wa
'a pyramid equal in height to the portion below, consisting of twenty-fou
steps, which grew narrower as they ascended. On the summit stands
four-horse chariot in marble, made by Pythis', perhaps identical witl
Pythius, the architect. Vitruvius states that each side of the building wa
supervised by a separate sculptor, namely Leochares, Bryaxis, Scopas
Praxiteles, or, according to some accounts, Timotheus; Pliny, on th
other hand, ascribes the east side to Scopas, the north to Bryaxis, the soutl
to Timotheus, the west to Leochares. The ruins were demolished, partl
for building material and partly to be burnt for lime, by the Knights o
St John and by the Turkish inhabitants, and in few instances has it been
possible to determine the side on which sculptures were placed—many o
them were picked out of the walls of the medieval castle and out of th
walls and chimneys of private houses by Newton's expedition: only
few were excavated from the ground upon which they had fallen from
their original positions. In any event the division of labour by sides could
only apply to certain classes of sculpture.

The remnants assembled in the British Museum include much of th
colossal chariot and horses of which Pliny writes, in addition to a number
of lions, the enormous statues of Mausolus and Artemisia (Pl. 52a), frag
ments of other statues of varying dimensions but mostly life-size, three
friezes, and some carved panels of no great merit which seem to have
formed part of the ceiling. The head of Mausolus was obviously intended

for a portrait, though idealized; his height—3 m.—is greater than would have been suitable for any other man, while the companion figure is likewise too large for any woman but Artemisia. The generally excellent preservation of the surface (only his head is weathered) indicates that they originally stood under cover; the unprecedented depth to which the folds of his drapery are cut must have been calculated to produce effects of light and shade in a position the sun could not reach. Probably, therefore, the statues were placed, like cult-images, within the cella. The jaggedness of their outlines (his especially) would then have been designed for liveliness when seen against the plain background of a wall, which would have caused a relatively straight-sided figure to look stiff. The Mausolus is composed as a balance of planes, each sharply defined by an abrupt change of level that is emphasized by shadow—in the case of minor changes, a thin slash of shadow. In the head, the lines of hair, brows and moustache flare away at exciting angles, likewise emphasized by shadow, in contrast to the wide smooth features that produce an effect of serene majesty. Identification of the sculptor among the four or five recorded to have worked on the Mausoleum can be attempted by elimination of those whose style is presumed to be incompatible; two then remain, Bryaxis and Leochares, and there are dubious grounds for eliminating the latter. Moreover the composition of the Mausolus resembles that of an Asclepius, known from copies, which might be Bryaxis' famous statue of that deity.

The story that each sculptor undertook one side of the building might, even if true, be inapplicable to figures in the cella. Praxiteles has left no trace of his questionable presence. A headless mounted Asiatic has been ascribed to Timotheus because the drapery bears some resemblance to that on the Amazon from the Epidaurus pediment and on another Amazon, now in Boston, that bridges the chronological gap between them. Several battered male heads recall the heroes of the Tegea pediments, and other heads and torsos might be shared between the remaining artists.

Each of the three friezes was certainly carved by many hands but could have been designed as a whole by a single artist; attempts to apportion the slabs to the four sculptors of the various sides have as yet been unconvincing (though admittedly collaboration between artists tends to result in something like uniformity of style, if their work is to be visible in conjunction). The largest frieze, 90 cm. high, was devoted to a battle of Greeks and Amazons; the slab illustrated (Pl. 52b), was found on the east side, Scopas' according to Pliny. Less remains of the narrower chariot-race or of the poorly-carved battle of Greeks and Centaurs, which must have been placed at a considerable height above eye-level. The original positions of

these friezes cannot be convincingly determined; some restorations locate
the Amazonomachia round the platform beneath the colonnade, others
above it as the frieze of the Ionic order, while the fine detail and smooth
surface of the chariot-race suggest a position on the cella walls. The wide
spacing of the Amazon frieze, though doubtless suitable to its original
position, has an air of poverty seen at close quarters, and the imaginative
fertility expended on varying the actions and groups does not obviate its
monotony. The heads have often been carelessly worked and offer no
stylistic criteria, but the Amazons, whose drapery parts to reveal their
shapely forms, recall the Maenad of Scopas. Similarly the heroes of Tegea
have been compared with the charioteers (Pl. 53a, b), slim youths who lean
forward over the reins with set, eager faces, their long chitons blown back
from their feet by the wind of their speed. But Bryaxis has equal claims, if
indeed a Victory, found in Athens, really stood on a signed base that lay
close to it, for the resemblance of this headless statue to the charioteers
passes beyond the limits of coincidence: according to an alternative theory,
however, the figure was an acroterion. The style of this Attic master is
otherwise unknown; the reliefs upon the signed base are negligent work
by some pupil.

Leochares is scarcely less nebulous. His portrait of Isocrates at Eleusis
was possibly the original of the quiet subtle bust inscribed with this name,
while a statuette in the Vatican answers better than any other Ganymede to
Pliny's description of his bronze group: 'the eagle, conscious what a prize
is Ganymede and to what high destiny it bears him, takes care to spare the
boy the sharpness of his claws, even through the clothing.' An eagle with
wings outspread lifts the boy by the shoulders, round which he wears
chlamys; the eye is carried upwards by the raised head, peering into the
sky, by the outstretched body and the dog that sits upon the ground watching its master's ascent. In view of the inadequacy of the Vatican group to
convey a true idea of the style, little weight attaches to the theories, devoid
of external confirmation, that credit Leochares with the original of the
Apollo 'Belvedere' (judged not by the Vatican copy, but by a head in
Basle), of the Capitoline Aphrodite, of the 'Alcibiades' head of the Conservatori, and of a related head, one version of which is placed upon the
Naples statue called 'Protesilaus'. A relief may reflect part of the group at
Delphi in which Leochares and Lysippus commemorated the lion-hunt of
Alexander and Craterus; this was dedicated after the death of Craterus in
321 and is the latest known work by Leochares.

Leochares was, perhaps, the sculptor of an original of which the head
exists on the Acropolis (Pl. 53c); there is also a copy of the Roman period

at Erbach. Although the subject must be Alexander in adolescence, with the swimming eyes and crooked neck that were his peculiarities, this is an idealized study of temperament and character, rather than an actual portrait of the ruthless egoist who was about to conquer half the world. His mane of hair is not so wild as in the 'Eubouleus' type, which probably represents Alexander at approximately the same age, in within a year or two of 336. The face is shaped with conventional simplicity; its larger expanses are quite smooth, the lines of eyebrows and lips are cut into perfectly regular grooves. The eye-sockets are overshadowed after the manner of Scopas, while the hint of a smile could have been borrowed from Praxiteles. In the Demeter of Cnidus (Pl. 54a) the same technique was used for another study of temperament and character. The shape of her mouth is almost identical with the Alexander's; the eyebrows and lips were chiselled into precisely the same clean lines. The goddess, though sorrowing over the loss of her daughter, retains a lingering trace of her normal half-smile of maternal tranquillity. Her matronly body is swathed in a himation with countless folds, which have suffered much damage, so diminishing the impact the statue originally made on spectators. Her head and neck were carved out of a separate block of marble; the neck is rounded underneath to fit into a hollow concealed by the edge of the drapery—a method employed in many later but few earlier statues.

Other notable sculptures from the coast of Asia Minor are the reliefs on the drums and bases of columns in the new temple at Ephesus, which retained this peculiarity of its predecessor. The most famous drum (Pl. 55) shows, among other figures of more than life-size, a woman, fastening her drapery, standing between Hermes and Death; the scene may be connected with the story of Alcestis. But there is nothing dramatic in the relief; nor even can it be called narrative, for the artist was concerned only with the decorative effect of his row of figures. The date is approximately fixed by the story that the construction of the temple was far advanced when Alexander offered to defray the cost of its completion. Two draped female statues, obviously of much the same time as the 'Alcestis' on the column-drum, are known from a pair of copies at Naples as 'the large' and 'the small Herculaneum women'; the finest copy of 'the small' (Pl. 56a) is a late Hellenistic work from Delos, harsher than the original, wherein neither the features nor the hair can have been so sharply defined. Both types were frequently copied in the Roman period; the smaller, at least, could be Lysippic.

The interest in drapery shown by sculptors of Alexander's lifetime is also exemplified in copies from three statues placed in the Theatre at

Athens in the 330s, which were ideal representations of the fifth-century dramatists Aeschylus, Sophocles and Euripides. The 'Lateran' copy of the Sophocles (Pl. 56b) conforms with the traditions that recalled a well-fed, well-dressed elderly gentleman, dignified and platitudinous; a restorer has added the left hand, the feet and the base with a scroll-box. The statue is composed on much the same principles as the Mausolus, with folds slashing across it at different angles, though the counterpoint of black and white is toned down by lesser changes of level between one plane and another. An original, the half-draped statue of an unkempt philosopher at Delphi, may be another imaginary portrait of the same period or somewhat later; it has, in fact, a general kinship with the British Museum statuette of Socrates which must have been freely copied (in the second century A.D.) from a fourth-century statue—possibly from the renowned work by Lysippus.

Lysippus and his Contemporaries

The activity of Praxiteles, Scopas and Euphranor apparently ended during the 330s, when Leochares must have been more than middle-aged, but Lysippus, the last great Master of the fourth century, was still fairly young. A Sicyonian, who grew to manhood among Polycleitus' successors, he surpassed them all. He had an unusually long career as a sculptor, although according to an author of the third century B.C. he began life as an artisan in a bronze-foundry and turned to original work after discovering that a painter had said that Nature was a better guide than any master—a remark which may then have seemed peculiar. His oldest recorded statue is perhaps that of Troilus, twice victorious at Olympia in 372 (or in 372 and 368); the base appears from the style of its lettering to be older than 350. An inscription that reads 'King Seleucus—work of Lysippus' is not of contemporary date and the portrait may therefore be older than Seleucus' adoption of the royal title in 306; an anecdote connecting Lysippus with the foundation of Cassandreia brings him to 316, and this is the last fixed point in his career.

Lysippus is recorded to have altered the proportions of the human body, 'making the head smaller than of old, the body thinner and leaner, thereby increasing the apparent height' (Pliny). In fact he modified the Polycleitan rule that the head should equal one-seventh of the total height, adopting a ratio of 1:8. He appears to have been amazingly prolific in spite of the minute finish which he bestowed upon every detail. Pliny tells a story that he set aside a gold piece from the price of every sculpture and when his heir opened his safe it was found to contain 1,500 coins. An average of nearly thirty statues a year is incredible, however large a share of the labour was entrusted to pupils, yet the productiveness of Lysippus must have been phenomenal for such a belief to become current. His recorded sculptures represent chiefly male deities or men; in fact he specialized in athlete types, following the normal practices of the Argive-Sicyonian school to which he belonged. Psychological subtlety appealed to him no more than to Polycleitus, to whom he had a striking affinity. Peloponnesian statues were perfect of their kind, but, like all completely successful work, had their strict limitations; the ideal figure was required to be well poised, admirably modelled, physically strong, and the face was mentally undistinguished.

No originals by Lysippus are preserved, with the hypothetical, and in any event unhelpful, exception of the gilt-bronze horses that embellish the frontage of St Mark's at Venice. (Pliny mentions a group of the sun-god in a four-horse chariot, made by Lysippus for the Rhodians, and it may have been the group of that subject they dedicated at Delphi, on an extant unsigned base; if so, some emperor presumably took it to Constantinople, where the Venetians obtained most of their best loot.)

Lysippus' style has become recognizable primarily from the somewhat discordant evidence, at second hand, of two statues. The Vatican 'Apoxyomenus' (Pl. 57a), the figure of a young athlete scraping the cleansing matter (oil and dust) off his skin, presumably reproduces Lysippus' bronze statue of that subject, exhibited in Rome; Tiberius, we are told, once had it removed to his own bedroom but yielded to popular clamour and returned it to its place outside the Baths of Agrippa. The marble copy, which is later than that episode, required the addition of a strut between the right wrist and the right leg, as well as of a tree-trunk beside the left leg. The other statue (Pl. 57b), carved in Lysippus' time, represents Agias (or Hagias) of Pharsalus, who had lived a century earlier. It was found at Delphi, but a counterpart formerly existed at Pharsalus, where the base has been discovered, inscribed with the signature of Lysippus in addition to an epigram almost identical with one on the Delphi base, which supported a row of nine statues. These were all erected by Daochus of Pharsalus, a Thessalian representative on the council at Delphi from 339 to his death in 334, between which years the statues must date. They represented himself and seven members of his family (Agias being an ancestor); the first statue had no inscription and its base is larger, hence it may have been an Athena. The workmanship is uniformly dull and poor. No difference in style can be detected between the Agias, a headless nude, and the head of another such figure; two statues wear the chlamys and one a short peplos, while the remainder have perished. The whole group has been claimed as a reproduction of a group by Lysippus at Pharsalus—a view not subject to effective criticism except on general grounds. Thus it may be urged that the dedication of a statue of Agias in his native place, more than a hundred years after his victories, would be a pointless proceeding unless it formed part of a large family monument such as the Delphian group. On the other hand tremendous expenses would be incurred in the transport of statues from Pharsalus to Delphi, so that if there were any such relation between the two dedications the second must have been based upon small clay models or have originated simultaneously with the originals in some more accessible part of Greece. A duplicate set, the carving of which was entrusted by Lysippus to inferior sculptors, would reproduce in the main the figures in the master's studio, with discrepancies in details, such as the hair, and in delicate points of style, which required the original cunning; if the copyists worked, independent of Lysippus, from small models, the correspondence would be less close. An examination of the group at Delphi reveals a contrast between efficient construction on the one hand and slovenly carving on the other—a strange conjunction in an original work but almost universal in copies. The statues seem, therefore, to be replicas of better originals; they offer but poor criteria by which to ascertain how many of these besides the Agias were by Lysippus.

The relationship between the Agias and the obviously later 'Apoxyomenus' must now be considered. Both figures seem as though about to shift their weight from one leg to the other, and the contrast between the solidity of the Agias and the springiness of the Apoxyomenus can easily be explained away, for the Thessalian had for the space of thirty years been a noted pancratiast, and displays the build necessary for that combination of boxing and wrestling, while the Apoxyomenus is a mere youth, with the light frame of the runner. More serious is the divergence in the treatment of surface markings. The Agias follows the normal method of the mid-fourth century, its sleek flesh undulating at the dictates of bone and muscles, but in the Vatican statue the skin is drawn tightly over the lumps of the structure, and muscles hitherto slurred over obtain their due prominence. Here attention should be called to the fact that Pliny considered 'the extreme definition of the work, even to the minutest details' to be characteristic of Lysippus. The original Agias may conceivably have adumbrated the new method, for the mason who carved the Delphi replicas was not the man to delay over refinements; neither, in all probability, did the Thessalian take any profound interest in the style of his advertisement. A fair comparison of the heads of Agias and Apoxyomenus can be effected only with great difficulty. The shape of the skull differs somewhat, but then neither copyist is completely reliable where improvisation entailed less trouble than imitation. The expression changes inevitably, for the one is a middle-aged boxer and the other an innocent youth of gentle pursuits, but the relative shallowness of the eye-socket in the later statue points to rejection of the style of Scopas, which has left such obvious traces in the Agias; moreover the profile of nose and forehead no longer runs straight, and the mouth and chin have receded. The rendering of the hair, in which respect, as Pliny remarks, Lysippus made considerable progress, can be studied only in the Apoxyomenus, because in the Agias is adopted a cursory technique available in marble alone.

A statue of a long-dead Thessalian athlete, Pulydamas, was set up at Olympia in memory of his victory in 408; this was perhaps another dedication of Daochus. The base has been recovered: it bears reliefs of the strong man fighting champions at the Persian court and struggling with a lion. The work is undistinguished.

A marble head at Olympia has been identified on insufficient grounds as a relic of the statue of an Acarnanian pancratiast, called perhaps Philandridas, an early work of Lysippus, which would accordingly form the one extant original from his hand. The head has much in common with the Agias and is of slightly finer quality, though deplorably damaged; the 'cauliflower' ears indicate a boxer. But the material is unusual for Lysippus and the work dull, hence the figure was perhaps an early school-piece like the Agias. To the same stage belongs another work, deeply influenced by both Polycleitus and Scopas, which is copied in a bronze bust from Herculaneum; the hair is modelled like that of 'Philandridas', but greater regularity has been introduced by the first-century copyist.

A different class of Lysippic statue is illustrated by the 'Farnese' Heracles, a statue copied on any scale up to 3 metres. The well-known colossal replica at Naples, with its heavy bearded face and ponderous body hung about with bunches of muscles, has a grotesque vulgarity, not entirely due to the Glycon of Athens who proudly signed it. The inscription of a lesser replica mentions Lysippus as its originator, which is confirmed by the style of the Uffizi and other copies. Perhaps the original of this weary Heracles, leaning upon his club, was the bronze figure of the god which stood in the market-place of Sicyon. The 'Epitrapezius', so called because Alexander used it to decorate his table, was a seated statuette of Heracles, known from several copies to have had the same physique as the 'Farnese'. In another seated Heracles, brought from Taranto to the Capitol and finally transferred to Constantinople, the shin alone was half as tall as a man. A Byzantine description suggests that copyists have seldom exaggerated the Strong Man aspect of a Lysippic Heracles: 'his chest was wide, his shoulders broad, his hair thick, his buttocks fat, his arms powerful.' This statue, large as it was, could not compare with the Zeus at Taranto, a figure so prodigious in size that the Romans made no effort to move it; they estimated its height at 58 feet.

Two lesser works have been recognized in marbles, the Poseidon of Corinth and the Eros drawing, or perhaps rather unstringing, his bow, which in pose resembles the 'Apoxyomenus' and has a slighter, childish build, with an even more ingenuous face. Of the allegorical statue of *Kairos* (Opportunity or Time), there remain lengthy descriptions and three adaptations in relief (Pl. 54b). The youth was running on tiptoe, like the Hypnos, with wings to his heels, his hair long in front and shaven behind, because he can be seized only by the forelock, while the razor and scales in his hand alluded to a Greek proverb, that the turn of events often balanced on an edge as fine as a razor's.

Lysippus also produced characterizations of Aesop, Socrates and the Seven Sages (none of which have been recognized with the possible exception of the Socrates), as well as portraits of Alexander from his boyhood upwards, and of members of his entourage. Some of the many extant portraits of Alexander must go back to originals by Lysippus, but they cannot be distinguished with certainty. The 'Azara' bust in the Louvre, inscribed with Alexander's name, is a miserable ruin, but together with its better replica in Geneva has a resemblance to the 'Apoxyomenus'. A bust in the British Museum answers best to a description by Plutarch:

> When Lysippus first made a portrait of Alexander with his face lifted up to heaven, just as he used to gaze, with his neck slightly on one side ... Alexander ordered that only Lysippus should make portraits of him, for Lysippus alone, it would seem, truthfully showed his character in bronze and portrayed his courage in visible form, while others in their anxiety to produce the bend of the neck and the swimming look of the eyes lost his masculine and leonine aspect.

Such praise of a portrait by Lysippus scarcely agrees with the impression derived from copies of his other works, though we may imagine that his Alexander had the fiery qualities of the Agias. Otherwise Lysippus now appears as an extremely able worker of little imaginative force, who displays no interest in the expression of mental life, but specializes in ingenious technical devices; he enlivens his figures by causing them to seem about to shift their weight from one leg to the other, and no single viewpoint suffices for appreciation, because the arms stretch out across the body and the trunk leans forward or backward. In his concentration on liveliness are foreshadowed the developments of Hellenistic sculpture.

The influence of Lysippus was already immense in his own lifetime. It is especially visible in the most ambitious of all Attic gravestones, the 'Ilissus' stela (Pl. 58a), which is 1.28 m. high despite the loss of its architectural frame. It was so greatly admired by contemporaries that craftsmen of Athens imitated it in humbler gravestones. The young man, resting upon his own tomb, has the fighting-machine character of the Agias; he is carved half in the round. The slave-boy, asleep at his feet, and his dog are naturalistic to an unprecedented degree; significantly Pliny includes 'dogs' among the most celebrated works of Lysippus. The drapery of the aged father, although much of it is lost, encourages the attribution of the 'small Herculaneum woman' to Lysippus.

The end of Praxiteles' career did not immediately entail the abandonment of his stylistic practices, at any rate at Athens. An original bronze statue of a youth, found in Marathon Bay, is a very competent work by some well-trained slavish follower, perhaps one of his sculptor sons.

Architectural sculpture was still produced in Greece. Pedimental groups, carved shortly before 329 for the temple of Apollo at Delphi, were the work of two obscure Athenians, Praxias and Androsthenes; since no vestige of these figures has been found, some Roman may have thought them worth removing. A miserable set of three Victories found in the Epidaurus Sanctuary must be acroteria from the temple of Artemis. The small circular monument of Lysicrates at Athens, built after his successful presentation of a chorus in 334, bears a gay frieze, only 25 cm. high, representing Dionysus' transformation of pirates into dolphins. Its composition is manifestly pictorial—indeed the action can scarcely be followed now the paint has vanished; the tall, slim figures are vaguely reminiscent of the 'Apoxyomenus'.

The use of paint in reliefs is uniquely demonstrated by the intact 'Alexander' sarcophagus; when found in the royal tomb at Sidon, the tints had only slightly faded (cf. p. 34). It is the latest of the series from Sidon and must have been commissioned by the last king, a Phoenician named Abdalonymus who was set on his throne by Alexander, probably in 332, and outlived him. The reliefs commemorate their association. Where Alexander himself appears (Pl. 58b), he might be unrecognizable but for the diadem, because neither his face nor his hair conforms with the official portraits, a fact which suggests that they had not yet become widely known. On that argument, Abdalonymus would seem to have ordered the sarcophagus very early in his reign, not long after the subjugation of

Persia; disregarding this argument, the latest possible date would apparently be 312, when Sidon was annexed by Egypt. The sarcophagus imitates faithfully the shape of a temple with acroteria, antefixes, gutters, and pedimental sculptures. One of the long sides contains a representation of a battle between Greeks and Persians, with Alexander wearing a lion-skin on the extreme left, pursuing with uplifted lance a Persian horseman; on the extreme right a Macedonian horseman has just given a death-blow to a Persian who falls into the arms of his squire. Between, the space is occupied by a confused struggle of horses and men (Pl. 58c). On the opposite side is a hunt, in which a huge lion holds the centre of the composition; already wounded, it is attacking the horse of a Persian, tearing its breast with its claws; from all directions rescuers arrive and one has raised his axe to knock the animal on the head from behind. From the right and left Greeks gallop to the scene, the one on the left being Alexander (Pl. 58b). The right corner represents another part of the hunt, where a stag is confronted by a Greek and cut off from safety by a Persian. One of the shorter ends contains a panther-hunt, and in its gable a battle between Greeks and Persians; the other has battles of Greeks and Persians both above and below.

The 'Alexander' sarcophagus is a purely Greek work but cannot be associated with a particular artist or even school. The design might conceivably have been supplied by a painter, rather than by someone who habitually undertook both sculpture and painting as Euphranor had done. The mêlée of the battle, which would be scarcely intelligible without the colours, is actually the most involved scene preserved in any Greek relief earlier than the Christian era, though lost analogies unquestionably existed because they inspired Etruscan imitation during the third century. No similarity to the sarcophagus appears in any contemporary reliefs—mostly Attic—which continued to show single figures or small groups linked by simple activity. More enterprising in composition are the many reliefs in local limestone from the cemetery of Taranto, but the persistent backwardness of southern Italy caused them to retain the blank faces and fluttering drapery of the Bassae frieze or the Epidaurus sculptures, although the bodies of combatants might be as strained as in the Mausoleum frieze. Work of such mixed derivation cannot be dated within narrow limits but the majority seem contemporary with Lysippus. An unusual example in Munich, which is certainly no earlier, shows Persephone and her husband, the deities of the Underworld, sitting on their thrones while behind them the shades of Danaus' murderous daughters perform their eternal task of filling a leaky water-pot; in front of them, Hermes rushes away, having accomplished his mission in Hades.

IX

The Hellenistic Climax

(323–133 B.C.)

WITH Alexander's conquest of the Persian Empire there commenced a new era in Greek history, the Hellenistic Age, when the political and economic centres lay outside Europe, expecially in Babylonia, Syria (including adjacent territory now torn from it) and Egypt, leaving Greece little importance other than cultural. On Alexander's death in 323, a committee of his officers divided the control of his empire among themselves; their rivalries soon turned to fighting. A lingering pretence of unity ceased in 306, when rulers in Macedonia (and its dependencies), Egypt and Syria (with which Babylonia was incorporated) declared themselves Kings, each aiming to gain possession of the intervening or outlying territories, where states of secondary consequence arose as occasion offered. Almost constant warfare persisted for a hundred and fifty years, during which art received but scanty and intermittent encouragement from the soldier monarchs. Only when a minor principality achieved domination over western Asia Minor (where Greek cities had revived on deliverance from Persia) did sculptors find employment on public works of any considerable scale, at its capital, Pergamon, where also were assembled copies of older masterpieces—the first instance of such collecting. The hellenization of the Oriental countries, initiated by the colonists planted by Alexander, evoked practically no demand for sculpture except at Alexandria, where the Greek element was swamped after a few generations by an influx of Levantines—mainly Phoenicians degraded in taste, or Jews, whose religion prohibited figurative art; in those conditions, metal-work, particularly silver-plate, alone continued to flourish. Moreover the coarse sandstone quarried near Alexandria could not be carved with precision, so that the sculptors there normally worked with imported marble, which restricted opportunities for local training; probably the more competent among them were always immigrants from the Aegean. The only large assemblage of Hellenistic statues elsewhere in Egypt, at the Serapeum of Mem-

phis, is so deplorable that its first excavator thought only one curious figure
worth salvaging. The few sculptures yet discovered in the interior of Asia
are little better, except for obviously imported bronzes. Recumbent
effigies from Carthage demonstrate that Greeks of some talent worked
there, while even the worst craftsmen could obtain employment in the
Carthaginian colonies of Sardinia, where hundreds of their life-size stone
or terracotta heads defile the Museums of Cagliari and Oristano. In short,
discriminating patrons were so rare except in Greece and the eastern
Aegean littoral that the sculptors of repute still congregated there, and only
rarely went to the Oriental countries to undertake some individual statue
intended to have an exceptional significance.

Changes in political and social life brought changes in the subjects and
style of sculpture. Although the Greeks still grouped themselves in city-
states, within the larger entities formed by the kingdoms, the average
citizen no longer shared in the policy and warlike enterprises of his state,
for policy and war alike had become the business of specialists. Therefore
art had no more concern with the types of the citizen-warrior or the
citizen-statesman, and a new subject arose in the war-lord, a semi-divine
being, whose tremendous passions express themselves in beetling brows
and ruthless jaws.

The few temples of the age were normally unsculptured. Civic monuments seldom took any other form than an honorific statue. At some date
between 317 and 307 Athens passed a sumptuary law which forbade the
erection of expensive gravestones, so that stelae depicting scenes of daily
life were no longer erected in memory of its citizens. They had already
become rare in the rest of Greece. The Attic form of stela was adopted for a
while at Alexandria, where, however, it soon lapsed into crudity, and was
abandoned. Sepulchral statues became increasingly popular. These cannot
easily be distinguished from honorific statues erected in a person's lifetime by his city or by a guild: the types are limited in number and based on
fourth-century creations, such as the Sophocles statue and the Artemisia of
the Mausoleum, reproduced again and again with slight variations until
late in the Roman Empire; but the heads, especially those of men, grow
steadily less ideal and more individual. Statues of writers and philosophers
also become abundant, for this self-conscious age studied literature with
avidity and drew from the sermons of their philosophers a consolation
which the popular religion of Greece could not offer. The great Olympian
deities declined in popularity, while Aphrodite, doubtfully admitted by
Homer to the Pantheon, and Eros inspire innumerable works, though few
of merit, and Oriental deities like Serapis, Isis and Harpocrates begin to

press into Greek life and art. Eros now degenerates from a sober youth into a sportive child, the Cupid of later times, and his representation indicates a taste for genre subjects rather than religious fervour. The cult of Aphrodite had greater religious import but she is usually treated merely as a subject for a study in the nude, not as a serious goddess. The female body begins to attract more attention than the male, while society turns at the same time from a homosexual to a normal basis.

A decay in amateur athletics contributed to the change, lessening the interest in boys which had naturally been felt when men of the upper classes exercised regularly in the gymnasia for pleasure or as training for their perennial little wars. Statues of young athletes, scarce even in the fourth century, practically cease to appear in the Hellenistic age; in their place occur statues of professional athletes, especially of boxers, whose muscles bulge from massive frames. There exist many essays in the male nude, illustrations of the Heroic Age, or, in a lighter vein, figures of satyrs, those gay incarnations of the qualities absent in great cities—perfect health, freedom from care. The courage of the Gauls who invaded the Mediterranean world in the third century gave art a new theme, treated according to the athletic tradition, which called forth the best that Hellenistic sculptors could produce; in general they achieved their good results merely by virtuosity. They were accomplished to a point hitherto beyond attainment; nothing surpassed their powers, for which they could barely find sufficient scope. They abominated simplicity. The faces they conceived run through the whole gamut of expressions, muscles become more strained, textures more different. The subjects range from infancy to decrepitude, from divinity to depravity; not content with two sexes, they imagine intermediate beings, hermaphrodites. Relaxed poses become unfashionable, unless the relaxation is so extreme as to offer a challenge; a tense figure is no longer balanced but twisted to a spiral. Instead of figures grouped side by side, we see a spidery composition wherein arms and legs thrust in all directions.

The Early Hellenistic Period

The development of sculpture during the Hellenistic Age has as yet been traced only in the broadest outline; it is least known for the first ninety years, actually the most obscure phase in the entire history of Greek and Roman art. The present state of ignorance is due not so much to the obvious fact that comparatively little sculpture was produced, owing to the small scale of patronage, as to lack of evidence for dating most works, but there is also reason to suspect that this was actually a period of artistic chaos.

Lysippus, who outlived every renowned sculptor of his time, may have remained active for twenty or even thirty years after Alexander's untimely death, while his influence, no doubt, was paramount in the absence of any rival. Continual warfare must have restricted his opportunities throughout his later period. He is not recorded to have worked on anything other than individual statues after his collaboration with the aged or ageing Leochares on a group commemorating a lion-hunt, in which Alexander's life had been saved by one of his generals, Craterus, who himself was killed in a battle of 321, leaving an infant son in whose name the dedicatory inscription was set up (probably by Craterus' executor). Since the group stood at Delphi, a relief of the same subject, found at Messene, is unlikely to be a truthful reproduction, but may convey a general impression of its appearance.

Praxiteles, Lysippus and their contemporaries left sons and pupils who worked till well after 300. Artistic traditions, therefore, continued without a break, though stagnantly. The school—or rather, perhaps, factory—of Lysippus apparently imitated him slavishly but otherwise the fusion of the previous separate styles proceeded to complete eclecticism. Accuracy in rendering the body was facilitated by the anatomical researches of the time. Realistic portraiture seems to have advanced owing to a practice of taking a mould from a human face, which, if Pliny be correct, Lysistratus, the brother of Lysippus, had instituted (apparently for the purpose of forming a wax mask which he could place upon his clay model, next working up the details until it became fit to be cast in bronze).

Mediocrity appears to have characterized the work of the sons of Lysippus. The bronze 'Praying Boy' in Berlin (Pl. 59a), found in the Tiber, may be the original, or a cast from it, of a 'Worshipper' which Pliny mentions as a work by Boedas, a son of Lysippus; both arms have been restored, approximately in their correct positions. The head and stance recall the 'Apoxyomenus', but the statue is a mawkish thing, probably intended to be erotically appealing. Another of Lysippus' sons, Daippus, a sculptor of athletes, requires mention only because some have held the Vatican statue to be copied from his 'Perixyomenus', not from the 'Apoxyomenus' of his father. A third brother, Euthycrates (who collaborated with Cephisodotus, son of Praxiteles, in a statue of the poetess Anyte), enjoyed a greater reputation, although, says Pliny,

he imitated the strength rather than the grace of his father's work, trusting to an austere rather than a pleasant style. He therefore achieved the most success in his Heracles at Delphi, Alexander hunting at Thespiae, a cavalry battle, the image of Trophonius at his own oracle, many chariots, a horse with forked poles, and sportsmen's hounds. Tisicrates, another Sicyonian, although actually the pupil of Euthycrates, clung so faithfully to the style of Lysippus that many of his works can scarcely be distinguished from that sculptor's including the old Theban [?Pindar], King Demetrius [306–283] and Peucestes, who saved the life of Alexander the Great.

A colossus by one of Lysippus' pupils, Eutychides of Sicyon, set a fashion for statues personifying the Tyche (Fortune) of a city; his represented the Tyche of Antioch, a city founded in 300, and Pliny gives 299–296 as the sculptor's *floruit*, probably with reference to this statue, his most famous work. The goddess sat on a rock with her feet on a swimming figure personifying the river Orontes (which flows past Antioch); on her head was a turreted crown symbolizing the walls of the city, adapted from that habitually worn by Cybele (following the precedent of Semitic goddesses). The existing copies are all much reduced in scale. The largest (Pl. 59b), in the Vatican, is less than 90 cm. high and differs both from the headless remnants of four others in marble and from several little bronzes in having a smoother rendering of the drapery; the Tyche's hands and Orontes' arms are restorations while her head does not necessarily belong, though ancient and of the right size, so that it is likely to be correct (a matter on which the bronzes are too small to be decisive). The Budapest statuette (Pl. 59c), 47 cm. high, is so ill-proportioned that the composition must be distorted; the bronzes, however, corroborate its treatment of the drapery with deep emphatic folds and a crinkly surface. In the huge bronze original the axial thrusts of the folds would have directed the eyes too violently off-centre but for the cross-lines on the surface; interest was sustained all over the statue, except apparently at the back, which may have been out of sight.

Eutychides must have excelled in the treatment of surface, for another statue from his hand, of the river-god Eurotas, was described as 'wetter than water': a torso in the Vatican has been conjectured to be a copy because the attitude resembles that of the Orontes, and the figure rises from the water in the same manner. Crinkly drapery is found in many statues of the early Hellenistic period and marks the beginning of the tendency to study drapery as an object of independent interest, the arrangement of folds becoming of greater importance than the body beneath. No fourth-century statue has its drapery planned with so little regard for the lines of the body. The direction of the limbs towards the left as well as forwards makes the pose less conventional; the swimming figure develops naturalistically the convention by which the elements had been represented by fauna (as beneath the feet of the Victory of Paeonius or the 'Nereids' from Xanthus).

On the evidence of coins, many Asiatic cities followed the example of Antioch in setting up their own Tyche. One such may plausibly be recognized in a statue of a girl sitting cross-legged in a posture as contorted as Eutychides used at Antioch, and draped with comparable cross-currents. The original might, therefore, have been another work by Eutychides; it is known from the Conservatori marble (Pl. 60a) and a bronze statuette in the Louvre. The hair is swept back in visibly separate locks to a roll on top—a favourite method in the third century.

Chares, another pupil of Lysippus and author of the famous bronze Colossus of Rhodes, is known only by repute; his statue was 105 feet high, and in spite of being weighted with huge blocks of stone inside the legs, it stood only fifty-six years, when an earthquake (of 227–222) threw it to the ground. It did not bestride the harbour: that fable dates from the Middle Ages. Lucian remarks that the work was delicate considering the size. The statue represented the Sun, the patron god of the Rhodians, whose head appears on coins of the city from 407 B.C. onwards; in the Hellenistic coins, presumably influenced by the Colossus, the face is of florid aspect and surrounded by tumbled hair from which emerge spikes to represent the rays of the sun. No other evidence of its style exists. Similar types occur in heads of Helios found on the Island and in heads believed to represent Alexander, whose features so deeply influenced the art of the third century in all parts of the Greek world that his portraits cannot always be distinguished from ideal heads.

Praxiteles' sculptor sons, Cephisodotus and Timarchus, followed that practice of collaboration in which Greek artists often indulged; Cephisodotus collaborates on one occasion with a son of Lysippus but generally with his brother. A female head at Cos may have belonged to the group of cult-images which they carved for the temple of Asclepius; it falls into a class supposed to have originated in the 'school of Praxiteles' with excessively smooth modelling to enhance a purely sensual appeal. The Cos head is of dull competent workmanship. Among the finest works of the school is the head of a young goddess, probably Aphrodite, from Chios in the Boston Museum (Pl. 60b). But the surface has been removed by cleaning with acid. The shallow modelling, dependent for its effect on the angle presented to the light (as in the Hypnos), and the shape of the face would be

compatible with the middle of the fourth century, but the spirit that pervades it seems later, for the artist aimed only at sweetness of expression.
The hair seems to have been built up in stucco, a practice especially
favoured at Alexandria as a means of saving marble as well as labour; the
head might have originated there. The best head in the Alexandria
Museum, found locally in the Serapeum, may also represent Aphrodite in
spite of its tragic air; the eyes, deeply set under overhanging brows like
those of a male head by Scopas, and the pouting lips produce a highly
emotional effect. The same style was applied, with sharper features to suit
a middle-aged man, to the supposed head (Pl. 60c) of a statue of Menander
by the two sons of Praxiteles, which stood in the Theatre at Athens. Since
over forty copies of the head are preserved, this must be the portrait of a
highly esteemed person, so that the identification is almost certainly
correct; it is supported, though not absolutely confirmed, by the features
of a mosaic bust labelled 'Menander' discovered at Mytilene. A Hadrianic
relief may record the whole statue.

If such was the treatment accorded to an author of comedies, it is no
surprise to find the decided expression very much intensified in the heads
of kings (recognizable by the diadems bound round the hair), of which
many survive. Identification is difficult in the absence of inscriptions,
despite the number of coin-portraits with which they can be compared;
the features all conform in some degree to the type of Alexander—no relation to any of them. The most lifelike of all these portraits is the bronze
bust in Naples which resembles Seleucus I (reigned 306–281), an identification confirmed by its obvious contemporaneity with the heads of
Menander, who lived from 342 to 291. Portraits of Seleucus by Lysippus,
Aristodemus and Bryaxis have been recorded; the first may be presumed
to belong to the fourth century, whereas this bust shows the king advanced
in years.

At the same time conventional work, scarcely differing from the fourth-
century productions of a similar class, was still being executed, especially
in Greece. The best instance is a statue of Themis, discovered at Rhamnus
in Attica; it bears the signature of a local sculptor, Chaerestratus, in lettering of about the year 300. Except for the unkempt hair and a crumpled
rendering of the undergarment this statue might easily be ascribed to the
same period as the Artemisia of the Mausoleum, in which the pose and
design are similar. Many sculptors adhered to the severer manner of the
fourth century in their portraiture, refusing to contaminate their dignified,
bearded subjects with the passionate style of the sons of Praxiteles. Thus
the head of Theophrastus (372–287), which from his apparent age belongs

to the last years of the fourth century rather than to the beginning of the third century, differs greatly in appearance from the Menander through the flat precision of its modelling, but resembles the Demosthenes by Polyeuctus, commissioned in the year 280, of which numerous copies survive (Pls. 60d, 61a). This notable statue was in reality a work of imagination, for Demosthenes had already been dead more than forty years; it is, of course, possible that Theophrastus too was portrayed after his death, as a younger man than he was at the close of his life.

The Vatican Demosthenes (Pl. 60d) is wrongly restored holding a scroll, for other copies prove that originally the hands were clasped in front of the body. In the pose is revealed the patriot, meditating on the downfall of Athens and his own approaching death at the hands of the Macedonians, rather than the orator; the nervous vitality differs vastly from the calmness of its fourth-century prototype, the Sophocles. In that the eye travels instantly to the head, whereas in the later figure the entire upper part of the body, all that comes level with the spectator's eyes, has its significance. This attraction of the eyes is obtained by a design based upon a series of right angles, in which lies an architectural balance of structure; the left leg is almost concealed but the end of the himation falls in the same line; the head turns, in harmony with the many folds of the garment, towards the right leg, which is paralleled by the folds along the left side. In the Sophocles, a work of 340, the lines had run principally in curves; in a transitional statue of Aeschines, who lived from 389 to 314, the lines run straighter and the folds are emphatically modelled, so that the body claims attention, but the head is merely an idealized type of the respectable citizen.

Portraits of Epicurus and his colleagues, Hermarchus and Metrodorus, are only known in copies, which in the case of the two colleagues are so much alike that a head of Metrodorus has even been published as that of Hermarchus. A strong resemblance between the Epicurus and the Demosthenes shows that Polyeuctus or another artist of the same group was employed upon this portrait, to which the statues of the two younger men may be regarded as pendants, probably by the same hand. The circumstance that such marked physical similarities occur in statues of unrelated philosophers points to unconcern with individual features so long as the specific aspect of the character was adequately rendered.

A headless statue of the woman Niceso, found at Priene and now in Berlin, presents the female counterpart to the statues of Aeschines and Demosthenes; the inscription belongs to the early third century. The outer garment is folded tightly round the figure, like Demosthenes' himation, so that folds run diagonally all across the front, but the undergarment falls in a crinkly cascade straight from neck to feet, and its lines can be dimly traced through the outer layer of cloth. The figure is strangely rectangular, and lacks the easy grace of the conventional female types.

The colossal seated Dionysus in the British Museum surmounted the Monument of Thrasyllus at Athens, a structure of 319, rebuilt with a more ornate frontage in 271, to which date the statue seems to belong. The head has been lost; the form of the body is not clearly indicated although the drapery fits closely, in broad swathes of slight projection. The statue is of surprisingly poor quality considering its pretentious size, and was ill-designed for its conspicuous position, backed against the cliff behind the Theatre, from which viewpoint it must have appeared as a clumsy lump with a surface undifferentiated except for troughs of drapery between the legs. A similar though better composition was used for the cult-image of Serapis at Alexandria, a colossus allegedly cast in some dark metal, though probably of bronze varnished with a tint appropriate to this newly Hellenized god of the Underworld. The date may be either before or after 250. The sculptor's name is recorded as Bryaxis; to him also was attributed the cult-image of Apollo at Daphne, near Antioch. The numerous copies of the Serapis vary so greatly that they must have been based on memory or on previous copies; probably no one was allowed to carve inside the temple. Conscious imitation of Pheidias' Olympian Zeus may be seen in the head, though with a heavier mop of hair and grim expression on the calm, pensive face. The drapery lay close to the trunk, seamed by thin wavering lines, but deep folds spread between the knees.

Another seated draped figure, obviously a product of much the same concepts, was the portrait of Menander's successor as a writer of comedies, Poseidippus, who died about 250. A copy of the whole statue exists in the Vatican; it gives a convincing presentation of cleverness in the wrinkled, sharp-featured countenance of an active man, still in the prime of life. An original marble statue of a woman named Nicocleia, in the British Museum, shows her with an aged face, standing erect in contorted drapery, such as the mediocre sculptor might have derived from studying Eutychides. His methods were definitely imitated in the 'Anzio Girl' (perhaps a young priestess), a standing but by no means erect figure (Pl. 61b). Her entire weight rests on the left foot while the right leg trails slackly behind it, and the head is bent downwards to the left so that she can read a scroll spread in both hands above the hip; the resultant twist of the upper part of the body is compensated by extending the drapery leftwards below the hip to fall in perpendicular folds equivalent, as in the Demosthenes, to an extra leg. The marble from Anzio appears to be copied from a bronze original, in which the crinkles on the lower part of the drapery would have been less conspicuous; folds in the upper parts are grouped in cross-currents, likewise in the manner of Eutychides. The date of the original is most uncertain; it can be ascribed to the middle or end of the third century, or even to the earlier half of the second century, depending on whether the clear-cut eyes and mouth acquired greater sharpness from the copyist. An argument that such vivacity would have been unattainable before the second century is based on lack of evidence, and might be disproved by new discoveries.

An even wider margin of chronological error must be allowed in the case of a marble statue at Copenhagen (Pl. 61c), presumably copied from a bronze original of a poet playing a lyre. Because another statue from the same site, outside Rome, represented Anacreon, the subject is probably some other poet of the distant past; the wrinkled face and chest indicate advanced age while the heavy drapery is so planned as to emphasize his vigour; its texture would have been better rendered in bronze.

Another statue obviously popular in antiquity, the Aphrodite crouching in her bath (Pl. 62a), has been ascribed to a Bithynian sculptor, Doedalsas, whose name and doings have been ingeniously worked out from circumstantial evidence and a series of emendations of corrupt passages in ancient texts; the result fits together but may be sheer fantasy. One emendation elicits the information that the artist made a cult-image of Zeus for the Bithynian city of Nicomedia, founded in 264; his statue was probably executed soon afterwards. A proof of the third-century date of the Aphrodite is afforded by the occurrence of an imitation on a relief epigraphically dated to the beginning of the second century. The series of copies and imitations thus inaugurated grew apace, three distinct variations of the type are represented and other alterations were constantly made for decorative purposes, while the proportions of the body follow the changing standards of taste. The crouching attitude produces ugly wrinkles on the plump abdomen. The merits of the head cannot be judged from the copies. In that illustrated, the top of the hair has been restored, as well as the fingers and toes; the copyist seems to have raised the left knee higher than in the original, because other copies make the thigh come almost straight forward.

A more remarkable product, probably of the middle or end of the century, was a group of the flaying of Marsyas, of which two members survive in good copies. Marsyas (Pl. 62b) is hanging by his hands, tied to a tree, about to be skinned for his presumption in challenging Apollo to a musical competition, while a slave (Pl. 62c) squats near by, sharpening his knife and gloating upon the victim: a seated Apollo may have completed the group, but no certain copy of this figure remains. A curious feature about the Marsyas type is the fact that the statue which seems to belong to the original composition has been copied in white marble, whereas a more sensational edition, best ascribed to the second century, has been copied in red marble, probably to imitate the sunburnt effect of the satyr, which may have been produced in the original by varnish. In the earlier form the bestial face is merely distorted with fright, and the body, stretched by its position, is painstakingly carved with the attention to detail seen in the Aphrodite of Doedalsas; in the later version the satyr is howling, his face is working frantically and the hairy body is damp with sweat. Such was the course upon which sculpture now embarked under the patronage of the kings of Pergamon.

The Pergamene Age

In the troubled years during which Alexander's generals were struggling for the possession of his dismembered empire, one of his successors, Lysimachus, selected the small town of Pergamon, north of Smyrna, for the storehouse of his treasury. In 283 Philetaerus, the officer in charge, revolted and established a minor state, which rose to sudden greatness under its third monarch after the repulse of a large horde of Gauls, who had for years ravaged Asia Minor with impunity. The decisive battle occurred in 241, but fighting persisted until 228. Attalus I celebrated his achievement by a set of bronze statues on the acropolis at Pergamon, presumably dedicated soon after 228 rather than after 241. In various collections, especially in Italy, there exist figures in the local marble of Pergamon, probably copied from these bronzes; the most famous is the Dying Gaul of the Capitol.

But Pergamon had become a centre of sculpture before the dedications, for new cult-statues had been required as the little town grew to an important capital; some had been executed by two celebrated Athenians, Niceratus and Phyromachus; the latter lived to take a share in what Pliny calls 'the memorials of the Gallic wars of Attalus and Eumenes' (it is doubtful whether by Eumenes he means the predecessor or successor of Attalus); the same author also mentions in this connection three other artists, Stratonicus, Antigonus and Isigonus, the last perhaps in mistake for Epigonus, whose name occurs elsewhere in his book as well as upon Pergamene inscriptions. The literary and epigraphical sources make it plain that the sculptors settled at Pergamon were drawn—and this continued to be the case—from all parts of the Greek world: the liberality of the Attalids first attracted them and then welded them into a school through common labours on subjects dictated by the court. Of works older than the great dedications it is doubtful whether any survive, even in a copy; the bare names remain of statues attributed by authors and inscriptions to the first sculptors of Pergamon. Thus Niceratus is credited with a group of Asclepius and Hygieia, a Nike, a group of Alcibiades and his mother, and 'Alcippe, mother of an elephant'; he is also said to have made portraits of the Argive poetess, Telesilla, and of athletes. Phyromachus, a younger man who collaborated with him at Delos (where both signatures appear on the one base), also made a group of Alcibiades driving a four-horse chariot, and a cult-statue of Asclepius so renowned that it was carried off by Prusias of Bithynia in an attack on Pergamon in 156. Existing types of Asclepius and Hygieia may reproduce originals by these sculptors.

Of the set of large statues dedicated at Pergamon after 228, only copies of Gauls survive, although Greeks were also represented; the original bases have been discovered and leave no room for doubt on the point. The famous statue on the Capitol (Pl. 63a) was formerly described as a gladiator, but the torque around the neck is Gaulish, and the trumpet that lies on the ground, together with the sword and shield, is proper to a victim of war, not of the arena. The nudity does not correspond to Gallic habits but to Greek convention. Blood flows from a wound in the right breast.

The 'Capitoline' Gaul had been partially restored in antiquity, which raises the question of the date at which the copies were produced; it has been suggested that they were almost contemporary with the originals, while others would ascribe them to the second century A.D., but a vast superiority over the general level of imperial copyists argues for a difference in time, not merely in school. If of Hellenistic date, strict accuracy on the part of the copyist must not be expected, for the copies of fifth-century statues executed at Pergamon under the kings differ considerably from their originals.

Almost certain is the attribution to Attalus' dedication of the Ludovisi group (Pl. 63b) in which a Gaul, who has killed his wife to prevent her falling into the hands of the enemy, now thrusts the sword into his own breast, as he glances over his shoulder at the pursuers. Among the restorations should be mentioned the man's left forearm, right arm and sword, the woman's left arm and right hand, and the noses of both; the hand grasping the sword has been restored upside-down in a fatuous position, the woman's left arm should droop parallel to the drapery, the man should hold his elbow further from his head. The flat surfaces of the woman's drapery recall the Dionysus from the monument of Thrasyllus. The region of the eye, in the woman and in the Capitoline statue, is sharply carved with little use of shadow; the eyebrows are omitted in the woman but marked in the Capitoline by a thin ridge, in the 'Ludovisi' man by a thicker ridge; the companion statues of Marsyas and the Knife-grinder exhibit a similar distinction, which may in every case be due to the copyist's inability to reproduce the hair incised on the bronze originals. The 'Ludovisi' heads are coarse-featured. The man's body is more forcibly modelled than is the case with other copies from the dedication, namely the Capitoline Gaul and a torso in Dresden. In these the detailed rendering of the surface anatomy is not allowed to break up the contours as in the Ludovisi figure. But the differences in style are no more than should be expected in statues due to different artists and copied by different hands. Stylistic divergences occur to a similar degree in the large number of heads which seem to be derived from the same dedication; the finest of these is the magnificent head of a Dying Asiatic (Pl. 64a), the rest are distributed between London, Paris and Rome.

At this point should be described a group frequently copied under the Empire, that of Menelaus carrying the body of Patroclus out of battle; such is its usual title, although possibly other heroes of the Trojan War may be represented. The best preserved replica is in Florence, but other examples of the heads, which offer a later style, are perhaps more accurately copied; the date cannot be decided until the style of the original is more clearly established; at present the variations in the heads would admit of any period in the long reign of Attalus (241–197), if not in the whole first hundred years of the Pergamene state. The motif is far older, appearing upon fifth-century vases.

The 'Ludovisi' head of a Sleeping Fury is an inadequate copy from an amazing original of the early Pergamene school. To the same period belong some of the finest portraits the Greeks have left. A pair of marble heads in Boston (Pl. 64b,c), found in Egypt, have been identified by the profiles on coins as Ptolemy IV (221–203) and his sister-consort Arsinoe, who was believed to have been murdered by his order. He was a worthless and vicious degenerate, a fact that the sculptor did not altogether conceal in spite of idealizing the features, but the queen evoked a sympathetic and probably faithful portrayal. The eyes retain some of the original paint; the hair must have been completed in plaster or metal from the diadem upwards, as also must the king's, while a row of holes along his jawbone held a metal beard. Another instance of identification by coin-portraits is the head in Rome (Pl. 65a) with the striking features and prototype sun-helmet of Euthydemus, a usurper who became king of Bactria (northern Afghanistan) about 230; the original was made, no doubt, in Asia Minor, which he visited towards the end of the century. Not less than three statues were executed of the philosopher Chrysippus, who died at the age of 73 between 208 and 204; one, at least, is known from copies to have shown him seated, with deeply folded drapery setting off his shrivelled face. No close dating is possible for an ill-preserved but seemingly original bronze head, recovered from the Anticythera ship; the uncouth bearded old man with the shaggy hair could have been a portrayal from life but is quite likely to have been an imaginary characterization of some long-dead personage.

A set of many small figures, known from copies, is recorded to have been dedicated on the Acropolis at Athens by a king of Pergamon named Attalus. Since Athena was the patron goddess of Pergamon, any of her kings might have felt impelled to put an offering in her home-sanctuary, and the prevalent confusion as to the development of Hellenistic sculpture gives scope for experts to dispute whether the donor was Attalus I, whose visit to Athens in 201 would have provided a likely occasion, or Attalus II (159–138), although the style of the intervening reign is exceptionally well documented.

The figures, on a scale of two-thirds life-size, were arranged in groups representing battles—of gods against giants, Greeks against Amazons, Athenians against Persians, Pergamenes against Gauls; the juxtaposition tacitly claimed for both Athens and Pergamon no less glory than for the gods. All the surviving statues are in marble, but the originals seem to have been of bronze, for one is recorded to have been blown off the Acropolis during a storm. Curiously enough, the marble is that used at Pergamon, but it is reasonable to suppose that duplicate bronzes were displayed there; they might, in fact, have occupied a series of pedestals which have been found at Pergamon, inscribed beyond question with the name of Attalus II. The singular dimensions of the extant figures correspond to Pausanias' 'two cubits' and to the measurements of pedestals discovered at Athens; further, the subjects agree with his list. Copies in the Naples Museum include a Dying Gaul and a Dying Asiatic, whose dress, often described as Persian, was used for all figures of Asiatics, including Paris the Trojan and other personages of Nearer Asia. There is an obvious relationship between this Gaul and the Capitoline Gaul of the First Dedication; but, as in all these smaller figures, the forms of the body receive greater emphasis, a development foreshadowed in the 'Ludovisi' group; the face too recalls that of the 'Ludovisi' Gaul, though in some of the companion statues the brows form deep wrinkles above the nose when contracted in pain. A statue of a dead Amazon, also in Naples (Pl. 65b), wears the short chiton of her tribe, fastened only on one shoulder, leaving a breast exposed; in a sketch of the sixteenth century a child is shown at the breast, and Pliny notes a group by Epigonus, 'a child pitiably caressing its dead mother'. The coincidence is so remarkable that it has been argued that the drawing may really give the motif of the original, though Amazons are not customarily represented as mothers, nor is the breast the right shape to contain milk.

Such considerations, however, may be irrelevant in view of the intensely theatrical character of the Second Dedication, in which the combatants take extravagant postures and the dead look ready to spring to life. The First Dedication had, indeed, been dramatic, and the Pergamene school of the early second century swung to melodrama (in the Gigantomachy); ascription of the Second Dedication to Attalus I puts its theatricality in an intervening phase, whereas the ascription to Attalus II would make it the last phase. The true sequence can, perhaps, be deduced by a series of arguments, though none is determinant in itself. Thus the Amazon's deeply modelled drapery is tumbled in a manner not found in early Hellenistic statues, and accentuates the spiral twist whereby the figure adheres to precedent; the limbs straggle, in contrast to the tightly-bound composition of the 'Ludovisi' Gaul and, to a lesser extent, of other members of the First Dedication. This loose type of composition has been claimed to be distinctive of the mid or late second century, though it could equally be due to a personal idiosyncrasy. The sharpness of the features is clearly derived from third-century tradition (as exemplified in the Demosthenes and other portraits), whereas Pergamene faces of the early second century tend to be fleshy; if the Dedication was really made by Attalus II, we must, therefore, postulate a return to the older convention.

Similarity both of face and body places in the same period as the Second Dedication the companion statues of an old and a young centaur, as captives of Love. The Capitoline copies in a dark grey marble are signed by Aristeas and Papias of Aphrodisias; they were discovered in Hadrian's Villa near Tivoli, and were probably carved in his reign; the hands of the elder centaur were shown tied together by an Eros formerly seated on his back (Pl. 65c). Other statues that resemble the Second Dedication include a fragment (in the Metropolitan Museum) consisting of the lower portion of a trousered Gaul in rapid movement, the later version of the Marsyas copied in red marble, and a spirally contorted Sleeping Hermaphrodite in the throes of an erotic dream. In hermaphrodite statues, for which the Hellenistic Greeks had a marked predilection, the attempt to combine male and female results in the predominance of the female element, but the sexual organs are invariably male, and the hips narrower than those of the average Greek woman.

Some of the many statues of satyrs, too, must belong to this period; it appears from their style that most of the types were produced at the time of the Pergamon kingdom but the untrustworthiness of the copies makes it difficult to assign them places in a series. The 'Barberini' satyr at Munich, by far the most striking of them all, comes closer to the First Dedication, while the popular bronze statuette from Pompeii of a dancing satyr resembles the Second, as does the satyr playing a flute in the Villa Borghese. A figure meant to be seen from all directions was attained in a satyr-boy turning to look at his handsome equine tail. A young satyr, wrongly restored with cymbals in his hands (Pl. 66a), is seen on a coin of Cyzicus accompanied by a seated nymph whom he is inviting to dance; the many copies of both figures and of their smiling heads suggest a date well after 200. Another popular work of the same class was the *symplegma* (embrace) of a satyr struggling with a hermaphrodite, whose playful resistance makes their arms and legs diverge in all directions.

A dating at approximately 200 or soon after has now been established for the great Nike (Victory) from Samothrace in the Louvre. A fragment of identical marble with the signature of Pythocritus, a known Rhodian sculptor of the time, belonged either to this monument or to some lost work in the vicinity. The Nike, 2.45 m. high in its headless condition, stood on the prow of a stone ship built in an artificial pool overlooking the island's sanctuary. The goddess was thus represented alighting on the war-galley as it advanced against the enemy fleet. Her head was thrown back, the left arm stretched downwards (perhaps to hold the frame of a trophy), the right arm seems to have been raised in front of the body and to have up-held a thin object, probably the metal band of a wreath, grasped between the thumb and the index finger. The torsion of the figure and the arrangement of the drapery are characteristic of the period, but the thinness of the cloth recalls the fourth-century conventions; a flying Victory in the slightly later Gigantomachy frieze of Pergamon wears garments of a more leathery texture but similarly wind-blown in opposing directions, whereas in the fourth century the drapery is blown all in one direction. Both figures were new editions of a type that went back to Pheidias and had constantly been revised in the meantime. A coin of Demetrius Poliorcetes, issued in cele-bration of a naval victory of 306, illustrates Nike blowing a trumpet on the prow of a galley; if he had dedicated a statue of this character, it might well have directly inspired the sculptor at Samothrace, whose apparently anachronistic rendering of cloth would thus be due to conscious imitation.

Again, imitation of his Nike may account for the drapery in a mediocre pedimental group which was added to the Hieron at Samothrace shortly after 150; it is now in Vienna.

A marble group that represented the slaughter of Niobe's children is preserved in copies of Niobe with her youngest daughter (Pl. 66b), the pedagogue slave with one of her sons, four (or possibly five) other sons and two elder daughters—one of whom is also known in the simplified 'Chiaramonti' version. The sculptor can best be placed, very tentatively, as a contemporary of the Pergamenes. The welter of datings that have been proposed, from the fourth to the first century, is really a tribute to his eclecticism, which was the cause of Pliny's remark that 'it is questionable whether Scopas or Praxiteles made the dying children of Niobe in the Temple of Apollo Sosianus at Rome'; since the Latin wording could also mean 'the death of the children' it need not imply the exclusion of Niobe herself. Sosius, after whom the temple was named, had been Governor of Syria and may have looted the statues there or in Cilicia. They are likely to have occupied a pediment, because they range from the tall Niobe to quite low figures and all were carefully designed to extend sideways rather than from front to back in order to fit a narrow base. The attitude and faces express despair, terror or defiance, as might be expected late in the third century or early in the second, while the drapery seems rather too restrained to be dated much after 200, although that worn by the youngest daughter is meant to be damp with the sweat of fear. The best copies of Niobe's head give reason to identify as another work by the same sculptor the 'Head from the South Slope' of the Acropolis at Athens (Pl. 66c). This head must be an original. Several copies of it exist but none is attached to a body; perhaps it belonged to a statue of the deserted Ariadne.

A great temple at Magnesia, begun in 201 and completed in 129, was decorated with a frieze which appears to have been designed soon after its inception; smaller friezes are preserved on Cos and at Teos. Their style is visible also in a gravestone from Chios, of a type represented only by one other example, and that from the same island.

The beginning of the second century was a time of tremendous artistic activity at Pergamon. Attalus' successor, Eumenes II, was endangered by an invasion by Antiochus of Syria, who was finally repulsed with Roman aid; this event of 190 probably offered the pretext for the enormous Altar decorated with a frieze representing the battle of the gods and giants. This Altar was infinitely the most striking of a group of buildings ranged round a crescent-shaped hillside; it took the form of a square platform, broken at one side by a flight of wide steps, which led up to the altar proper; below

the colonnade, surrounding the platform, ran the great frieze in one continuous band, 2.30 m. high and 130 m. long. Most of it survives and has
been removed to Berlin.

To assist the spectator to follow all the incidents of the Gigantomachy, in
which the obscurest gods and little-known giants take part, the name of each
figure was written beneath. The artists' signatures were also inscribed,
each on the slab entrusted to him, but these have almost entirely perished;
it has proved possible to restore only one complete signature, that of
Orestes, son of Orestes, the Pergamene, but there remain fragments that
have been read as 'Dionysiades and Menecrates, sons of Menecrates',
members of a large family of sculptors connected with Tralles and Rhodes.
Fragments recorded other sculptors of Athenian, Pergamene and probably
Trallian nationality. The design of the whole frieze must have been by
one man, who had obviously made an intensive study of fifth- and fourth-
century sculpture, for he reproduced many of its type-figures and imitated
groupings he had observed in the Parthenon pediments.

The frieze as a whole gives a realistic impression of a writhing mass of
figures engaged in a desperate struggle. The upper parts of the giants are
human in shape, of magnificent muscular development and equipped with
great wings, but their legs turn below the knees into serpents, which fight
an independent battle of their own, fill gaps and add continuity to the
crowded composition, which in any case is bound together by overlapping figures. On four of the best-preserved slabs (Pl. 67a), Athena pulls a
giant's hair, Victory flies towards her, and Ge (Earth) emerges from the
ground to make a grief-stricken appeal for clemency towards her sons, the
giants. Throughout the Gigantomachy every face registers the utmost
possible emotion, muscles bulge with strain, bodies are contorted, yet the
scenes fail to horrify because they are clearly unreal.

The east side of the frieze opens with the combats of Hecate and Artemis
(Pl. 67b). At the corner a giant raises a rock with both hands to hurl at his
triple-bodied opponent, Hecate, while one of the snakes, in which his legs
terminate, pulls away the end of her shield with its teeth; Hecate's dog
attacks him in the thigh. The foremost body of the goddess stands fully
revealed, of the other two only the arms and parts of the heads can be seen;
the first holds a shield and brandishes a torch; the central figure, of which
the hair alone is visible, thrusts with a spear; while the furthest, whose face
is disclosed below her helmet, waves a sword in the right hand and strikes
with its scabbard in the left. Otus, who is opposed to Artemis, has a purely
human body and carries a richly decorated shield and a long-plumed
helmet; between the combatants another giant with reptilian extremities

lies struggling with a dog, which has seized him by his neck, but he gouges out its eyes with his finger; a third giant is stretched dead on the ground. Artemis plants her foot upon the corpse, loosing an arrow at Otus before he can get to close quarters with his sword. The sculptor's care extends to such details as the hairy armpits of the giants and the ornamental hunting boots of Artemis.

If the frieze is in questionable taste, it was at least successful for its purpose, for a work of more refinement and less varied surface would have been inconspicuous in such a setting. The speed with which Pergamene sculpture had developed was phenomenal; the Altar was created about 188, only forty or fifty years later than the Dying Gaul of the First Dedication. Yet the over-emotional character of the frieze could have been predicted from the dignified and older figure; the constant increase of sculptors' skill brought with it an ever greater extravagance of detail, from the motive of technical display. The groundwork of Pergamene art remains the same throughout, only in the frieze the bodies are more heavily muscled and more contorted, the features more agonized, the hair wilder, the eyebrows more strikingly contracted. Many of the figures, however, are types of the fifth century, brought up to date.

The execution of the frieze is more effective than conscientious in accordance with its dimensions, and the smaller works of the school are of finer quality, especially the female head (Pl. 68a), which probably represents a goddess. The majority of the statues discovered at Pergamon and datable to this period represent gods or goddesses, although some of the female types may conceivably be portraits of ordinary women. Of the remaining sculptures the most notable are a head that perhaps represents Attalus I, a work of approximately the end of the third century, fitted simultaneously or later with a wilder mane of hair; a head of Alexander, of an older type, revised in the sensational manner of the day; reliefs of dancing girls, which surrounded a circular base, and small statues of the same subjects, imitating to varying degrees the mannerisms of late archaic drapery.

Originals and copies in the style of the Gigantomachy have been discovered in all parts of the Mediterranean world, for it became cosmopolitan—a fact due to the habitual wanderings of artists. A statue, of which copies exist in Munich and the Capitoline, has strong claims to be considered identical with the 'drunken old woman' which Pliny attributes to a sculptor named Myron, apparently of Boeotian origin like his more famous namesake, but settled at Smyrna; his signature has also been found on a pedestal at Pergamon, of second-century date, and the statue is imitated on vases, one of which bears an inscription of the later half of that century. The drapery may be compared with that of the Gigantomachy; the Munich statue alone preserves the head, with a shrunken wrinkled face and a fatuous gap-toothed smile; the arms hug a wine-jar of the Hellenistic type called a *lagynos*. The subject is no new one, for drunkenness had long held a place in the repertory of artists, and old age had provided the caricaturists of the previous two centuries with abundant material of the same nature. It is a statue intended to exhibit the perfection of the sculptor's technique; artists now rioted in the freedom which their skill had given to them.

A dignified treatment of old age is seen in the 'Centaur' head (Pl. 68*b*) to which a restorer added a bulbous nose, removed since the photograph was taken. Comparison with the Gigantomachy establishes that the original was Pergamene of that date, with fleshy features in contrast to the clear-cut lines of the Old Centaur ridden by Eros. The innumerable busts of old blind Homer, made for ancient libraries, are likely to be derived from a statue of which the base was found at Pergamon, inscribed in second-century lettering, but the style of the original has been transmuted by the copyists and adaptors.

The Gigantomachy is likely to have been carved about twenty years before the death of Eumenes II in 159, so that he should have had ample time to complete the Altar. Its enclosure was lined internally with a frieze, two-thirds as high and astonishingly different. It illustrates the life-story of Pergamon's mythical founder, Telephus, the son of Heracles by Auge, a priestess of Athena, who was set adrift in an 'ark' when her pregnancy became known. In the scene illustrated (Pl. 68*c*) she is seated on a rock watching the construction of the vessel, while other women in the background mourn her fate. Some figures are cut almost in the round, others project very little and are indistinct without the original colour. The designer was surely one of the painters who added to the renown of Pergamon; his design even includes such features as a bird in flight. The whole frieze is a pictorial narration, divided by rocks and trees into separate scenes, many of which are crowded with figures arranged in depth, receding one behind another. The subject matter is necessarily quieter than the Gigantomachy's and offered no opportunity for exuberance of fancy, but the action is always treated calmly even where it could legitimately have been hectic. The style itself is calm without the pomposity of the Gigantomachy. The drapery forms linear patterns, many simply repetitive but some complicated by folds of an inner garment shown through the outer. Previous sculptors had revealed only an occasional underlying fold here and there, whereas the Pergamenes now composed the whole figure in terms of both layers. The device was not used in the Gigantomachy though it must have been introduced almost contemporaneously on the evidence of statues found at Pergamon.

The transition in draped figures from the time of the Gigantomachy to that of the Telephus frieze and slightly later can be very closely followed by means of a series of female statues from Pergamon. One of these, a Muse wearing a sword-belt, is the original, or perhaps one of the originals, of a type copied among a set of Muses very dubiously attributed to Philiscus, a Rhodian artist. A relief of the Apotheosis of Homer (Pl. 71a), itself a work of twenty or thirty years later, represents several of these Muses among those on the slopes of Olympus, but in reality their drapery does not offer such marked contrasts of light and shade as in these small reproductions, which are simplified in accordance with later taste. The existence of numerous copies in the round as well as on reliefs establishes that the originals of the 'Philiscus' Muses greatly resembled the statue in the British Museum from Erythrae (Pl. 69a). This figure is remarkable for the manner in which the body is ignored, and its place as the constructive element taken by the drapery, which is plotted out in bars of light and shade; these build up the form by their vertical direction, while their almost horizontal curves bind it solidly together. A sense of impermanency, valued by the Pergamene artists, is preserved by the incomplete character of these curves, which fade away, lacking the perfect sweep of those on the Sophocles statue. Absolute reliance on the vertical folds to suggest the form would of course be impossible with a thick himation, and is indeed scarcely found in the most advanced cases of transparency, such as the statue from Magnesia (Pl. 69b). Doubtless many of these draped female figures can be explained as honorific or sepulchral statues, for the same types occur on the gravestones known as 'Eastern Greek Reliefs', especially frequent in Smyrna and Samos from this time onwards. The carving is very shallow; usually two or three figures stand or sit in a panel framed by an arch.

At Delphi, a frieze of more historical than artistic interest commemorates the Roman conquest of Macedonia in 167; the general in command, Aemilius Paullus, put it, together with an equestrian statue of himself, on a monument which King Perseus of Macedonia seems to have erected to his own glory. The scenes on the four sides illustrate successive episodes, beginning with the incident of the runaway horse that was reported to have touched off the fighting, and continuing with a mounted figure that may be a portrait of Paullus; the battle that followed is treated conventionally, except for the accurate rendering of the types of helmets and shields that distinguish the opposing armies. Perhaps the frieze was designed by Metrodorus of Athens, whom Paullus took to Rome to execute the pictures of the campaign displayed at a Triumph; at any rate it is unquestionably Greek work, and it is significant as an early instance of Roman patronage for an artistic record of actual events.

A few portraits may be contemporary with the last kings of Pergamon, though a headless statue found in a temple built there by Attalus II is not so likely to represent him as Zeus. A bronze statue in the Terme stands in the usual heroic nudity with one hand resting on a lance above the head; the extremely heavy build of the body matches the brutality of the face (Pl. 69b). The features have been identified from a resemblance to coins as those of Demetrius I of Syria (162–150), or preferably, of Alexander Bala (150–146), the usurper who displaced him; the absence of a diadem should imply that the king is deified.

The influence of archaic work has already been noted in Pergamene sculpture: it was, no doubt, largely exerted through the Attalid collection of antiques, which included even a sixth-century piece, the Graces of Bupalus. In Greece the same tendency was evident; the bulk of the sculpture produced in that country during the Hellenistic Age follows older models of one period or another. In the second century a movement towards the simplicity of Pheidian art spread through Greece and Asia Minor; its chief protagonist seems to have been Damophon of Messene. Excavation at Lycosura, a sanctuary of Demeter in the Arcadian hills, disclosed the remains of cult-statues which had formed one of his principal groups. Two seated figures of Demeter and Persephone were flanked by subsidiary standing figures of Artemis and of a Titan, Anytus. The drapery is designed with extreme care; the portions covering the body recall Pergamene work, while a hanging end of Demeter's robe is carved to represent embroidery, showing Nereids riding sea-monsters, winged Victories, and a row of animal-headed creatures, deities from a primitive stratum of religion which survived in no other district of Greece. The heads of three figures have been recovered and placed with this fragment in the Museum at Athens, while the rest remain in a museum built on the site. Damophon treated the heads in a cursory manner, unlike the Pergamenes; obviously he was deeply influenced by the fifth century, especially in the faces, which are derived from Pheidian types though enlivened by the parting of the lips (Pl. 70b). But the actual cutting of the marble has been done by inefficient hands; Damophon entrusted the reproduction of his clay models to others.

Damophon seems to have worked exclusively in the Peloponnese, in the cities belonging to the Achaean and Arcadian Leagues. According to Pausanias, in his own city of Messene he made an image of the Mother of the Gods for the market-place, a large number of marble statues for the sanctuary of Asclepius, and an Artemis Laphria; of all these, only a head of Apollo has survived and been identified by its resemblance to the Artemis of Lycosura. At Aegion he made a cult-statue of Eileithyia, the body being of wood and the face, hands and feet of marble; the whole image was clothed in a finely woven garment. In the same town he was responsible for the images of Asclepius and Hygieia: and for the sanctuary of the Great Goddesses at Megalopolis he carved both the cult-images and the subsidiary figures as well as the decorations. He also restored the Olympian Zeus of Pheidias when the ivory cracked open, probably about 170; no recorded work of his can be later than 146, when the cities lost their independence and declined into poverty.

The partial return to the simplicity of early sculpture coincides, it would seem, with the supreme achievements of the Pergamene school. Complete mastery of technique had at last been attained; as happens in every age when the fruits of liberty prove rotten, art wilted, and many sculptors relapsed into imitation of a period when restraint had been imposed by incompetence. The fact that Greece and Pergamon now became Roman territory, in 146 and 133 respectively, contributed to the temporary sterility of ideas.

X

The Hellenistic Anticlimax and the
Roman Republic

(133–23 B.C.)

The Delos Period

W HEN the last king of Pergamon died in 133, leaving his possessions to Rome, Greek art became almost totally dependent on the patronage of rich individuals: although other kingdoms survived into the next century—Cyrene was annexed only in 96, Syria in 65, Egypt in 30—Cyrene alone has yielded any sculptures of merit which might belong to the last years of independence. The commonest varieties of sculpture in Greek lands were at this period the portrait statue and the diverse adaptations or imitative pieces of archaistic conception. The former class may be divided into honorific and sepulchral statues, but actually members of both subdivisions looked alike: they had conventional bodies, nude or draped according to the sex or occupation of the person represented; the heads, however, had in many cases pronouncedly individual traits. This interest in portraiture may be seen most plainly at Delos, which maintained a large colony of Italian merchants, and it is conceivable that the demand for realistic likenesses found in them its strongest supporters, for the Etruscans, whose art dominated Central Italy, specialized in portraits. Side by side with realistic portraiture there flourished several varieties of imitative work, which cannot be rigorously separated from one another; Neo-Attic decoration becomes increasingly merged with the usual archaistic class, both of which had a long and not always inglorious career, continuing far into the Roman empire. Other sculptors produce new editions of old types, altering the style to taste, especially making the heads conform to the Pheidian characteristics recently popularized by Damophon and his associates. In statuary, therefore, the effect depended upon technical ability, the creative faculty being confined to abolishing the stiffness of older statues, allowing the limbs to spread themselves unconstrainedly and twisting the bodies out of their eternal immobility. But experiments continued in other directions;

the landscape element was developed into a separate branch of sculpture (doubtless following a similar move in the art of painting), while a pictorial treatment of details can be traced in the carving of drapery. Both these tendencies were to find their full development under the early empire.

Childhood was, perhaps, the only theme that had not already been fully explored. A sculptor habituated to the bulging muscles of the Giganto-machy could have taken a rococo delight in the proportions of babies, the lumps and dimples of their flesh, their pouting cheeks and mouths. The lesser frieze of the Altar included a scene of a doe giving suck to the infant Telephus, of whom only the upper half remains, much damaged, but the form might easily be that of an older child; figures of the sort had been conventional ever since the latter part of the fourth century. Accurate portrayal of babies seems to have followed almost immediately. The most popular of such figures was a Sleeping Eros of perhaps two years old, sprawled on his back with one arm under his head and the other laid across his chest. The more deserving figure of a chubby little boy hugging a goose, best known from the Capitoline copy, may be identical with a statue by Boethus mentioned by Pliny, though the text as preserved describes it as 'a child of six years strangling a goose', whereas the Capi-toline type looks two or three years younger; the manuscripts, however, appear to be corrupt, reading variantly *sex annis* or *sex anno*, perhaps instead of *amplexando*, which would give the requisite meaning, 'a child strangling a goose by hugging'. The Capitoline type is infinitely superior to the other statues of children playing with toys or pets—usually geese or smaller birds, less often puppies because the average Greek dog was a beast unfit for the nursery. These are votive figures, nearly always of boys; they occur in Greece and other countries (in Cyprus by the hundred) dedicated to a number of deities linked only by concern with childbirth, and must therefore be parental offerings. The series demonstrably (at Sidon) begins in the fifth century but for the most part dates from the third century; since it includes no figure more infantile than the Telephus of Pergamon, the naturalistic Capitoline type seems to have been an innovation of com-paratively late date. One at least of the two sculptors named Boethus lived, apparently, in the middle and latter half of the second century. His signature, 'Boethus, son of Atheneius of Calchedon', appears on a bronze herm with an archaic head, a meretricious decorative piece found in the ship wrecked off Mahdia in the first century B.C. From the same wreck came quite a good bronze statue of a winged teenage boy, tentatively identified as a personification of *Agon* (Contest), because he is placing a victor's wreath on his head with his right hand, while his left elbow could have rested on the herm. Boethus, if we accept that conjunction, was an academic sculptor, an eclectic imitator of the fourth-century masters. But Pausanias noticed in the Heraeum at Olympia a gilt-bronze statue of a seated boy, which he (or a copyist of his text) ascribes to Boethus of Carthage. Since the adjectival forms of Calchedon and Carthage differ in Greek by only one letter—*Kalchedonios* and *Karchedonios*—a textual emendation met with applause until the discovery of an inscription referring to work at Ephesus by Boethus, son of Apollodorus, of Carthage. If the manuscripts of Pausanias preserve the correct reading, the Capitoline type should be associated with him rather than with the more renowned Calchedonian.

The supreme figure of a child, though well advanced towards his teens, is the bronze boy-jockey in the National Museum at Athens, recovered from the ship in which also lay the 'Zeus of Artemisium'. The face, distorted with effort, the wind-ruffled hair and immature arms, put it later than the Kingdom of Pergamon, either shortly before 100 or preferably in the first century B.C.

A pleasant marble statue of a boy, whose swollen ears identify him as a boxer (Pl. 70a), was an adaptation of a figure that can be ascribed to Lysippus or one of his followers; the chlamys is treated as in members of the Daochus group to which the Agias belonged. Another copy of the body exists, but none of the head; we may suppose, however, that the later sculptor increased the mobility of the features, while he certainly hardened the outlines to obtain a severity like that of Pheidias. In so doing he conformed with the archaizing tendency of his own time. Actually the date cannot be determined within narrow limits; there is nothing to show that it is earlier than the first century, though the provenance may suggest otherwise. This is one of a number of archaizing statues found at Tralles (the modern Aydin). From it the Istanbul Museum acquired an Athena head in the manner of Pheidias, an Apollo of semi-Praxitelean composition but with hard-outlined features, and a caryatid which must have originated as an archaistic concept (and is known from a copy in Algeria); a head recognized as akin to the Venus of Milo went to Vienna, but other sculptures with an intentionally old-fashioned flavour were destroyed in the Great Fire of Smyrna. Whether, like the Berlin archaistic statuette from Pergamon, the bulk of the Tralles collection could be contemporary with the Altar is at present questionable but it certainly need not be much later because some Greek carved typical mock-archaic drapery at Carthage, which was destroyed in 146; it occurs on the sarcophagus of a priestess who is enfolded by the wings of a vulture-goddess.

On the extinction of its dynasty, Pergamon ceased to attract artists; their new centre became the island of Delos, where the Romans opened a free port in 166. It had long been important as a shrine of Apollo, and the temple lent money at the low rate of ten per cent, a help to business. Here the Pergamene kings had dedicated statues of themselves and of Gauls, so that the style of Delos was at first identical with that of Pergamon. The city that suddenly arose on this barren island had an aristocracy of business-men, drawn from all parts of the Mediterranean world. Such citizens required the services of sculptors to supply portrait statues for erection in public or private places, genre and decorative pieces for their spacious houses, images of deities for the guildhalls and shrines. Sculptors came from Samos, Miletus, Ephesus, Heraclea, Athens, Calchedon, Cyrene, Cilicia, and other regions.

But Mithradates' thorough sack of Delos in 88, followed by a pirates' raid in 69, ended the prosperity of the place; traffic was diverted to Rhodes and the new Italian ports, leaving on Delos a small village, which gradually decayed until the site relapsed into desolation. Excavators have uncovered houses and public buildings with many sculptural contents, but the few bronzes had already been sought out and melted down. The best pieces have been removed to Athens, but the greater part of the material can only be studied on the island. With its help approximate dates can be ascribed to similar works elsewhere, for the vast majority belongs to the period of highest prosperity, the half-century before 88 B.C.

Thus the Aphrodite from Melos, better known by its latinized title, the Venus of Milo, stands in a peculiarly contorted attitude which relates it to one of the statues at Delos, an Isis of 128–127, while the cold serenity of the head is akin to the archaizing copy from Delos of the 'Small Herculaneum Woman' (Pl. 56a). The Venus is indeed based upon a prototype of the Praxitelean age, but the face has been cut with a fifth-century severity, while the body, on the other hand, has been placed in a later and more complex attitude. The rapture with which this statue has been laden sounds absurdly exaggerated to students of ancient sculpture. It is, of course, a clever piece of work and it is possible to read into it a sentimental morality; its popularity may be further due to the supple and twisted pose. In both the Cnidian and the Melian Aphrodite, the hips and shoulders are very far from parallel, while the median line bends so that the direction of the body changes three times, from right to left, from left to right, and finally the legs lean from right to left. But in the later statue the twists are more violent; from almost any viewpoint, therefore, it shows to equal advantage. The excuse for the many contortions lies in a necessity to support the drapery on the hips, a feat which requires an awkward and strained position in the wearer, for it was not upheld by either hand. The position of the arms and the occupations of the hands are a matter for conjecture: very probably the right arm was pressed close to the breast and bent at the elbow over to the left, while the left upper arm cannot have been raised above the shoulder line. A hand holding an apple, found with the statue, may belong to the Venus. The Aphrodite of Capua appears to have been copied from the same fourth-century prototype, and in this case the arms were restored in 1820; the right arm is held across the body while the left is raised to shoulder level. Probably the Venus of Milo was in much the same attitude.

In complexity of pose the statue resembles other works from the Aegean islands, especially the Isis at Delos, which is inscribed with a date corresponding to 128–127 B.C. No stylistic objection, therefore, exists to the theory that it originally stood upon a base inscribed with lettering of about 100 B.C., and discovered in the same grotto. The beginning of the inscription is missing, but the sculptor's name may be restored as either Alexander or Hagesander and his place of origin is stated as Antioch on the Maeander, a small town in Asia Minor. On the other hand, a drawing made soon after the discovery attaches the base to a herm of which no other record is preserved; this does not necessarily mean that the two were connected. The Venus fits the base as well as is usual for an antique work—an accurate join was not required since the block out of which the feet were cut was fixed in position with lead.

Another statue from Melos, the colossal half-draped Poseidon in Athens, must be a product of the same school as the Venus; the impressive embodiment of majesty was attained by skill of a similar nature. This, again, is a new edition of a long-established type. A strange instance of adaptation can be seen in a perfectly competent figure of a youth from Eretria, not earlier than the Delos period; it combines the draped body of one fourth-century type with the athlete's head of another, although the statue was probably sepulchral, and it might therefore be expected to bear a portrait head.

The relief of the Apotheosis of Homer (Pl. 71a) can be roughly dated about 130 by the lettering of its inscriptions. The artist gives his name as Archelaus of Priene, but may have left his native Asia Minor. In the upper rows the action takes place on Olympus, where Zeus sits on the crest of the mountain attended by his eagle. Below, Homer is received by the nine Muses (mostly of the 'Philiscus' group) and by Apollo (dressed according to the manner of musicians in the long Ionic chiton and identified by his lyre and the omphalus at his side). In the lowest band, mortals are shown sacrificing to the new god, on either side of whose statue rest personifications of his two creations, the *Iliad* and the *Odyssey*; two figures, labelled Time and *Oikoumene* (The Civilized World), place a crown upon his head. The heads of these two seem more like portraits than ideal types, and since the male head wears a diadem, they have been thought to represent a king and queen. Of the identifications proposed with the aid of coin-portraits— with Ptolemy II (284–247), Ptolemy IV (221–203), and Alexander Bala (152–144)—none can be taken as certain. Ptolemy II is most suitable on historical grounds, for he was the greatest of Hellenistic patrons of literature and in particular financed the Homeric studies of Alexandrian scholars, while Ptolemy IV is known to have dedicated a temple to Homer, but his features have least resemblance to those of the head on the relief; the identification of Alexander Bala has the single merit that his date undoubtedly comes near that of the relief. If Ptolemy II be the monarch represented as Time, then the sculptor must have been instructed to copy his features (familiar from the coins still in circulation), as a tribute to the patronage which gave to the world the first critical text of Homer. The relief was discovered at the point where the Appian Way leaves the Campagna, but may, of course, have been removed from Alexandria or elsewhere. Incidentally a fragment with similar drapery, comprising the lower half of a statue, has been found at Canopus. The alternation of deep troughs of shadow and flat bands of highlight instances the preoccupation with pictorial effects characteristic of late Hellenistic work, and the adaptation to this simple scheme of the complex design of the 'Philiscus' drapery (even more elaborate than that of the Gigantomachy) points to the influence of archaic work, now becoming still more prominent.

Pictorial influence again declares its presence in a large relief at Eleusis; the donor, Lacrateides, held a high civic office in 97 and must then have been an elderly man, so that the date is fixed within a narrow margin. The relief contains a group of the Eleusinian deities, as well as a portrait of Lacrateides; sitting and standing figures are superimposed. The drapery has an almost flat surface cut by thin lines of shadow, a method of treatment found in other sculptures on the site, including the pair of Caryatid busts dedicated by a Roman, Appius Pulcher, who died in 48. The heads of these colossal works, which presumably belong to the Attic school, are dull imitations of the later fifth-century manner, which inspired, too, the design of the drapery, though not its method of execution.

The excavations of Delos have thrown light upon another celebrated statue in the Louvre (Pl. 70c), the 'Borghese Warrior', signed by Agasias, son of Dositheus of Ephesus. Another Agasias, the son of Menophilus, like-wise an Ephesian, whose signature was attached to thirteen portrait statues at Delos towards the years 100–90, was probably a cousin, for Greek custom presumes the existence of a third Agasias as the paternal grandfather of both sculptors. The head is of Lysippic character (most youthful heads at Delos are in the style of Polycleitus or Lysippus), and the whole may well be derived from an original of the school of Lysippus, but the sculptor has certainly introduced his own variations into the pose and treatment of details. The outstanding muscles that cover the body do not coalesce into great waves as in the figures on the Gigantomachy of Pergamon; each is carved distinct, in a hard dry manner which reflects more credit on the sculptor's knowledge than on his taste. The figure has been carefully posed to display all the muscles to the greatest advantage, like the models of skinless men used for teaching surface anatomy. The subject has been interpreted as a hero parrying the attack of a mounted opponent by means of the shield worn on the left arm, while the right arm (now restored) drew back a spear or sword; another suggestion is that the figure represents a competitor in a relay race for men in armour, holding the lighted torch which was to be passed from one member of the team to another.

A gilt-bronze colossus in the Conservatori may portray Mithradates the Great (121–63) as Heracles. The prototype, known from other copies, was probably by Lysippus, but here the brutal countenance and receding fore-head recall to some extent the head on the coins of Mithradates. His features are dubiously recognizable also in a group from Pergamon; during Mithradates' residence at Pergamon from 88 to 85 the subject of Heracles delivering Prometheus might easily have been chosen as an allegory of his deliverance of Asia from Roman tyranny, and coins depict him under the guise of Heracles. On the other hand it seems strange that the Romans should have allowed a piece of such offensive symbolism to be preserved after they regained control. Possibly the features are those of Attalus II or III, and the monument would then commemorate the preserva-tion of the Pergamene kingdom from its enemies. A clumsy piece of in-competent sculpture, this group consisted of upright figures of Heracles, shooting at the vulture, and of Prometheus, crucified on the rock of Mount Caucasus, personified by a recumbent figure below; the landscape back-ground probably resembled that on the Apotheosis of Homer.

A decline in technical ability is conspicuous in the latest of all Greek friezes; it comes from the temple of Hecate at Lagina, in western Asia Minor, and is likely to date from after rather than before 100. The figures stand in affected postures and are poorly grouped; folds in the drapery were intended to compose linear patterns but rarely form anything better than a series of unrelated strokes. Even at Delos the standard of carving fell; many portraits are hack work, while a sculptor of little ability produced the largest group found there, an utterly vulgar gift by a merchant of Beirut to the assembly-hall of the Poseidoniasts, a guild of Syrian businessmen. It can be dated between 110 and 88. Aphrodite stands naked, holding up a slipper to repel the embraces of an ithyphallic Pan, whose face is as bestial as his goat's legs; a childish Eros lies on her shoulder and fends him off by pushing one of the horns that grow out of the semi-human forehead.

The smooth treatment of Aphrodite's flesh in the Poseidoniasts' group is enhanced by a high polish, such as Praxiteles had introduced; this enabled the carving of her features to be skimped—a blur concealed inadequacies. This use of polish to save labour had long since become habitual at Alexandria; it is seen especially in the statuettes of Aphrodite that seem to have been common there in matrimonial bedrooms (perhaps for magical purposes), but some faces of either sex are as vaguely shaped as if they were modelled in melting snow or butter. The Delos group is almost the only instance in Greece of a blurred surface, while even a high polish is a rarity (though erosion may often have removed it). Its occurrence in some Aphrodites of merit found in Libya was presumably due to Alexandrian influence. The best, in the Terme, was uncovered by floods on the site of Cyrene; the head is missing. Here again a type of the fourth century has been brought up to date. The right shoulder is lowered and the right hip pushed out, rather as in the Venus of Milo, but the pose is not contorted in the like manner because the drapery is independent of the body; it hangs by the side of the figure on a dolphin's tail—the dolphin suggesting the birth of the goddess from the sea.

The portraits at Delos by no means form a homogeneous group. Some have in style an obvious relationship with Pergamene heads, gaining their effect by lumpy modelling, a method illustrated in the only remaining bronzes, probably of a ruler (Pl. 71b). Others mark a distinct advance on the Pergamene ideals, dispensing with the emotional expression and with its accompanying bulging forehead and deep-set eyes; these substitute line-drawing for chiaroscuro, by cutting thin black lines on a white face, which can be compared with the system of black lines on a white garment by which the Attic sculptors of the first century B.C. carved their drapery. This black-on-white style presumably developed before 100, from its prominence at Delos; but its progress continued after the fall of Delos, apparently at Athens. It is employed in a head of Pompey (106–48), which obviously represents him towards the close of his life. One of several examples from

Attica is on the relief of a family group in Berlin. An undeviating adherence to the truth, however ugly, marks the portrait sculpture of this school; a sketchy rendering of the hair occurs frequently, yet not invariably—it is for example carefully executed in the head of Pompey.

The statues with which this class of head is associated are of many types. Some stand in heroic nudity; and of these Delos has yielded the most remarkable, a life-size figure of a Roman (Pl. 71c). Some, who stand, or ride on horseback, wear the military cuirass; examples of both varieties are found in Delos, one of the former being of a Roman, Billienus. Others sit or stand, wearing civilian dress. The bodies are always conventionally modelled, serving only to support the head; interest in the male body had perished. Portraits of women are invariably draped.

Half-length figures of women have been found at Thera and at Magnesia—in the latter case on a stela with an inscription of the early first century. The use of busts was not yet fashionable, but circumstances were advancing in that direction. The momentous step was finally taken in Italy, for the Romans were becoming the chief patrons of art. The Etruscans, whose art had now reached its last stage of decay, had clung to full-length portraits, but the Romans required heads alone, and the limitation of portraits to the bust quickly became regular throughout the Greco-Roman world, although occasional full-length statues occur at all periods and in all places.

The Growth of Sculpture in Rome

The art of early Rome is known only from incidental references by much later authors; few monuments can be older than the first century B.C. The city in its infancy was politically and culturally subject to Etruria and an artistic subjection may safely be presumed. At the archaic period, Etruscan art was permeated by Greek influence; hence there is no reason to doubt the legend that the Romans of that time employed two Greek sculptors, Damophilus and Gorgasus, to decorate the temple of Ceres in the Circus Maximus. Such occasional visitors from the Greek cities of Italy could not outweigh the constant influence exerted by Rome's Etruscan neighbours, and the majority of the older statues and architectural sculptures of the city must have been executed by artists trained in the Etruscan style. The Forum, which seems to have contained the pick of these works, was destroyed by fire in 210 B.C., which accounts for the scarcity of such remains at the present day.

In the second century Etruscan sculpture reached its height; a Pergamene element manifests itself in the design and the details, although the

Etruscans clung to the subjects which suited their mentality and customs. The typical products of their Hellenistic period are the sarcophagi and their smaller editions, the crematory urns, which bear as a rule reliefs on the lower half while a reclining figure on the lid represents the deceased holding a wine-cup. No example of either class is known from Rome. There survives one good portrait statue, the bronze '*Arringatore*' (Orator) found near the Etruscan city of Clusium (Chiusi); it is inscribed in the Etruscan alphabet with the name of a Roman, Aulus Metellus, but might be Greek work. The drapery is treated as in a marble statue of the merchant Dioscurides which stands headless in his own house at Delos, on a base dated by its inscription to the year 138–7.

Nothing comparable has been found in Rome, although there exist records of early statues—such as those of Manlius, Camillus, the mother of the Gracchi, an Augur, and the Vestal Virgins—which may have followed Greek models as closely. It is at least certain that the influence of the Delian school, which is so evident in that statue, extended to Rome, for two Athenians, Dionysius and Timarchides, whose signatures remain upon the nude portrait at Delos of a Roman official, Gaius Ofellius, supplied cult-statues for temples built in Rome soon after 150. From this time onwards, especially after the annexation of Greece and Asia Minor in 146 and 133, so many of the wealthier Romans were obliged to visit the Aegean, either in an official capacity or on private business, that a large proportion of the potential patrons of art at Rome must have acquired some first-hand knowledge of Greek sculpture.

A statue of Orpheus, found in Rome, resembles Etruscan work of the worst quality; it may be a trifle earlier than 100. A large and pretentious monument erected by the Fluteplayers' Guild shows that the native sculpture of Rome remained abysmal into the first century; the inscription can be roughly dated about the year 80. The two headless draped statues of men holding flutes are imitations of Greek types. Like the Orpheus and many later Republican sculptures, they are carved in *peperino*, a volcanic stone with the texture of coke, but the surface was covered with stucco, which may conceivably have been modelled to produce a less barbarous effect. The craftsmen of Rome should have been skilled in modelling, because wax masks of ancestors (*imagines*) were then worn at funerals; there is no reason to suppose that any of these were portraits from life, but some may have originated as death-masks and been worked up to a lifelike appearance.

The extinction of Etruscan sculpture in the first century, and the absence of any native sculpture worthy of the name of art, forced the more hellenized members of Roman society to employ Greeks. Their ideals of portraiture were slightly different, it may be, but the Italians at Delos had been given what they wanted—perhaps (like Cromwell) only by instructing the artists to be unusually naturalistic—and the Greek sculptors who flocked to Rome in the first century found no difficulty in giving satisfaction. They had a great advantage over native Italian sculptors in that they habitually carved in marble and thus attained cleaner, finer modelling than could be effected in the coarse stones, discoloured alabaster or terracotta in which the Etruscans and Romans were accustomed to work. The presence of a certain number of portraits made by Greeks served to leaven the mass of Roman portraiture, raising its level far above that reached by the Etruscans.

To what extent the portraitists of the late Republic were themselves of Greek origin cannot be decided, but a large proportion had received a training in Greek methods. A few works, mostly later than the lost original of the Pompey, can only be described as purely Greek, whereas others seem to display Greek and native Italian elements mingled in varying degrees, on average with a preponderance of Greek. No Italian touches are apparent in the Dresden head (Pl. 72a), which should be compared with Delian work and with a standing figure of the Attic family-group in Berlin. A head from the purely Latin town of Praeneste (Pl. 72b) affords the clearest signs that its sculptor retained Etruscan rather than Greek proclivities, but such examples are rarer than those of obviously foreign influence and technique. Few Republican heads of any merit could be *unhesitatingly* ascribed to Italian workmen, though in actual fact Italians may well have carved at least fifty per cent of them.

The prominent Greek sculptors of Rome commanded a high price for their work but seldom signed their names, with the result that personalities now appear but faintly. Most celebrated of these artists was Pasiteles, whose energies were chiefly given to metal-work; in his efforts in marble he followed the evil custom of preparing clay models to be reproduced by other men's hands. To a large extent his rivals and pupils adapted or imitated older sculptures; their work in this line has already been discussed (page 57). The athlete signed by Stephanus, pupil of Pasiteles, suggests that to this school should be assigned such statues as the Resting Hermes, and the boy removing a thorn from his foot (Pl. 72c). The latter, usually known as the *Spinario*, combines an old type of head with a Lysippic type of body which bore in the original a less pretty head, such as that seen on a copy in the British Museum. A replica of the eventual head forms part of a standing figure in Leningrad, copied apparently from a statue of the middle of the fifth century. The hair of the *Spinario*, whose head is bent forward so sharply, should of course fall over the face instead of maintaining its original position. The Resting Hermes, discovered at Herculaneum, is frequently described as copied from an original of the Lysippic school, if not itself the original, but the face has no Lysippic character and seems definitely later. Apart from this statue and a marble variant at Merida, the type has only been observed in the minor arts, appearing in bronze statuettes and on a gem signed by Dioscurides, who is known to have carved Augustus' signet. The Naples statue differs from the rest in that the torso leans forward, thus producing an impression of alertness which greatly improves the effect.

A preoccupation with prettiness marks the sculpture of the first century; its growth may be traced through the severer archaistic work of the latter part of the previous century, and it now reaches its height, with an exaggerated care for daintiness, elegance and grace. But there remains a certain dignity in bronzes from Herculaneum, such as the bearded head of Dionysus or the five dancing girls. These sculptures may be either new creations or free copies from works of about 470–450. Some bronzes may actually have been cast from earlier originals; the necessary touching-up would usually betray the copyist but he might be knowledgeable enough to avoid incongruity. A sculptor of some standing would presumably be needed; the name of one such, Menodotus of Tyre, was inscribed (together with his obscure Rhodian collaborator's) on a tablet inside the 'Piombino Apollo', which may possibly be a cast from a late archaic original. A few marble statues, such as the Artemis from Pompeii, seem true to lost archaic originals except for a disgusting cheapening of spirit, whereas the 'Chigi' Athena at Dresden is a pastiche in pseudo-archaic manner with undisguisedly late scenes on the embroidered robe.

The conjunction of prettiness and archaistic mannerisms has a long pedigree, springing from religious conservatism and the attempt to transform the formal incompetence demanded by conservatism into pleasantly quaint decoration. The movement began, so far as can be seen, in the large painted vases that were given as prizes in the Panathenaic Games; athletic festivals were all held in honour of some deity, who at Athens was naturally Athena, and a figure of the goddess fills one side of the vase, the other bearing a scene of wrestling or whatever else the event might be for which the prize was awarded. Throughout the fifth and fourth centuries the painting continues in the awkward process, black on a red ground, that was generally abandoned in the sixth century, and mannerisms appear; herein lies the beginning of an archaistic fashion. One of the most typical mannerisms was the swallow-tail end to floating drapery, and one of the favourite themes was the relief bearing figures almost exactly alike, placed flatly in rows—an idea so successful that it held its ground for five hundred years without any fresh display of originality, other than the addition of further types to the common stock.

A relief in the Louvre (Pl. 73a), of Dionysus leading a procession of the Seasons, was copied from an original of approximately the middle of the second century, when archaistic carvings still retained the same conventions as in the fourth century. The bodies are elongated, the heads unnaturally small; fingers too are elongated and bend in affected gestures. But most of the drapery is allowed a fluidity unknown in the archaic period, while even the definitely archaistic patterns formed by the edges of the garments are roundly modelled instead of lying flat on several planes. In a later variety of archaism (Pl. 73b) the mannerisms become less conspicuous while the drapery is composed throughout in accordance with archaic precedents; the cold precision of the carving emphasizes the antiquated character of the whole. The example illustrated is a fragment from a long procession of deities; Poseidon, identified by the little dolphin he carries, is followed by a goddess and by Ares, who wears a fringed 'anatomical' cuirass (moulded to conform with the human figure) and 'anatomical' greaves on his shins; his helmet is suspended on the strap in his right hand, the left hand grasps a spear behind the shield (worn strapped, as usual, above the elbow). The faces approximate to the convention of the mid-fifth century; prototypes of the figures of Poseidon and the goddess are found in the sixth century, but the Ares is of fourth-century style, apart from the drapery with its swallow-tail end. The drapery and figures form lifeless but agreeable patterns; the intention was to please, not to convey an impression of reality, and with the exception of the Ares the figures do not impress one as genuine personages. Perhaps for that reason most carvings of this class, which is termed Neo-Attic, contain few, if any, figures of archaic derivation; types that originated not earlier than Pheidias were preferred, and only rarely are they tricked out, like the Ares, with markedly archaistic details.

Neo-Attic decoration was commonly applied to large marble vases as well as to rectangular or curved slabs. It received the name because several works are signed by Athenians; in actual fact Athens does seem to have been the centre of production, for an unfinished vase has been found there, and a ship, wrecked near Mahdia on its way from Athens, contained several completed vases. The craftsmen worked almost exclusively for export, above all to Italy, where demand persisted from shortly after 100 B.C. far into the first century A.D. The origin of the style can be traced to the fourth century; a pair of dancing youths, placed as handles to the water-pot carved on an Attic gravestone, are slimmer and even more elegant than the many Neo-Attic satyrs, and executed with equally cold precision. Some old types were reproduced unchanged for the Roman market, but the majority required adaptation; the total repertory amounted to over fifty types, some of which are repeated scores of times. There exist, for instance, several replicas of separate groups adapted from the shield of Athena 'Parthenos', as well as a complete set of them, which formed part of the cargo of a ship that was burnt in Piraeus harbour. But the most popular types were borrowings not from Pheidias himself but from his successors, whose thin floating drapery was more readily converted into chilly decoration. The Attic Maenads (Pl. 41a) were special favourites. Sections of the Nike Temple Parapet were imitated rather than copied, also necessarily at Athens; the Neo-Attic versions include the Victory fastening her sandal (Pl. 40a), but the freshness of the original drapery is transformed into graceful artificiality. Where a Neo-Attic craftsman modified a pose, the result was a figure that strikes a self-conscious attitude; when he invented a composition of his own he merely juxtaposed unrelated figures at regular intervals, forming a harmonious but meaningless parade. Just as a ritual performed after belief has been lost can still be beautiful, so Neo-Attic carvings can be very attractive pieces of decoration. Keats's 'Ode to a Grecian Urn' did one of them a great deal more than justice, but the vision he derived from it, of a Golden Age of simplicity, differed from a Roman's only through being over-credulous.

While Neo-Attic craftsmen could work better in Greece, many able sculptors necessarily went to Italy for employment, chiefly as portraitists. At Rome, in particular, this influx caused a rapid advance in sculpture in the last generation of the Republic, when artisans of Italian birth learnt to avail themselves of Greek methods. Of ideal work in the round there exists nothing of genuine merit. In portraiture a definite change can be noted; thus in the busts of a married couple in the Vatican (Pl. 74a), a flat appearance, common in the previous generation, has been superseded by a more colourful treatment, in which shadow plays an important part. Like most other examples of the style, which lasted into the beginning of the Christian era, the Vatican busts are probably Augustan rather than Republican in date; in any case they should be somewhat later than the assassination of Julius Caesar in 44. Some portraits of him in the earlier style may be originals executed in his own lifetime or else copies therefrom; the portraits in the later style are apt to be posthumous creations to satisfy a demand that persisted long after Augustus had secured his deification. The lifetime of Caesar seems to have been the crucial period in the development of Roman reliefs. Coins of the Republic employ a very shallow relief, so that their types resemble outline drawings, but this style was rarely adopted for sculpture, the only instance worth quoting being the large slab at Munich showing a trumpeter and soldiers or gladiators. The great majority of republican reliefs have a considerable depth, and contain squat, stiff figures, childishly arranged; this style survived in many of the western provinces, even under the empire, but was now superseded at Rome. The oldest large set of reliefs in the improved manner obviously belonged to a single monument; the scenes, 72 cm. high, are divided at regular intervals by pilasters, from the positions of which it can be assumed that all four sides of an oblong base are extant, one in the Louvre, the others at Munich. The wedding of Poseidon and Amphitrite, attended by a rollicking procession of lesser marine deities (Pl. 74b), fills all the Munich slabs, which are purely Greek in concept, whereas the side in the Louvre (Pl. 75a) illustrates the Roman theme of a quinquennial census and the sacrifice of purification (*lustrum*) that followed it. The monument, therefore, was erected by a Censor, probably one who held office in the year 70; the reliefs may have been carved about 65. The design, if not the actual carving, must be due to a sculptor trained by a Greek of the eastern Aegean, though he himself may have been Italian. In the Louvre section he reproduces pompous types of figures such as occur on late Hellenistic gravestones or on the Lagina frieze, while provincialism is evident from the proportions of the figures and the rather clumsy execution, though the other sides have a more sophisticated, competent air; here in fact the artist was on sure ground, but when confronted with the necessity to improvise a representation of Roman official life his training did not help him, and he could only adapt the strutting heroes of Greek sentimentality to the recent event. The *Suovetaurilia*, or sacrifice of a pig, sheep and bull on behalf of the state, formed henceforth one of the favourite subjects of Roman art. The relief lacks the sure touch of the imperial artist, his confidence to depict a Roman scene in a Roman manner; as in so much work of its century, the artist had been told what he must represent and felt that he needed only to consider which of the recognized styles to imitate, but there was as yet no tradition for the representation of Roman official life. His task was easy in the case of the Munich slabs, for the rout of sea monsters offered no novelties to a Hellenistic artist, though seldom indeed does the writhing troop call forth such exuberance; we know of nothing so imaginative since the Gigantomachy of Pergamon, by which he may have been influenced. If so, the influence did not affect his details; faces, bodies and drapery alike are dully conventional. The child Eros, perched on the tail of a hippocamp, is also of a conventional type, afterwards reiterated on innumerable sarcophagi; it owes little to such figures as the 'Sleeping Eros' or the 'Boy with the Goose'.

The style of the Gigantomachy had endured only for a short time at Pergamon and there is not the slightest indication of persistence elsewhere; hence its recrudescence late in the first century, apparent in several pretentious sculptures in Italy, has been variously explained as due to copying from Pergamon originals or to imitative new creation, while some experts even believe the masterpiece among these works, the Laocoon, to be an original of the Pergamene age. There can, however, be no denying that a demand for unusually expensive copies would imply that Pergamene art pleased Roman taste, so that commercially-minded sculptors would be tempted to revive the style in their own ambitious products, which in this period would necessarily be destined for Romans, Greek patronage being generally limited to small commissions. The success immediately obtainable with a pseudo-Pergamene original may have measured up to the rapture expressed by Pliny in 79 A.D.:

> The Laocoon, placed in the house of the emperor Titus, should be rated above all works of art, whether in painting or sculpture. The brilliant Rhodian artists, Hagesander, Polydorus and Athenodorus, collaborated in an agreed design, carving out of one block of stone the man and his children and the intricate coils of the snakes.

(The group was in reality composed of seven or eight different blocks, but the joins had been carefully concealed and only became apparent in recent times.)

The three sculptors are also named in an inscription found in the so-called 'Grotto of Tiberius' at Sperlonga; Agesander (Hagesander) was the son of Paeonius, Athenodorus the son of Agesander, Polydorus the son of another Polydorus. The inscription is in signature form but might be a replacement; the lettering would be appropriate to Tiberius' time. Sculptors of these names are recorded in Rhodian inscriptions of both the second and the first century but never as collaborators, so that the trio cannot be distinguished with certainty from their relatives. Possibly, however, it was the same Athenodorus, son of Agesander, who in 42 signed a portrait group and in 24–23 held the distinguished office of priest of Athena, in which he was succeeded by a different Agesander, the son of Agesander, who might have been the father of this Athenodorus and the senior partner of the trio. On this hypothesis, his two sons were already men of substance in 24–22, and his own activity was about to cease, if indeed he was still alive. The Laocoon group would not, then, be earlier than (say) 60 and not appreciably later than 22, at which time the trio might have carved it in order to profit from the notoriety Virgil had just conferred on the subject (*Aeneid* ii); till then the myth of the killing of Laocoon and his two sons by constrictor snakes had attracted little attention, in spite of descriptions by Greek poets. The Rhodians' work at Sperlonga may likewise have illustrated an epic, for among the five thousand fragments of sculpture excavated in 1957 are remains of several large groups, two of which seem to be in the style of the Laocoon and to treat subjects from the *Odyssey*. One may have represented the blinding of Polyphemus, the other the seizure of Odysseus' shipmates by Scylla, whose lower limbs writhe in snake-like form; pieces of human figures from both groups are likewise reminiscent of the Laocoon, but judgement must be suspended till more pieces have been joined together. Meanwhile the general question may be raised of whether sculptures of such complexity would have been carved at a distance from their eventual place of exhibition, which in every case was in Italy. The block of Italian marble behind Laocoon (in the representation of an altar) is quite as likely to be original as a later insertion.

Scrutiny of the Laocoon group reveals defects, some of which are hardly compatible with the suggestion of Pergamene date. The raggedly pyramidal composition was ill-balanced (though not so lop-sided as it appears in photographs taken before 1961, when the wrongly restored right arms were removed from all three figures and the father regained his original right arm, bent inwards to his neck). The muscles of the father's body, strained to the utmost, are treated in a perfunctory and unconvincing manner compared with the broad bands of muscle on the Pergamene giants or the anatomically accurate bulges of the 'Borghese Warrior'. The sculptors were not concerned with anatomical accuracy; the lines of the father's ribs are impossible, while one of the sons has three joints of the thumb. The snakes are absurd—too thin to crush a human body, too long to be venomous—and one is biting like a dog. The body of the younger boy is sleekly elegant, his elder brother (Pl. 73c) is slightly built with even less muscular development than was usual in the fourth century. In all three heads the envelope of flesh is as thin as in the Second Pergamene Dedication, which was imitated slavishly; the foreheads are wrinkled in its manner, forming an inverted V on either side above the nose, regardless of the difference in age between father and sons. The drapery is unlike any in Pergamene work but comparable to Augustan.

The huge 'Belvedere' torso in the Vatican is signed by an Athenian, Apollonius, son of Nestor, in first-century lettering, but his rendering of the extremely powerful physique conforms with the style of the Gigantomachy, so that the statue might be a copy from a Pergamene original. But if the subject has been rightly identified as Polyphemus seated on a rock looking out to sea, it accords with the Roman, rather than Greek, liking for illustrations to the classics. Possibly Apollonius' figure is an adaptation from a Pergamene original of a different subject. The torso is in marble; the bronze statue of a boxer (Pl. 75b) may also be by Apollonius because the letter A is clearly legible on both feet while the eye of faith can discern his complete signature in some blurred markings on the left gauntlet. This statue must, in any event, date from Apollonius' time; it cannot be a copy, though it may have been freely adapted from an earlier figure. The monstrous slabs of muscle and the battered face parody the style of the Gigantomachy.

A bronze bust from Herculaneum (Pl. 76a) likewise ranks as virtually an original, so much does it exaggerate the farouche character of the 'Pseudo-Seneca' type, known from a host of marble heads which seem to be copies from a Pergamene statue. None of the many guesses at the subject of this doubtless imaginary portrait has yet carried conviction, though he must have been a very famous personage.

It may seem strange that sculpture of horrors should flourish contemporaneously with Neo-Attic and other archaistic prettiness. But when, throughout history, art has passed a climax it tends to flounder between opposite extremes. The last century of the Hellenistic Age was one of these barren periods when dexterity took the place of inspiration. Indeed the situation bore some resemblance to that provoked in the eighteenth and nineteenth centuries by a similar reaction against a violently passionate school; the reaction took several forms in each case—the archaistic movement is paralleled by the pre-Raphaelite, the Neo-Attic school by Flaxman, Leighton and Burne-Jones; the comparison cannot be pressed further to cover every manifestation of the two unguided periods. The basic point of resemblance is that style did not come naturally to an artist, he was forced to choose what scholastic formula he would adopt, with a resultant artificiality. Normally, the subject of a first-century sculpture was set by a patron of private means and no permanent official position; his choice rarely gave scope for originality. The novel application of Greek ability to Roman subjects alone promised to relieve the tedium; the brief dictatorship of Caesar, and his munificent patronage, showed what benefits might have ensued if his office of ruler of the world had become legalized as a permanent feature of the Roman constitution. This change was effected by Augustus, through whom classical art took a new lease of life.

XI

Imperial Classicism: Augustus to Nero

(23 B.C.–A.D. 68)

WHEN Augustus founded the Roman empire in 23 B.C. art became the expression of Roman aspirations through a Greek medium. Without imperial Rome Greek art would have continued to die its lingering and inglorious death, in purely eclectic and imitative work. The Greek or Roman birth of individual artists is irrelevant; what is important is the existence of a subject in the glorification of the emperor and his achievements. Naturally the new age inherited the style and technique of preceding ages—inheritance cannot be avoided—but a great change lay in the fact that art now gained the purpose and confidence hitherto conspicuously lacking. Artists from all regions were not slow to seize the opportunity, for state patronage was again forthcoming after a lapse of a century and a half since the last great period, that of the Pergamene kings. But for some reason the sculptors of the empire chose to sink their identities: their names are not recorded in literature, which might be explained on the ground that such manual labourers were not thought worthy of a gentleman's attention, but it is clear that their anonymity was deliberate because they rarely signed their works. The Neo-Attic craftsmen (and, in the second century, sculptors of Aphrodisias) occasionally carved their names, perhaps when they intended to export a piece executed in their native place and used the signature as a guarantee of authenticity. Sculptors of other regions scarcely ever signed.

Coinage and portrait-statues had been used by Hellenistic monarchs to advertise their semi-divine status, though to a negligible extent compared with Augustus, whose example was followed by subsequent emperors. But there can have been few precedents for the official reliefs carved in his honour, and the content was almost entirely novel, with a range of subjects that was not appreciably extended, it would seem, before his dynasty, the Julio-Claudian family, became extinct in A.D. 68. This innovation proved exceptionally valuable as an advertising medium because the

Romans and most provincials did not share the Greek respect for the human body and consequently preferred relief sculpture when it illustrated matters of interest; the designers too found it interesting because problems of depth and spacing arose that had not troubled Hellenistic artists, who worked in simpler compositions. Upon all kinds of official sculpture was imposed a new style which must have been chosen to conform with Augustus' own wishes. Basically it involved rejection of Hellenistic practice in favour of an artificial set of conventions, more akin to those prevalent in the time of Pheidias. In portraits of the emperor, fifth-century methods of execution were employed, but the intention differed essentially; the individual features of Augustus were dignified to express the beneficent majesty of empire, whereas portraits of Greek citizen-statesmen, such as Pericles, had stressed the wisdom that made a leader among his peers. Some vague similarity to Augustus himself must have been requisite but his individual traits were not paramount as in Republican portraiture. Similarly, in portraits of members of the upper classes, the actual features of the subject, whether ugly or pleasant, ceased to be mapped and were toned down to resemble the features of Augustus. (In the same way, English ladies dyed their hair auburn or wore wigs of that colour in the days of Queen Elizabeth I, and in Nattier's pictures French court ladies look like their Queen.) This essentially imperialistic tendency had been foreshadowed in the imposition of Alexander's features on the portraits of his successors.

The capital of the empire would inevitably have been the centre of sculpture, and was the more so because portraits of the imperial family were disseminated to the provinces in duplicate bronze casts and marble copies, or even perhaps by piece-moulds; hence any stylistic change at Rome quickly became known to sculptors at whatever distance. Gradually, therefore, a close approach to uniformity came to prevail throughout the empire in work of good quality; the poorer craftsmen retained local peculiarities, but scarcely any of the provincial schools mustered enough vitality to produce ambitious carvings with a distinctive character. Greece was impoverished (and the depopulation so advanced by Pausanias' time may have already been apparent); great technical skill persisted there but was directed almost exclusively to the export of copies from the Old Masters and of Neo-Attic ornamental pieces. Asia Minor was in a rather better state. A set of metopes from Ilium, a little town on the site of Troy, are so purely Hellenistic in inspiration that they have even been ascribed to the temple built by Lysimachus in the third century B.C., but must surely be due to Augustus' reconstruction of it. Sculptors continued to make a living in several parts of Asia Minor, following the Hellenistic tradition, while a school of some originality flourished at Aphrodisias for centuries; its first notable relic, a long relief in honour of a citizen named Zoilus, has proved to be at least a hundred years earlier than the reign of Hadrian (A.D. 117–138) to which it was quite reasonably ascribed on its discovery in 1961. In the western provinces a Hellenistic tradition had been implanted only in Provence, owing to the existence of wholly or partially Greek cities there. It is manifested almost exclusively in reliefs carved in limestone; the finest are four great panels on a cenotaph (probably commemorating Augustus' nephews) at Glanum, near St Rémy. The crowded scene of a battle between Greeks and Amazons (Pl. 76b) anticipates genuinely Roman attempts at representation in depth, the figures in the background being visible only in part behind those in front, and carved in very shallow relief; each is outlined by a sharp-edged groove, according to a persistent local convention rarely adopted elsewhere (though there is an Augustan instance in Rome). This Hellenistic style of Provence is last found in battle-scenes on the Triumphal Arch at Orange, built in Tiberius' reign. But when, in 6 B.C., a king of the Alpine region erected a Roman-style Commemorative Arch at Susa, friezes were carved in a crude simulation of the archaic Greek manner, which had doubtless lingered in the Po valley since the Etruscans introduced it. All the western provinces turned to the cosmopolitan style of Rome during the first century A.D.

The greatest sculptural monument of Augustus' reign, the *Ara Pacis Augustae*, survives in many fragments. This Altar of Augustan Peace was decreed by the Senate in 13 B.C., to celebrate the final pacification of Gaul and Spain, and was dedicated four years later. It stood in the Campus Martius. Some of the fragments were unearthed during the Renaissance and others in more recent times; the excavation of 1903 resulted in the discovery of new pieces and a credible revelation of the general plan, with which a coin of Nero agrees. The altar itself stood in a rectangular enclosure entered on the east and west sides, which were over eleven metres long, whereas the north and south sides were a metre shorter. On the base of the altar ran a frieze, 39 cm. high, showing various types of civil and religious functionaries and the animals they would lead there annually to sacrifice. Garlands were carved on the inward face of the enclosing wall. On its exterior, two bands of more important and, as it happens, better-preserved sculpture were framed by mouldings; the upper part, 1.55 m. high, was devoted on two sides to a frieze of the dedicatory procession but on the others was divided into pairs of long separate scenes, while the lower part consisted throughout of a slightly taller series of panels carved with stylized foliage. Most of the figures in this larger procession are not types but portraits, though greatly idealized; they include the entire imperial family, the main officials of the state, and a number of senators (Pl. 76c), behind whom walks a *camillus* (acolyte), holding a jug and a casket. Here, then, were seen the living re-founders of Rome under its new imperial constitution. Between the two wings of the contemporary procession were shown the original founders and the joint achievements of past and present. These scenes on the intervening sides represent Aeneas making an offering to his Penates, Mars watching Romulus and Remus suckled by the wolf, Roma seated on a pile of weapons beside several allegorical figures (too fragmentary to be interpreted with certainty), and the bounty of the land (Pl. 78a). The central figure in this scene may be either Tellus (the Earth goddess) or a personification of Italy; she is seated with her cornucopia, holding two children who typify the human race. The figures on either side of her may represent Air and Water, or else salt water, riding the dolphin, and fresh water, riding the swan, but swans are particularly associated with the Po. A relief from the Roman colony at Carthage might almost be termed a replica and is possibly contemporary; the central figure would be Africa, if that on the Ara Pacis is Italia, but the older identification of both as Earth remains equally plausible. This concept, of the Earth happy under the peaceful rule of the emperor, recurs in later art, even into the Christian empire (for a disk in Madrid represents Theodosius with his sons enthroned above Earth and her children).

The frieze of the Ara Pacis has often been compared with that of the Parthenon and was perhaps designed as a Roman edition of that great monument of the Attic state. The technique and objectives vary in each relief on the Ara Pacis; it is an agglomeration of academic stiffness and experiment. The heads are based upon the style of the Pheidian school, which also inspired the figure of Aeneas; while the Tellus relief is up to date, like the landscape reliefs so popular among the Romans, whose sentimental interest in country life expresses itself also in their literature. In the procession scenes, a new technique is introduced in the carving of figures with their heads at the same level but at different depths in the block, so that the last row fades into the background. But the faces float along on top of the drapery, under which no signs of a body exist. The members of the procession have no individuality; only the children have any freedom of movement, the rest are carried on in the stream formed by the mingled drapery of them all. This unhappy result could be avoided by increasing the apparent distance between front and rear ranks of figures; thus in an

altar, dated A.D. 2, which represents in quite low relief the sacrifice offered
by *Vicomagistri*, the figures are clearly distinguished by a series of different
planes.

Parallels to many figures of the Ara Pacis have been noted in the form of
statues. The best known is the bronze *camillus* in the Conservatori, of more
classical style than the boy of Pl. 76c, the head indeed resembling that of a
fifth-century woman. Another life-size bronze, found in Rhodes and now in
New York, represents a boy whose features identify him as a member of
the imperial family—probably Augustus' nephew, Lucius, who died young
in A.D. 2; the portrait could be posthumous.

The most remarkable statue of Augustus himself (Pl. 77a) is almost certainly posthumous. It was found in his wife's villa at Prima Porta, outside
Rome; it must once have stood isolated but after damage to the back was
fixed against a wall, apparently on a terrace in the garden. The surface of
the marble has become worn in places, and a few small portions are lost.
If the fingers of the right hand have been correctly restored, the emperor
was represented addressing the army, but they may possibly have held
some object; the left hand certainly grasped something, perhaps a staff or a
lance. The cupid and dolphin, which support the right leg, reminded
spectators of the family's descent from Aeneas, Venus' other son. The
dolphin, no doubt, was painted in its natural sombre colour; the cloak
around Augustus' waist seems to have been dark red, while a bright red
distinguished the tunic that protrudes beneath the cuirass, the fringes of
which retain traces of yellow paint, probably a foundation for gilding. An
actual cuirass of this type, suitable only for ceremonial parades, would have
been bronze, possibly gilt all over except for enamelled decoration. The
sphinx on the shoulder was a personal touch, recalling the emblem on
Augustus' seal; other reliefs on the front, and (at the back) one of a trophy,
allude to the security he enabled the civilized world to enjoy. At the top,
the sky-god Caelus spreads the mantle of the heavenly vault above the
sun-god, who drives his chariot in pursuit of two goddesses identifiable as
Dew and Dawn by the jug and torch they carry. Below, at the sides, a pair
of seated figures may be assumed to personify recently subjugated peoples.
Under them are seen deities of Augustus' special devotion, Apollo and
Diana, appropriately mounted on a griffin and a deer for careering across
the Earth, which is symbolized (in the middle) by a figure bearing the
cornucopia of prosperity and accompanied by two babies; loss of the
original colour on objects near the feet hinders further definition of the
allegory, which cannot have been quite the same as on the Ara Pacis. This
set of peripheral scenes was evidently of less import than the central group,

which must refer to the immensely valuable success obtained against Parthia in 20 B.C., when Tiberius commanded the army on the eastern frontier. The figure in Roman uniform is receiving the Parthian royal standard from a diademed king wearing Oriental trousers, whose right hand grips it (one may suppose) at a symbolic fracture in the staff, on which the eagle finial sits crooked. The Roman representative, who is attended by—presumably—the allegorical watch-dog of the frontier, has been identified as the deified Romulus, or even as Mars, unlikely though it seems that a Parthian king, however divine in the estimation of his own countrymen, would be shown obviously equal in status to any member of the Roman pantheon. But the alternative explanation, that the king is presenting a token of his broken power to a mere general, involves an out-rage to mundane protocol, because none but the Emperor, in his capacity of commander-in-chief, could be portrayed in such circumstances. An impasse can only be evaded by assuming that the statue of Augustus was carved after his death, which occurred in A.D. 14. His successor, Tiberius, could then justifiably appear in person, idealized as the juvenile officer; he had been aged twenty-two at the time. The concept of the statue fits with that supposition; in particular, living emperors were regularly shown booted if wearing a cuirass, while the bare feet should indicate deification. The face, then, was not simply idealized but also made younger than the actual age—seventy-six—at which Augustus died. Alternatively there is a possibility that the statue was a revised copy of an earlier type.

The Augustus from Prima Porta is not merely the earliest but also the most interesting of the imperial cuirass statues which remained in vogue into the Christian empire. Its antecedents can be traced in reliefs back to Attic gravestones of the fourth century but true predecessors are known only at Delos, where a dull statue of a Roman named Billienus is well preserved apart from the loss of the head; its cuirass is not ornamented. The motive of Cupid riding the dolphin occurs beside some statues of Aphrodite, Hellenistic in concept though possibly Roman in execution. The Prima Porta Cupid is but superficially modelled; it, as well as the right arm and left leg of Augustus, may be ancient restorations. The delight in the execution of decoration, and the cold definite lines of the face, neatly cut and free from the soft transitions of previous centuries, indicate the influence of archaic work, which would naturally appeal to the precise mind of Augustus. Such a style of portraiture is obviously official, the expression of a superhuman perfection which does not admit of emotion; it announces to the empire the magnanimity of its semi-divine ruler. There exist many less ornate portraits of Augustus, discovered in all parts of the empire, but the face always expresses the same inhuman calm, so that a collection of them is a wearisome, monotonous sight; a head of the emperor in old age forms a pleasing contrast to the rest. Some of the marbles were, no doubt, carved in the provinces, but copies are likely to have been mass-produced in Rome from the latest official portrait. A bronze head in the British Museum is surely an example of the latter sort; it must have been hacked off a statue in Egypt by invaders from the Sudan, who carried it back as a trophy to their capital, Meroe.

Of Livia, the consort of Augustus, there exist many portraits; the best being a head in Copenhagen (Pl. 78b). The ridge of the nose only has been restored and in other respects the head is in excellent condition, with the original painting of the eyes still visible as well as traces of colour on the hair. The empress seems to have worn a wig, for the stiff elaboration of the hairdressing contrasts with the simpler fashion which she affects a little earlier in her life. Born in 57 B.C., she is represented in this head as she must have appeared towards the beginning of the Christian era; although her face is unlined (by her own artifices or the artist's complaisance), the mouth betrays the approach of old age, and a lack of freshness marks this from her earlier portraits. The precision of the carving, together with the cold serenity of the mask and the absence of all personal touches, places Livia on the same exalted level as Augustus, who may then have been already deified, for she outlived him by fifteen years.

Slightly more human are the portraits of Agrippa, Augustus' trusted minister and friend (63–12 B.C.), a man of energetic personality; but in the bronze head at New York the strong features have more resemblance to Augustus than truth could have admitted; indeed if the head had not been found with an inscription, its identity might not be suspected, for other portraits give Agrippa a beetling brow and sullen eyes set at a sharp angle. This variation should be noted as a warning against the dogmatic denials of identity in which archaeologists frequently indulge; ancient artists claimed greater latitude than moderns, and required few sittings or none from great personages.

In portraits of commoners greater fidelity to nature prevails. On the tombstone of two freedmen (Pl. 79a), the head of the older, Demetrius, is practically Republican in style whereas only the harsh realistic treatment differentiates Philonis' from heads on the Ara Pacis procession. The fact that shoulders are included in the busts indicates a date very early in the Christian era. Both men should, from their names, have been Greeks. Their employer and former owner, Licinius, had held the office of Lictor, as is shown by the fasces carved on the left margin; the metallurgical equipment in the pediment may refer to his magisterial duty of supervising the coinage, while in the right margin we probably see the tools of his own business—a bow-drill, knife and anvil, it would seem. Portraiture of women and children likewise fluctuated or compromised between the styles of the Republic and of contemporary officialdom. A pair of heads in New York, evidently of a mother and her young daughter (Pl. 77b), are slightly under life-size and formed part of a relief, for each is attached at the back to a slab, the rim of which curls forward over the head; the stump that rises from the smooth surface of the girl's hair is a relic of this projecting border. The heads, therefore, come from a family group, probably sepulchral. They are finely modelled, with fair distinction between the texture of flesh and hair. The feathering of the eyebrows, which in the average marble head of this period were left plain, to be marked in paint, abolishes the unnatural sharpness of other early imperial portraits. The bones of the faces are delicate—a feature of portraits of the Augustan Age—and the nose of the elder woman is inclined to be aquiline. The girl's hair is parted down the middle and drooped over either ear, while the mother wears twisted side curls and a tress along the top of the head, in the fashion which was favoured in late Republican days and continued into the reign of Augustus; it may be seen in coin types of Fulvia or Octavia. The head of a young boy in the Barracco Museum further illustrates the Augustan treatment of children.

Equestrian statues, with which the Greeks had rewarded outstanding services ever since the fourth century, were by no means reserved for emperors or even officials during the first century A.D. Two, buried at Herculaneum by the eruption of 79 and now in the Naples Museum, are unusually well preserved. The horses are of Greek type, probably copied from originals of, roughly, Alexander's time. One statue (Pl. 79b)—a much better piece of work than the other—is presumed to represent a local citizen, Marcus Nonius Balbus; it is patched here and there, and the right hand is restored, while the head is a modern copy from a standing statue of him. A dating in the first rather than the second quarter of the century is preferable; uncertainty is the greater because Marcus' son, of the same name, a praetor and proconsul, may have commissioned this simultaneously with other family portraits when the inferior equestrian statue was erected in his own honour. An inscription identifies another statue at Naples (Pl. 80a) as Viciria, his mother and wife of the elder Marcus. This is of a type that had been used for ideal figures, commemorative or otherwise, since the fourth century, but the grim face is unquestionably a portrait; in similar figures in Asia Minor the features too are idealized.

The drapery, none too well executed, supplies one of the few Roman examples of a trick of showing the folds of an under garment through a transparent upper garment; in this respect, and in the pyramidal design of the whole, the statue follows late Hellenistic prototypes (Pl. 69a).

It should be noted that the drapery of Viciria has a comparatively smooth surface, upon which shallow channels have been cut to reproduce the shadow cast in Greek work by projecting folds. These two opposite principles, 'tactical' and 'optical' as they have been called, flourished side by side during the early years of the empire; afterwards the 'optical' method predominated in Italy, while in Greece and the East the older tradition was preserved. The source of the new method is obscure; it may be of Etruscan origin or it may be a Greek experiment towards labour-saving in the carving of the more voluminous Roman garments; in Italy, where clients were less critical than in the East, it was adopted with alacrity. An Attic relief (p. 239) of about 100 B.C. is the first reputable work in which the method is adumbrated; and although as a short cut its use may retreat to a remote age, its full and frank development was reserved for the Italian school, in which, however, the better workmen at first resisted temptation.

Portraits of later emperors are less thoroughly idealized than those of Augustus. A statue of Claudius (Pl. 80b), who was born in 10 B.C., shows him with features so aged that it must be dated late in his reign of A.D. 41–54. It was found at Leptis (more properly Lepcis) in Libya; the eagle and the globe in the hand are restored on the evidence of fragments. Half-draped figures of emperors, either seated or standing, were already common and remained so till late in the century; fully-draped standing poses are also characteristic, whereas heroic nudity is less frequent. Statues of private persons are nearly always fully draped unless they are represented as deities.

The 'Ludovisi Juno' head, over a metre high, resembles posthumous coin-portraits of Claudius' mother, Antonia; on these issues of 41 and 42 she is described as Priestess of the deified Augustus. The enormous size did honour to him as well as to her own deification.

Restoration of the nose limits comparison of a head in Copenhagen (Pl. 80c) with profile coin-portraits, but the identification as Agrippina the Younger can be accepted with little doubt. Since she is represented mourning, the date should be not very long after the death of her husband Claudius in 54, when she became regent of the empire during the minority of Nero, her son. She was beautiful and intelligent but licentious, cruel and ambitious; in 59 Nero procured her assassination as the only means of stopping her interference. More youthful portraits of her, or of her mother,

Agrippina the Elder, are dubiously recognizable; among them is a small head in the translucent green silica termed emerald plasma. The fashion of hairdressing establishes the approximate contemporaneity of other fine portraits, including two heads of girls, a woman's head from Albania, and a statue of a princess as Artemis, discovered at Ostia.

One of the best toga statues, the Fundilius found at Nemi (Pl. 80d), dates from roughly the middle of the first century A.D. The inscription, C. FUNDILIUS DOCTUS APOLLINIS PARASITUS, identifies the man as the leader of some theatrical company who took Apollo as their Protector. The head and upper part of the bust are carved in a separate piece of marble, which fits into the rest of the statue; more usually a head and neck alone form the separate block, so that the junction may be concealed by the edges of the drapery. The arms were also carved in separate pieces and affixed by metal dowels, for the holes into which they fitted can be seen. The plinth is ancient, carved from the same block. Care was taken that the supports at the base should fall naturally into the design; indeed the prop between the feet harmonizes with the drapery as if it were a loose end of the toga. The face is less idealized and the drapery less exquisite than in official art; and the presence of the body is clearly indicated by the arrangement of the folds, which in their vertical fall suggest the form of the left leg, while the right leg and upper part of the body are allowed to show. In the statue of his wife, inscribed FUNDILIA F. C. PATRONA, some glimpses of the body can be caught; the head is manifestly a portrait, although the body belongs to an old type, commonly found in female statues from all parts of the empire; the lifting of the hand to pull a bunch of the palla up over the chest is a slight variation.

The statues of Fundilius and his wife must have been carved by a sculptor from Rome, and exemplify the highest standard of portraiture among the middle classes at the capital. The eruption of Vesuvius in 79 has preserved small-town equivalents, wherein the Republican tradition of unflinching accuracy still prevailed. In the extreme instance of a bronze bust from Pompeii, the hideous face of Caecilius Jucundus is mapped in every detail; a banker, he flourished under Nero, so that the bust can be dated about 60 or 70.

Meanwhile imaginative statues fluctuated between similar realism and feeble prettiness. An example of the latter tendency, the Apollo Belvedere, long held an undeserved reputation, because it was discovered as early as the fifteenth century when it had few competitors; at the present day, comparison with many statues of greater merit makes the encomiums of older critics appear ridiculous. The statue shows, however, some originality and more technical ability. A faulty restoration of the left hand and right forearm is largely responsible for the affectation of the pose. The right hand should be further forward and not so far extended; from a prop, which joined the hand to the hip, hung the fillet and bay leaves, Apollo's attributes as the god of purification. The left hand almost certainly carried a bow. Since the crisp elaborate hair would be more easily executed in metal, it is possible that the original was a bronze, but this copyist was an accomplished virtuoso who might have altered the treatment of the hair according to his own tastes. Supposing the material in the original to have been bronze, the chlamys need not have fallen so stiffly from the left arm; the tree-trunk would have been unnecessary, for the fillet and bay leaves could hang loose from the hand and these attributes would have been sufficient to balance the bow on the opposite side of the figure, and the statue would thereby have been freed from a clumsy accumulation of foreign matter on the right side. The fact that it would be improved in bronze may be taken as evidence that this was the original material; moreover the absence of pubic hairs, so easily engraved on bronze, points to the same conclusion—in marble copies the hairs of the body were sometimes added in paint. No other copy of the body has yet been noted, but a damaged head at Basle appears to reproduce the same original; it is, however, free from the imitation of bronze technique which spoils the 'Belvedere'. The original belonged most likely to the time of Alexander the Great and has been attributed to Leochares, on the ground of a resemblance to the poor copy of a Ganymede by which that sculptor's style may be known. To judge by its attenuated proportions the Belvedere variant originated under one of the early emperors.

A bronze statuette of Dionysus, better known as 'Narcissus', from Pompeii, seems to be a reduced version of a statue, life-size copies of which exist in Florence and Cherchel; the head is superior to the 'Belvedere' (partly because the material is more suitable to unruly hair) and should be compared with the heads of Julio-Claudian aspect on a pair of terracotta medallions.

If, however, the foregoing class of sculptures was predominantly imitative, there remain certain lines in which Roman artists developed ideas of their own, notably in their studies of old age. When the subject occurs in Greek art, as it does from the sixth century onwards, the intention is often comic; it is frankly so in the case of the old woman nursing a wine-pot, and the Greek sense of humour could appreciate other instances which appear merely painful to modern sensibility. But under the empire sculptures of decrepitude are serious essays in an aesthetic problem. There are a few main types—old peasants, fishermen, and market women—from which a large number of variants evolved. Most of the prototypes date perhaps from the period of the Laocoon, with which they have much in common stylistically, while in feeling they may be compared to the pastoral reliefs; the development of both subjects proceeds together.

Perhaps the best of these statues is that of the Old Market Woman at New York (Pl. 81a). The face has been considerably restored, but correctly, on the lines of another copy at Dresden. The face is sunken, the neck skinny and the breasts flabby, while the whole figure is arthritic; only in the legs and feet is there any tempering of the harsh realism. At her left side are some chickens and a basket of fruit, and probably her right arm (now missing) held other produce for sale. The ivy-wreath encircling the handkerchief on her head may point to the celebration of some Bacchic festival. A few traces of colour are still preserved—a bright pink on the border of the himation, and a dark green on the strap of the left sandal. From the gentle, rippling lines of the drapery, the work can be tentatively ascribed to the middle of the first century, when the study of sculptures like the Nike Parapet led to similar results.

A sentimental interest in country life is very marked in Latin literature, and the pastoral reliefs, numerous under the early empire, express the same spirit. Present data make it unlikely that such reliefs existed during the Hellenistic Age; the conventions which governed Greek bas-reliefs for generations prevailed till the first century B.C., when the simple groupings on one or two planes gave way to a pictorial treatment, helped by foreshortening, which represented a greater depth than could be effected previously. A parallel transformation took place in this century in painting, for frescoes too had been confined to a few planes and the mastery of the third dimension was only now acquired.

The Ara Pacis provides the earliest sculptures that can be properly described as landscape; once initiated, the idea spread rapidly and is developed in countless panels of marble, stucco and terracotta, as well as in paintings. The fresco of a garden from Livia's villa at Prima Porta is, of course, datable, and the more elaborate pictures at Pompeii belong to the middle of the first century A.D. The vaulted ceiling and walls of an Augustan house in Rome, unearthed near the Palazzo Farnesina, were covered with stucco reliefs (now in the Terme Museum), whereon some panels contain figures dotted about fantastic landscapes which recall the willow pattern and other chinoiseries of our ancestors, while intervening panels are completely filled by figures on a larger scale; a more archaistic variety of the Neo-Attic style is employed for the latter than for the smaller figures.

A similar type of wall and ceiling occurs at a slightly later date in an underground basilica discovered in Rome near the Porta Maggiore; but here the reliefs have a religious import in harmony with the purpose of the building, which was dedicated to some mystic cult. Closely related in style is a pictorial relief at Munich (Pl. 81*b*) in which the illusion of depth is more adeptly contrived than in the Ara Pacis; it may be of about A.D. 50. A peasant, carrying some of his goods in a basket and a dead hare slung from a stick over his shoulder, is driving a cow to market; on its back lie a couple of sheep, tied upside down by the feet. Behind them is a circular shrine, containing a pillar sacred to Diana, most of which is visible as the wall has broken down. On the right an arched gateway has been built over an old oak-tree; further back a ledge of rock crops out, and upon it stands a shrine of Priapus, whose image appears in the doorway.

The first century was indeed the great age of Roman decoration, the charm of which does not always survive its loss of colour. But in one class of terracotta architectural ornament (imitated in Adam decoration) in which Neo-Attic figure subjects played the main role, there remain plentiful traces of the paint. These plaques, known as 'Campana Reliefs', were produced from about 50 B.C. to A.D. 150 but most abundantly under the first emperors. Mouldings are usually painted yellow or reddish brown, the background blue, tree-trunks and woodwork a reddish brown, tree-tops green and water blue; nude figures were left plain, except for touches on the eyes, lips and hair. It will be realized that the clarity of pictorial reliefs, like the Tellus scene and the Munich pastoral, largely depended upon such colouring.

Reliefs of figure subjects were more truly sculptural, although they too have lost by the fading of paint. The style is long faithful to that of its Neo-Attic originators; a style of elegant affectation, of sleek bodies, and of drapery extended by a perpetual breeze and crinkled into innumerable parallel folds. A Perseus who takes Andromeda's arm, as she steps from her rock, has the air of an exquisite handing a lady from a carriage; Endymion sits dozing on the mountain, with nodding head, while his dog barks at the sky, whence no doubt the goddess was descending; a nymph, dressed in the height of fashion, gives a satyr-child a drink, shaded by a tree that contains a whole menagerie of beasts, birds and reptiles. A fondness for caves with rocky borders, manifest in the Ara Pacis, is carried furthest in two slabs in Vienna, called the 'Grimani' reliefs (after a former owner): in each a cave occupies the centre of the foreground, in one stands a ewe suckling a lamb, from the other a lioness and her cub growl at the spectator. The distance is treated in much the same manner as in the Ara Pacis, though here it is more developed and the date may be as late as about 70; the slabs, which seem to have decorated a curved fountain, are carved in low relief, except for the caves and their occupants, which stand practically in the round. Animals, rare in Greece except as sepulchral symbols, become favourite subjects under the empire, when almost every known species was represented: the Vatican owns the largest collection, but entertaining pieces have been distributed over all Europe, one of the quaintest among them being a hippopotamus in red marble, in the Ny Carlsberg Glyptotek (No. 187). There also exist copies of a group in the round, comparable to the Munich relief; a peasant sits on a rock and holds a rope encircling the neck of his cow.

Characteristic, too, of early Roman decoration are elongated figures of deities, many thoroughly archaistic while in others the archaism is confined to the proportions. A frieze from the theatre at Fiesole, executed in this manner, dates from the reign of Claudius. The column of Jupiter at Mainz, of Nero's reign, bears figures of deities around the shaft, in zones placed one above the other, to conform with the drums of which the column was composed. Here types of Greek origin predominate, but they have been transformed in accordance with the spirit of the first century, in a praiseworthy attempt to conceive new and living forms for Latin deities.

A less important branch of religious decorative art is afforded by the sepulchral altars, very numerous throughout the first hundred and fifty years of the empire, after which they were superseded by sarcophagi. The study of these monuments has been facilitated by the fact that inscriptions frequently give the date of the death, hence their historical value is out of all proportion to their artistic merits. In the majority of Julio-Claudian instances the decoration consists wholly of festoons or similar motives; the altar of greatest sculptural interest, that of Livia's freedman, Amemptus, bears a relief of centaur musicians ridden by Cupids, a subject related to the Hellenistic group of the Capitoline but treated in a Roman manner.

As an instance of the recasting of ancient types for decorative ends, a favourite practice of the early empire, may be quoted the little head of a sphinx (Pl. 81d), which terminated the arm of a marble chair. An imitation of late archaic work, its Roman date becomes obvious with a glance at the eyes, for here the artist's deliberate *gaucherie* did not take him as far as the incompetence of the Primitives; he was faithful to them in the regular ripple of the hair, the sharp-edged plane that includes the forehead and nose, the pronounced eyebrows, the high cheek-bones. The mouth was probably significant, for in archaistic heads the 'archaic smile' is habitually exaggerated.

The appearance at Rome of imitations of Egyptian works can always be explained on either decorative or religious grounds. The only piece of real merit, a head, was found in a temple of Isis, and is thought to represent the goddess rather than a mortal woman; it is a mere translation into marble of an Egyptian granite original, the style being that of native sculpture of the late Ptolemaic age. But in most instances Oriental influence occurs in the minor arts, and went no further than the employment of an exotic motive for the sake of quaintness, just as a Chinese scene may be painted on English pottery. Thus terracotta plaques often bear designs like those on the base of the Nile statue; pygmies chase crocodiles on a river that swarms with the creatures, while cranes and hippopotami march along the bank. Equally untrue to facts is the design on the support of a marble table (Pl. 81c). The tree is intended for a date-palm, but its branches do not spring from one point in the correct manner, nor does the fruit droop below the lowest branches as it should; it is the conception of a date-palm of a man accustomed to pines or deciduous trees. The griffin by its side is derived from one of the mythological creatures of Mesopotamian origin, though transformed; the type was habitually used under the early empire for table supports—trestles translated into marble—on which the flat top of the table was laid. The griffins sit in the pose of a cat, front feet close together, chest curving out; they are always placed back to back, and a scrap of the companion figure on the Chicago slab is just visible on the projecting corner of the stone beyond the tree.

XII

Roman Experiments: Vespasian to Trajan

(A.D. 69–117)

THE assassination of Nero in 68 was followed by rather more than a year of civil war, which ended in the triumph of Vespasian, who had previously been entrusted with the suppression of a Jewish rebellion. The extinction of the Julio-Claudian house and the foundation of a new dynasty —the Flavian—by a man of insignificant birth brought among its concomitants the disappearance of the refined Hellenic style patronized by the late rulers and the fashionable society which imitated them. A gradual mitigation of the academic qualities of Augustan sculptures had been effected in the course of time; it now became pronounced. In the reaction arose a style of baroque tendencies, in which the accuracy of portraiture was almost untouched by idealism, and the reliefs were enlivened by light and shade.

In the province of portraiture, the head of Vespasian himself (Pl. 82a) reveals the magnitude of the revolution. Vespasian was a man of tough sense, and his are the most lifelike of imperial portraits of the first two centuries; this particular head, carved in Italian marble, shows him not long before his death (in 79). None of his successors was so irreverent towards the shams beneath which emperors could be veiled; he refused to conceal his humble birth and occasionally visited the farm of his ancestors in the Sabine hills. His sons, Titus and Domitian, may have relapsed somewhat into the beautifying manner of the earlier empire, but the shortness of Titus' reign and the destruction of Domitian's monuments, after his murder in 96, result in a scarcity of evidence for them.

The photographic accuracy of the true Roman portrait rarely occurs in the eastern provinces: it sufficed there if a man's public repute were revealed, while sepulchral statues of women were almost invariably fitted with stock heads rather than portraits. Monotony is, on the whole, the impression gathered from a collection of Greek statues of the early empire, although the execution often reaches a high standard of merit and

267

occasionally an interesting piece comes to light. The ambitious artist had too often migrated to Rome, the more lucrative field of activity.

The realism of Flavian portraits did not extend to the body, for which the conventional fourth-century types were used; moreover mortals took on the types of deities from this century onwards in an increasing number. In Pl. 82b, a middle-aged Roman lady is identified as Venus and supplied with a cupid—his feet remain on the base of the statue—to remove all doubt as to the impersonation. The 'Capitoline' type was selected, but the head is a portrait; the hair is dressed in the manner of the later Flavians and thus dates the work at the end of the century. The sculptor, being of his period, could not abstain from a modification of the flesh, too plentiful but at least firm in his prototype, to suit the middle-aged face above it. Though possibly a member of the ruling house, the woman may equally well have been a private individual since Roman husbands often invested the memorials of their dead wives with the attributes of the goddess of love. There is a half-draped figure, inscribed to the memory of Ulpia Epigone, whose hair is similarly arranged and who holds a fat hand in the approved pudic manner.

No finer example of a Flavian statue has yet come to light than the bronze Victory at Brescia, found there in the ruins of a temple built by Vespasian in 72. The type of the figure is based on that of an Aphrodite, who stood almost in the position of the Venus of Milo; a half-draped copy, found at Capua, now belongs to the Naples Museum, while a fully-draped variant exists in the Louvre. As befits a Victory, this figure is fully draped and equipped with a pair of great wings, which spring from the shoulders in a direction more backwards than sideways. In style it recalls the reliefs of the column at Mainz, and is another example of the endeavour to recast old types.

The statue of the Nile in the Vatican was found on the site of a temple of Isis, from which a companion statue of the Tiber (now in the Louvre) was also recovered, in addition to a number of sculptures in the Egyptian manner. A sphinx, emblem of the land of Egypt, supports the river-god, whose infants symbolize the seasonal inundation on which Egypt's irrigation system depended; there are sixteen children, one for each cubit's rise in the water level (the height of 16 cubits being the accepted maximum), while their dispersal higher up or lower down on the body carries the allegory further. One group of children on the left is playing with a crocodile, another with an ichneumon; the sixteenth rides in a cornucopia, which is crammed with the fruits and flowers of the prosperity given by a full flood. The water flows from the pointed end of the cornucopia under cover of the drapery (for the sources of the Nile were a mystery in anti-quity), and surrounds the base. Here are carved scenes from the life along the river banks, on every side except the front where there was enough to see without calling attention to the base. Combats between crocodiles and hippopotami, with aquatic birds as spectators, start the reliefs on the left side; next come boat-loads of pygmies hunting crocodiles; another croco-dile has his tail in the grip of a hippopotamus while a watchful ichneumon is waiting to jump into his open mouth and bite his vitals; last of all come herds of cattle grazing quietly beside the stream.

The sculptor has suggested the fluid nature of the god in many ways—by his smooth body, which is also powerfully built as befits a river of such importance, by his flowing hair and his air of inability to raise himself from his watery bed. His sixteen children frolic wildly, but he lies indolent, only troubling to hold out some ears of corn, a sample of the crops he pro-duces with such ease. The point is significant, for Egypt was the country on which Rome chiefly depended for its bread. The workmanship of the Nile statue is so superior to that of the Tiber that it has been thought to be a reproduction of an older Hellenistic statue, whereas the Tiber was considered to be merely a companion produced by a Roman sculptor. But the Egyptian type of the Nile god, Hapi, was the only personification of the river until fairly late in Hellenistic times, when a seated figure in the Greek manner was invented, and that is the sole position in which the god is found in Romano-Egyptian terracotta work. The Vatican Nile is a Roman type, based possibly on a picture; for parallels to the general conception one need only turn to the Tellus scene and to terracotta plaques and mosaics of 'Nile life', manufactured in Rome. The type may have arisen under the Julio-Claudian dynasty, it was certainly in use under the Flavians, but the date of the Vatican statue can be only vaguely ascertained—as is true of many Roman statues.

The originality of the Flavian Age is best displayed in the reliefs on the Arch of Titus, which was completed during the reign of Domitian (81–96), although it commemorates the fall of Jerusalem in 71; at least, it was not supplied with its inscription until after the death of Titus. Of the two main reliefs on either side of the passage of the Arch, one represents the spoils of the Jewish temple carried in procession, the other the emperor driving, accompanied by Victory, in his triumphal chariot, past soldiers marching with lances sloped over their shoulders. In the centre, only the lances appear above the chariot and horses; the figures in the foreground are rendered distinct by deep shadows cast between them, and a general play of light and shape prevails, but the soldiers are outlined in such low relief that, although clearly distinguished, they cast no shadow upon the background. The artist aimed at conveying the illusion of a procession seen through an open frame, with merely air and no wall behind it, all its members clear cut as if against the sky. A simpler, more successful and therefore more pleasing relief is the sacrifice scene found at Pompeii, and thereby dated before the eruption of 79.

Another product of unfettered art and dizzy perspective, a relief 1.31 m. high (Pl. 82c), was discovered outside Rome at a tomb of the Haterii family, which is probably identical with the building depicted. Such tombs were composed of a brick core faced with marble or stucco: an effort of the imagination is required at the present day, when every Roman tomb is but a shapeless mass of bricks, to realize the original appearance when cased with gay reliefs. The main portion of the tomb, in the shape of a Corinthian temple, served no doubt as the chapel for the cult of the dead. In its pediment is seen the bust of a woman, on the side wall are the busts of three children, members of the family; figures below represent the three Fates, and on the intervening strip cupids are playing (this band apparently running right round the building). The substructure, built of large square blocks by the side of the steps, is elsewhere overlaid with decoration, including a Hercules seated on a basket within a shrine; his drinking cup decorates its pediment while his bow and club fill the triangular spaces alongside. The doorway next to him presumably led into the vault, which may have received light and air through the grille of upright pillars further to the left. Above the grille is an altar on which a sacrifice is burning. But in accordance with custom the altar should have stood further to the left, in line with the steps; the sculptor had to move it in order to squeeze in the crane, moved onwards by a treadmill, by which two workmen are approaching the roof to add a finial to the gable. Above the roof is a further collection of objects. Here we see a woman with a bird in her hand reclining on a couch placed against a curtain close to a large stand, on which an offering burns violently. An altar in front of the couch also bears a fire tended by an old woman; three children are playing on the ground. An erection on the right, like a triple arch, holds in its central niche a nude female figure, while above it are three colossal masks roughly blocked out. These objects all use the same base, decorated with eagles carrying garlands, so that they formed one entity to the sculptor's mind; they can scarcely have stood on the roof of the tomb and it has been suggested that they actually stood inside, but are shown in this position because it was impossible to represent them indoors. They would in this view be reproductions of miscellaneous monuments dedicated to the dead. It is of course conceivable that they were arranged upon a different section of the exterior. The problem has not yet been solved and even to contemporaries, unless some explanation were given to them, it must have been puzzling. In the anxiety to fit in everything relevant, both the end and the side of the tomb are carved almost frontal, and this is true of most representations of buildings in reliefs. In Pompeian paintings the drawing is generally more correct.

Domitian's villa on the Alban hills has yielded a fair number of sculptures, but none is particularly striking, the better pieces having no doubt been removed after his death. When he was murdered in 96, Domitian was engaged upon building a Forum with a temple in honour of Minerva, which was completed two years later by Nerva, presumably without alteration to the plans, which must have been already half realized. The frieze is composed of a single row of figures monotonously carved and badly co-ordinated, whose pursuits have yet to be satisfactorily explained but appear to have reference to the cult of the goddess. The river-god, seated in a bed of reeds, should be noted for comparison with the Nile. The height at which the reliefs are placed may excuse their perfunctory character. The two 'Cancelleria' reliefs, discovered in Rome in 1938 and now exhibited in the Vatican, are not only better in both design and carving but also of quite a different style. They form a pair, one illustrating Domitian's first public appearance in 70, welcoming Vespasian's arrival in Rome, the other Domitian's own departure for a campaign. Unmistakable portraits of the dead and living emperors are interposed in a medley of deities, personifications and idealized human beings, dramatically posed with much gesticulation. The figures stand overlapping, with their feet all on the same level but their heads at somewhat uneven heights; the manner of composition was derived largely from the Parthenon frieze, while the types of many individual figures were borrowed or adapted from Greek art of periods ranging from Pheidian to Pergamene. The drapery shows the same influences, though predominant among them is the style of the Nike Parapet, especially as rendered in Neo-Attic work. The sculptor may be assumed to have been trained in Greece. The drapery of a statue at Olympia, identified as a portrait of the reigning empress Domitia, gives a more accurate reproduction of the style of 400 B.C.

Nerva reigned only from 96 to 98, and therefore few portraits of him exist, but in so far as they are known his features correspond with those of a standing half-draped statue in Copenhagen, although in its case they are much idealized. The grandeur of the figure is due to the heavy mass of the toga, which forms thin, close-pleated folds, in contrast to the severity of the nude torso, and almost doubles the width of the statue by falling from the raised left arm to near the ankle-level. The concept of heroic semi-nudity was, of course, derived from the art of the fifth century, but no Greek precedent is known for drapery of such lateral extension above the waist, though in the Demosthenes (Pl. 60d) it had doubled the width of the composition at the ankles.

The influence of the Old Masters was waning. Partial or complete nudity ceased, therefore, to be common in figures of emperors, despite the impressive results achieved thereby in the supposed Nerva and, still more, in a magnificent statue of his successor, Trajan (Pl. 82d). In this the treatment of the nude was derived from Polycleitus but the pose comes from the slightly earlier 'Diomedes', while the cloak (paludamentum) on the shoulder defines the wearer as a general. The statue, which was found in Rome, shows Trajan in his early fifties; the head corresponds with the second portrait-type on his coins and should therefore be not later than 108, when a third type was introduced upon the tenth anniversary of his accession, and a few years later the sculptors of his Column represented him with a face like a bulldog. In some of the numerous heads and busts extant he appears much younger, with his features idealized according to the Julio-Claudian tradition, of which there is little trace in the statue. (Busts, it should be noted, extend lower than had formerly been customary; they now terminate just below the breasts.)

Trajan's work at Rome was concentrated on the new Forum that bears his name; it seems to have been built between 111 and 114, by a Greek architect, Apollodorus of Damascus, who also planned a bridge over the Danube for the Dacian campaigns of 102-5. Four slabs of battle-scenes in the Arch of Constantine may have been part of the wall decorations but their damaged condition does not allow the emperor's face to be identified. The Arch is adorned, too, with statues of barbarians resembling those discovered in Trajan's Forum, where they seem to have stood in a long series of parallel niches. The motive of the barbarian prisoner, at first used only in female figures to personify conquered races, is now turned to good account for decorative purposes. Dacians, the most formidable race subdued by the emperor, are probably represented here, wearing a thick native dress; their captive condition is inferred from their dejected attitudes and lowered heads. From a statue of this description came the head in Berlin (Pl. 83a), which is reported to have been found in Rome and from its style and type may have stood with the other figures in Trajan's Forum. The nose is restored and the surface rather worn, so that a metallic effect, caused in other examples by the liberal use of the drill to separate the locks of unkempt hair, is disguised by time.

In a statue in the Loggia dei Lanzi (Pl. 83b) is seen the female counterpart of such figures. The nose, the fingers, the upper part of the left arm and the right arm are restored. The dress, long hair and full development of the body suggests a German—the size of the women of that race much impressed the Romans—and for this reason the statue was at first named 'Thusnelda', after the wife of Arminius, who was captured and led in a Triumph through Rome, but it is now supposed to be a personification of Germania. The arrangement of the drapery may be compared with some on the Arch of Benevento (Pl. 84a) but the figure of the goddess was intended to be seen from afar and is therefore more cursorily treated; the fine detail of 'Thusnelda' occurs in works of about 100 A.D., including the frieze of Nerva's Forum. A Trajanic is more probable than a Julio-Claudian date, when such intensity of grief as is revealed by the contracted brows and heavy mouth would be unexpected; but, like the figures of captured races on the Augustus of Prima Porta, a prototype of 'Thusnelda' in a less pathetic style may have been conceived under an earlier emperor.

The Ara Pacis had given an allegorical representation of the peace bestowed by Augustus, but Trajan, a devoted soldier, commemorated his conquest of Dacia by a narrative, perhaps inspired by paintings of episodes exhibited in his triumphal procession. He achieved his purpose with the first instance of a solitary column decorated with a continuous band of sculpture, which climbs spirally up to the summit. The designer (possibly Apollodorus of Damascus) was clearly influenced by the only precedent for a sculptured narrative, the Pergamene frieze that told the life-story of Telephus, but he invented a peculiarly harsh style to allow for distant viewing. The experiment was evidently thought successful (otherwise it would not have been repeated for Marcus Aurelius), but the modern spectator is more impressed with the disadvantages. The scroll of narrative is over 200 m. long, and no one could have been expected to walk twenty-two times around the column to watch it all unfold. Furthermore, though the height of the sculptured band increases from 90 cm. at the base to 1.25 m. at the top, so that the figures grow larger on the ascent (of, vertically, 100 Roman feet), only the most long-sighted of eyes can distinguish those in the upper portions.

In antiquity, however, the court in which the Column stood was surrounded by arcades of two stories, which might have mitigated this last objection. The depth of the bands could not be greater nor the figures larger than they are, unless the Column were very much thicker; had a deep band and large figures been substituted, very little of each scene would have been visible at a time and the effect would have been far from continuous. A fault which could have been corrected, however, is the over-crowding of each scene (Pl. 83c). Excuses, even here, lie ready to hand; Michelangelo, when he had completed one panel on the roof of the Sistine Chapel, could rectify his mistake of overcrowding, but no such break in the design of a stone column could be effected. Furthermore the use of colour and metal accessories may have enormously increased the visibility of the reliefs.

The Column tapered towards its summit on which stood a colossal statue of Trajan, represented on coins after the year 110: coins before this date show an eagle in its place. The change in the design was probably made on the emperor's decision to be buried in the base, where a small chamber was accordingly prepared. An inscription built into the base records the decree of the Senate, together with a date in 113, doubtless that of the dedication of the completed monument.

While the influence of older compositions in the form of friezes, and of the pictures or modelled figures carried in triumphal processions, can undoubtedly be traced, there prevails in the Column a tendency to form larger masses and groups, each tightly bound up, of rhythmically placed members. The greater mastery of perspective acquired during the preceding 150 years—forced on the sculptor of Roman monuments in order to accommodate a crowd, a problem not presented in Greek art—enabled the designer to accumulate deep blocks of figures where before he would have been compelled to spread a thin line over a larger expanse. The Trajanic designer had no scruples in altering the size of people or inanimate objects to suit his purposes, and the buildings on his reliefs are invariably made much smaller than they should be, sometimes no larger than the figures immediately beside them. Figures in the background, even if pressed close to those in the front row, are habitually placed higher up, whereas they were represented on the same level in the Ara Pacis and Arch of Titus; here can be traced the influence of the narrative pictures carried in triumphal processions, in which the figures behind were raised to a higher level.

Battle-scenes are given less space than might be expected in a narrative of Trajan's campaign, far less than would be accorded in a Greek monument. The Romans were interested in the course and results of the battles rather than the actual fighting; in both the Arch of Titus and the Arch of Trajan at Benevento, only one relief of the set is devoted to a battle-scene. The Column transforms the subject into the concerted operations of troops, sometimes in a mêlée, but plainly engaged on a general advance instead of in the series of single combats usual in Greek friezes (although individual figures often have Greek prototypes). In sieges too the old simple composition (such as we find at Gjölbaschi, where the line of a high wall divides the scene into two distinct halves), is broken up; figures are so massed in front of a low wall as to mark its importance to the design, though it runs up and down hill with violent twists, compelling the troops on either side to fall into large bodies of men pressing in definite directions, symmetry being carefully preserved by balancing the movements of one section against another. The drapery is important to the design; it both binds together the masses of men, and emphasizes, by the systematic direction of its lines, the calmness or desperation of the combatants or the moods and feelings of important personages. But drapery so treated tends to become formalized to such an extent that it loses its meaning as clothing; stock patterns of folds are repeated in figure after figure, line for line, with a mechanical dullness from which the eye turns.

Clearly the reliefs were all designed by one mind, however many hands were employed on the execution. The story is told with due regard to the emotions and artistic interest aroused by each section, with a gradual quickening as a crucial moment approaches, and a gradual relaxing when it has passed. Strongly contrasting episodes are placed side by side; on the one hand is seen civilization, on the other barbarism. Trajan, seated on a stool, dispenses rewards to his soldiers, one of whom is kissing his hand, while two others are embracing in their happiness: but in the following scene Dacian women are torturing Roman prisoners. An obviously intentional counterpart to this episode occurs beyond that of Trajan and his soldiers, where a group of captured Dacians is seen under unobtrusive guard inside a humanely-conducted prison-camp. The composition here, as in several other places, takes the form of a triptych, with the image of imperial beneficence in the centre, flanked by two pieces of propaganda.

The narrative of the whole Column is divided in half by the truce that actually separated the first and second Dacian wars; the division is marked by a figure of Victory. So far its arrangement might seem genuinely historical, but the order of the episodes does not correspond with those of literary sources and the designer must have aimed more at giving a fine impression of the successful war, than at a factual account. He includes all the regular incidents of a Roman war—the emperor's addresses to the army, sacrifices, construction of buildings and engines of warfare, the capture of prisoners, the emperor's interviews with prisoners or embassies, troops on the march, journeys by land and sea, the flight and pursuit of the enemy, the removal of the spoil; in the suicide of the defeated Dacian chiefs a favourite motive of ancient art is introduced.

The direction of advancing troops is from left to right, in accordance with the revolving of the spiral: and when occasionally the Dacians take the offensive they too move in the same direction. Herein lies that appearance of continuity which pervades the Column, though in reality the composition can be divided into separate scenes, with trees or other scraps of landscapes interspersed, like the trees placed in the Gjölbaschi frieze to mark the end of each section. The frequency of painted or modelled scenery in triumphal processions perhaps inclined the artist to afford more space to this element than is given in other Roman monuments, but it must be noted that in size the natural features and buildings are invariably subordinated to the human elements, for man is still 'the measure of all things'. Pure landscape is only employed at the extremity of the relief-spiral, where the height of the relief field is not enough to admit figures. Moreover linear perspective is completely ignored, and this Trajanic master returns to the conventions of painters of the late fifth century, who painted almost 'bird's-eye views' in which figures were drawn without relation to the height of the horizon. A high horizon and a tendency towards perspective characterizes the painting of the two previous centuries, but, with the rest of the illusionist technique, were rejected by the Trajanic artist in favour of the archaic method of placing the back row of figures higher than the front row, undiminished in size. But unlike the archaic artist the Trajanic designer took as his unit not one man but a group of men, and thus gained a means of composition by which to play with symmetry and antithesis, parallelism and rhythmical division. The result is geometrical, but the different actions of individual figures in the groups prevent the monotony of the archaic geometric compositions. The Column has the same surface treatment for all kinds of objects—flesh, hair, drapery, wood, stone, earth, leaves—and all are cut clearly from one another. In this, as in other points, is seen the resemblance to archaic art and the rejection of the experiments in illusionism, which together make the Column a forerunner of the art of the fourth century A.D.

Another large monument was erected after the Dacian war on the lower Danube, where the city of Tropaeum Trajani was built on the site now known as Adamklissi. In 1837 its ruins were examined by von Moltke, then attached to the Turkish army: he recognized the nature of the building, but no further investigations took place until the district was annexed to Romania. The trophy, which gave the town its name, was raised high above a solid cylindrical base, 100 m. in circumference. The trophy itself took the usual form of a tree-trunk hung with a helmet, a cuirass, two shields and two greaves, all on a gigantic scale; by its side were relatively inconspicuous figures of prisoners, themselves of more than life-size.

Around the top of the base were set sculptured metopes illustrating the campaign, and on a line of crenellations above were reliefs of captives with their hands tied behind their backs. Whereas the form of the building is impressive, and may be compared with the tomb of Cecilia Metella or of Hadrian, the sculpture was crude to the point of becoming comic. Its primitive nature led at first to conjectures that attributed it to an anachronistic provincial school of the Augustan Age, or to decadent provincials of the Constantinian Age; but the motives are frequently paralleled on the Column, so that the backwardness must be due to inexperienced hands of Trajan's own time. Moreover the survival of large fragments of that emperor's dedicatory inscription ought to have prevented wild speculations as to its date; in addition a neighbouring rock was inscribed in 109, by order of Trajan, to the memory of the Roman soldiers who fell in his Dacian campaigns.

The Monument of Philopappus at Athens, built in 114–116, retains damaged and worn reliefs of conventional competence; the processional scene with the consular chariot is so reminiscent of the Arch of Titus that the sculptor must surely have been to Rome.

In the twelve huge reliefs that ornament the Arch erected in honour of Trajan at Benevento, the terminus of a road he constructed, the influence of the Arch of Titus is clearly apparent, as was almost inevitable since the design and carving alike would certainly have been entrusted to sculptors from Rome. The duplicate inscriptions do not cite the last title, *Parthius*, that was conferred upon Trajan; these reliefs seem therefore to have been composed in 115, but two panels in the attic row can scarcely have been carved before the accession of Hadrian in 117, because his figure appears on the same superhuman scale as Trajan's although he had never been acknowledged as heir-apparent. The Arch was put up by the Senate, which had voted Trajan the title of *Optimus* in recognition of his beneficial government, hence most of the reliefs illustrate his routine activities in Rome (or at any rate in Italy); these scenes of receiving deputations, giving alms to children, and the like, are appropriately concentrated on the frontage towards Rome and in the passage. On the outward frontage we see indirect references to his military successes but no battles; gratitude for his addition of more provinces to the empire is expressed by scenes of their submission or pacification, without so much as a hint at the grievous process of conquest. A narrow frieze, between the top of the piers and the attic, does indeed represent a triumphal procession but is inconspicuous. The reliefs of the attic, carved in higher relief as befits their greater elevation, were evidently intended to attract most attention. Here two panels, separated by the inscription, form a single composition on the inward frontage; in one of them Trajan is welcomed home by (among others) Roma, while in the next (Pl. 84*a*) his arrival is awaited by the Capitoline triad—Jupiter, Juno and Minerva—and lesser deities. They appear crushed together because all are carved in high relief, with their heads on the same level.

The experiment in illustration presented by Trajan's Column distracts attention from the real artistic achievements of his reign, which was evidently a period of rapid transition. Just as the Parthenon metopes are due to craftsmen twenty years apart in outlook, so carvings on the Arch at Benevento span the gap between the first-century style and the Hadrianic, while in the portraiture of individuals unconnected with the imperial household the Flavian tradition prevails far into Hadrian's reign. The masterpiece in this respect, whether it be Trajanic or later, is part of a statue identifiable by its costume as a Vestal Virgin (Pl. 85*d*); she was, no doubt, the abbess of the convent, the spiritual custodian of Rome.

XIII

Virtuosity: Hadrian to Caracalla

(A.D. 117–217)

The Reign of Hadrian

HADRIAN's cultured personality affected Roman art as deeply as Augustus', bringing into fashion a classicist style of Greek rather than Roman creation, but less dependent on the remote Hellenic past; types borrowed from the antique are disguised by a contemporary treatment. This certainly is Greek though derived less from Greece itself than from Asia Minor, where the Hellenistic tradition had retained greater vitality. Its influence had already appeared in Flavian reliefs at Rome and on the Arch of Benevento; its triumph was now accelerated by, if not due to, its consonance with the emperor's personal taste. The nickname *Graeculus* (the little Greek), which conservative Romans gave him, was as apt in artistic as in other respects. Since, however, Hadrian spent most of his reign (117–138) outside Italy, there is no reason to think that his approval was obtained for the design of every sculptured monument erected in Rome to his honour or even at his order. He is unlikely to have given detailed instructions for the purchase of the countless statues that ornamented his Villa near Tivoli; in any event, no predilections can be discerned from the impartial copying of works of all periods, from the fifth to the second century B.C. But Hadrian must have approved all the official portraits of himself and the empress. Unlike previous emperors, who almost invariably had been clean-shaven, Hadrian wore a beard and moustache; these, in conjunction with heavy features, result in a head reminiscent of the fourth or third century. He is habitually portrayed standing in a cuirass ornamented with allegorical scenes after the manner of the Augustus of Prima Porta (Pl. 77*a*). The extraordinary number of these statues—many of which were afterwards re-used, bearing the heads of other emperors—might imply only that he enjoyed displaying himself in full-dress uniform, but they were probably intended as a reminder of his military career under Trajan, in order to quash cavilling at his inglorious though eminently practical frontier policy. Hadrian, in fact, never started a war, and when he became embroiled involuntarily in one he stopped it by giving way to the enemy's wishes. His surrender of Trajan's newly-won (and perhaps untenable) province of Mesopotamia must have especially outraged Roman pride, and the only rejoinder open to him was to emphasize his capacity to assess a military problem.

Further unquestionable evidence of Hadrian's personal taste is offered by representations of his dead favourite, Antinous. This young man, a native of Asia Minor, drowned himself in the Nile during Hadrian's visit to Egypt in 130, in order to prevent by a human sacrifice the fulfilment of a prophecy against the emperor. Hadrian decreed him a god, justifying his apotheosis by his death in the sacred river. His cult was accepted at Delphi and Olympia, where it long survived, while in Egypt the number of cheap amulets testify to the popularity of his worship, but all the Antinous types, even if they do not embody the actual appearance of the youth, are of almost contemporary date. He is best represented in the Delphi statue (Pl. 84b), one of several which seem to be copied from the first cult-image of the new god. The posture was derived from a supposedly Pheidian Apollo, of which copies have been found in the Tiber and at Cherchel, but the details reproduce the physical peculiarities of Antinous himself. He is recorded to have been pigeon-breasted, hence the outward curve of the heavy chest; the sculptor also hints at sexual immaturity or impotence. The body is unmuscled and smooth, whereas the prototype Apollo has the broken contours of an athlete; the face too is smooth and fleshy.

A more idealized type is preserved in the enormous 'Mondragone' head (Pl. 84c) and two smaller copies. In this case the treatment of the hair was adapted from the fifth century, while the features are more refined than in the Delphi type. The forehead and level brows, almost meeting above deep-set eyes, give an impression of severity to the face, which is contradicted by the sensuous half-parted lips, and the shortness of the space between the mouth and nostrils. A resemblance to the Bologna head of the Lemnian Athena (Pl. 34d) has been noted, but is superficial; in fact it establishes the Hadrianic date of that copy almost as much as it proves that a Pheidian type was adapted to portray Antinous. The Hellenic influence is of course profound, but the nose has a slightly aquiline form instead of the classic straight line.

In both the 'Mondragone' head and the Delphi statue the underlying Pheidian type is blurred by a high polish. The resulting combination of material softness and sensuousness with severity and purity of line not only immortalized the features of a handsome imperial favourite, but also embodied the sensuality, melancholy and youth which his contemporaries found so attractive a combination; to a less romantic age he might appear overfed and spoilt. As regards technique, the 'Mondragone' head had the eyebrows only faintly indicated, while the eyes were inlaid in enamel or precious stones, and metal leaves were affixed to the band of ivy that surrounded the hair. In the Delphi head the eyebrows and hair are less distinctly modelled; in a statue at Naples the brows are represented by a light feathering, the hair consists of a crisp mass in which each lock describes an arc of a circle, and the eyeballs are carved as circles within which lies a crescent-shaped trough to indicate the pupils.

Antinous has many roles. In the 'Mondragone' head and the Braschi statue in the Vatican he is the mystic Dionysus; in the Lateran statue he is Vertumnus, a god of the seasons and fruits of the earth; at Eleusis he is Apollo with the omphalus, and in Egypt he is Osiris or Serapis. In two reliefs he is identified with Silvanus: the half-length in the Villa Albani may be closely compared with the Delphi statue, from which it diverges mainly in the more emphatic curve of the breast-bone, but the other, signed by Antonianus of Aphrodisias, departs altogether from the usual type; the pose recalls Attic gravestones of the end of the fifth century B.C., on which a young man stands in an easy attitude with a dog at his side, but here an altar hung with many bunches of grapes is carved in very low relief in the background. The drapery is subordinated to the body, for the Greeks had not lost an appreciation for the human form such as the Romans never really felt.

Aphrodisian sculptors signed their work more frequently than other artists of the empire, no doubt because their reputation ensured a higher price in Rome. In fact, the Capitoline centaurs in grey marble (Pl. 65c), carved by two Aphrodisians in collaboration, show infinitely greater skill than the average copyist's and possibly some ingenuity in addition, since the elaborate support under the belly would not have been needed in the bronze originals. Ingenuity is a characteristic of much sculpture actually found at Aphrodisias, where an unusually plentiful supply of white marble was cheaply available; the other characteristic of the local school can best, perhaps, be described as flamboyance. It is more successful in relief than in the round; a typical piece of decorative work (Pl. 84d), on a pilaster from Baths of Hadrian's reign, shows the infant Heracles strangling the snakes that attacked him. In this period the influence of Aphrodisias extended throughout Asia Minor and even into Macedonia but rarely affected sculptors in southern Greece, Italy or the western provinces.

The classicist style of Rome is exemplified in a set of eight circular reliefs built into the Arch of Constantine but obviously derived from some

Hadrianic monument. The heads have been re-carved or replaced to give likenesses of Constantine and his associates, but there are still incompletely obliterated traces of the beards for which Hadrian set a fashion. Figures of both Hadrian and Antinous are recognizable. The subjects all relate to hunting, to which Hadrian was so devoted that he even issued coins illustrating his exploits. The eight reliefs seem to have been designed for arrangement in a narrative order. At the start of the series the party enters the hunting-field with a sacrifice to Silvanus. After a medallion showing the hunting of a bear comes another whereon it is offered to Apollo; similarly a boar is killed and offered to Diana, the hunters stand beside a dead lion and then make an offering to Hercules (Pl. 85a), while finally we see the return of the party. That the designer was Aegean-trained appears from the structural solidity of most figures, and from the drapery which forms simple patterns of small rounded folds, clearly outlined by shadowy depressions. The shortness of the clothing leaves powerful legs displayed; in the medallion with the lion Hadrian and his retinue look sturdy enough to have killed it. At the centre of the other medallion is the slim Antinous, taller than the rest because he has already become a god; Hadrian, confronting him across the altar, stands contrastingly four-square. The distant figure of Hercules is an instance of perspectival diminution, which had long been accepted by painters but was seldom emphatic in sculpture. The relief fails to suggest depth; the backgrounds are merely background, on which overlapped figures do not impinge because their feet are placed level with the foreground.

Reliefs of other subjects attributable to the close of Hadrian's reign have been preserved, among them two large reliefs in the Palazzo dei Conservatori. One of these represents the apotheosis of an empress, who is carried up to heaven by a winged female figure which stretches diagonally across the slab; below sits the emperor watching the burning pyre, by which reclines a youth personifying the Campus Martius, scene of the funeral. The next relief shows the emperor delivering a speech, no doubt the proclamation of the apotheosis; it is remarkable for the awkward manner in which figures varying in size are distributed at different levels, filling the entire panel except for the space in one of the top corners, occupied by a small temple.

The Dresden head (Pl. 85b) resembles a number of similar portraits from Athens, which from the long disordered hair were at first taken for barbarians, though it is more likely that the fashion was the mark of a group of residents; a town largely composed of persons engaged in literary or learned pursuits might well indulge in oddities. The most curious of these heads was at various times identified incongruously as Christ, Commodus, Herodes Atticus, a Thracian king, or a sophist; its likeness to the Dresden head is so close that the latter, too, can safely be described as Greek work. These heads date before A.D. 150, and some at least are Hadrianic, for the execution is not unlike that of some heads of Antinous in the eyes, eyebrows and hair.

The Capitoline centaurs in grey marble (Pl. 65c), found in Hadrian's villa at Tivoli, probably belong to his reign, to which, too, can be assigned other instances of the use of coloured marble such as the red satyrs from the same villa. An admirable head of a young African (Pl. 85c) is also executed in dark grey marble with eyes inlaid in white and dark grey. The lumpy treatment of the hair suggests the liberal use of butter still practised by certain tribes of the Sudan, a district with which the Romans were in close touch, although it retained its independence. He wears his hair in the national manner, and as that privilege would have been denied in Roman territory to a slave, he may have been a chief, a visitor to the empire, or one of those travelling adventurers whose acceptance by society was derided by the satirists. The presence of a replica in the same materials in the Terme suggests the favourite of fashion, whose busts might be multiplied during his tenure of power.

Another effective piece of coloured sculpture from Rome (Pl. 90a) is the statue of an old fisherman, carried out in black marble with a strip of yellow marble to represent the single article of clothing round his hips. The restorations include both arms, the inlay of the eyes, and probably the head itself, but they were based on a dull version in ordinary marble; the right arm is almost correct (the fingers should be grasping a fishing-net), the left hand held a basket of fish at arm's length. Rheumatism was inevitable in the life of a poor fisherman and the knees and back are distorted accordingly. His sole rag, wrapped round his hips, reveals a body wrinkled with age and underfeeding, and overgrown with veins; his face is hopelessly brutalized. There is no touch of idealism, and every unpleasant detail is scrupulously carved. It is another example of the native Roman love of realism, which is expressed in many statues, and affected even the more educated classes. Such a *reductio ad absurdum* of their ideals seems to have glutted even the Roman appetite for the lifelike, with the result that a progressive reaction towards stylization can be traced in sculptures of the next few centuries.

A more normal example of fine decorative sculpture is given by the Venus at Syracuse (Pl. 86a), inspired by a type of Aphrodite which originated later than Praxiteles. The goddess is rising from the sea, which is symbolized by the dolphin at her side, and leans slightly forward to hold together the two ends of her garment; the right arm is bent across the body. The pose is therefore related to the 'pudic', initiated by Praxiteles and followed by countless lesser artists, but here the position of neither hand depends entirely upon modesty or coquetry; the right hand must have been occupied with the loose hair that would fall over the breasts, by which are lumps on the surface of the body, marking the ends of tresses. The real function of the drapery, which had no logical right to be present at the birth of the goddess from the sea, lies in its providing an admirable foil to the smooth body, for which purpose the cloth is creased in the centre and much crumpled round the legs. On the whole the folds are coarsely carved and the drapery is only roughly worked at the back. The legs and feet are almost without modelling, although great care was devoted to the nude parts of the back, which reach to the top of the thighs, while the surface is excessively smooth and polished. The date of this very able statue cannot be decided within narrow limits.

The principate of Hadrian marks the commencement of a period of mass-production of decorative sculpture (especially in the round) which endured till the end of the century. Hundreds of statues—copies or adaptations more often than originals—were required by wealthy citizens throughout the empire, for the adornment of their houses or their gardens, or to be erected in public places as monuments of their generosity; quality became a matter of slight importance, and in truth the vast majority of second-century sculpture has no right to be considered as art. Very rare are the statues equal to the Syracuse Venus, while its subject is typical of the age. An instance of Oriental art being adopted for decorative ends is given by two supporting figures carved in red granite in the Egyptian style, used for architectural purposes in Hadrian's villa. Closely related is a statue in red marble showing Antinous in the guise of a Pharaoh, where the face and costume are purely Egyptian, but the modelling of the body purely western; there can be little doubt that the artist was a Greek or a Roman, and the fact that Antinous was drowned in the Nile suffices to account for this exotic representation of him.

In most respects Hadrianic decorative reliefs differ little from those of the preceding century. Elegant mythological scenes were still produced; when the study of this class of subject has advanced it will perhaps be found necessary to date the majority in the second rather than in the first century. A celebrated set of eight reliefs, housed in the Palazzo Spada, appears to contain more Hadrianic than other elements, though indeed the copyist has selected type of various dates and schools and reduced them all to the same shape to form a series. Peaceful sentimentality is the prevailing note, the situations are seldom dramatically rendered, though in such subjects as the Theft of the Palladium or the Serpent killing the child Opheltes, the artist naturally practises less restraint than in groups of mythological personages conversing. Two of the reliefs introducing Paris, with Eros and Oenone respectively, exhibit later characteristics than the others, but it is questionable whether they alone can be assigned to the Antonine Age, leaving the rest to Hadrian. A similar problem attaches to the sarcophagi which abound later in the century and which must have started by Hadrian's reign; the repeated use, without alteration, of the same motifs prevents any accurate dating of sarcophagi and it is better to treat the development as predominately Antonine, while admitting the Hadrianic origin of some motifs.

The Antonine Age

The Antonine Age was one of wealth and calm, despite the invasions of barbarians driven against the empire's borders by the pressure of other hordes pouring out of the Steppes. In art the Hadrianic style persists in a modified form; a more schematic treatment of drapery matches the lifeless composition; the hair becomes elaborately curled, the eyebrows are usually carved, and exceptions to the custom of marking the pupils become rarer.

Hadrian died childless in 138, after nominating as his successor Antoninus Pius, who simultaneously adopted two boys, Marcus Aurelius and Lucius Verus, to be his heirs. These events were commemorated in one of a great set of reliefs at Ephesus. Another of the slabs (2.03 m. high and 3.10 m. long) represents the apotheosis of an emperor in military uniform, whose head has been lost. He is shown stepping into the chariot of the Sun, who stands at the head of his impatient horses, accompanied by Virtus; beneath her feet sits Tellus (Earth) with her cornucopia and a child. Since Victory holds the reins and helps the emperor into the chariot he should logically be identified as Trajan, the last conqueror, although more than twenty years had passed since his death; on the other hand the pacific Hadrian's insistence on portrayal in uniform might, in Antoninus' reign, have encouraged a tactful fiction that made him also a victor—a claim that might justifiably have been made for Antoninus himself, but the reliefs are unlikely to be later than his death in 161. The apotheosis scene is balanced by a slab on which the Moon, accompanied by the Evening Star, drives her chariot-team of deer, following the lead of Night, into the stream of Ocean, who is personified as a youth with a rudder. The designs are treated pictorially, in terms of light and shade without delicately carved transitions; the slabs, therefore, look better in photographs than in reality in the Vienna Museum, to which all but a few fragments were taken.

The Hadrianeum in Rome, a temple of the deified Hadrian, was dedicated seven years after his death. Near the foot of its walls stood a row of draped female figures in very high relief, personifying provinces; sixteen remain, distributed between the Naples Museum and various Roman collections. In spite of carefully varied attitudes they are not a lively spectacle, and are far from well carved.

A Greek plutocrat, Herodes Atticus, was distinguished at the middle of the second century by his munificence in erecting huge buildings all over Greece. At Olympia he celebrated his provision of a water supply (about 155) by filling an *exedra* (rounded recess) at the fountain with dull statues of members of the imperial family and his own. The portrait of Herodes also occurs elsewhere in Greece.

A large base, now in the Vatican gardens, had supported a plain column, dedicated, in the joint reign of Marcus Aurelius and Lucius Verus, to Antoninus and his wife Faustina. One of the main sides is occupied by the inscription, the other by a relief, in which the deified couple, attended by eagles, ascend to heaven on the back of a winged genius, whose figure crosses the field diagonally; below it sit Roma and a personification of the Campus Martius, the scene of the funeral pyre (identified by the obelisk held on his hip). The bold composition, well adapted to a public monument, is more balanced than its Hadrianic prototype, where the actions of the flying figure are confused with drapery, wisely omitted by the later sculptor to obtain definite lines from a clean-limbed body. But an overloading with accessories damages the general effect. On the two other sides a military parade takes the curious form of detachments of infantry encircled by galloping cavalry, like a roundabout at a fair.

The skill displayed in this flying genius was never equalled in the round. A statue of Victory, dedicated by one Marcus Satrius for the campaigns of the two emperors (161 and 168), is clumsily adapted from Greek prototypes; the figure, of gilt bronze, was found at Calvatone and acquired by the Berlin Museum. But good portrait statues were produced, for example the bronze equestrian statue of Marcus Aurelius on the Capitol.

The portraits of Marcus Aurelius (161–180) do not improve the reputation of that philosopher—he appears physically weak and mentally indecisive; those of Lucius Verus, the colleague of his first eight years, have an enlivening touch of madness. A bust in Copenhagen (Pl. 86b), well preserved apart from the restored nose, differs from the usual Verus portrait, so that its identity has been disputed; on the other hand it was found in Rome together with a number of coins stamped with his effigy, and the work is roughly contemporary with his reign. Moreover such a temperament as the bust reveals cannot have existed outside the imperial house, and is not proper to any other member at the time; the brooding eyes and loose mouth belong to an irresponsible egoist stricken with the insanity that has held so many autocrats. But the fleshiness of Verus as he was usually portrayed has in this bust been refined away, and the features seem almost emaciated within the ring of tumbling hair that rises above them. Verus used to powder his hair with gold dust, so it was probably gilt in portraits. Perhaps the divergency from the regular type of this bust and another in Leipzig, apparently a replica, is explicable on the same grounds as the variations in the Antinous portraits—that is the licence allowed to sculptors who were working after the apotheosis of their subject. Since the line of the drapery breaks off abruptly instead of being rounded off, it has been surmised that the bust was copied from a complete statue.

The mode of hairdressing places an ivy-wreathed female head from Amorgos (Pl. 86c) in Aurelius' reign; a wide face is accentuated by the centre parting, and as the Empress Faustina the Younger seems to have had the same width of face, it is likely that the characteristic was introduced into non-imperial portraits of her time. The simplicity of female heads, compared with male heads of the period, results from the method of carving the hair in parallel wavy lines instead of by elaborate undercutting. Male portraits are at this time extremely common in Greece, especially at Athens, where developments can be followed in a large series of named, and often dated, busts of *Cosmetae*, officials of the gymnasia. In general, the Greeks followed hesitatingly and belatedly the alterations in style and technique that portraiture underwent at Rome in the second and third centuries; they avoided the strengthless Antonine elegance.

The sculptors of Greece and Asia Minor, whose influence had previously been expressed spasmodically at Rome, were now busy in their own countries carving sarcophagi for export as well as for local purchasers, with the result that their style became familiar throughout the empire, influencing the sarcophagus-sculptors of Rome, and consequently of all Italy and such western provinces as kept abreast of the times. In the course of the second century the upper classes in every advanced region abandoned cremation, for motives at which we can only guess, and took to laying their dead full-length in these stone receptacles, which were usually placed out of sight, in a tomb built above ground, yet were always sculptured as lavishly as the purchasers' resources allowed.* This change of practice may have started as early as A.D. 100, but did not gather momentum before the Antonines. At Rome, the first sculptured sarcophagi found in a datable context come from a family tomb built late in Hadrian's reign, as is known from stamped bricks of the years 132 and 134. In the cemetery under the Vatican cremation prevailed, with only one exception, till the middle of the century, but throughout the second half all the bodies were deposited full-length. This preference for burial seems to have spread to Italy from Asia Minor, where ornate sarcophagi had been made in the sixth century for local Greeks and subsequently for non-Greeks; the marble funerary couch of an early Hellenistic king or noble is also relevant because it bears a figure of the deceased (still in his tomb at Belevi, near Ephesus). To wealthy Greeks under the empire, burial in a sarcophagus obviously became a means of display. The earliest dated example, at Salonica, is again Hadrianic, but of 120; in shape it conforms with the Proconnesian type.

The various shapes of sarcophagus originated in different regions, where the marble was quarried or carved or both quarried and carved. The deposits which caused Proconnesus afterwards to be called Marmara (from which the Sea is named) lay more conveniently for shipment than any elsewhere, and were exploited as an imperial monopoly; whether sarcophagi were ever sculptured on the island is uncertain but vast numbers were exported blank, though ready-shaped, and gave rise to even more imitations. A gabled lid confers a vague similarity to a built tomb (as in the fifth- and fourth-century sarcophagi made for Kings of Sidon). To facilitate decoration on the upright sides of the chest, these were cut in two planes, both of which the quarrymen left rough to be carved overseas. The higher plane could be converted at slight cost into garlands of foliage, flowers and fruit, swung between masks or bunches of grapes or mythological figures—cupids for choice; in the third century medallions with portrait busts often took their place. The Proconnesian output may thus have been largely responsible for determining the principles on which garland sarcophagi were designed but had no effect on sculptural style; in

* In Republican times the Scipio family (and conceivably a few others of patrician rank) laid their dead in sarcophagi carved with a frieze of alternate triglyphs and rosettes, but this custom must have been an aristocratic eccentricity; there is no evidence that it endured under the empire. It may have originated as a result of Etruscan connections. The interval of at least two centuries between the latest Etruscan sarcophagi and the earliest of imperial Rome gives reason to suppose that the two types are unrelated; the difference in the lids also points to that conclusion. The Etruscan type, with a reclining figure on the lid, must be of Greek derivation whereas the imperial Roman seems an independent creation.

fact, garlands swung between the same ostensible means of support had long been used to decorate Roman altars and cinerary urns.

Athens, though quantitatively a less important centre, exported sarcophagi ready-sculptured, not only with garlands, etc., but frequently with mythological scenes. As a rule all four sides are equally ornate; the lid is sometimes shaped into a funerary couch on which reclines a figure of the deceased, which was left rough-cut until the final wishes of the purchaser were known. The distant recipients must therefore have themselves been sculptors (or at least competent monumental masons); on occasion, they apparently ordered a sarcophagus merely blocked out, with the raised spaces left blank for carving on arrival. For Attic sarcophagi made long voyages; they are found from Catalonia and Cyrenaica to the Crimea, though most were distributed over the Greek mainland and islands. The example illustrated (Pl. 87a) was discovered near Sidon; the battle of Greeks and Amazons continues on the ends, but the back is occupied with the battle of the Lapiths and Centaurs—ancient subjects in contemporary treatment.

The importation of Attic sarcophagi stimulated the sculptural development—almost entirely at Rome itself—of the 'Roman' type, which was prevalent throughout Italy and the western provinces. This differed in shape because it was intended to stand against a wall; the back, therefore, was always left plain, while the lid might either be flat or else slope gently upwards to the front, where it ended with an upright edge (Pl. 87b). This strip is sculptured in shallower relief, and necessarily with figures on a smaller scale, than is the front of the sarcophagus; the ends, too, since they could scarcely be noticed inside a tomb, are usually carved in shallower relief, but in their case less care was taken and the most slovenly work might be acceptable. Garland compositions abound; for more expensive products there was an extensive repertoire of subjects drawn both from mythology and from contemporary Roman life, including many that can be (and possibly were) interpreted as referring to the joys the soul might experience after death. But the choice must generally have depended on the sculptor's caprice; anyone so inclined can (and, no doubt, could then) perceive symbolism in everything, whereas sceptics may conclude that any theme capable of decorative treatment was liable to be chosen irrespective of whether an esoteric meaning could be read into it. The purveyors, no doubt, endeavoured to satisfy their customers' hazy mysticism (for which there is ample evidence, both literary and archaeological), but it must have been incomprehensible to many of the better sculptors, who evidently were immigrant Greeks.

Only a Greek can have possessed the detailed knowledge of Bacchic topics exhibited on the 'Casali' sarcophagus (Pl. 87b), one of the finest Antonine examples of the 'Roman' type. Related subjects were chosen for the lid and chest, as is very often the case, but the scenes on both are distinctly unusual. In the centre of the box Bacchus and Ariadne are seen reclining on a bank to drink, overshadowed by a vine; their attendant leopards lie at their feet. Below a fight between Pan and Cupid has taken place on a plot of ground sprinkled with a basketful of sand for the purpose; Cupid, holding the palm of victory, is now hustling off Pan with his hands tied behind his back, while Silenus and another cupid drive him onwards from the rear. Neither Bacchus nor Ariadne takes any interest in the affair, but Mercury has watched in his capacity of patron of prize-fights (*Enagonios*) and the troop of maenads and satyrs is intent on the sport. The venerable priests of Bacchus, holding torches, look on with ecclesiastical unconcern. Scattered about the ground are the animals and ritual apparatus proper to Bacchus—snakes, panthers and goats, a winnowing fan (*vannus*), casket (*cista mystica*) and altar carved with the image of the god. On the edge of the lid Bacchus and Ariadne again appear carousing, with a satyr drinking from a horn and a maenad playing the double flute and dancing with sounding-boards (*kroupezia*) fastened to her feet. To the left enters a chariot drawn by two leopards, one of them ridden by a cupid playing the lyre; to the right comes a troop of maenads carrying off Pan's wine. Beyond are two more maenads engaged with the *cista* and *vannus*, which have been placed on a rock; a satyr starts back at the sight of the snakes that crawl out of the *cista* when the lid is lifted. For the most part the figures on the lid have a cramped appearance, though the sculptor availed himself of the antique convention which allowed a figure to alter in size to fit the space it must occupy. As in other sarcophagi, the play of light and shadow is very evident, though the excessive use of the drill produces an unpleasant, worm-eaten effect.

That the Antonine artists excelled in the expression of emotion may be learnt by a fragment in New York. The dying Meleager, nude among a crowd of draped figures, is being carried home by a friend and two barefooted slaves, while an old slave leans grieving over his master, and other mourners behind bury their faces in their garments. (Titian's picture of the burial of Christ resembles the scene both in design and in some of the details, and a duplicate may have come to light during the Renaissance.) The relief probably formed the central portion of the front of a 'Roman' sarcophagus, in which the neighbouring panels contained other incidents in the story, placed side by side in the continuous manner introduced in Trajan's Column and popular on sarcophagi.

Another type of sarcophagus, free-standing like the Attic but with a lid that simulates the roof of a building (Pl. 87c), was produced in Asia Minor, where isolated examples have been found in most districts and a much larger number on the south coast; probably, therefore, the industry was centred in one or more of the Pamphylian cities—Attaleia (Antalya), Perga or Side. All four sides of the chest alone are sculptured, with compositions that tend to be less crowded than their Italian or Attic counterparts, while the individual figures depend more on form than on pictorial effects of light and shade, in spite of the liberal use of the drill. In other words the Hellenistic tradition still operated; the details, however, were up-to-date—early Antonine in the case of the sarcophagus illustrated, which now belongs to the Rhode Island School of Design. The parody of a big-game hunt, enacted by cupids with their pack of hounds, is framed at the corners by images of rustic deities, up which grow acanthus plants. The relief on the opposite side, of Hector's body being dragged after Achilles' chariot, shows the heroes in cuirasses of Antonine army issue; subjects totally unrelated to either side are treated on the ends. The gabled lid is ornamented with palmette 'acroteria' to disguise the strengthening function of the upturned corners (a regular feature of Proconnesian and other exported sarcophagi), but the lion-head water-spouts are incongruously placed against the rows of cover-tiles instead of beside the intervening flat portions that would drain a roof; all is pretence, to be taken no more seriously than the sporting cupids.

When the 'Asiatic' type had been established a generation or more, during which time sculptors in several parts of Asia Minor had, no doubt, adopted it, the practice arose of substituting columns for the corner figures, and soon was elaborated into converting the whole chest to a semblance of an ornate building; for that there had been occasional precedents over the previous seven centuries, but now the scheme entailed the addition of intermediate columns linked by alternate arches and lintels, to accord with a fashion in contemporary architecture. The architectural features, which could be carved quite rapidly with the aid of templates, gave these 'Asiatic Column Sarcophagi' a deceptively expensive appearance, thus commending them to overseas as well as local customers. The initial stages of development are, in fact, seen most clearly in Italy, by means of two sarcophagi, one of 165 from Torre Nuova, and one of a few years later at Melfi. (No outstanding intact example exists in Asia Minor earlier than one of about 190 or 200, which was found at Sardis, the ancient capital of Lydia; hence the term 'Lydian' used to be applied to distinguish Asiatic sarcophagi of the second from those of the third century, in the mistaken belief that different schools were involved.) The classic calm and dignity of the Torre Nuova groupings obviously spring from familiarity with monuments of the fifth and fourth centuries B.C., while the frame of the relief consists only of a column at each corner and mouldings above and below. In the Melfi sarcophagus (Pl. 88a) the front panel is broken by four columns in addition to those at the corners, thus forming no less than five niches, which are connected at the top by bands of ornament; these form a peak over the central niche and a horizontal bar over the two on either side of it, while the two exterior niches are arched. Each niche houses a figure, thus reproducing the ornamental façades of second-century buildings in Asia Minor. The ends are similarly divided into niches but the central niche of one end is carved in the shape of a door—the false door used in the tombs of Asia Minor since the archaic period. On the lid lies a recumbent full-sized figure of the deceased, a woman whose hair is dressed in a style represented on coins of 169 and so can be dated almost exactly, for she had every chance of keeping up with changes of fashion since she lived near the Appian Way—the sarcophagus was found in a tomb built actually beside it, presumably on her country estate. The mythological subjects underneath bear no relevance to her; the niches, in fact, contain reproductions of famous statues and the only allusion to death occurs inconspicuously, the false door being flanked by figures of Hermes in his capacity of gate-keeper and a woman bringing gifts.

Sarcophagi from Greece and Asia Minor were brought not only to distant ports but also to places far inland; the Melfi district, for instance, lies midway between the east and west coasts of Italy on a road that led obliquely across the country. In many regions of the empire a mixture of styles resulted from local imitation, so that the historical importance of sarcophagi exceeds their artistic value, which is not always negligible; many of them show a freshness lacking in the more formal reliefs commissioned officially by an emperor or by the Senate.

Three historical reliefs in the Conservatori relate to Marcus Aurelius' Triumph in 176. They are less enterprising than a set of eight reliefs which must have come from some monument in his honour—posthumous, it would seem—but are built into the Arch of Constantine. The emperor's head was replaced by that of Constantine, then in turn by a Renaissance imitation; the heads of other principal figures have been re-cut to resemble courtiers of the later reign. In the scene illustrated (Pl. 88b) Marcus sits on a canopied platform, receiving money handed to him by a boy to give to the populace below. Extreme diversity in costume and posture is enhanced by the varying treatment of drapery, except in the case of the emperor's adult attendants, whose consequent similarity must have been calculated to bring him into greater prominence; they are so placed that the canopy is seen to be at a distance from the edge of the platform. Contrasts of light and shade are achieved by lavish use of the drill, especially to deepen parallel folds in the clothing and to impart texture to the hair.

The 'Antonine Column' at Rome, commemorating the frontier wars of Marcus Aurelius, may have been designed, like Trajan's, in his own lifetime but is more likely to be entirely posthumous, because the scaffolding had not all been erected as late as thirteen years after his death. Although an obvious imitation, the Column was intended to improve on the Trajanic prototype. The narrative is, in fact, relatively comprehensible when seen from a distance owing to the much greater depth of relief and the coarser execution (Pl. 89a). Individual figures attract less attention; they are frequently placed in a row, with so little variation in pose that the effect is monotonous, but it makes the nature of the activity easy to perceive. Instead of the massed battle-scenes of Trajan, we find double lines of combatants. The field is often divided into two horizontal planes, which are unmistakably separated; for instance, the ox-cart full of shields and spears moves along a brief upper plane (terminated by one of the windows that light the internal staircase) while the plane below is longer at both ends, so that it accommodates both another ox-cart and a mule-cart laden with a dismantled catapult and a stack of the stone balls it was to shoot. Confused details may have been clarified by paint; on that supposition, a contemporary spectator would have more readily distinguished the emperor among the cavalry on the left of the carts. The abrupt change of scene from cavalry to baggage-train is typical of the Column; the story unrolls in the form of a series of illustrations rather than a connected narrative, and justifiably because the expanse displayed was at every viewpoint wider than in the Trajanic prototype. This Column was necessarily thicker because the top bore a pair of statues—of the emperor and empress—whereas Trajan's stood alone. The height is the same. The Column itself rests on a torus moulding decorated with oak leaves; the spiral of reliefs begins at once and reaches the top in twenty-three turns. It is divided in the centre by a Victory in the act of adorning a trophy, showing that there were two campaigns represented, with ethnographical data on the barbarian races. But comparison with the historical records fails to establish beyond question which campaigns were chosen out of those Marcus conducted in 169–172, 172–3, 174–5 and 177–180; a combination of 172–5 and 177–180 seems most plausible, in which case the whole concept must be assigned to the reign of Commodus.

The fully developed Antonine style, based on the lavish use of the drill, is seen at the highest point of its virtuosity in an extraordinary bust in the Conservatori (Pl. 89*b*). During the latter years of his reign (180–192), Commodus identified himself with Hercules *Romanus* and was worshipped in this form. The sculptor accordingly gives him the club and lion-skin proper to the god—the muzzle of the skin lies on top of his head, the paws are tied in front; in his left hand he holds the apple of the Hesperides. The allegorical designs of the base refer to the emperor alone. Upon a block of Oriental alabaster kneels an Amazon holding a cornucopia full of fruit, while a similar object on the other side was originally grasped by a companion figure; above, an Amazon's shield, with a Gorgon's head as its central device, ends in two eagles' heads, while below lies a globe on which are engraved a ram and a bull—astronomical signs. The stress laid on Amazons can be accounted for by the name *Amazonius* which he assumed at the extreme end of his reign, and which he pressed into the calendar as a substitute for January. But the bust can hardly have been completed in the short space of time between the assumption of that name and his murder, after which his monuments were blotted out by the Senate's decree of *damnatio memoriae*. It has been suggested that it is a work of Severus' reign commissioned after 197, when Commodus was 'consecrated'; for it was discovered in a building owned by the descendants of Severus. The head is an idealized portrait, in expression and features surprisingly like Marcus Aurelius, the philosophic father of this profligate; indeed the whole Antonine family has a strong resemblance in spite of differences in character. The curly hair is common to all its members; in the bust it would be gilded, for Commodus had golden hair, so bright that it required no brightening gold-dust. It is executed in a novel manner, by boring holes so deeply that they form pits of darkness (whereas previously lumps of hair stood up plainly from the scalp, visible in the hollows left between them). The surface of the stone is polished so highly that it gleams like porcelain. Another stroke of the chisel would have broken the marble where the lion-skin overhangs the hair, so finely is it trimmed. The skill of ancient sculptors is nowhere displayed to greater advantage than in this bust, in which some critics see also great artistic merit.

The Dynasty of Severus

Another piece which gave full play to the Roman love of photographic accuracy, and to the skill of sculptors at the close of the second century, is a female portrait in Copenhagen (Pl. 89*c*). The brown-tinted hair is further distinguished from the flesh by the careful polishing of the latter. An uncertain identification sees in the portrait the wife or daughter of Didius Julianus, who is reported to have bought the throne by auction in the camp of the Praetorian Guards and who held it for part of 193. As the instigators of his ambition, both women appear on the coins of his short reign, but their features are not sufficiently distinguishable to guarantee any identification, especially since the nose of the Copenhagen head has been restored. Its date, at least, is certain—the last few years of the second century.

A pitiful decline in standards is manifested by a collection of statues now replaced in the House of the Vestals. On this site lay numerous bases—all of them erected in the third or fourth century, except for two of the early empire—commemorating the Chief Vestal Virgins whose statues had once stood above. Their headdress is peculiar; a long woollen fillet is bound many times round the hair and falls in a loop over each shoulder, while above they wear a veil (suffibulum) composed of a four-sided white cloth with a (formerly) purple border, and fastened at the neck by a brooch. Other insignia as well are represented on the sole earlier example (p. 278, Pl. 85d) but every late figure lacks one or more, and the omissions can only be due to slovenliness. The sculptors' incompetence is the more significant because of the veneration in which the office was held.

The Arch of Septimius Severus at Rome commemorates his capture of Ctesiphon and Seleucia-on-Tigris; it was erected in 203 to celebrate also the tenth anniversary of his accession. On the summit stood a bronze group of a chariot drawn by six horses, as well as two equestrian statues; all these have disappeared but the Arch itself remains complete. Through it run three passages, over two of which there was space for reliefs up to the level of the tall central arch. On either façade four columns stand on bases decorated with reliefs of Parthian prisoners led by legionaries (Pl. 91a). Facing the Capitol, on the keystone of the central arch, is the figure of Mars, on the triangular spaces at either side are the Genii of Summer and Autumn, river-gods decorate the tympanums of the two lateral arches, above them stretch narrow bands of minute figures: while larger reliefs above record incidents of the war. On the façade towards the Forum, the reliefs are too worn for identification. In this Arch the combined influence of Trajan's Column and the Arch of Benevento is visible: the reliefs are disposed in two lines corresponding to the panels of the latter, but the division is marked only by an irregular line, composing the floor of the upper relief. In the play of light and shade and the compression of figures is seen the continuance of the technique found in Hadrianic work; there is no attempt at pictorial illusion. The depth and style of carving vary between one part of the Arch and another, depending on the distance from which it would be seen. The Parthians and their guards (Pl. 91*a*), near ground-level, are cut shallower than the reliefs of Marcus Aurelius (Pl. 88*b*), in a rather similar style, though with less delicacy. The group of Roman soldiers (Pl. 90*b*), high above the northern lateral arch, is almost in the round; only a minimum of detail is represented and that in a cursory repetitive manner derived from the 'Antonine' Column. The effect, however, verges on caricature, presaging developments late in the century.

A flat, practically two-dimensional technique of relief is found on a small Arch at Rome called the Porta Argentariorum; it was dedicated to the imperial family in 204 by the Guilds of Bankers (*Argentarii*) and Cattle-merchants. On two panels there remain the stiffly-posed figures of Septimius and his wife Julia Domna and of their son Caracalla. The rich floral decoration on the pilasters is better; it influenced the development of Renaissance ornament.

In 203 Septimius paid a state visit to his birthplace Leptis, probably in order to inspect the monstrous series of buildings erected at his cost. His entry is represented on an Arch which is likely to have been ordered on that occasion and completed before his death in 211. Like the pilasters of his basilica at Leptis, which bear a harsh edition of Hadrianic decoration at Aphrodisias (Pl. 84*d*), the sculptures of the Arch are in Asia Minor marble and were obviously carved by craftsmen from Asia Minor. The whole set of reliefs—a frieze on each side and panels on each pier—is homogeneous; a typical piece shows the crowd attending a sacrifice in honour of Julia Domna (Pl. 91*b*). Deadly monotony results from the predominance of frontal postures and a greater reliance on the drill than on Septimius' Arch at Rome. Frontality had, of course, been habitual for portrait busts on the tombstones and sarcophagi upon which most sculptors relied for their regular livelihood; the designer's incapacity for free composition would be explicable if he too had never before had a chance to attempt it.

A higher standard of technique persisted in Macedonia where, from the beginning of the second century, the usual form of private monument had been a tombstone carved with portrait busts in medallions; as many as eight members of a family are represented together on Severan slabs, the medallions being arranged in rows. In most other provinces the standard of carving varied from bad to competent while the designs were conventional. But a re-emergence of the Celtic spirit in Gaul and Britain is shown in works of such originality as to be undatable within half a century; in the largest and finest of them, the astonishing pediment at Bath, Antonine or Severan technique was applied to un-Roman subjects treated in an utterly un-Roman manner, while in minor reliefs a local deity may be distinguished, not merely by costume, but by the crude vigour of the presentation.

Sarcophagi of the early third century differ from the Antonine in their more crowded compositions; several figures are fitted in one behind the other and even less free space than before is left. An interesting sarcophagus in the Palazzo Riccardi at Florence has its front carved in imitation of the Asiatic style, while the sides are covered with very low reliefs, of an emperor inspecting a prisoner and a sacrifice scene. The architecture of the front differs from Asiatic examples, and its central niche holds a representation of a Roman wedding. These Roman subjects make it plain that the sarcophagus and its like were made in Italy, in spite of the Asiatic elements. In the sarcophagi now produced in Asia Minor the use of the drill was still more pronounced, but since these were not exported in appreciable numbers and did not attain their full development till later, discussion of them should be reserved for the next chapter, in dealing with the best sarcophagus, that from Sidamara (Pl. 92*b*).

In portraiture the extinction of the Antonine house led at first to little change. Honorific statues had become rare; even emperors were normally represented in busts, yet a bronze nude of Septimius Severus (at Nicosia) is of fine quality. In style the heads of him are practically indistinguishable from those of Marcus Aurelius. Most heads of his son Caracalla conform with Hadrianic and Antonine conventions, but occasionally a harsher treatment demonstrates that the transition to the style of the late empire had begun.

The greatest work of Caracalla's reign, the enormous Baths built in Rome between 211 and 216, was decorated with sculptures and mosaics on a gigantic scale to match the building. Of the statues the most noteworthy is a 'Flora' in Naples, ultimately based on the style of 400 B.C., and the 'Farnese' Hercules, 3 m. in height, signed by Glycon the Athenian; the original of the Hercules was Lysippic, and the existence of another copy on the same scale implies that Lysippus' statue too was of this size. It has been argued that Glycon's statue cannot have been carved expressly for the Baths, on the ground that so good a work could not have been produced by an age which carved the poor and minute copy on one of the capitals. Apart from the obvious fact that a capital executed by a stonemason does not fairly represent the art of his day, the head of the colossus appears no older than late Antonine and has most resemblance to the style of the Caracalla portraits; the hair is drilled and the eyes are deeply bored. It is true that the head, as well as the arms and legs, is made from separate blocks but there is no reason to suppose that a later sculptor replaced a new head on an older statue. The body is disfigured by bulging muscles, the responsibility for which rests as much with Lysippus as with Glycon.

The group known as the 'Farnese Bull' in Naples, another of the ornaments of the Baths of Caracalla, is the largest surviving sculpture of antiquity (Pl. 92a). It illustrates the story of Dirce, who was tied to a bull by the youths, Zethus and Amphion, in return for her cruelty to their mother Antiope, who stands watching the proceedings; the rocky ground of the mountain Cithaeron, whose Genius sits on the right between the legs of one of the youths, is covered with flora and fauna carved in relief. A group of this subject is mentioned by Pliny as comprising the figures of the two sons, Dirce and the bull; his silence concerning the subsidiary figures is significant, implying that they were added to the Naples group by a Roman copyist. The original was the work of Apollonius and Tauriscus of Tralles, and was brought to Rome from Rhodes; the artists' father, Menecrates, is doubtfully identified as one of the sculptors of the Gigantomachy of Pergamon, but the recurrence of the same names through several generations of this family of sculptors leaves the epigraphical evidence indecisive. Of the two presumably later figures, Antiope and Cithaeron, one is similar to the 'Flora' from the Baths and the other is obviously a Roman type. The peculiar structure of the group must be due to the late artist; composed in the form of a pyramid, the base is built up in three levels. On the highest, which occupies the centre, stand the bull and Amphion, whose body is propped up by the tree-trunk against which he has laid his lyre; on the middle level stands Zethus, pulling down the bull's head by means of a rope attached to its horns, and Dirce is seated near an altar of Dionysus with one foot resting on the lowest plane. The group has been thoroughly restored at various times, and of the figures practically half is new, so that the details do not assist in disentangling the original from the accretions, although the simpler group recorded by Pliny may be that illustrated on Lydian coins. The Roman group has more historical value; in spite of the restorations it can confidently be ascribed to a period after A.D. 150 and may belong to Caracalla's reign as well as any other. The cursory treatment of the drapery of Antiope is one of the most decisive features that contribute towards this verdict. As to the aesthetic value, it was a more impressive piece of decoration because of that elaboration which annoys the modern critic.

In addition to the Baths, Caracalla built extensively at Baalbek, the sanctuary of the Baal whom the Romans called Jupiter Heliopolitanus. The gigantic temples on this site remain in a fair state of preservation, but they yielded not more than two or three statues, of a provincial standard, and very few reliefs. The most ambitious decorate the rims of two extensive fountain-tanks, whereon Tritons swim with Nereids seated on their tails, holding up cloaks that the wind blows around them; these mediocre reliefs are exactly paralleled on sarcophagi in Asia Minor, from which the sculptor must have come. Since they were left unfinished, they can be ascribed with the utmost probability to the reign of Caracalla, the last emperor to undertake seriously the task of completing the sanctuary. A well-deserved assassination cut short his activities in 217, and with Caracalla perished the lingering Antonine tradition of sculpture. Henceforth the small extent to which imperial patronage was available limited the activities of artists.

XIV

The Transition to Byzantine Art: Decline
of the Pagan Empire

(A.D. 217–337)

SCULPTURE was almost entirely confined to portraits, sarcophagi and small decorative reliefs during the last hundred years in which Rome remained the capital of the Empire. Ruffians of ephemeral power, rushed into the purple by their own ambition and the greed of their armies, had neither the time nor the impulse to carry out historical reliefs, while the few meritorious emperors were confronted with more urgent calls on their depleted treasuries. Of portraits, both of private persons and of emperors, there is no lack, but it is rare to find more than one head of each individual, hence identifications proposed for those which seem to represent emperors can seldom be certain in the absence of inscriptions. Apart from portrait busts, the best work of the age is to be found on the sarcophagi, on which the heads deserve considerable praise. Rome was the headquarters of the industry, exporting sarcophagi to the western and, more rarely, to the eastern provinces. In this 'Roman' type of the mid-third century the composition of reliefs was often so crowded as to look confused (though not to the degree occasionally reached under the Antonines). The supreme example is the 'Ludovisi' sarcophagus (in the Terme) which probably contained the body of Hostilianus, the young prince who became nominally emperor in 251 and died later in the year; the features of the commanding officer certainly resemble his coin-portraits. Here the figures are seemingly piled in a heap, though actually those at the top were intended to be in the background. By contorting the figures it was possible to crowd in as many as four, one above the other, each large enough to cover, if extended, half or more of the total height of the relief: the deep undercutting feasible by means of the drill helped to distinguish the various layers of human bodies, but the use of this instrument produced unpleasant, spongelike hair, and coarsened the treatment of drapery.

The possibilities of this technique were fully explored in the 'Sidamara' sub-type of Asia Minor, which developed early in the third century from such precedents as the Sardis sarcophagus, and culminated, but did not end, about 250, with the enormous sarcophagus (about 3.50 m. long) found near Sidamara. Two figures, of a man and a woman, recline on the lid, along the edge of which runs a frieze with unrelated subjects—cupids fighting wild animals, athletes training and chariots racing. The chest, as usual, is faced with a colonnade throughout, and a doorway is represented on one of the ends; the other end and the side beneath the faces of the recumbent couple are filled by hunting scenes, incongruous in their architectural setting, but since the stage of a Roman theatre was given just such a background the absurdity would not have struck an ancient spectator. The back contains the principal relief (Pl. 92b). The dead man occupies the central niche; seated on a stool ending in lion's paws, he reads a half-unrolled scroll which he holds in the left hand, while the right rests on the lion-skin covering the stool. The head reproduces without individual traits the conventional type of the philosopher, poet or rhetorician; the pupils of the eyes are incised, the short, curly hair stands up from the forehead, where the frontal sinus is accentuated. He is raised upon a dais, so that his head falls level with those of the standing figures; this seated figure is, however, too wide for the niche, and in order to avoid spoiling the colonnade design the dais is placed to the left of the exact centre, so that the left column shows only between the legs of the stool, and the whole of the right column is visible except where the outstretched leg passes over it. The effect is clumsy and painfully unsymmetrical. The female figure to the right of the dead man, of matronly aspect, therefore perhaps his wife, is of a fourth-century Hera type; contrary to the general practice on the sarcophagus the eyes are not incised. Behind him on the left is another female figure dressed as Artemis, but which may represent his daughter. The arched niches at either end are each occupied by a Dioscurus holding a horse, much telescoped and reduced in size; their forefeet rest on a small tree-trunk which grows out of the column, a comic device which lamentably confuses the design at the end of the composition where simple contours and firm lines are most needed. Excessive use of the drill produces violent juxtapositions of light and shade, and transforms classical mouldings into nothing better than vermiculation. Anti-classic tendencies are expressed in the taste for a continuous motive without beginning or end, like an arabesque, as against the ancient use of the independent and fully developed incident. Every available space of the background is covered with decoration.

No examples of the 'Sidamara' group are known to have been exported, because sculptors in Rome and elsewhere in the west now fulfilled the demand for the 'Asiatic Column' type by producing substitutes of their own; these apparently sold more readily if pure Roman elements were blended into the decoration. The central niche (Pl. 93a) of one such Romanized version of an 'Asiatic' sarcophagus contains the group of a Roman bride and bridegroom clasping hands in front of a curtain; a child genius stands between them holding a cornucopia to suggest the fruitfulness of marriage. On a much restored panel to the left stands Artemis in her capacity of goddess of marriage and childbirth, accompanied by another female figure, perhaps the wife; the corresponding panel to the right is occupied by a bearded man of philosophic mien, probably the husband (fatuously restored with a sword), and by his side stands another small figure. These side niches more often contain figures of Dioscuri, as on Asiatic sarcophagi. Coins frequently represented the emperor and empress clasping hands at their wedding ceremony; since this is a sarcophagus, the hand-clasp should be interpreted rather as that of the last separation, or of a 'mystic marriage' in the After-life. Both man and wife have reached a considerable age, to judge by their faces, but these are idealizations, not portraits. The man wears his toga in the third-century manner, with a band of folds across the breast: the treatment of the drapery is a good example of the Roman habit of cutting hollows for the shadows instead of raising the highlight folds above the general surface. The form of the woman's body is skilfully shown through her drapery and the contrast between the curtain and the clothing is clearly expressed. This Roman sculpture has a sense of life absent in the traditional Hellenism of Asia Minor, where, however, there prevails a finer sense for pattern. Apart from the borrowing of the general scheme, no specifically Greek touches can be traced; the work and subjects are characteristically Roman and related to such sculpture in the round as the capital could offer at the time.

Into portraiture a great change entered, soon after Caracalla's death. The contrasts in the modelling of Antonine heads diminished under the Severus dynasty, to be then abandoned completely for a sterner, harder treatment; similarly the tired, peevish expression of the late second century was strengthened by Caracalla into one of ferocity, and whatever the character of the individual, the expression remained forceful and definite. The germ of the new modelling can be traced in some heads of Caracalla; its full development appears in the bust of Philip the Arabian, emperor from 244 to 249 (Pl. 93b). Owing to a fashion of wearing the hair smooth and close-cut, the hair and beard could now be represented by means of short strokes or points on a smooth surface, raised only slightly over the level of the face; this method had been used from the Republican period onwards for heads of almost bald men or the shaven priests of Isis, but it is now applied to hair trained to lie close to the head. Shallow grooves are cut where Antonine sculptors would require greater depth, the lips are thin, the eyes bulge from the head and the eyebrows no longer project. The whole effect is flat and dry. The bust now reaches to the waist; the umbo of the toga is folded thickly across the chest in the new fashion, found also on the sarcophagi. With the exception of the edge of the left ear and the point of the nose, the bust of Philip is in good preservation, and the identification, based upon coin-portraits, may be taken as assured; the guileful nature of the adventurer, who rose to power through an obscure conspiracy, is well expressed.

A bronze head of comparable quality in the Deva Museum, found outside the Dacian provincial capital, is identifiable by coins as a portrait of Trajanus Decius, who spent his reign of 249–251 fighting to save Dacia from barbarian invasions. Coins of Trebonianus Gallus, who reigned from 251 to 254, may justify recognition of a bronze portrait of him in New York; the head is disproportionately small for the statue, which stands in heroic nudity. Naturally the features of these bronzes are modelled to a greater extent than the marble Philip's, but the degree of simplification is practically the same. The steps whereby sculptors had learnt to simplify their technique have not yet been satisfactorily investigated. In the supposed bust of Pupienus, who died in 238, the long beard is merely channelled with the drill, and the toga is arranged in the same manner as in the bust of Philip. Another remarkable portrait is the bronze head at Munich, questionably recognized as Maximin the Thracian, who reigned from 235 to 238. The structure of this head, in planes set at an angle one to another, has been conjectured to be imitated from the porphyry sculpture of Egypt; but until porphyry work of undoubted contemporaneity is available for study, nothing should be built on the suggestion. It is possible that the long bony face of Maximin himself was responsible for such a treatment. He was a man of extraordinary physique, 8 feet in height and of prodigious strength, if the stories related about him be true; his coins are sufficiently striking to justify an unusual technique in a larger portrait. But an equally harsh treatment of the face may be noted in a marble figure of Egyptian provenance, representing an old man carousing on a couch in the attitude of sarcophagus-lids; it must be remembered that no marble existed in Egypt, and no one can decide whether the raw material or the finished statue was imported.

For the female type that corresponds to the bust of Philip the Arabian a head in Copenhagen (Pl. 93c) must serve as an example; from the hair-dressing it dates probably from the decade in which his reign fell, although no identification can be conjectured. The neck is rounded for insertion into a statue. In the polished flesh-surface lingers the tradition of the previous century, but perhaps greater emphasis is laid on the eyes; in essentials the style is far closer to that of the late Antonine Age than is customary in contemporary male portraiture.

An interesting school, much influenced by the sculpture of the late archaic period, flourished in Greece towards the mid-third century. Its masterpieces are the heads of a youth (Pl. 94a) and a boxer in Copen-hagen. In details such as the eyes and hair, the rendering cannot be dis-tinguished from ordinary Roman work, but in general effect the head resembles the Discobolus of Myron (Pl. 29a) of seven hundred years before; intervening periods had demanded a more sentimental or more intellectual type of athlete. The difference between the early and the late artist lies in this; the rough treatment of the hair was due to incompetence in Myron, whereas the late artist was an impressionist desiring to give an effect to be seen from a distance or gathered from a rapid glance. He was anxious to avoid prettiness, and the decision of the athlete's features is un-marred by any touch of the grace that characterized the work of fifty years before. In its return to archaic treatment, this style is a forerunner of the fourth century.

Soon after the middle of the third century portraits returned to a slightly contrasting and colourful style, although the dotted rendering of the hair remained in some heads. Gallienus, whose father appointed him co-emperor in 253, may be responsible for the reaction, for he was a dandy and would, in particular, have disliked a sober representation of the hair which he wore powdered with gold-dust. Less elegant than his other por-traits is the colossal head in Copenhagen (Pl. 94b), in which he appears as an older man, less idealized; the surface lacks the polish of other heads. It belonged to a statue of nearly twice life-size. The more youthful types probably date from the period in which he was his father's colleague, but this certainly should be assigned to his own reign (260–268), during which the anxiety caused by no less than nineteen pretenders to his throne, the news of whose rebellions he always received with a careless smile, must have aged even this singular character. If he had any solid qualities they escaped the observation of ancient historians, whose account Gibbon has summarized as: 'He was a master of several curious but useless sciences, a ready orator, an elegant poet, a skilful gardener, an excellent cook, and a most contemptible prince.' Although art must have profited from an emperor avowedly devoted to culture, whose reign of fifteen years was the longest since Septimius Severus, talk of a 'Gallienic renaissance' over-estimates the sculptural achievements; there may, however, have been some increase in private as well as official patronage. At any rate, the latest set of statues that has survived from the pagan empire must have been com-missioned by some distinguished family of Gallienus' reign. The three figures are obviously products of one workshop, if not of one sculptor; presumably they were found together, since they are all in the Villa Doria-Pamphili at Rome. One man stands wearing a toga and tunica; an-other, standing nude except for a paludamentum over his shoulder, is accompanied by a dog, an indication that he was hunting, while a third stands nude, sword in hand, to kill the boar beside him. The work is effec-tive in an uncouth manner.

A head identified by coins as Probus (276–282), does not depart so far from the treatment of the Philip, perhaps because the features and character of the two men were more alike; the hair is more prominent in the Probus. On the other hand, another head, recognized from coins as Carinus (283–285), follows the type of Gallienus. The portraiture of the later third century shows therefore a slow development towards formality, modified by the characteristics of the individual portrayed.

The final stage in this process can be seen in a head in Copenhagen (Pl. 95a) which should date from near the end of the century or even after 300. It must represent one of the co-rulers responsible for the administration and defence of different parts of the empire, a system introduced by Dio-cletian a couple of years after his own accession. He began in 286 by taking one partner, Maximian, and in 293 appointed Galerius and Constantius as assistant emperors, entitled Caesars. The tetrarchy ensured stability, so that in 305 Diocletian and Maximian were able to retire after an orderly hand-over to the Caesars. The tetrarch portrayed in the Copenhagen head (and another in the Doria-Pamphili collection) cannot be identified with cer-tainty because the coin-profiles of the time are travesties, which distin-guish Diocletian from Maximian merely (if at all) by showing three wrinkles in the forehead instead of the other's one; on that tenuous ground the man should be Diocletian if he is one of the older pair, in which case his apparent age would put the date well before the appointment of the Caesars in 293. He cannot be Constantius, whose extremely individual features are recognizable in a head of which two copies remain, both colossal (Pl. 95b). In this case the trend towards simplification has advanced so far that only the major features are represented; the sculptor must have eliminated lesser natural markings such as abound on the 'Diocletian'. So great a change in the conventions of official portraiture may seem unlikely to have occurred quickly, but the maximum we can allow for it is some twenty years if the original of the Constantius be placed between 293 and his death in 306—disregarding the faint possibility that it was posthumous, made to the order of his son Constantine. Had it been posthumous, it would surely have been idealized to express his reputation; 'clemency, temperance and moderation distinguished the amiable character of Constantius,' says Gibbon.

The return of settled government brought a revival in the output of large monuments. A successful war against the Persians, ending in 297, was commemorated by the erection of a triumphal arch at Salonica in honour of Galerius. The accumulated rubbish of centuries raised the ground around it until the reliefs came within easy reach, a fact of which devoted Moslems took advantage to mutilate the representations of the human form; the figures of Galerius had probably been attacked long before by Christians, in revenge for his persecution of the Church. But although their condition is deplorable, these reliefs are among the most instructive relics of the later empire. On the three exposed sides of each inner pier of the triple arch were placed four strips of relief superimposed, but horizontally divided by carved mouldings; the reliefs on each side formed self-contained compositions as on a sarcophagus. The narrative can be followed only on one pier, where it begins at the top, with the opening of the campaign, and continues in the second strip with the defeat of the Persians; the third and fourth are devoted to the triumphant aftermath. A quiet scene often alternates with one of activity. For sheer turmoil, none exceeds a panel of the second strip, where Galerius rides down the enemy general, striking him with a lance while an eagle helps by shooting a well-aimed flash of lightning. In a quiet panel on the third strip (Pl. 95c) the two Caesars offer sacrifice at an altar, holding out their right hands to personifications of Armenia and Mesopotamia. On one of the adjoining crowded panels, the two emperors sit on thrones supported by the river-gods Tigris and Euphrates, while the other is filled with genii and gods between reclining figures of Ocean and Earth at either corner. Figures of Victories in the lowest strip stand in the niches of a colonnade, each below a shell canopy, as on an Asiatic sarcophagus.

The technique of the reliefs is anomalous for the period in two respects, their great depth and the sparing use of the drill. Probably all the sculptors concerned made their living from sarcophagi; they must have been brought to Salonica from a distance, and the designer seems to have been familiar with historical reliefs of the past, presumably in Rome. Following their lead he was indifferent to decorative value and took liberties with the size of objects, reducing towns to the height of men, and representing the enemy smaller than the Romans. At close quarters it can be seen that many portions are not raised above the background, but are merely surrounded with a furrow cut in the stone to produce at a distance the effect of a shadow cast by a projecting mass: this convention of 'optical contours' is seldom found in Roman work (except in Gaul in the first century) and has been assigned to Oriental influence, for it was a method long used both in Asia and Egypt. But it may as plausibly be attributed to acquaintance with the technique of painting, although the subjects and composition fairly closely resemble those of third-century Persian rock-carvings.

In 303 a row of statues on columns was put in the Roman Forum in honour of the tetrarchs. The one remaining base is carved with the subjects of an Emperor or a Caesar sacrificing to Mars and Roma (Pl. 94c), the *Suovetaurilia*, a procession of Senators, and two Victories displaying a shield inscribed '*Caesarum Decennalia Feliciter*'. The drapery is intersected by deep channels to indicate shadows, and similar lines are cut round the figures, making them stand out from the background; the long hair of the Victories is represented simply by a network of pits spread over a flat surface. Throughout very few planes are used; the relief largely dispenses with modelling in favour of a flat surface and dark grooves.

In expensive sarcophagi of about 300 the same style appears as in this base; technique had become gradually simplified since the mid-third century, just as composition had lost the exuberance of that era, and the human figure was now conventionally represented. A steadily increasing proportion of sarcophagi was produced for Christians, who concealed their illegal creed by such devices as equating Orpheus with the Good Shepherd, so that they could choose from quite a wide range of apparently pagan subjects; nor is there anything distinctively Christian in the style of presentation. Local peculiarities are not often conspicuous. In the most notable exception, the obviously pagan 'Dumbarton Oaks' sarcophagus, a decadent offshoot of the 'Sidamara' school is unexpectedly found to have been still active in 330 or even a trifle later. A medallion with portrait busts of a man and wife occupies the centre of the front, in the manner of the previous century; underneath is a swarm of cupids busy vintaging. A pair of winged Seasons stands to either side; low down between Winter and Spring is a diminutive shepherd, milking a goat, while a peasant cutting a sheaf of wheat fills the corresponding gap between Summer and

Autumn. The clumsy and lifeless Seasons, badly carved, project far beyond the background; the smaller-scale work is done so largely by drill as to give an effect of vermiculation.

The next large monument to require sculpture was the triumphal arch erected in honour of Constantine's victory in the civil war of 312; in addition to the assorted older sculpture incorporated, a great deal of new work was needed. This was probably completed soon after 313, when the edict of toleration legalized the practice of Christianity. That Christians were employed on the carving of the reliefs has been suggested to account for their childish character, compared, for instance, with the tetrarch base in the Forum; certainly the Victories on the Arch piers exhibit a different technique, with drapery crinkled into innumerable small channels, while masses of it run in sweeping folds at right angles across the rest. This method occurs eight hundred years before in Acropolis *korai*. Christian sarcophagi of the fourth century employ the style of the long reliefs of the Arch (Pl. 96*a*), but this is by no means proof of the sculptor's religion, for in the pagan sarcophagi of Diocletian's time occur parallels both to the base of 303 and to the various sections of the Arch. A significant point is the rapidity with which art was altering in the West, where the revolution from classical to Byzantine art progressed more rapidly than in the East.

All the sculptures of Pl. 96*a* belong to the reign of Constantine himself, for their mixture of styles is accountable in a time of transition, and the technique of their details is identical. The little figure over the cornerstone of the Arch, an emperor in a cuirass and military cloak, follows the conventional type of centuries, but the treatment is more formal and rectangular. The reclining figures in the spandrels of the Arch are derived from equally conventional types of greater antiquity, and again the difference is in the execution; a straight cut divides finger from finger, the graceless drapery is intersected by indiscriminating and meandering runs of the drill; the faces are out of shape, and the bodies merely adumbrated. Interest in the human body had perished. Ivory carvings from Alexandria frequently bear figures like the one on the right spandrel, better if anything, for Rome no longer led the provinces. But in the scene above, the break from tradition is complete; such a grouping might be found above the doorway of a medieval cathedral. The Emperor sits enthroned in the midst, like Christ on the Judgment Day, his staff of nine Senators and two Lictors behind him; in front are lines of dumpy figures in naïve attitudes of acclamation, recipients of the Emperor's bounty; eight of these are dressed as Senators, the rest are ordinary citizens. Constantine holds a closed scroll in his left hand, with his right he empties a plate, holding twelve coins, into the end of a toga which one of the Senators extends with both hands. A Senator on the tribunal passes the Emperor the money for distribution. In four small tribunals, officials are attending to the common people, who are only entitled to six coins apiece; in each case a clerk verifies the names of the recipients while another records the payments.

A childish simplicity prevails throughout the relief, in composition and perspective, in grouping and proportions and details of the figures. The loss of most of the skill that classical art had gained in every direction should probably not be attributed in its entirety either to the employment of incompetent sculptors or to deliberate abandonment, but to a mixture of the two with a greater element of incompetence. Perspective and natural-ism are lacking because they could not be attained; the power had been lost by a century's disuse. It must also be remembered that the reliefs were high up on the Arch, where defects would not be visible; many of the figures have no feet, for the sculptor knew that the omission would be screened by the mouldings below the reliefs.

Crude though they may be, these reliefs possess some merits foreign to classical art. In spite of incompetence, the populace seems more lifelike than in older works with their stereotyped copies of ideal heads; there exists a childlike desire to capture the characteristics of real people, but it ends, in the lack of any standard of beauty, in caricature and vulgarity. The sil-houette is raised above the background, but all attempt to mould the figures in the round is avoided. Figures are allowed to vary in size according to their importance, a principle which developed further in medieval art so that any part of the body, perhaps an accusing finger, which needed emphasis was enlarged out of all proportion. The figures of each group move in concert, in an axis assigned to it; the true prototype for this con-vention existed in ancient Egypt, although a hint of it is found in Trajan's Column. The whole work is an example of that movement which was to leave ancient sculpture very much in the condition in which it started.

A dull cuirass statue of Constantine, guaranteed by inscription, stands at the church of St John Lateran in Rome but has become so weather-worn that the face is less helpful than coins for identifying other portraits. These include heads originally of Hadrian or Marcus Aurelius, re-carved into his own likeness, on the reliefs incorporated in his Arch. Marble pieces of a colossus, found in the Basilica he completed, can be accepted without ques-tion as the remains of a seated statue of him, not earlier than 324. The head and neck (Pl. 96*b*) are 2.60 m. in height; fragments prove that the arms and lower parts of the legs consisted of marble, while the remainder was pre-sumably composed of wood. The head can scarcely be described as competent. Its main characteristics are common to all the high-class work of the age: details are neglected, only the outlines of the face and of such parts as the eyebrows, eyelids and lips are modelled with the utmost distinction and with as regular lines as possible; the eyebrows and fringe form thick masses while the rest of the hair is marked out into a multitude of close-set locks; the melancholy eyes look upwards and somewhat to the side, though the head itself does not turn as in third-century portraits but is held rigidly straight to the front. This return to the 'frontality' convention of Oriental and archaic art was completed later in the fourth century, when the eyes too follow the direction of the head and body. But the style of Constantine's reign had already come to bear a superficial resemblance to that (Parthian by origin) found at the desert cities of Hatra, which was destroyed in 240, and Palmyra, destroyed in 273; the last sculptors of the pagan empire can scarcely have been subjected to influence from that direction, but the attenuation of their Greek heritage makes their works seem akin to those of Orientals who had lived beyond the frontier and never been more than partially hellenized.

It is noteworthy that the gigantic head of Constantine has a more nearly Byzantine aspect than the rather later bronze head (also in the Conservatori) from a smaller colossus believed to portray one of his sons; nor was that by any means the last occasion when the seesaw of development raised up the ancient heritage. The Hellenistic tradition retained some vitality into the fifth century or even later (when copies of the antique were still being carved at Aphrodisias), but an infusion of Byzantine spirit is evident in the best of the last attempts to recapture the pagan mode—such as the marble statues in the museums of Athens, Corinth and Chalcis, or the bronze colossus at Barletta. No date can truthfully be said to mark the turning-point between Roman and Byzantine art but events in the latter years of Constantine (who died in 337) proclaim its cause and meaning. The ancient world ended, and a new began, in 325, on his recognition of Christianity as the state religion, and in the next decade with his transference of the capital to Constantinople. In 334 he issued the first edict of a series (continued in 337, 344 and 374) intended to encourage the training of sculptors, architects and other artists or craftsmen, of whom there were too few to carry out the work required of them; after a thousand years of fruitfulness the arts seemed doomed to extinction. False as that impression proved to be as regards architecture, painting and mosaic, it was almost true of sculpture, which became a subordinate art of dwindling output.

APPENDIX I

Deities, Their Attributes and Types

AESCULAPIUS. See ASCLEPIUS.

APHRODITE (Latin VENUS)

In Greece the goddess of love and beauty, as Aphrodite Pandemus of licence and lust, as Urania of married love: in Asia Minor she was associated with fertility and vegetation. *Attributes*. Eros, the dove, the dolphin; the goat as the symbol of Pandemus, the tortoise of Urania, the partridge and pomegranate of fertility. *Types*. After the time of Praxiteles usually nude in the 'pudic' attitude; sometimes she holds a piece of drapery over her lower limbs.

APOLLO

The god of music, youth, athletics and the chase, the leader of colonies, the guardian of flocks and streets, the bringer and averter of plagues and sudden death; more especially he was the god of purification and expiation, and the lord of oracles. His solar aspect grew till in Roman times he was actually identified with Helios. *Attributes*. His most constant and distinguishing attributes are the lyre, bow, bay leaves, fillet and tripod (the last three belong to him as god of expiation and oracles). The griffin and omphalus are common, recording his victory at Delphi over the Python; the griffin was also his attribute as sun-god. Less common are the oak-wreath, palm-branch, agonistic urn, apple and pomegranate. Animals are sacred to him, such as the ram, deer, mouse, lizard, wolf, snake, cock and dolphin. *Types*. Usually nude, often of effeminate physique, with long hair tied up in a knot on the top of the head. As musician he wears a long Ionic chiton.

ARES (Latin MARS)

The god of war. *Attributes*. Helmet, spear, lance, shield and dog; the torch and oak tree are sometimes found, and the occasional presence of Eros beside him is a reminder of his connection with Aphrodite. *Type*. Youthful; middle-aged if Mars.

ARTEMIS (Latin DIANA)

Protectress of young vigorous maidenhood, but also the goddess of marriage and childbirth; closely associated with the moon. Occasionally she is identified as Hecate. In Asia Minor she was the younger form of the Anatolian mother-goddess. The Roman Diana is especially a woodland deity and the protectress of wild nature. *Attributes*. The bow, quiver and deer or hound distinguish her as the huntress, the torch as Hecate and the crescent as the moon-goddess. In early times the lion was also her animal. *Types*. A vigorous young woman, wearing a short chiton, and high hunting boots. In early art she wears a high crown, later a mere bandeau.

ASCLEPIUS (Latin AESCULAPIUS)

The god of medicine and healing. *Attributes*. The staff or sceptre with a snake coiled round it, and a cock. Sometimes he stands by an omphalus. *Types*. Except in late Roman times he is represented as a Zeus-like bearded man.

ATHENA (Latin MINERVA)

The goddess of wisdom, and of the arts of peace and war; as chief deity of many places in early times she has manifold activities. *Attributes*. The owl, aegis (goat-skin) bearing the head of Medusa, Attic or Corinthian helmet, lance, eagle or Nike, olive-tree, cock and snake; occasionally a double-axe (common to many deities). *Types*. Either seated and unarmed, or armed, erect and stern. After the second half of the fifth century she wears a Doric peplos with the peculiarity of a long overfall and an extra girdle outside.

CASTOR AND POLLUX. See DIOSCURI

CERES. See DEMETER

CUPID. See EROS

CYBELE

Anatolian mother-goddess. *Attributes*. Lions, a mural crown, a timbrel, and a shallow bowl (*phiale*). *Types*. Seated or standing between two lions, or in chariot drawn by lions.

DEMETER (Latin CERES)

Earth-goddess and mother of Persephone. *Attributes*. Ears of corn, a tall basket (*kalathos*), torches, a pig, a snake, a chest, poppies. *Types*. Chiefly seated, with the himation drawn over the head.

DIANA. See ARTEMIS

DIONYSUS (Latin BACCHUS, LIBER)

A god concerned with the seasons, animal and vegetable life. *Attributes*. The two-handled wine-cup (*cantharos*), staff tipped with a pine cone (*thyrsus*), ivy-wreath, leopard, snake, grape-cluster, box (*cista*), winnowing-fan basket (*vannus*). *Types*. In a car drawn by panthers; seated as a lyre player; standing with a bunch of grapes in his raised right hand and the wine-cup in his left hand; as a child he is carried by Hermes or Silenus, nursed by nymphs, or surrounded by Curetes. Bearded in Hellenic art, except in archaistic work; in later times always juvenile and beardless.

DIOSCURI—CASTOR AND POLYDEUCES (Latin POLLUX)

Calm the sea and send favourable winds. *Attributes*. They may always be distinguished by their caps with stars, sheathed swords, horses, although they have numerous other attributes, not found in better known sculptures. *Types*. Two young men in various positions or two young heads.

EILITHYEIA

The goddess of childbirth. *Attributes*. Girdle, torch and mantle. *Type*. Youthful, seated or standing.

EROS (Latin CUPID)

The god of love and son of Aphrodite. *Attributes*. Wings growing on the shoulders, torch, bow and arrow. *Types*. At first as a youth; from Hellenistic times as a child.

HECATE

The goddess of night. *Attributes*. Torches and a crescented *kalathos* head-dress. *Types*. Usually she stands, holding torches; sometimes triplicate.

HELIOS (Latin SOL)

The sun-god. *Attributes*. Rays and nimbus, chariot, snake. *Types*. He is represented by a bearded radiate head or bust, or by a young male head, or as a charioteer.

HEPHAESTUS (Latin VULCAN)

The artisan god. *Attributes*. Anvil, hammer, double-axe and oval cap. *Types*.

Vigorous, bearded, with one leg shorter than the other; wears a short chiton fastened on one shoulder only.

HERA (Latin JUNO)

She is principally the consort of Zeus, the patron of marriage and childbirth. Sometimes she is the earth or female principle in nature. *Attributes.* Sceptre, sometimes surmounted by a cuckoo, crown, pomegranate, peacock. *Types.* A mature woman, sometimes enthroned, wearing full drapery, with a veil or himation drawn over her head.

HESTIA (Latin VESTA)

Goddess of the home and hearth. *Attributes.* Torch, hearth. *Types.* Well-draped, seated, or leading a procession of the gods.

HERACLES (Latin HERCULES)

A hero deified for performance of feats of strength. *Attributes.* Club, bow and lion-skin. *Types.* Middle-aged man with a powerful frame and small, bearded head.

HERMES (Latin MERCURY)

The messenger of the gods; as local deity, shares many of the functions of Apollo. His early symbol was the phallus, and he was especially connected with fertility. He was also the god of commerce and prize-fights. *Attributes.* The herald's staff (*kerukeion*), at first entwined with ribbons and later with a snake, a winged hat or cap (*petasos*) and winged sandals; as the god of commerce, a purse; as patron of prize-fights, the agonistic urn. *Types.* A youthful male figure in various attitudes: bearded in archaic work and on herms.

HYGIEIA

Asclepius' assistant, the goddess of health. *Attributes.* A snake and a sceptre. *Types.* A young woman, often feeding a snake from a saucer.

IRIS

The female messenger of the gods. *Attribute.* Wings. *Type.* Youthful.

ISIS

Her worship spread from Egypt in Hellenistic times, as a universal goddess. *Attributes.* Head-dress of solar disc and feathers, a fringed mantle knotted in peculiar manner on the breast, a sistrum and poppy. *Types.* Fairly young, sometimes enthroned or on a couch.

JUNO. See HERA

JUPITER. See ZEUS

MITHRAS

Of Persian origin; cult favoured by Roman imperial army. God of the sun and light, friendship; also a mediator. *Attributes.* The zodiac, stellate tiara, the bull, a tree entwined by a snake, a Phrygian cap. *Types.* Appearing from a tree; dragging or slaying a bull.

MERCURY. See HERMES

NEMESIS

The dispenser of divine justice; also in charge of birth and death. In Roman times often identified as Diana. *Attributes.* Measuring rule, a wheel, a crown of stags and small victories, a griffin, apple branch, sword, crescent, bowl and disk. *Types.* On a coin of Cyprus which perhaps represents the cult statue at Rhamnus, she stands wearing a peplos like that of Athena; at Carnuntum she is dressed in a short peplos and high hunting boots like the Diana at Nemi; in a relief from Piraeus she is winged and standing on a naked man; according to Pausanias, however, no ancient statue of Nemesis bore wings.

NIKE (Latin VICTORIA)

Victory, an attendant of Zeus and Athena. *Attributes.* A palm-wreath, trumpet. *Types.* Striding with a chiton open at both sides, generally winged.

PAN

Especially an Arcadian god: protector of flocks. *Attributes.* Pipes. *Types.* Seated on a rock, usually in a cave, with goat's horns or legs and hoofs; hairy body and face, slanting eyes: sometimes a young shepherd.

PERSEPHONE (Latin PROSERPINA)

Goddess of vegetation. *Attributes* shared with Demeter. *Type.* Girl in late teens.

PLUTO

God of the underworld. *Attributes.* Oak-leaves and acorn, Cerberus. *Types.* Carrying off Persephone, or seated with Cerberus beside him.

POSEIDON (Latin NEPTUNE)

God of the sea, rivers and springs; also the tamer of horses. *Attributes.* Trident, dolphin, tunny. *Types.* Has the features of Zeus, but is not enthroned; frequently standing with the trident in his outstretched hand, and later with one foot resting on a rock; or riding in his chariot over the waves.

PRIAPUS

God of gardens. *Type.* A herm.

PROSERPINA. See PERSEPHONE

SATYRS (Latin FAUN)

Familiars of Dionysus. *Attributes.* Ass, ivy-wreath. *Types.* Youthful; pointed ears; sometimes horse-tailed and hoofed.

SERAPIS

An earth deity identified with Zeus and Pluto; his cult spread from Hellenistic Alexandria. *Attributes.* Those of Zeus and Pluto but distinguished by the *modius* (*kalathos*), worn on the head like a high crown and decorated by olives or ears of corn. *Types.* Bearded and Zeus-like.

SILENUS

Attendant of Dionysus. *Attributes.* Ass and ivy-wreath. *Types.* Snub-nosed, coarse-featured old man, always inebriated.

SELENE (Latin LUNA)

Moon-goddess. *Attributes.* Nimbus, chariot, horse, narcissus, partridge. *Type.* Youthful, driving a chariot.

VICTORY. See NIKE

ZEUS (Latin JUPITER)

Functions. The sky-god; the father and ruler of the Olympian deities. He was connected with all the celestial luminaries, but only in Hellenistic and Roman times was he identified with any in cults like that of Zeus Helios: identified with the Egyptian king of the gods, as Zeus-Ammon, and with an Anatolian god as Zeus Dolichenus. *Attributes.* Those common in sculpture are the eagle or Nike, the sceptre and thunderbolt; the Olympian Zeus was crowned with an olive-wreath and his himation was embroidered with lilies; as a child his attribute is a pomegranate, as Zeus-Ammon, ram's horns in his hair; Dolichenus holds thunderbolt and double-axe and stands on a bull. *Types.* His aspect varied with his epithets, *Soter* (the Saviour) or *Meilichios* (the amiable), but usually in early times he was represented striding, with the thunderbolt levelled and threatening. Later his beneficent aspect predominated. In the metopes of Selinus he is enthroned, with the himation drawn only over the lower limbs: the later type followed the image by Pheidias, likewise enthroned and with the torso bare, but of benign expression, dignified by the flowing hair and beard and the impressive eyebrows suggested by Homer's description; the thunderbolt is lowered. There were also sculptures of Zeus as a youth and as a child surrounded by Curetes.

APPENDIX II

Greek and Roman Dress

In Greece both sexes wore the same dress except for slight differences to allow greater freedom of movement to men. Two main types are found, the Doric and the Ionic, each consisting of an inner garment, called the peplos and the chiton respectively, and an outer garment, the himation: the term 'peplos' applies only to the Doric undergarment, whereas the term 'chiton' may be applied to either Doric or Ionic. Men frequently wore, instead of the himation or in addition to it, an extra cloak, the chlamys, which was especially used for riding or travelling: and in rare archaic female statues is found the epiblema, a shawl worn over the Ionic himation or veiling the head.

21. The peplos, or Doric chiton

Originally the only female dress in the Greek mainland was the Doric, if Herodotus be correct, but the Ionic was introduced at least as early as the sixth century. The Acropolis *Korai*, of the end of the century, wear the Ionic chiton and himation, with rare exceptions. After the Persian wars female statues habitually wear the Doric chiton, otherwise called the peplos. A long Ionic chiton, like a woman's, was always the customary dress of charioteers and musicians. Late male statues are found with himation, chiton and chlamys, singly or in conjunction.

It now remains to describe the garments in detail (see diagrams). The Doric, as might be expected, is the simpler type. The peplos consists of a

318

large oblong piece of material, usually woollen, in length exceeding the
height of the wearer by about one foot, and in breadth equal to twice the
distance from elbow to elbow when the arms are outstretched horizontally. The material is folded round the body and pinned once on each
shoulder, the side being either left open or fastened by brooches or sewing:
in order to dispose of the superfluous foot, the upper edge is folded over,
so that the material is double from neck to waist, forming the overfall
(*apoptygma*). A girdle is worn round the waist, and any remaining length
is pulled over this, forming the pouch (*kolpos*). This is the ordinary femi-
nine method of wearing the Doric peplos.

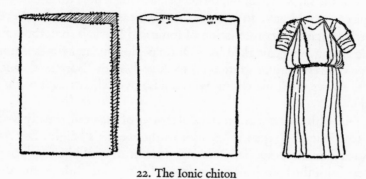

22. The Ionic chiton

Some other Doric fashions must be noticed. The peplos of Athena has a
longer overfall with girdle worn over it. In the Victory of Paeonius an
opening is left on both sides, and the garment is fastened only on one
shoulder. In statues of consistently active personages the peplos is modified
to give greater freedom. Artemis' peplos tends to be very short, with no
overfall and only slight pouch, which is held by an extra girdle round the
shoulder. Amazons dispense with both overfall and pouch. Men wore the
peplos with the modifications found in statues of Artemis and athletic
women: for slaves and workmen, the shortest possible garment, fastened
on shoulder and without pouch or overfall, is the only clothing allowed.

The Ionic chiton differed from the Doric in material, method of fastening and volume. It was usually of linen, and either pinned on the shoulder
in several places along the upper arm or sewn: though of varying length
and width, always longer and wider than the Doric. In its simplest form it
was cylindrical, formed by a rectangular piece of cloth, folded over, with
the two side edges sewn together; next the top edges were sewn or drawn
together by several brooches, leaving a hole in the middle for the head
and a hole at either end for the arms. When the garment was in position

the arms of the wearer forced the arm-holes to fall parallel with the body; the loose material thus pushed under the arms was generally controlled by a band, crossing either at the back and front or at the back only and attached to a girdle; if the length was greater than the height of the wearer, a pouch was made over the girdle. We have perfect examples of the simple chiton, on the 'Nereid' (Pl. 44b), with a kolpos and fastened with brooches, and on the Delphi charioteer, without a kolpos and sewn. Vases distinctly show a chiton with a separate sleeve, in which case either a longer piece of material was doubled over, a hole cut for the head, and the sides sewn up as far as the armpits, or else two smaller pieces were taken and joined together at the sides and on the shoulders, leaving a hole for the head; two small pieces would have to be added in each case to make the sleeves.

In archaic statues a combination of Ionic and Doric is sometimes found, an Ionic chiton being overlaid by a Doric peplos. In later times features of one type of dress may be grafted on to the other; the Boston 'throne', for instance, shows the Ionic chiton with a false overfall attached to the neck (Pl. 25b).

The Doric himation was a rectangular piece of material, usually woollen, 7 or 8 feet long and equal in breadth to the wearer's height. Its arrangement varied greatly, especially among women; it could be worn over the shoulders with the ends hanging in front (Pl. 22c), or with an end thrown back over one shoulder for additional warmth (Pl. 23a); sometimes the head also was covered. In the sixth century men might wear the himation like a shawl, but afterwards the favourite manner was to place one end on the left shoulder, drawing the rest round the back of the body under the right arm to the front, then to throw the other end over the left shoulder. The Ionic himation too was rectangular, but usually of linen and differently adjusted. The material was first doubled over to make an overfall, then wrapped round the body under the left arm and fastened on the right upper arm with brooches from the shoulder to the elbow; probably a girdle lay under the overfall to keep it in position. Occasionally the himation was caught up on the left shoulder by a brooch. It could also be worn like a shawl with two ends hanging in front.

The smaller cloak, the chlamys, worn only by men, consisted of an oblong piece of woollen cloth, folded so that the middle line came at the left shoulder, while the two edges were fastened on the right shoulder.

Roman dress differed for men and women. Indoors, women wore first the tunica, which is never visible, and over that the stola, which consisted of two oblong pieces of cloth sewn together as far as the armpits and fastened on the shoulders with a brooch. It reached the feet, and in the case of matrons carried a border on the bottom hem; a girdle passed under the breast, over which a pouch was pulled if necessary; there were no sleeves unless sewn on separately. The palla, which formed the outdoor clothing of the women, resembled the himation in shape and the variety of ways in which it could be arranged. The fully-dressed woman of Plate 80a wears the palla, with enough of the stola showing to reveal its shape.

Roman men wore an undergarment of uncertain shape (subucula) and a tunic with a belt. The toga, to judge by a remark of Quintilian, was semi-circular, about 18 feet in diameter and 7 feet in depth. The straight edge was taken at one-third of its length and placed on the left shoulder, allowing the end to touch the ground between the feet; the remaining two-thirds was then carried round the back and under the right arm; next the toga was taken about one-third down its depth and flung over the left shoulder, so that the straight edge now fell over the front, forming circular folds which reached the knee (sinus). A belt (balteus) was formed by the folds round the waist, and finally the end, which at first had been left touching the ground, is raised so that the point hangs between the legs, forming yet another mass of folds (umbo). This full toga was not worn before late republican times and was found to be so cumbersome that it was only used for ceremonial occasions. A variation known as the cinctus Gabinus gave freedom to the left arm, as the belt of folds was carried round the waist and tucked in at the front; this method also displayed the purple border which was woven on the straight edge. It is seen in the procession of senators on the Ara Pacis (Pl. 76c). In the later empire, the toga is sometimes arranged across the left shoulder in a broad band. For ordinary wear a less cumbersome garment (resembling the chlamys), the laena or lacerna, was used; another type, the paenula, seems to have been like a poncho, having a hole cut in the middle for the head. The paludamentum, a cloak worn by generals, resembled the Greek chlamys.

APPENDIX III

Important Museums

*An asterisk indicates that the publication of a very informative and fully illustrated catalogue has been at least begun.

ACROPOLIS MUSEUM, ATHENS.* Greek sculptures, other than bronzes, found on the summit and slopes of the Acropolis.

AGORA MUSEUM, ATHENS. Sculptures, mainly Greek, found in the Agora.

ALEXANDRIA: GRAECO-ROMAN MUSEUM. Local Hellenistic and Roman finds, mostly of poor quality.

ARA PACIS MUSEUM, ROME.* Reassembled slabs of Augustan monument.

ASHMOLEAN MUSEUM, OXFORD. Polycleitan bronze head.

ATHENS: NATIONAL MUSEUM. Selected finds of all periods from most parts of Greece; bronzes alone from Acropolis.

BARRACCO MUSEUM, ROME.* Small choice collection, mainly of copies.

BERLIN (EAST): STATE MUSEUMS, ANTIQUITIES COLLECTION (formerly in Old Palace).* Individual Greek and Roman sculptures. Reconstructed Pergamon Altar.

BORGHESE VILLA, ROME. A few notable copies. (Other sculptures known as 'Borghese' are in the Louvre.)

BOSTON, MASS.: MUSEUM OF FINE ARTS.* Choice works of all periods.

BRAURON (VRAONA) MUSEUM. Local finds of Greek period.

BRITISH MUSEUM, LONDON.* Most of the sculptures now exhibited are Greek.

CAPITOLINE MUSEUM, ROME.* Local Hellenistic and Roman finds.

CAPITOLINO NUOVA see NEW CAPITOLINE

CASSEL, ANTIQUITIES COLLECTION.* Copies.

CERAMEICUS, ATHENS. Fifth- and fourth-century gravestones *in situ*.

CHALCIS MUSEUM. Pediment from Eretria.

CHERCHEL MUSEUM.* Copies etc., collected by King Juba of Mauritania at the time of Augustus.

CONSERVATORI PALACE, ROME.* Local finds of all periods.

COPENHAGEN see NY CARLSBERG GLYPTOTEK

CORFU MUSEUM. Local finds, including archaic pediment.

CORINTH MUSEUM. Local finds, mainly of first century A.D.

CYRENE MUSEUM.* Local finds, mainly of Roman period.

DELOS MUSEUM and site. Local finds, archaic to Hellenistic.

DELPHI MUSEUM.* Local finds, archaic to second century A.D.

DRESDEN, STATE ART COLLECTIONS, SCULPTURE GALLERIES (ALBERTINUM). Mainly of Roman period.

EPIDAURUS MUSEUM. Local finds, largely of fourth century B.C.

FITZWILLIAM MUSEUM, CAMBRIDGE.* Small collection, including Greek and Roman originals as well as copies.

FLORENCE: ARCHAEOLOGICAL MUSEUM.* A few Greek bronzes in Etruscan collection. See also LOGGIA DEI LANZI and UFFIZI GALLERY.

HERMITAGE, LENINGRAD (St Petersburg).* Copies.

IRAKLION: NATIONAL MUSEUM. Daedalic finds from Crete; an unpublished Roman bronze statue.

ISTANBUL: ARCHAEOLOGICAL MUSEUM (formerly Imperial Ottoman Museum, Constantinople).* Finds of all periods from previous Turkish Empire.

KASSEL see CASSEL

LATERAN PROFANE MUSEUM, ROME, transferred to separate gallery in VATICAN. Roman sculptures, some of exceptional importance.

LOGGIA DEI LANZI, FLORENCE. Trajanic colossus.

LOUVRE MUSEUM, PARIS. Archaic to Roman.

METROPOLITAN MUSEUM, NEW YORK.* Choice works of all periods.

MUNICH: GLYPTOTHEK. Archaic to Roman, Aegina pediments.

NAPLES: NATIONAL ARCHAEOLOGICAL MUSEUM (in process of repair and rearrangement). Regional finds, mainly from Pompeii and Herculaneum; sculptures of fifth century B.C. to third century A.D. collected at Rome by the Farnese family.

NEW CAPITOLINE MUSEUM, ROME (formerly Mussolini Museum).* transferred from Communal Antiquarium. Local finds of more historical than artistic value, some Republican.

NY CARLSBERG GLYPTOTEK, COPENHAGEN.* Great collection of all periods, richest in portraits.

OLYMPIA MUSEUM.* Local finds, archaic to second century A.D.

PAESTUM (PESTO) MUSEUM. Archaic local finds and metopes from Sele.

PALERMO: ARCHAEOLOGICAL MUSEUM. Finds from W. Sicily, including Selinus.

PIRAEUS MUSEUM: Greek bronze statues; adaptations of reliefs on shield of Athena Parthenos.

APPENDIX III

SALONICA: ARCHAEOLOGICAL MUSEUM. Finds from N. Greece, almost all of Roman period.

SAMOS MUSEUM. Local archaic finds.

SPARTA MUSEUM.* Finds from Laconia, largely archaic.

SPERLONGA MUSEUM. Reassemblage of fragments from 'Grotto of Tiberius'.

SYRACUSE: ARCHAEOLOGICAL MUSEUM. Finds from E. Sicily, almost all of Roman period.

TERME, NATIONAL MUSEUM OF THE, ROME.* Mainly finds from Central Italy; some of all periods from former Ludovisi collection.

TARANTO: ARCHAEOLOGICAL MUSEUM. Regional finds, mainly Greek.

TRIPOLI: CASTLE MUSEUM. Roman finds from W. Libya.

TUNIS: BARDO MUSEUM.* Selected Roman sculptures from all Tunisia; Hellenistic bronzes from Mahdia wreck.

UFFIZI GALLERY, FLORENCE.* Statues and busts of Roman period.

VATICAN MUSEUM.* Vast display of sculptures of Roman period, mostly commercial products and over-restored; a few earlier pieces.

VIENNA: KUNSTHISTORISCHES MUSEUM. Gjölbaschi frieze; Roman sculptures from Ephesus.

SELECT BIBLIOGRAPHY

GREEK ARTS IN GENERAL

J. Boardman, J. Dörg, W. Fuchs and M. Hirmer, *Art and Architecture of Ancient Greece* (1967)
R. Carpenter, *Greek Art* (1962)
J. Charbonneaux, R. Martin and F. Villard, *Archaic Greek Art* (1971); *La Grèce classique* (1969); *La Grèce hellénistique* (1970)
R. M. Cook, *Greek Art* (forthcoming)
G. M. A. Richter, *Handbook of Greek Art* (6th edn. 1969)
T. B. L. Webster, *Hellenistic Art* (1966)

GREEK SCULPTURE

L. Alscher, *Griechische Plastik* (i, 1954–iv, 1963)
M. Bieber, *Sculpture of the Hellenistic Age* (1955; 2nd enlarged edn. 1961)
R. Carpenter, *Greek Sculpture* (1961)
J. Charbonneaux, *La Sculpture grecque archaique* (1938); *La Sculpture grecque classique* (1943)
A. Conze, *Die attischen Grabreliefs* (1893–1922)
W. Fuchs, *Die Skulptur der Griechen* (1969)
A. Furtwängler, *Masterpieces of Greek Sculpture* (1895); revised by A. N. Oikonomides (Chicago 1964— not generally accessible in Europe)
G. Lippold, *Die griechische Plastik* (Handbuch der Archäologie iii 1, 1940)
R. Lullies and M. Hirmer, *Greek Sculpture* (1957)
Ch. Picard, *La Sculpture antique* (i, 1935–iv. 2, 1963)
G. M. A. Richter, *Greek Sculpture and Sculptors* (4th edn. 1970)
F. Winter, *Kunstgeschichte in Bildern* I (1900)

ROMAN ARTS IN GENERAL

R. B. Bandinelli, *Rome, The Centre of Power: Roman Art to* A.D. 200 (1970); *Rome, The Late Empire: Roman Art* A.D. 200–400 (1971)
G. M. A. Hanfmann, *Roman Art* (1964)
J. M. C. Toynbee, *Art of the Romans* (1965)

ROMAN SCULPTURE

Donald E. Strong, *Roman Imperial Sculpture* (1969)
Eug. Strong, *La Scultura romana* (i, 1923; ii, 1926)

REFERENCES

In references to books, an author's initials precede the surname (or if it is a very common one, a Christian name may be spelled out), and the title is followed by the year of publication in parentheses. In references to articles, authors' initials are not stated; the year cited (not in parentheses) for a periodical forms part of the title of the volume and is liable to anticipate the date of publication. Only the first page of an article or first relevant page of any publication is cited.

ABBREVIATIONS

AA	*Archäologischer Anzeiger* (supplement to *JdI*)
AAA	*Athens Annals of Archaeology*
ADelt	Archaiologikon Deltion (*'Αρχαιολογικὸν Δελτίον*)
AD	*Antike Denkmäler*—plates
AE	Archaiologike Ephemeris (*'Αρχαιολογικὴ 'Εφημερίς*)
AJA	*American Journal of Archaeology*
AM	*Mitteilungen des Deutschen Archäologischen Institut, Athenische Abteilung*
AP	*Antike Plastik*
ASAA	*Annuario della Scuola Archeologica di Atene*
BAB	*Bulletin van de Vereenigung tot Anticke Beschaving*
BCH	*Bulletin de Correspondance Hellénique*
Bie	M. Bieber, *Sculpture of the Hellenistic Age* (1955, 2nd enlarged edn, 1961)
BMC	*British Museum Catalogue of Sculpture in the Department of Greek and Roman Antiquities*
Boll d'A	*Bolletino d'Arte*
BrBr	H. Brunn, published by Bruckmann, *Denkmäler griechischer und römischer Skulptur*—plates
BSA	*Annual of the British School at Athens*
BSR	*Papers of the British School at Rome*
Bull Comm	*Bulletino della Commissione Archeologica Communale*
Bull Metr Mus	*Bulletin of the Metropolitan Museum of Art*
Cat	*Catalogue, Catalogo*
D	École française d'Athènes, P. de la Coste-Messelière, *Delphes* (1957)

F de D	*Fouilles de Delphes*
GrPl	G. Lippold, *Die griechische Plastik* (*Handbuch der Archäologie* iii 1, 1940)
Hek	A. Hekler, *Greek and Roman Portraits* (1912)— plates
Hel	W. Helbig (and successors), *Führer durch die öffentlichen Sammlungen klassicher Altertümer in Rom* (4th edn, i, 1963–iii, 1969) — no plates
Hesp	*Hesperia*
JdI	*Jahrbuch des Deutschen Archäologischen Instituts*
JHS	*Journal of Hellenic Studies*
JRS	*Journal of Roman Studies*
K	*Katalog*
Korai	G. M. A. Richter, *Korai* (1968)
Kou	G. M. A. Richter, *Kouroi* (3rd edn. 1970)
LGS	A. W. Lawrence, *Later Greek Sculpture* (1927)
LH	R. Lullies and M. Hirmer, *Greek Sculpture* (1957) — the references are to plates; see also 'Notes' to them (at end)
MA	*Monumenti Antichi ... Accademia dei Lincei*
Mem Am Ac	*Memoirs of the American Academy at Rome*
M	A. Furtwängler, *Masterpieces of Greek Sculpture* (1895). American readers will find better illustrations in the edition by A. N. Oikonomides (Chicago 1964).
MPiot	*Monuments et Mémoires ... Fondation Piot*
NCP	F. Imhoof-Blumer and P. Gardner, *Numismatic Commentary on Pausanias* (1887), reprinted from *JHS* 1885–7. A re-issue edited by A. N. Oikonomides (Chicago 1964) is not generally accessible in European libraries.
NM	National Museum, Athens
NSC	*Notizie degli Scavi di Antichità*
ÖJh	*Jahreshefte des Oesterreichischen Archäologischen Instituts*
Overbeck	J. Overbeck, *Die antiken Schriftquellen zur Geschichte der Kunste* (1868)
PAE	Praktika tes Archaiologikes Hetaireias (Πρακτικὰ τῆς ᾿Αρχαιολογικῆς ῾Εταιρείας)
Por	G. M. A. Richter, *Portraits of the Greeks* (i–iii, 1965)
Poulsen	F. Poulsen, *Delphi* (1921)
PY	H. Payne and R. Young, *Archaic marble Sculpture from the Acropolis* (1936)
RA	*Revue Archéologique*
Raub	A. E. Raubitschek, *Dedications on the Athenian Acropolis* (1949)

RM	Mitteilungen des Deutschen Archäologischen Institut, Römische Abteilung
ScR	Eug. Strong, *La Scultura romana* (i, 1923; ii, 1926)
ScSc	G. M. A. Richter, *Greek Sculpture and Sculptors* (4th edn. 1970)
SkGr	W. Fuchs, *Die Skulptur der Griechen* (1969)

CHAPTER I: CONTENT AND FUNCTIONS OF THE SCULPTURE [Pages 19–28]

Page 22 Sepulchral reliefs: C. W. Clairmont, *Gravestone and Epigram* (1970); Pauly, *Real-Encyclopädie* iii A2 (1929) 2307 'Stela'.

Reliefs of meals: Thönges-Stringaris, *AM* 80 1965 1 *Beilagen* 1–30.

Votive reliefs: U. Hausmann, *Griechische Weihreliefs* (1960).

23 Athletes: H. A. Harris, *Greek Athletes and Athletics* (1964); W. W. Hyde, *Olympic Victor Monuments* (1921)—illustrates many statues not definitely connected with Olympia.

24 Architectural sculpture: W. B. Dinsmoor, *Architecture of Ancient Greece* (1950); A. W. Lawrence, *Greek Architecture* (2nd edn 1967); R. Demangel, *La frise ionique* (1932); H. Kähler, *Das griechische Metopenbild* (1949); E. Lapalus, *Le Fronton sculpté en Grèce* (1947).

26 Greek setting of statues: Ridgway, *Hesp* xl 1971 336.

27 Roman setting of sculptures: A. Boethius and J. Ward-Perkins, *Roman Architecture* (1970); Vermeule, *Burlington Magazine* 110 1968 545, 607.

CHAPTER II: MATERIALS AND METHODS [Pages 29–43]

MARBLE AND OTHER STONES

29 Greek marbles: Ashmole, *BSA* 65 1970 1; Young, *Boston Museum Bulletin* lxvi no. 346 1968 141.

30 Roman marbles: Ballance, *JRS* lx 1970 134; Ward-Perkins, *JRS* xli 1951 89.

31 Portraits in Egyptian stones: Adriani, *RM* 77 1970 72, pls 32–51.

Sculptors' procedure: Sheila Adam, *Technique of Greek Sculpture in the Archaic and Classical Periods* (1966); C. Bluemel, *Greek Sculptors at Work* (1969).

32 Pointing: Richter, *RM* 69 1962 52.

Egyptian and Archaic grid: see references to p. 78.

33 Hellenistic grid: von Bissing, *AM* xxxi 1906 55, fig. 1.

Colour: P. Reuterswärd, *Studien zur Polychromie der Plastik—Griechenland und Rom* (1960).

34 Lycian painted tomb: Ch. Fellows, *An Account of Discoveries in Lycia* (1841), coloured pl. after p. 198.

Paint on sarcophagus: F. Winter, *Der Alexandersarkophag aus Sidon* (1912)—coloured pls.

35 *Ganosis*: Langlotz, *AA* 1968 470, 1969 231.

BRONZE

Statue with 'Chatsworth' head: Haynes, *RA* 1968 101. **Page 37**

Draped statue from the sea: Ridgway, *AJA* 71 1967 329 (especially 332), pls 97–100.

Casting procedure: Haynes, *RA* 1968 104.

Extant moulds: Thompson, *Hesp* vi 1937 82, fig. 43 (face); Shear, ibid. 343 fig. 8 (legs); Heilmeyer, *JdI* 84 1969 12, fig. 17. Cf. for technique K. Kluge, *Die antiken Grossbronzen* i (1927).

WOOD AND ADJUNCTS

Extant wooden statuettes: Ohly, *AM* 68 1953 77, *Beilagen* 13–42. **40**

Wood and sheet metal: Amandry, *BCH* lxiii 1939 109, 116, pl. xxxviii.

Delphi ivory: ibid. 90, pls xix–xxii.

Olympia workshop: Deutsches Archäologisches Institut, *Neue Deutsche Ausgrabungen* **41** (1959) 281, figs 15–33.

Ivory faces: Albizzati, *JHS* xxxvi 1916 373, pls viii, ix (Vatican); Lethaby, *JHS* xxxvii 1917 17 (British Museum).

TERRACOTTA

Temple terracottas: E. D. van Buren, *Archaic Fictile Revetments in Sicily and Magna* **42** *Graecia* (1923); *Greek Fictile Revetments in the Archaic Period* (1926); A. Åkerstrom, *Die architektonischen Terrakotten Kleinasiens* (1966).

Ganymede group: K. Schefold, *Classical Greece* (1967) 96—coloured plate.

Acroteria of Victory in Acropolis Museum: *PAE* 1956, pl. 30.

Paestum Zeus: Sestieri, *Boll d'A* xl 1955 193; E. Langlotz, *Art of Magna Graecia* (1965), pls iii, iv; *JHS* lx 1970, pl. viii.

Corinth statues, technique: Weinberg, *Hesp* xxvi 1957 289.

Locri plaques: H. Prückner, *Die lokrischen Tonreliefs* (1968).

Statuettes: R. A. Higgins, *Greek Terracottas* (1967).

'Spinario' parody: *Opus Nobile* 8, W. Fuchs, *Der Dornauszieher* (1958), fig. 7.

Roman statues: A. Levi, *Terracotte figurate del Museo Nazionale di Napoli* (1926). **43**

'Campana' reliefs: see references to p. 264.

Polychromy: Higgins, *Studies in Conservation* 15 1970 272.

Plastered mummies: K. Parlasca, *Mumienportrats und verwandte. Denkmäler* (1966); *Cat…* *Cairo Museum*, C. C. Edgar, *Graeco-Egyptian Coffins* (1905), pls vii–xxx.

CHAPTER III: AIDS AND HINDRANCES TO KNOWLEDGE [Pages 44–60]

LITERARY SOURCES

Collected passages: Overbeck—practically complete, in Greek or Latin (1868); H. Stuart **44** Jones, *Ancient Writers on Greek Sculpture* (1895)—short selection with English translations.

Pliny: K. Jex-Blake and E. Sellers, *The Elder Pliny's Chapters on the History of Art* (1896)—
with translation.

Page 47 The sculptor's profession: B. Schweitzer, *Der bildende Kunstler und der Begriff des kunstler-
ischen in die Antike* (1925).

INSCRIPTIONS

48 Inscribed signatures: E. Lowy, *Inschriften griechischer Bildhauer* (1885); Raub; J. Marcadé,
Recueil des signatures de sculpteurs grecs i, 1953; ii, 1957.

49 Piombino Apollo: Ridgway, *AP* vii 43, pls 24–34.

EVIDENCE FROM OTHER ARTS

49 Greek coins: G. F. Hill, *Select Greek Coins* (1927); C. M. Kraay and M. Hirmer, *Greek
Coins* (1966); Ch. Seltman, *Masterpieces of Greek Coinage* (1949).

Late coins: *NCP*; L. Lacroix, *Les reproductions de statues sur les monnaies grecques* (1949).

50 Hair styles: A. Carandini, *Vibia Sabina* (1969)—19 pls of drawings; (le R.P.) Delattre,
Musée Lavigerie 39, pl. ix—busts in Hadrianic tomb.

Gems: G. M. A. Richter, *The Engraved Gems of the Greeks, Etruscans and Romans* (1971).

Vase-painting: R. M. Cook, *Greek Painted Pottery* (1960; 2nd edn forthcoming) E.Pfuhl,
Malerei und Zeichnung der Griechen (1923)—iii for pls; Martin Robertson, *Greek Painting*
(1959).

INTRINSIC EVIDENCE

52 Forged portraits: Recognized examples include the heads of Julius Caesar in London
(*BMC* iii (1901), pl xiii 1) and Berlin (*Hek 158a*) and the 'Farnese' bust of Caracalla in
Naples (*Hek* 290). I personally suspect a supposedly Hadrianic 'Farnese' bust of an
unidentified man, also in Naples (*Hek* 233).

Boston 'Throne': Young and Ashmole, *Boston Museum Bulletin* lxvi (No. 346) 1968 124—
scientific investigation.

54 Head of Earth: Istanbul Museum No. 609; *RA* 1899 1 329, pl. xii.

Bust shapes: *Enciclopedia dell'arte antica* ii (1959) 227; Hekler, *ÖJh* xxi–xxii 1922–4 186.

55 COPIES: G. Lippold, *Kopien und Umbildungen griechischer Statuen* (1923).

56 Guild inscriptions: *Corpus Inscriptionum Graec.* No. 3067.

58 Copies of extant originals: Despinis, *AAA* iii 1970 407—Nemesis; Richter, *Bull Metr Mus*
30 1935 216—Eleusis relief; Schefold, *Antike Kunst* 14 1971 37, pl. 16—Piraeus Athena
(see also Waywell in forthcoming BSA 66); *AE* 1953–4 3 30, figs 3–5, pls i–ii—Apollo
of Euphranor.

Pointing: Richter, *RM* 69 1962 52.

Baiae moulds: Richter, *AJA* 74 1970 296, pl. 74; Squarciapino, *Boll d'A* 39 1954 10.

59 Herculaneum bronzes: Ethel R. Barker, *Buried Herculaneum* (1908); Ch. Waldstein and
L. Shoobridge, *Herculaneum Past Present and Future* (1908).

CHAPTER IV: THE BEGINNINGS OF GREEK SCULPTURE [PAGES 61–74]

ANTECEDENTS: E. Akurgal, *The Birth of Greek Art* (1968); J. Boardman, *The Greeks* Page 61
Overseas (1964); A. M. Snodgrass, *The Dark Age of Greece* (1971).

Pottery centaur: Desborough, Nicholls and Popham, *BSA* 65 1970 21, pls 8–10.

Vase-painting: J. N. Coldstream, *Greek Geometric Pottery* (1968).

Bronze statuettes: B. Schweitzer, *Greek Geometric Art* (1971)–'Morgan' centaur, pl. 85.   62

Dipylon ivories: ibid., pls 146–8; Kunze, *AM* 55 1930 147, pls 5–8; *Korai* 21, figs 16–24.   63

Corinthian ivories: H. Payne and T. J. Dunbabin, *Perachora* ii (1962) 403, pls 171–82.   64

Spartan ivories: *JHS Supplementary Papers* 5; R. M. Dawkins, *Sanctuary of Artemis Orthia*
(1939), pls xci–clxviii; Boardman, *BSA* lviii 1963 4–for dating.

Phoenician-Attic jewellery: Higgins, *BSA* 64 1969 143.

Phoenicians in Rhodes: Coldstream, *University of London Institute of Classical Studies
Bulletin* 16 1969 1–for head, 3, pls 11 a–c.

Orientalizing bronzes: Korti-Konti, *AAA* 4 1971 273, 281.

Cretan shields: E. Kunze, *Kretische Bronzereliefs* (1931)–for cymbal-clashers 48, pl. 49,
cf. J. Boardman, *The Greeks Overseas* (1964), pl. 4b; *Dädalische Kunst auf Kreta* (1970) 14.

Reliefs on pottery: Kontoleon, *AE* 1969 215, pls 38–58.   66

DAEDALIC SCULPTURE: R. J. H. Jenkins, *Dedalica* (1936); Cook, *JHS* lxxxvii 1967 24.

Apollo on Athenian coins: *NCP* pl. CC. xi–xiv.   68

Hera on Samian coins: P. Gardner, *Samos and Samian Coins*, pl. v. 1–9.

Nicandra: NM No. 1; *Korai* 26, figs 25–7.   69

Dreros group: Marinatos, *BCH* 60 1936 485, pl. 63; *Korai* 32, figs 70–75.

Auxerre statuette: *Korai* 32, figs 76–9, pl. xxiia; LH 6.

Gortyna fragment: G. Rizza and Scrinari, *Il Santuario sull'Acropoli di Gortina* i (1968) 156,
pls ii, iii.

Gortyna terracottas: *ASAA* xxiii–iv 1955–6, figs 39–82, pl. iv.   70

Mycenae reliefs: Rodenwaldt, *Corolla L. Curtius* (1937) i 63, ii, pls 7–10; LH 7–goddess.

Terracotta plaque: *Korai* 33, fig 85.   71

Gortyna reliefs: G. Rizza and Scrinari, op cit. i 156, pls iii–iv; *JHS* xci 1971, pl. x.29.

Prinia frieze: Pernier, *ASAA* i 1914 48, fig. 19.

Prinia stelae: P. Demargne, *La Crète dédalique* (1947) 284, fig. 52; R. W. Hutchinson,
Prehistoric Crete (1968) 341.

Prinia goddesses: Pernier, *ASAA* i 1914 54, 60, figs 20–21, pl. v.

Eleutherna statue: Joubin, *RA* 1893 i 10, pls ii, iv; Ch. Picard, *La Sculpture antique* i (1935)   73
448, fig. 124.

Delos nude fragments: *Kou* 27, figs 20–24.   74

Delphi bronze: *F de D* v, C. Rolley, *Les statuettes de bronze* (1969) No. 172, pls xxviii–
xxix; *Kou*, figs 14–16.

Delos belted fragment: *Kou* 53, figs 94-5.

Page 75 W.-H. Schuchardt, *Archaische Plastik der Griechen* (1957); E. Akurgal, *The Birth of Greek Art* (1968); E. Langlotz, *Frühgriechische Bildhauerschulen* (1927)—attempt to distinguish local styles by comparison with small objects; Deyhle, *AM* 84 1969 1, pls 1–30—on attempts to distinguish individual Attic sculptors.

THE MAINLAND AND CYCLADES: STATUES

76 Sunium *kouros*: *Kou* 43, figs 33–8, 91.

New York *kouros*: *Kou* 41, figs 25–32; LH 11–13.

77 Dipylon head: *Kou* 46, figs 50–53.

78 Grid: Iversen, *Mitteilungen des Deutschen Archäol. Instituts, Kairo* 15 1957 134.

Delphi Twins: *D* 34–7; *Kou* 49, figs 78–83; Heidenreich, *Corolla L.Curtius* (1937) i 67, ii, pl. II—grid.

79 Boeotia: F. R. Grace, *Archaic Sculpture in Boeotia* (1939).

Dermys and Cittylus: *Kou* 48, figs 76–7; G. M. A. Richter, *Archaic Gravestones of Attica* (1961) 13, figs 31–3.

80 Boeotian head: *Kou* 48, figs 72–5; LH 26–7.

Boeotian *kouros*: *Kou* 66, figs 151–3; *BMC* i. 1 (1928) No. B474, pl. xlii.

Megara torso: *Kou* 99, figs 297–9; BrBr 791–3.

Tenea kouros: *Kou* 84, figs 245–50; LH 34–6.

Melos colossus: *Kou* 96, figs 273–9; LH 32–3.

Piraeus bronze: *Kou* 66, figs 478–80.

Anavysos *kouros*: *Kou* 118, figs 395–6, 400; LH 53–7.

Munich *kouros*: *Kou* 118, figs 391–4, 399.

Aristodicus *kouros*: *Kou* 139, figs 489, 492–3; C. Karusos, *Aristodikos* (1961).
'Strangford' *kouros*: *Kou* 136, figs 461–3; LH 84; *BMC* i. 1 (1928) No. B475, pl. xliii.

81 'Critian Boy': *Kou* 149, figs 564–9 & opposite fig. 593; PY, pls 109–12; LH 85–7.

Archaic asymmetry: Rolley, *RA* 1970 12.

82 'Moschophorus': PY, pls 2–4; LH 23; *Opus Nobile* 11, W. Schiering, *Der Kalbträger* (1958).

'Rampin' horseman: PY, pls 11 *a–c*; LH 28–9.

'Sabouroff' head: C. Blümel, *Die archaisch griechischen Skulpturen zu Berlin* (1964) No. 6, figs 16–19.

'Blond Boy': *Kou* 141, figs 570–71; PY, pls 113–15.

83 Head of Hera: *Korai* 38, figs 118–21; LH 10.

Naxian Sphinx: *F de D* iv. 1 (1909) 41, pls iv–v; Poulsen 97; *D* 47–9; *Korai*, pls xi *f–h*—head.

'Hydrophore': *Korai* 41, figs 151–4.

Berlin goddess: C. Blümel, *Die archaisch griechischen Skulpturen zu Berlin* (1964) No. 1, **Page 83n**
figs 1–8; LH 18–21; *Korai* 39, figs 139–46. Acropolis No. 593: *Korai* 40, figs 147–50.

Archermus Nike: *Korai*, pl. xiv; Raub 484.   **84**

Phaedimus base: *Korai* 58, figs 284–5; Dörig, *AA* 82 1967 15, figs 1–3 – cf. stela attributed
to Phaedimus, figs 4–7, 12–13.

Peplos *Kore*: No. 679: *Korai* 72, figs 349–54; PY 29–33; LH 41–3.   **85**

    Kore, No. 682: *Korai* 73, figs 362–7.

    Kore, No. 674: *Korai* 81, figs 411–16; LH 75–7.

    Kore, No. 683: *Korai* 77, figs 381–4; Karouzos, *BSA* 39 1938–9 102.

Antenor's *Kore*: *Korai* 69, figs 336–40; PY 31, pls 51–3; Raub 481.   **86**

Euthydicus' *Kore*: *Korai* 99, figs 565–72; PY 40, pls 84–7.

'Aphrodite of Lyons': *Korai* 57, figs 275–81; PY, pls 22–6.   **87**

Endoeus' Athena: PY 46, pl. 116; Raub 491.

Seated Dionysus, NM No. 371: Schuchhardt *AP* vi 7, pls 1–8.

'Scribes': PY 47, pl. 118.

Callimachus' Nike: PY 72, pl. 120: Raub No. 13.

THE EASTERN AEGEAN: E. Buschor, *Altsamische Standbilder* i (1934)–v (1961); Him- **88**
melmann-Wildschütz, *Istanbuler Mitteilungen* xv 1965 24—chronology of statues;
Istanbuler Forschungen 27, K. Tuchelt, *Die archaischen Skulpturen von Didyma* (1970).

Ephesus priest: E. Akurgal, *Die Kunst Anatoliens* (1961) 198, figs 158–9.

Thasos colossus: Picard, *BCH* xlv 1921 113, figs 10–13; *Kou* 51, figs 84–6, 106.

Cheramyes' statue, Louvre: *Korai* 46, figs 183–5; LH 30–31; E. Buschor, *Altsamische* **89**
Standbilder i–iii (1934) 83, figs 86–9, v (1961) fig. 340.

Acropolis head and torso, No. 677; *Korai* 47, figs 198–200; PY, pls 18–19.   **90**

Chios torsos: *Korai* 38, figs 122–8; Boardman, *AP* i 43, pls 38–44.

Cheramyes statue, Berlin: *Korai* 46, figs 186–9; E. Buschor, op. cit. v (1961), figs 341–4.

Geneleus' base: E. Buschor, op. cit. i–iii (1934) 26, figs 90–101, v (1961) 84, figs 345–50;
Korai 49–50, figs 217–24.

Draped male statue: E. Buschor, op. cit. i–iii (1934) 46, figs 160–62; *Kou*, figs 624–7. **91**
Cf. headless statue from Myus, C. Blumel, *Die archaisch griechischen Skulpturen zu Berlin*
(1964), No. 69, figs 2171–9.

Istanbul head and Samos torso: Eckstein, *AP* i 47, pls 45–52; *Kou* 110, figs 369–70, 632–4.

Branchidae/Didyma statues: *Istanbuler Forschungen* 27, K. Tuchelt, *Die archaischen Skulp-* **92**
turen von Didyma (1970); *BMC* i. 1 (1928), pls vi–xv—with head, No. B271; E. Akurgal,
Die Kunst Anatoliens (1961) 218, figs 187–92; Möbius, *AP* ii 23, pls 14–19.

Aeaces statue: ibid. 26, figs 3–5.

Didyma fragment: *Kou* 110, figs 371–2.

Ephesus columns: *BMC* i. 1 (1928) 47—female face No. B89, pl. iv; female head B91, **93**
pl. v; draped legs, B121; *Korai* 56, figs 263–8.

Page 94 Didyma columns: *Korai* 60, figs 296–300; C. Blümel, *Die archaisch griechischen Skulpturen zu Berlin* (1964) No. 59 162–6.

Statuette of Apollo: British Museum *Catalogue of Bronzes* (1899) No. 209, pl. 1; A. S. Murray, *Greek Bronzes* (1898) 10, fig. 3.

95 'Lion Tomb': *BMC* i. 1 (1928) No. B286, pls xviii–xx; E. Akurgal, *Griechische Reliefs des vi Jahrhunderts aus Lykien* (1941) 3, pls 1–5.

Isinda tomb: ibid. 52, pls 6–14.

96 Dorylaeum stela: Istanbul Museum No. 526; J. Boardman, *The Greeks Overseas* (1964) 254, fig. 68; Koerte, *AM* xx 1895 1, pls i–ii.

Thasos gate reliefs: *Études Thasiennes* viii, Ch. Picard, *Les Murailles* i (1962) fig. 15—Heracles; fig. 35, pl. xvi—Silenus.

97 Xanthus sphinxes: *BMC* i. 1 (1928) 132 Nos B290–91, pl. xxvii.

'Harpy Tomb': ibid. No. B287, pls xxi–xxiv.

Basel stela: E. Berger, *Das Basler Arzt relief* 1970; Neumann, *AA* 1971 183.

98 Persia: Richter, *AJA* 50 1946 15—fig. 1 Pasargadae drapery; John M. Cook, *The Greeks in the East* (1962) 127—Telephanes.

Etruscan sculpture: P. J. Riis, *Introduction to Etruscan Art* (1953)—Veii Apollo 66, pl. 34; M. Pallottino, *La Scuola di Vulca* (2nd edn 1945).

Cypriot sculpture: *BMC* i. 2 (1931); T. Spiteris, *Art of Cyprus* (1970); *Deutsches Archaologisches Institut, Samos* vii, Gerhard Schmidt, *Kyprische Bildwerke aus dem Herzaion von Samos* (1968)—dedications by Cypriots.

ARCHITECTURAL SCULPTURE AND GRAVESTONES: E. Lapalus, *Le fronton sculpté en Grèce* (1947); K. F. Johansen, *Attic Grave Reliefs* (1951); G. M. A. Richter, *Archaic Gravestones of Attica* (1961).

99 Athena on Spartan coins: *NCP* 58, pls iv, xiii, xv.

Spartan incised reliefs: Arthur B. Cook, *Zeus* ii. 2 (1925), fig. 915.

100 Sele earlier metopes: P. Zancani Montuoro & U. Zanotti-Bianco, *Herzaion alla foce del Sele* ii (1954) —Tityus 320, pls xlviii, xciii.

Assos temple: BrBr 411–12; Sartiaux, *RA* 1913 ii 26, corrected by G. Mendel, *Catalogue ...Constantinople* i (1912) 20.

Thermon terracottas: *AM* xxxix 1914, pls xiii–xv, *AD* ii 49–53a; *EA* 1900, pls 10–11, 1903 pls 2–6.

Corfu pediment: G. Rodenwaldt, *Altdorische Bildwerke in Korfu* (1938); LH 14–17; *PAE* 1911, figs 1–20; Kunze, *AM* 78 1963 74 *Beilagen* 36–7—analogies in bronze.

102 Small *poros* pediments: Lapalus, op. cit.; T. Wiegand, *Die archaischer Porosarchitektur des Akropolis zu Athen* (1904)—'Hydrophore', fig. 221; *Korai* 41, figs 151–4.

'Hekatompedon' *poros* pediments: Lapalus, op. cit.; LH 24–5—coloured pl. of three-bodied monster, restoration in 'Notes' (at end); Broneer, *Hesp* 8 1939 91, figs 1–6—Heracles and Triton, with coloured pl. of head then recently found; Schuchhardt, *AM* 60–61 1935–6 86—restoration fig. 14.

Sicyonian Treasury: *D* 40–41; Poulsen 73, figs 19, 23–5; P. de la Coste-Messelière, *Au* **Page 103**
Musée de Delphes (1936).

Chrysapha stela: C. Blümel, *Die archaisch griechischen Skulpturen zu Berlin* (1964) No. 16, 104
figs 42–4. Cf. M. N. Tod and Wace, *Cat ... Sparta Museum* (1906) 75, fig. 65–almost a
duplicate.

'Hekatompedon' marbles: PY, pls 36–7; LH 65–head of Athena. 105
Caryatids from unidentified Treasury: *D* 55–9; *Korai* 57, figs 270–4, 282–3.

Siphnian Treasury: *D* 63–91; *F de D* iv 2 (1928) 57, pls vii–xxv; P. de la Coste-Messelière,
Au Musée de Delphes (1936); *Korai* 66, figs 317–20–caryatids; LH 44–51; *F de D* iv
(1909) pls xxi–xxiv–coloured restoration of frieze.

Sele dance metopes: P. Zancani Montuoro and U. Zanotti-Bianco, *Herzaion alla foce del* 107
Sele i (1954), pls xli–lix; E. Langlotz, *Art of Magna Graecia* (1965), pls 9–11.

Selinus 'C': ibid., pls 14–15; BrBr 286–7, 292, 741; A. W. Lawrence, *Greek Architecture*
(1967), fig. 68–gorgon.

Boeotian stela: Caskey *AJA* xv 1911 293, pl. viii. 108

'Brother and Sister' stela: *Metr Mus Journal* 3 1970 89–photograph after latest joins;
Korai 85, figs 439, 440; G. M. A. Richter, *Archaic Gravestones of Attica* (1961) 27, 159,
figs 96–109, 190, 204.

Eretria pediment: LH 62–4; *AD* iii 27–8.

Hoplitodrome stela, NM No. 1959: *Gr Pl* 84, pl. 27.4.

Aristion stela: G. M. A. Richter, op. cit. 47, figs 155–8; LH 68. 109
Statue base, NM No. 3476: LH 58–61; Casson, *JHS* xlv 1925 164, figs 5–6, pl. vi, cf. fig.
9 pl. vii–hockey base; *GrPl* pl. 28.1–2, cf. pl. 28.3–hockey. Cf. *AM* 78 1963 *Beilage*
66–almost a duplicate of athletes.

'Rayet' head: *Kou* 141, figs 409, 410; Schuchhardt, *AP* vi 18. 110
Delphi temple: *D* 138–47; Poulsen 150, figs 58–63; *F de D* iv 3 (1931); *Korai* 67, figs 322–6.

Megarian Treasury: E. Curtius and F. Adler, *Olympia* iii (1897) 5, (1894), pls 2–3; N.
Gardiner, *Olympia* (1925) 228, figs 58, 65; *Gr Pl* pl. 25.2.

Athenian Treasury: *D* 107–25; Poulsen, 158, figs 66–93; *Korai* 64–dating. 111
'Leonidas': Delevorries, *ADelt* B.1 1969 132, pl. 123; Woodward and Hobling, *BSA*
xxvi 1923–5 253; BrBr 776–8.

Aegina pediments: D.Ohly, *Aigineten* (forthcoming), LH 69–73, 78–84; A. Invernizzi, 112
Frontoni del Tempio di Aphaia (1965); A. Furtwängler, E. R. Fiechter and H. Thiersch,
Aegina (1906).

'Aeginetan' bronze head, NM No. 6446: BrBr 2; *AE* 1887, pl. 3. 113

CHAPTER VI: THE EARLY CLASSICAL PERIOD (430–370 B.C.) [PAGES 114–157]
THE FIRST POST-ARCHAIC GENERATION

Tyrannicides: Raub 513; S. Brunnsåker, *The Tyrant-Slayers of Kritios and Nesiotes* (1955); 114
J. Charbonneaux, *La Sculpture grecque archaique* (1938), pl. 86; A. Blanco, *Cat ... Prado*
i (1957) No. 78, pls xxxv–xxxvi.

Page 115 Statuette of armed runner: BrBr 351; O. Neugebauer, *Antike Bronzenstatuetten* (1921), pl. 31; W. W. Hyde, *Olympic Victor Monuments* (1921), fig. 42.

116 Florence torso: *Kou* 150, figs 585–6.

Alxenor's stela: BrBr 41; K. F. Johansen, *Attic Grave-Reliefs* (1951) 124.

117 Sofia stela: Welkow, *AA* 1932 97, fig. 1.

Naples stela: BrBr 416.

Archaistic votive relief, Acropolis Museum No. 581: Pfuhl, *AM* xlviii 1923 132, fig. 4; W. H. Schuchhardt, *Archaische Plastik de Griechen* (1957), pl. 46; PY, pl. 126.

Delphi Charioteer: *F de D* iv 5, F. Chamoux, '*L'Aurige*' (1955); LH 98–101; *D* 149–59; BrBr 786–90.

119 Calamis: Overbeck 508–32; L. P. Orlandini, *Calamide* (1950); Raub 505—younger Calamis 507; Shear, *Hesp* v 1936 311, fig. 17—coins showing Alexikakos.

Pythagoras: Linfert, *AA* 1966 495.

120 Sculpture in Italy: Ashmole, *Proceedings of the British Academy* xx (1934); E. Langlotz, *Art of Magna Graecia* (1965); H. Prückner, *Die lokrischen Tonreliefs* (1968)—terracotta plaques.

Taranto goddess: C. Blümel, *Die archaisch griechischen Skulpturen zu Berlin* (1964) No. 21, figs 55–9; LH 93–7; *AD* iii 33–44; H. Herdejürgen, *Untersuchungen zur thronenden Gottin aus Tarent* (1968).

Crimisa Apollo: Orsi, *Atti e Memorie della Societa Magna Grecia* 1932 135, pls xvi–xviii —head, xix—hands, xx–xxi—wig, cf. 160, pl. xxiii—Vatican head; de Franciscis, *RM* 63 1956 96, pls 45–7, cf. pl. 48—Terme head.

'Ludovisi' head of goddess: Hel iii No. 2342; Langlotz op. cit., pls 62–3.

Selinus Heraeum 'E'; ibid., pls 100–13; LH 124–7; *Korai* 80, pls xix, xx; Fuchs, *RM* 63 1956 102, pls 50–56—heads, *RM* 64 1957 230.

'Esquiline' stela: Ashmole, *JHS* xliii 1923 248, pl. 230; R. Lullies, *Griechische Bildwerke in Rom* (1955), figs 5–6; Hel ii No. 1506.

121 'Leucothea' stela: Johansen, op. cit. 143; BrBr 228.

122 Thasos 'Banquet' relief, Istanbul Museum No. 578: E. Akurgal, *Die Kunst Anatoliens* (1961) 273, fig. 240; U. Hausmann, *Griechische Weihreliefs* (1960) 27, fig. 13.

'Ludovisi' and Boston 'Thrones': Young and Ashmole, *Boston Museum Bulletin* lxvi (No 346) 1968 124; E. Simon, *Die Geburt der Aphrodite* (1959).

123 Xanthus aged couple: *BMC* i. 1 (1928) 130 No. B289, pl. xxv.

Olympia metopes and pediments: B. Ashmole and Yalouris, *Sculptures of the Temple of Zeus* (1967)—replacements at corners 22; M. L. Säflund, *The East Pediment of the Temple of Zeus at Olympia* (1970), and Kardara, *AJA* 74 1970 325, pl. 78—proposed rearrangements; LH 105–23; Rodenwaldt, *JdI* xli 1926 205 — relationships.

127 Xanthus Peplos Korai: *BMC* i. 1 (1928) 147 Nos B316–18, pls xxxii–xxxiii; *Korai* 109, figs 652–4.

'Penelope': Eckstein, *JdI* 74 1959 137; Langlotz, *JdI* 76 1961 72; *AD* i 31–2; Hel i Nos 123, 343.

'Chatsworth' head: Wace, *JHS* lviii 1938 90, pls viii–ix; Haynes, *RA* 1968 104, figs 1–9. **Page 128**

'Choiseul-Gouffier'—'Omphalus' Apollo: Dörig, *JdI* 80 1965 138, 230—arguing against **129** Calamis; *Kou* 151, figs 589–91; *SkGr*, figs 59–60.

Cassel Apollo: Schmidt, *AP* v 7, pls 1–53; Hel ii No. 1788.

'Tiber'—Cherchel Apollo: Hel iii No. 2253; *MPiot* xxii 1916, pls vii–viii; *SkGr*, figs 70– 71; *GrPl*, pl. 36.1.

Mantua-Pompeii Apollo: *M*, fig. 10; BrBr 302–3.

'Zeus of Artemisium': LH 128–31; H. G. Beyen, *La Statue d'Artemision* (1930); Karouzos, *JHS* xlix 1929 141, pls vii–viii.

Copies of female draped statues: F. Hiller, *Formgeschichtliche Untersuchungen zur griechis-* **130** *chen Statue* 1971.

Calamis' Aphrodite, Sosandra, 'Aspasia': Raub No 136; Dörig, *JdI* 80 1965 214; Berlin *K* iv (1931) Nos 166–7, pls 51–4.

Terme-Iraklion female type: Hel iii No. 2324; *Bull Comm* xxv 1897, pls xii–xiii—Irak-lion; *SkGr*, fig. 199.

'Giustiniani Hestia': BrBr 491; *GrPl* 104 n. 8, pl. 47.1.

Myron: Raub 517; P. E. Arias, *Mirone* (1940); *GrPl* 136.

'Discobolus': Hel iii No. 2269—'Lancelotti' and headless Terme copy; *AA* 1925 22, figs **131** 5–7—head at Basle; *ScSc* 208, figs 579–80—Munich statuette; *SkGr* 73.

Marsyas group: Pollak, *ÖJh* xii 1909 154, pls 2–5; *ScSc* 209, figs 584–93; Hel i No. 1065; Carpenter, *Mem Am Ac* xviii 1941 3, pls 2–3, 4–5.

'Mourning Athena': Acropolis No 605; LH 137; BrBr 783. Cf. for style, LH 92—stela of **132** boy victor from Sunium, NM No. 3344.

Other works of Myron: Dörig, *AP* vi 21; Berger, *RM* 76 1969 66, pls 23–40.

Minotaur groups: *SkGr* 349, fig. 386; Hel ii No. 1757, iii No. 2264; NM Nos 1664, 1664*a*—variant from a fountain.

Perinthus-Cyrene athlete: L. Polacco, *L'atleta Cirene-Perinto* (1959); BrBr 542 and *M* fig. **133** 70—Perinthus (in Dresden).

Discobolus herm: ibid., pls xiv, xvi–xix; Hel iii No. 2325.

PHEIDIAS: G. Becatti, *Problemi fidiaci* (1951); E. Langlotz, *Phidiasprobleme* (1947); H. Schrader, *Phidias* (1924); *ScSc* 215.

Promachus: Raubitschek and Stevens, *Hesp* 15 1949 107—base and restoration; Stevens, *Hesp* 26 1957 350—technique; *NCP*, pl. Z. i–vii, *Hesp* 5 1936, pl. viii—coins; Jenkins, *JHS* lxvii 1947 31, pl x—Byzantine drawing.

Parthenos: Overbeck 645–99; *Opus Nobile* 11, F. Brommer, *Athena Parthenos* (1957); **134** N. Leipen, *Athena Parthenos: A Reconstruction* (1971); Schuchhardt, *AP* ii 31—Varvak-eion, pls 20–34, Lenormant, pls 35–7; C. Blümel, *Die klassisch griechischen Skulpturen* (1966) No. 92, fig. 126—Berlin relief; Hel ii No. 1980, iii No. 2328—copies in Rome; Carpenter, *EA* 1953–4 B 41, pls 1–2—possible copy of Nike.

Parthenos' shield: V. M. Strocka, *Piräusreliefs und Parthenosschild* (1967); Harrison, *Hesp* 35 **136** (1966) 107, pls 36–41; Schlörb, *AM* 78 1963 156 *Beilagen* 75–82.

Olympian Zeus: J. Liegle, *Der Zeus des Phidias* (1952); Richter, *Hesp* 35 1966 166 — copy on gem; Deutsches Archäologisches Institut, *Neue Deutsche Ausgrabungen* (1959) 281, figs 15–33 — finds in Workshop (full report to appear in *Olympische Forschungen*).

Page 139 The Parthenon: A. H. Smith, *The Sculptures of the Parthenon* (1910) — complete for its time; P. E. Corbett, *The Sculpture of the Parthenon* (1959); British Museum, *An Historical Guide to the Sculptures of the Parthenon* (1962); *Inscriptiones graecae* i, 2nd edn 339–53 — for building inscriptions.

Eleusis copies from Parthenon: Travlos, *ADelt* 16 1960 *Chron* 56.

140 Parthenon metopes: F. Brommer, *Die Metopen der Parthenon* (1967) — pls 230–35 for south side Nos 30–31; C. Praschniker, *Parthenonstudien* (1924) — east and north sides; Praschniker, *ÖJh* 41 1954 5 — west side.

141 Acropolis head No. 699: H. Schrader, *Phidias* (1924) 128; *GrPl* 161 n. 12.

144 Parthenon frieze and Persepolis: Lawrence, *JHS* lxxi 1951 118.

Parthenon pediments: F. Brommer, *Die Skulpturen der Parthenongiebel* (1963), and *AM* 84 1969 103, pls 40–56 — identifications of subjects; BrBr 362 — Laborde head.

149 Athena 'Lemnia': *M* 4; *ScSc* 227; *SkGr* 191, fig. 204; *GrPl* 145, pl. 51.3.

'Medici' colossus: *M*, fig. 6; *GrPl* 155 n.14, pl. 56.3.

'Hope' Athena (now in Getty Museum, Malibu): *M* 73, figs 25–8; *JdI* xxvii 1912, pls ix–xi; *GrPl* 190 n. 10, pl. 66.4.

Dresden Zeus: *GrPl* 190 n.9, pl. 66.3.

Seated goddess: Bieber, *AM* xxxvii 1912 159, pls xi–xii.

150 'Farnese' Diadumenus: BM No. 50; BrBr 27; *GrPl* 154 n. 6, pl. 51.2; Marwitz, *AP* vi, pl.21.

'Aphrodite Urania': C. Blümel, *Die klassisch griechischen Skulpturen* (1966) 91, figs 161–9; S. Settis, *XEΛΨNH Saggi sul'Afrodite Urania di Fidea* (1966).

Aphrodite with image: Blümel, op. cit., figs 192–5; BrBr 673.

'Barberini Suppliant'; Herscher and Ridgway, *AJA* 75 1971 184.

CONTEMPORARIES OF PHEIDIAS

'Theseum' metopes and friezes: Morgan, *Hesp* 31 1962 210, pls 71–84; BrBr 152–3, 406–8.

Frieze from Ilissus: *AD* iii 36; C. Blümel, *Die klassisch griechischen Skulpturen* (1966) 88, figs 148–54.

151 Agora silvered head: Thompson, *Athenian Studies presented to W. S. Ferguson* (1940) 183.

Cresilas: Raub 510; *Por* i 102, figs 429–43 — Pericles.

Diomedes: *GrPl* 184 n.2, pl. 48.4; Hel ii No. 2096; *M* 146, figs 60–62; B. Maiuri, *Il Diomede di Cuma* (1930).

'Protesilaus', Diitrephes: Raub No 132; *GrPl* 173 n. 1–3, pl. 62–3 — bronze statuette; Carpenter, *Mem Am Ac* xviii 1941 8, pl. 4.

152 Amazons: D. von Bothmer, *Amazons in Greek Art* (1957) 216, pl. lxxxix; *Opus Nobile* 1, V. Poulsen, *Die Amazone von Kresilas* (1957) — ascribing 'Lansdowne' type to Cresilas, 'Capitoline' to Polycleitus; Richter, *Archaeology* 12 1959 iii — perhaps a fifth type; see also books on Polycleitus and Pheidias.

Polycleitus: C. Vermeule, *Polykleitos* (1969); P. E. Arias, *Policleto* (1964); *GrPl* 162; *ScSc* **Page 153** 246; R. B. Bandinelli, *Policleto* (1938)—literary sources, pls; Marwitz, *AP* vi 31, figs 5–15, pls 15–20—Diadumenus; Gardner, *JHS* xxxix 1919 69, pl. 1—Oxford bronze head.

Boeotian gravestones: Rodenwaldt, *JdI* xxviii 1913 309, pls 24–30.   155

Niobids: R. M. Cook, *Niobe and her Children* (1964) 30, 43 n.8; BrBr 706–14; LH 172–5— Terme; *GrPl*. pl. 65. 1–3; Hel iii No. 2279.

'Giustiniani' gravestone: C. Blümel, *Die klassisch griechischen Skulpturen* (1966) No. 2, **156** figs 2, 4, 6, 9; LH 138–9.

Sabouroff stela from Carystus: Johansen, *Attic Grave-Reliefs* (1951), 125, fig. 60.   157

Thessalian stelae: H. Biesantz, *Die thessalische Grabreliefs* (1965)—Polyxena 17 *K* 27, pl. 8, 'Exaltation' 22 *K* 36, pl. 17, youth with hare 13 *K* 19, pl. 10; Johansen, op. cit.—Polyxena 134, fig. 67, youth with hare 130, fig. 64.

CHAPTER VII: THE MIDDLE CLASSICAL PERIOD (430–370 B.C.) [PAGES 158–184]

ATTIC SCULPTURE, 430–390 B.C.: T. Dohrn, *Attische Plastik vom Tode des Phidias zum* **158** *Wirken der grossen Meister des IV Jahrts* (1957); B. Schlörb, *Untersuchungen zur Bildhauergeneration nach Phidias* (1954).

Villa Albani relief: LH 177–9; H. Diepolder, *Die attischen Grabreliefs* (1931), pl. 9.

Agoracritus: Schefold, *Freundesgabe für R. Boehringer* (1957) 543.   159

Nemesis of Rhamnus: Despinis, *AAA* iii 1970 407—identification of fragments and copies; *JHS* xxxi 1911 70, fig. 5—head; cf. Karouzou, *AM* 77 1962 182—supposed acroteria and pediments. Base: E. Kjellberg, *Studien zu den attischen Reliefs* (1926); BrBr 464.

'Velletri' Athena: Hel ii No. 1773; D. Mustilli, *Il Museo Mussolini* (1939) 120, pl. lxxvii; **161** *SkGr* 211, fig. 227; *GrPl* 173, pl. 62.3; *M* 141, figs 58–9; Pfuhl, *JdI* 41 1926 1.

Vatican Demeter: Hel i No. 36; BrBr 172; W. H. Schuchhardt, *Die Epochen der griechischen Plastik* (1959), fig. 59.

Eleusis Demeter: ibid., 543; BrBr 536; Lehmann-Hartleben, *Die Antike* 7 1931 331, fig. 1; *SkGr* 201, fig. 215; *GrPl* 191, pl. 70.1.

Gravestones in Rhodes and Cyprus: Frel, *AAA* iii 1970 367; LH 183.

'Venus Genetrix': BrBr 473; *SkGr* 207; F. Hiller, *Formgeschichtliche Untersuchungen zur griechischen Statue* (1971), pl. 1.

'Theseum' cult-group: Papaspyridi-Karusu, *AM* 69–70 1954–5 67 *Beilagen* 31–3, pl. x; **162** *AA* 1941 475—best copy of Athena; Hel i No. 377, ii No. 1991—others.

Alcamenes: L. Capius, *Alkamenes* (1968); Hecate: Eckstein, *AP* iv 27, pls 12–14. Hermes Propylaeus: Willers, *JdI* 82 1967 37; *The Athenian Agora* xi; E. R. Harrison, *Archaic and archaistic Sculpture* (1965) 122, 130—also for herms in general. Procne and Itys: *AD* ii 22; Praschniker, *ÖJh* 16 1913 121, figs 61–6, pl. iii; *SkGr* 200, fig. 214.

Erechtheum Caryatids: *GrPl* 192, pls 70–72.   163

Orpheus and three other reliefs: Thompson, *Hesp* 21 1952 60, pl. 17; Harrison, *Hesp* 33 1964 76, pls 11–12.

Hegeso stela: LH 185; BrBr 436; *GrPl* 196, pl. 72.1.

Page 164 Vatican horseman relief: *JdI* xxviii 1913, pl. 28; R. Lullies, *Griechische Bildwerke in Rom* (1955), fig. 19.

'Borghese' Ares: Freyer, *JdI* 77 1962 211; *SkGr* 95, fig. 86; BrBr 172.

Strongylion: Raub 524, and No. 176—base of horse; *Hesp* v 1936 460—restoration of horse.

Nike Temple frieze: C. Blümel, *Fries des Tempels der Athena Nike* (1923), and *JdI* 65–6 1950–51 135; Harrison, *AJA* 74 1970 317.

165 Acroteria of Athenian Temple: *Exploration archéologique de Délos* xii, F. Courby, *Les Temples d'Apollon* (1931) 237, pls xiv–xvi, xxvii; *SkGr* 353, fig. 392.

166 Nike Temple parapet: LH 187–9; R. Carpenter, *The Sculpture of the Nike Temple Parapet* (1929)—but his restoration is incompatible with one of the fragments published by Welter, *AA* 1939 15, figs 6–11; Thompson, *Hesp* 17 1948 176, pl. lii—head.

Callimachus: W. Fuchs, *Die Vorbilder des Neuattischen Reliefs* (1959)—'Laconian Dancers' 91, Maenads 73; G. Caputo, *Lo Scultore del grande bassorelievo con Danza delle Menadi in Tolemaide* (1948); Hel ii No. 1590—Conservatori; *LGS*, pls 84–5—Villa Albani.

167 Erechtheum friezes: Boulter, *AP* x 7, pls 1–30.

168 Dexileus stela: LH 191; K. F. Johansen, *Attic Grave-Reliefs* (1951) 48.

NON-ATTIC SCULPTURE IN GREECE 430–390 B.C.

Argive Heraeum: C. Waldstein, *Argive Heraeum* i (1902); *NCP*, pl. I. xii–xiv—Hera on coins; *JHS* xxi 1901, pls ii–iii—possible copy of Hera's head, BM No. 1792.

169 Polycleitan School: *JdI Erganzungsheft* 25, D. Arnold, *Die Polykletnachfolge* (1969); P. E. Arias, *Policlito* (1964); BrBr 700—Terme basalt boy; *AD* iv 24–9—Pompeii bronze.

Nike of Paeonius: BrBr 444–5; *ScSc* 244, fig. 637, cf. figs 639–41—heads; Hofkes-Brukker, *BAB* 34 1959 1 and 35 1960 63—derivation, 37 1962 52—novelty, 36 1961 1 —relation to Bassae, 42 1967 10—relation to other works.

171 Thasos gate relief: *Études Thasiennes* viii, Ch. Picard, *Les Murailles* i (1962) 149, fig. 66, pl. xlii.

Bassae frieze: Hahland, *ÖJh* 44 1959 5; Dinsmoor, *AJA* 60 1956 403; Yalouris, *AE* 1967 187, pls 30–53—additional fragments; Hofkes-Brukker, *BAB* 36 1961 1—ascription to Paeonius. Cf. Hofkes-Brukker, *BAB* 38 1963 52—metopes, 40 1965 51—identifying acroteria.

SCULPTURE IN ASIA 430–360 B.C.

173 Locri acroteria: E. Langlotz, *Art of Magna Graecia* (1965), pls 122–3; de Franciscis, *RM* 67 1960 1, pls 1–6; *SkGr* 354, figs 393–4.

Sidon sarcophagi: O. Hamdy Bey and T. Reinach, *Necropole royale de Sidon* (1892); G. Mendel, *Cat. ... Constantinople* ii (1914).

Sidon boys: Dunand, *Festschrift für K. Galling* (1970) 61, pls 1–4, and *Bulletin du Musée de Beyrouth* xviii 1965 106, pl. ii.

'Satrap' sarcophagus: I. Kleeman, *Der Satrapen-sarkophag aus Sidon* (1958); Pfuhl, *JdI* 41 1926 147; *GrPl* 207 n.12, pl. 75.1.

174 'Lycian' sarcophagus: *GrPl* 210, pl. 75.2.

Lycian monuments: G. Rodenwaldt, *Griechische Reliefs in Lykien* (1938)—especially for non-Greek elements; Borchhardt, *AA* 1970 383—dating.

Tombs in London; *BMC* ii (1900) No. 950, pls vi–xii—Payava, No. 951, pl. xiii—Merehi; **Page 174n** Borchhardt, *AA* 1968 198—Payava inscription, cf. 174—rock-cut tombs at Cadyanda.

Gjölbaschi: F. Eichler, *Die Reliefs des Heroon von Gjölbaschi-Trysa* (1950); Praschniker, **175** *ÖJh* 28 1933 1.

Nereid Monument: *Fouilles de Xanthos* iii, Coupel and Demargne, *Le Monument des* **177** *Nereides, l'Architecture*. Statues: Bielefeld, *AP* ix 47, 56. Friezes: Gottlieb, *AJA* 1956 177; Schuchhardt, *AM* 52 1927 94 *Beilagen* xiii–xvi; Schröder, *JdI* xxix 1914 123—parallels in painting.

Views of towns at Pinera: *JHS* lviii 1938 213, fig. 4.   **178**

Limyra: Borchhardt, *AA* 1970 353.   **179**

SCULPTURE IN GREECE 390–360 B.C.

Lysias: *Por* ii 207, figs 1340–45.

Antisthenes: ibid., 179, figs 1037–56.

Lysimache: *Por* i 155, figs 878–9—possible copy of head.

Epidaurus inscribed accounts: A. Burford, *The Greek Temple Builders at Epidaurus* (1969) 212; Roux, *BCH* lxxx 1956 518.

Epidaurus cult-image: *NCP*, pl. L. iv–v—coins; Ridgway, *AJA* 70 1966 217, pl. 49—reliefs.

Epidaurus pediments and acroteria: *JdI Erganzungsheft* 22, B. Schlörb, *Timotheos* (1965); **180** J. Crome, *Die Skulpturen des Asklepiostempels von Epidauros* (1951)—for illustrations alone; *ADelt* 19. B2, pls 192–4—additional fragments; *BCH* 90 1966 783, figs 1–8—new joins; G. Roux, *L'Architecture de l'Argolide* (1961) 102, fig. 22, pl. 32a—restoration of Amazon.

Statues of Epidaurus affinites: Schlörb, op. cit.; Arnold, op. cit.—Aphrodite with sword- **181** belt, pl. 20a.

Eleusis Pan, NM No. 254: *AE* 1890, pls 10–11; F. Hiller, *Formgeschichtliche Untersuchungen* **182** *zur griechischen Statue* (1971), pl. 5.11.

Fogg head: *AJA* xxvi 1922 204, fig. 2.

'Joven Orador': A. Blanco, *Cat...Prado* i (1957) No. 39, pl. xxi; *The Athenian Agora* xi, E. R. Harrison, *Archaic and Archaistic Sculpture* (1965) 135, 163, pl. 56—fragment of similar statue, arguments against ascription to Cephisodotus.

Eirene and Plutus: G. M. A. Richter, *Cat...Metropolitan Museum* (1954) No. 98, pl. lxxx; J. Boardman and others, *Art and Architecture of Ancient Greece* (1967), pl. 247—Munich.

'Hope' Hygieia: R. Kabus-Jahn, *Studien zu Frauenfiguren des vierten Jahrts* (1963) 85, 109, **183** pl. 15; Ashmole, *Papers of British School of Rome* x 1927 1, pls i–iii.

Piraeus bronze Athena: Schefold, *Antike Kunst* 14 1971 37, pl. 16; Waywell, *BSA* 66 **184** (forthcoming).

CHAPTER VIII: THE LATE CLASSICAL PERIOD (370–323 B.C.) [PAGES 185–210]

Page 185 L. Alscher, *Griechische Plastik* iii (1956); A Conze, *Die attischen Grabsreliefs* (1893–1922).

PRAXITELES: G. Rizzo, *Prasitele* (1932)—illustrates all supposed works.

Hermes: LH 220–23; J. Boardman and others, *Art and Architecture of Ancient Greece* (1967), pl. 249.

186n Date of Hermes: Sheila Adam, *Technique of Greek Sculpture* (1966) Appendix; *AJA* 35 1931 248–97—controversy.

187 Brauron girls: *BCH* 83 1959 595, figs 25, 27; 84 1960 665, figs 5–7; 85 1961 639, figs 4–5, 9.

188 Dating of Praxiteles' career: *ScSc* 259; *GrPl* 234.

Apollo Sauroctonus: *ScSc* 262; *GrPl* 240 n. 6; L. Budde and R. Nicholls, *Cat...Fitzwilliam Museum* (1964) No. 51, pl. 15.

Hypnos: *GrPl* 252 n. 7, 91.4—ascribing to Scopas: BrBr 529—Madrid; A. Blanco, *Cat... Prado* i (1957) No. 89, pls xliii–xlv.

189 Statuette of nude girl: *Opus Nobile* 9, A. Greifenhagen, *Das Mädchen von Beröa* (1958); LH 194.

Cnidian Aphrodite: C. Blinkenberg, *Knidia* (1933); *Opus Nobile* 10, T. Kraus, *Die Aphrodie von Knidos* (1957); *ScSc* 260, figs 668–72; Hel i No. 207—Vatican.

191 Eros of Centocelle: *GrPl* 264 n. 11; Hel i No. 116, ii No. 1586—ascribing to a Peloponnesian of early fourth century.

Capitoline satyr: Hel ii No. 1429; *GrPl* 240 n. 9; BrBr 126–7—Louvre.

192 Dionysus, 'Sardanapalus': Ashmole, *BSA* xxiv 1919–21 78, pls iii–iv; Hel i No. 496.

Satyr pouring wine: Hel iii No. 2338—Terme; *ScSc* 266, figs 682–4—Dresden.

Eros of Parium: *ScSc* 263, fig. 674—coin.

'Diana of Gabies': *ScSc* 265, fig. 686; *GrPl* 239 n. 7 pl. 83.4; A. Furtwängler, edited by A. N. Oikonomides (1964) 423, pl. lxxxiv—incompatible relief at Brauron.

'Leconfield', head; Vermeule, *AJA* 59 1955 145.

193 'Aberdeen' head, BM No. 1600: Pfuhl, *JdI* 43 1928 23.

Mantinea base, NM Nos 215–7: *ScSc* 265, figs 679–81; *GrPl* 238 n. 2, pl. 85.1–3.

SCOPAS: P. E. Arias, *Skopas* (1952).

194 Tegea fragments: C. Dugas, J. Berchmans and M. Clemmensen, *Le Sanctuaire d'Aléa Athéna à Tegée* (1924), pls xcvi–cxvi; *ScSc* 270, figs 690–93, 696; *ADelt* 20 B. 1, pl. 151a—winged acroterion; Delevorrias, *ADelt* 24 B.1 130, pl. 117.2, and *AAA* 1968 117 —additional fragments from pediments.

195 Dresden Maeand: *ScSc* 276, fig. 709; *GrPl* 251 n. 5.

'Ludovisi' Ares: Hel iii No. 2345; *GrPl* 289 n. 11, pl. 102.2; Praschniker, *ÖJh* 21–2 1922–4 203, figs 73–9, pl. ii.

Pothos: Hel ii Nos 1392, 1644; *GrPl* 252 n. 5, pl. 91.3; G. A. Mansuelli, *Cat...Uffizi* i (1958) Nos 31–2 (illd).

'Lansdowne' Heracles (now at Malibu) and 'Townley' bust, BM No. 1733: *J. Paul Getty Museum Publication* 1, S. Howard, *The Lansdowne Heracles* (1966); cf. D. Mustilli, *Il Museo Mussolini* (1939) 80, pl. lv.

Meleager: Hanfmann and Pedley, *AP* iii 61, pls 58–72; Hel i No. 97; Sichtermann, *RM* 69 1962 43, pls 18–21, and 70 1963 174.

Scopas' Apollo: Amelung, *RM* xv 1900 201, fig. 2; *GrPl* 221 n. 12 pl. 89.1.　　　　**Page 196**

Sorrento base: *Ausonia* iii 1908 94, fig. 1; *ScSc* 275, fig. 706.

Ostia Nereid: *JdI Erganzungsheft* 22, B. Schlörb, *Timotheus* (1965), fig. 171; *GrPl* 253 n. 8–9; J. D. Beazley and B. Ashmole, *Greek Sculpture and Painting* (1932), fig. 117.

LESSER-KNOWN CONTEMPORARIES OF PRAXITELES

Corinna: *RA* 1900 i, pls ii–iii; *Por* i 144, figs 780–82.

Plato: R. Boehringer, *Platon—Bildnisse und Nachweise* (1935); *Por* ii 164, figs 903–75.　　　**197**

Naples 'Apollodorus': Schlörb, op. cit., 292, pl. 257.

Bologna portrait: Ducati, *Ausonia* ii 1907 235, figs 1–2.

Olympia head of boxer, NM No. 6439: LH 224–5; *GrPl* 233 n. 1, pl. 77.4.

Cyrene head of Libyan: LH 198; *LGS*, pl. 27.

Aristonautes stela, NM No. 738: *GrPl* 221 n. 16, pl. 79.4.

'Les Pleureuses': Ch. Picard, *La Sculpture antique* iii.2 (1954) 208; *GrPl* 231 n. 9, pl. 82.1.

Metope of mourners, NM No. 1688: E. Löwy, *Polygnot* (1929), fig. 60; Wolters, *AM* **198** xviii 1893 1, pl. 1.

Argive-Sicyonian statues: *JdI Erganzungsheft* 25, D. Arnold, *Die Polykletnachfolge* (1969); F. P. Johnson, *Lysippos* (1927)—for pls; Dorig, *AP* iv 37; Hel ii No. 1759, and Willemsen, *AA* 72 1957 25—Naucydes' Discobolus.

Euphranor: *GrPl* 260.

Apollo Patrous: Thompson, *AE* 1953–4 iii 30, pls i–ii; Shear, *Hesp* v 1936 310, fig. 17—　**199** coins.

Paris: Hel i Nos 120, 571; Ch. Picard, *La Sculpture antique* iii.1 (1948) 781; Dacos, *BCH* 85 1961 371; Jantzen, *JdI* 79 1964 241; *M* fig. 155.

'Eubouleus': Hel i No. 75, ii No. 1240; Harrison, *Hesp* 29 1960 382—ascribing original of ten listed copies to Leochares.

Anticythera bronze: *GrSk* 117, figs 107–8; R. Carpenter, *Greek Sculpture* (1960) 161; LH 208–9, 213; Karouzos, *AE* 1969 59, pls 1–4—new restoration.

The Mausoleum: E. Buschor, *Mausollos und Alexander* (1950); LH 201–4—Amazon frieze, **200** 205–7—Mausolus and Artemisia; forthcoming British Museum publication of statues, by G. B. Waywell, and friezes, by B. Ashmole and D. E. Strong.

Bryaxis: Ch. Picard, *La Sculpture antique* iv.2 (1963) 854; *ScSc* 281, figs 723–6—base and **202** Nike.

Leochares: Picard, op. cit. 754; *Por* ii 208, figs 1346–8—Isocrates; Hel i No. 528, and *ScSc* 285, fig. 737—Ganymede.

Prototype of Apollo 'Belvedere': Tölle, *JdI* 81 1966 142; K. Schefold, *Basler Antiken im Bild* (1958) 37, pl. 28.

Conservatori 'Alcibiades' and related head: *Ausonia* iii 1908, pl. v; Graef, *RM* xii 1897 30, pl. ii.

Lion-hunt: *JdI* iii 1888, pl. vii.

Page 203 Acropolis Alexander: *Por* iii 255, fig. 1727; Ashmole, *JHS* lxxi 1951 15, pls xi–xii.

Demeter of Cnidus: ibid. 13, pls i–ix, xii; LH 216–17.

Ephesus columns: LH 214–15; *ScSc* 273.

'Herculaneum Women': see references for Lysippus; Bie, 2nd (1961) edn only, figs 748–53; *LGS*, pls 72–3 — Delos 'Small'.

204 Aeschylus: *Por* i 121, figs 577–610.

Sophocles: *Por* i 124, figs 611–716.

Euripides: *Por* i 133, figs 717–79; *LGS*, pl. 80—relief.

Delphi philosopher: *D*, figs 155–6; *SkGr* 132, fig. 119.

Socrates: *Por* i 109, figs 461–573; BM statuette: ibid. 116, figs 560–62; *JHS* xlv 1925, pls x–xiii.

LYSIPPUS AND HIS CONTEMPORARIES

Lysippus: E. S. Sjöqvist, *Lysippus* (1966); *ScSc* 287; F. P. Johnson, *Lysippos* (1927); Dörig, *AP* iv 37, pls 15–19—ascribing oil-pouring Athlete to youthful Lysippus; Schauenburg, *AP* ii—75 pls 46–56 possible copies of Pulydamas head, 78 pls 60–71 copies of Apoxyomenus; Hel i No. 254—Vatican copy.

205 Horses at St Mark's: Crome, *BCH* lxxxvii 1963 209; K. Kluge and K. Lehmann-Hartleben, *Die antiken Grossbronzen* (1927) ii 78, figs 5–7, iii pl. xxiv.

Daochus group: Dohrn *AP* viii 33, pls 10–35; *D* 181–9—Agias 182–5; Sheila Adam, *Technique of Greek Sculpture* (1966) 97.

207 Pulydamas base: *ScSc* 291, fig. 752; *GrPl* 284, pl. 94.2.

'Philandridas', Olympia head: Dohrn, *AP* viii 44, figs 17–19; *GrPl* 284—against ascription to Lysippus.

Herculaneum bronze head: BrBr 364; Arnold, op. cit. 172, pl. 24d—ascribing to Daedalus.

'Farnese' Heracles: *GrSk* 101, fig. 95; *GrPl* 321, pl. 101.1; BrBr 284–5.

Heracles Epitrapezius: F. de Visscher, *L'Antiquité classique* 30 1961 67, pls iv–xxvi; Dörig, *JdI* 72 1957 19, figs 16–21.

208 Eros with bow: Hel ii No. 1231; *GrPl* 281, pl. 100.4.

Kairos: Picard, op. cit. 553–65; *ÖJh* 26 1930, pl. 1—Trogir; J. Boardman and others, *Greek Art and Architecture* (1967), pl. 261—Turin; Acropolis Museum No. 2799, cf. Walter, *Beschreibung* No. 125.

Alexander: *Por* iii 255, figs 1724–40; M. Bieber, *Alexander the Great in Greek and Roman Art* (1964).

209 'Ilissus' stela: LH 218; N. Himmelmann-Wildschütz, *Studien zum Ilissosrelief* (1956)—related subjects.

Marathon bronze, NM No. 15118: LH 210–12; *GrPl* 274 n. 12, pl. 96.3; *ScSc* 267, figs 46–8; Chamoux, *Études d'archéologie classique* 2 1959 38.

Epidaurus Victories: P. Cavvadias, *Fouilles d'Epidaure* (1893) 18, pls ix–x.

Lysicrates frieze: Ch. Picard, *La Sculpture antique* iv. 2 (1963) 1132.

'Alexander' sarcophagus: F. Winter, *Der Alexandersarkophag aus Sidon* (1912)—coloured pls; K. Schefold, *Der Alexander-Sarkophag* (1968)—ascribing to before 323; *Istanbuler Forschungen* 27, V. von Graeve, *Der Alexandersarkophag und seine Werkstatt* (1970)—ascribing to after 317.

Taranto reliefs: J. Bernabó Brea, *Rivista dell'Istituto d'Archeologia* (1952) 1; P. Wuilleumier, **Page 210** *Tarente* (1939); H. Klumbach, *Tarentiner Grabkunst* (1937); cf. Carter, *AJA* 74 1970 125, pls 27–34—third-century.

CHAPTER IX: THE HELLENISTIC CLIMAX (323–133 B.C.) [PAGES 211–233]

L. Alscher, *Griechische Plastik* iv (1957); Bie; *LGS* 99—list of sculptures published by **211** 1927; E. Buschor, *Das hellenistische Bildnis* (2nd edn 1971).

THE EARLY HELLENISTIC PERIOD

Alexandrian Sculpture: A. Adriani, *Repertorio d'arte dell'Egitto greco-romano* Ai–ii (1961); Lawrence, *Journal of Egyptian Archaeology* xi 1925 179—pls of better finds; I. Noshy, *The Arts in Ptolemaic Egypt* (1937).

Memphis Serapeum: J.-Ph. Lauer and Ch. Picard, *Les statues ptolémaiques du Serapeion de Memphis* (1955).

Sculptures from Inland Asia: Roland, *Art Quarterly* xviii 1955 174—finds from Iran; LH **212** 264—bronze head in British Museum from Satala, Armenia.

Athenian sumptuary law: H. K. Süsserott, *Griechische Plastik des IV Jhts* (1938) 120 n. 136.

Messene lion-hunt relief: *GrPl* 284 n. 8; Ch. Picard, *La sculpture antique* iv.2 (1963) 741, **214** 750, figs 314–15.

'Praying Boy': Bie 39, fig. 93; *GrPl* 296 n. 8, pl. 105.2; BrBr 283.

Tyche of Antioch: T. Dohrn, *Die Tyche von Antiochia* (1960); Hel i No. 548—Vatican; **215** BrBr 610—Budapest.

Eurotas: *RM* viii 1893, pls v–vi; Hel i No. 54.

Conservatori Tyche: *GrPl* 297 n. 1; Hel ii No. 1480—ascribing to rather later period. **216**

Heads of Helios: *SkGr* 570, fig. 697; Shear, *AJA* xx 1916 283, pls vii–viii; cf. Maryon, *JHS* 76 1956 68—other evidence for Colossus.

Cos head: Bieber, *JdI* xxxviii–xxxix 1923–4 242, pl. vi; Bie 20, fig. 33.

Chios head: LH 228–9; *LGS*, pl. 6.

Serapeum head: *LGS*, pl. 23; *GrPl* 325 n. 2. **217**

Menander: *Por* ii 224, figs 1514–1643; *Antike Kunst, Beiheft* 6, S. Charitonides, *Les mosaiques de la maison du Ménandre à Mytilène* (1970), pls. 2.1, 15.1.

Seleucus I: *Por* iii 269, figs 1867–8; Bie, figs 142–3; Hek 68.

Themis of Chaerestratus, NM 231: Bie 65, fig. 516; *GrPl* 302, pl. 108.1; BrBr 476.

Theophrastus: *Por* ii 176, figs 1022–30, Hek 96*a*.

Page 218 Demosthenes: *Por* ii 215, figs 1397–1531.

Aeschines: ibid. 212, figs 1369–96; Hek 53–5.

Epicureans: *Por* ii 194, figs 1149–1225—Epicurus, 203, figs 1268–1324—Hermarchus, 200, figs 1226–67—Metrodorus.

Niceso: Bie, fig. 517; T. Wiegand and H. Schrader, *Priene* (1904), figs 118, 120.

219 Dionysus of Thrasyllus: BrBr 119; *ScSc* 66, fig. 213; Bie 213.

Serapis: Kraus, *JdI* 75 1960 88; Bie 83, figs 296–7; *GrPl* 258 n. 6, pl. 93.3—ascribing to the Mausoleum Bryaxis.

Poseidippus: *Por* ii 238, figs 1647–50.

Nicocleia: LH 231.

'Anzio Girl': LH 232–3; Bie, figs 97–100; Carpenter, *Mem Am Ac* xviii 1941 70, pl. 23.

220 Seated poet: *Por* i 66, figs 231–42—identifying as Archilochus.

Crouching Aphrodite: *SkGr* 304, fig. 334; Linfert, *AM* 84 1969 158—ascribing to Polycharmus by emendation of Pliny and denying existence of Daedalus; R. Lullies, *Die Kauernde Aphrodite* (1954); Hel i No. 205, iii No. 2292; *LGS*, pl. 25*a*—bronze; Wiegand, *AM* xxxvi 1911 295, fig. 3—relief.

Marsyas group: Bie 110, figs 438–44, cf. 445—presumed Apollo; *LGS*, pls 29–30*a*, 39; G. A. Mansuelli, *Cat ... Uffizi* i (1958) Nos 55–7 (illd).

THE PERGAMENE AGE

221 Asclepius and Hygieia: Mariani, *Bull Comm* xliii 1914 3, pls 1–2; Bie 107, fig. 423; Hel iii No. 2227.

Ist Dedication: Bie 108; Hel ii No 1436—Capitoline Gaul, 2337—'Ludovisi' Gaul and wife, iii No. 2240—Dying Asiatic.

223 Menelaus and Patroclus: Bie 78, figs 272–7; *GrPl* 362 n. 17, pl. 122.2.

'Ludovisi' Fury: Hel iii No. 2343; Bie 112, figs 452–3; *LGS*, pl. 35.

Ptolemy IV and Arsinoe: *Por* iii 264, figs 1829–30, 1833–4; *LGS*, pl. 36—Arsinoe.

Euthydemus: *Por* iii 278, figs 1970–71; Bie, figs 311–13, cf. 310—coin.

224 Chrysippus: *Por* ii 190, figs 1113–47; Ingholt, *Berytus* xvii 1968 143, pls xxxviii–xli—distinguishing at least three prototype statues.

Anticythera head, NM No. 13400: LH 236–7.

Second Dedication: A. Scholer, *Die Kunst von Pergamon* (1951), figs 99–102, 106–115; Bie 109, figs 430–37; *LGS*, pl. 37*b*—wounded Greek.

225 Old and Young Centaurs: BrBr 5*a*, 392; Bie 140, figs 581–4.

Red Marsyas: Hel ii No. 1587.

Trousered Gaul: *LGS*, pl. 38; G. M. A. Richter, *Cat... Metr Mus* (1954) No. 205, pl. cxlv.

Sleeping Hermaphrodite: Bie 112, figs 623–5; *LGS*, pl. 40; BrBr 505; Hel iii No. 2243—Terme.

'Barberini' satyr: LH 234–5; Bie 112, figs 450–51; *LGS*, pl. 34*b*; *SkGr* 318, fig. 354. **Page 226**

Dancing satyr: Bie 35, figs 95–6; BrBr 435; Hel ii No. 1995.

Flute-playing satyr: Bie 59, fig. 94; *GrPl* 298 n. 6, pl. 104.3.

Satyr looking at his tail: *Boll d'A* xiv 1920 47, fig. 8; J. D. Beazley and B. Ashmole, *Greek Sculpture and Painting* (1966), fig. 165.

Invitation to dance: *LGS*, pls 30*b*, 31; Bie, figs 562–7; Deonna, *Studies presented to D. M. Robinson* i (1951) 664, pls 68–9; G. A. Mansuelli, *Cat… Uffizi* i (1958) Nos 51–2 (illd).

Satyr and hermaphrodite: B. Ashmole, *Cat.. Ince-Blundell Hall* (1929)—No. 30, pl. 21 now in Walker Gallery, Liverpool; BrBr 731; *GrPl* 113.1; Hel ii No. 1715.

Nike of Samothrace: J. Charbonneaux, *La Sculpture grecque au Musée du Louvre* (1936), pls 219–22, and *Hesp* xxi 1952 44, pls 12–13—identifying right hand; *SkGr* 229, fig. 250; R. Carpenter, *Greek Sculpture* (1960) 201; Bie 125, figs 493–6.

Samothrace pediment: *Samothrace* 3, P. W. Lehmann, *The Hieron* (1969), or advance **227** extract, *Pedimental Sculptures of the Hieron* (1962).

Niobe group: Bie, figs 253–65; R. M. Cook, *Niobe and her Children* (1964) 19, 47; Weber, *JdI* 75 1960 112, figs 1–9; G. A. Mansuelli, *Cat… Uffizi* i (1958) Nos 70–83 (illd); *LGS*, pls 12–'Chiaramonti', 13—son; Hel i No. 312—'Chiaramonti'.

'Head from South Slope', NM No. 182: BrBr 174*a*; *GrPl* 304 n. 16, pl. 109.3.

Magnesia frieze: K. Humann and C. Watzinger, *Magnesia am Maeander* (1904) 84, 185, pls xii–xiv; Bie 164, figs 702–3.

Cos frieze: O. Benndorf, *Reisen in S.-W. Kleinasien* i (1884) 13, pls ii–iv.

Teos frieze: Hahland, *ÖJh* 38 1950 6, figs 27–43.

Chios gravestone: *LGS* 23, 115, pl. 42.

Gigantomachy: *Altertümer von Pergamon* iii.2, H. Winnefeld, *Die Friese des groszen Altars* (1910); LH 238–47; H. Kähler, *Der grosse Fries von Pergamon* (1948); Evamaria Schmidt, *The Great Altar of Pergamon* (1962).

Female head from Pergamon: Bie 119, fig. 475; *LGS*, pl. 44. **229**

Head of Attalus I: Bie 113, figs 454, 456–7; *Por* iii 273, fig. 1915; Hek 75.

Head of Alexander: Bie, fig. 455; *LGS*, pl. 46*a*.

Dancing girls: Bie 120, fig. 479; *LGS*, pls 45, 71.

Drunken old woman: Hel ii No. 1253; Bie 81, fig. 284; BrBr 394.

'Centaur' head: BrBr 535; Hel ii No. 1483; *Pedimental Sculptures of the Hieron* (1962), fig. **230** 41, cf. figs 39–40—centaur from ceiling at Samothrace.

Homer: R. and E. Boehringer, *Homer—Bildnisse und Nachweise* i (1939).

Telephus frieze: K. P. Stähler, *Das Unklassische im Telephosfries* (1966); Bie 120, figs 477–8; E. Schmidt, op. cit., pls 60–67.

Statues from Pergamon: Stähler, op. cit.; A. Schober, *Die Kunst von Pergamon* (1951); **231** *Altertümer von Pergamon* vii, F. Winter, *Die Skulpturen* (1908).

Muses: D. Pinkwart, *Das Relief des Archelaos von Priene und die 'Musen von Philiskos'* (1965), and *AP* iv 55, pls 28–35.

Draped female statues: *RM Erganzungsheft* 2, R. Horn, *Stehende weibliche Gewandstatuen in der hellenistischen Plastik* (1931); Bie, figs 498–502, 510–15, 520–21.

Erythrae draped female statue: Krahmer, *RM* xxxviii–xxxix 1923–4 175, pls 15–16.

Magnesia draped statue: *LGS*, pl. 50; Bie 131, fig. 520.

'Eastern Greek Reliefs': Pfuhl, *JdI* xx 1905 47, 123, figs 1–28, pls 4–6.

Frieze of Aemilius Paullus: *Monumenta Artis Romanae* v, H. Kähler, *Der Fries vom Reiterdenkmal des Aemilius Paullus* (1965).

Page 232 Zeus of Attalus II: R. Carpenter, *Greek Sculpture* (1960) 204, pl. xxxviii; *LGS*, pl. 52; Bie, figs 471–2.

Terme bronze Ruler: Hel iii No. 2273; *LGS*, pl. 51; *Por* i, figs 880–81.

Lycosura group: Dickins, *BSA* xii 1905–6 109, and xiii 1906–7 357; *LGS* 30, pls 54–5; Bie 158, figs 665–70.

233 Damophon at Messene: Paus. iv. 31.10; Despinis, *AA* 1956 378, figs 1–2; *SkGr* 572, fig. 698.

CHAPTER X: THE HELLENISTIC ANTICLIMAX AND THE ROMAN REPUBLIC [PAGES 234–251]

234 L. Alscher, *Griechische Plastik* iv (1957); Bie, and last chapter added in 2nd edn (1961); *LGS*—for references prior to 1927.

THE DELOS PERIOD: J. Marcadé, *Au Musée de Délos* (1969).

235 Sleeping Eros: Ashmole, *JHS* xlii 1922 244, pl. x; *LGS*, pl. 41*b*; Hel ii No. 1461.

'Capitoline' boy and goose: Bie, fig. 285; Hel ii No. 1410.

Hellenistic votive children: Lawrence, *BSA* xxvii 1925–6 113; *LGS*, pl. 21.

Boethus' herm and *Agon*: W. Fuchs, *Der Schiffsfund von Mahdia* (1963) 12, pls 1–8; Bie, figs 286–9.

236 Boy jockey: E. Buschor, *Plastik der Griechen* (1958) 155; Bie, 2nd edn (1961) only, fig. 645.

Tralles boy boxer: *LGS*, pls 74–5; Sichtermann, *AP* iv 71, pls 39–49, cf. pls 50–52—Terme torso.

Tralles head of Athena: *LGS*, pl. 53; *BCH* xxviii 1904 68, pl. iii.

Tralles female head, Vienna: Tralles caryatid: *LGS*, pl. 70; P. Arndt and W. Amelung, *Einzelaufnahmen* 864–5.

Carthage priestess: *LGS*, pl. 90*a*: Héron de Villefosse, *MPiot* xii 1905 96, fig. 7, pl. viii (in colour).

237 Aphrodite of Melos: *Opus Nobile* 6, J. Charbonneaux, *La Vénus de Milo* (1958).

Delos Isis: Marcadé, op. cit., pl. lvii.

Delos 'Small Herculaneum Woman': *LGS*, pls 72–3.

238 Aphrodite of Capua: BrBr 297; B. Maiuri, *Museo Nazionale di Napoli* (1957) 30–31 (illd).

Melos Poseidon: Schäfer, *AP* viii 55, pls 38–44.

Eretria youth, NM No. 244: BrBr 519; Lippold, *JdI* xxvi 1911 275, fig. 6—head.

Apotheosis of Homer: D. Pinkwart, *AP* iv 55, pls 28–35.

Canopus drapery, Alexandria Museum: E. Breccia, *Monuments de l'Égypte greco-romaine* **Page 239** i (1926), pl. xxix. 4.

Lacrateides relief: *LGS* 124, pl. 78.

Eleusis caryatids: *LGS* 129, pl. 65b—Eleusis Museum; L. Budde and R. Nicholls, *Cat...* *Fitzwilliam Museum* (1964) No. 81, pls 24–5; H. Hörmann, *Die inneren Propyläen von Eleusis* (1932) 64, pls 50–2, cf. restorations, pls 21–3, 27–9, 33–4, 36.

'Borghese Warrior': BrBr 75; F. P. Johson, *Lysippos* (1927) 177.

Bronze Heracles: Hel ii No. 1804; Krahmer, *JdI* xl 1925 183, figs 13–14, pl. ix; British **240** Museum, H. B. Walters, *Select Bronzes*, pl. 50—statuette; cf. Krug, *AA* 1969 189, figs 1–3, 5—identifying a bust of Helios as Mithridates.

Prometheus group: Ridgway, *Hesp* xl 1971 349; Krahmer, op. cit., figs 1–2, 10–12; Bie, figs 485–7.

Lagina frieze: A. Schober, *Der Fries des Hekateions von Lagina* (1933).

Poseidoniasts' group: Marcadé, op. cit. 393, pl. l; *LGS*, pl. 63; *BCH* xxx 1906, pls xiii– **241** xvi.

Cyrene Aphrodite: *LGS* pl. 76; Hel iii No. 2278.

Delos portraits: *Exploration archéologique de Délos* xiii, C. Michalowski, *Les portraits hellénistiques et romains* (1932).

Bronze head from Delos: ibid., pls i–vi; LH 258; *LGS*, pl. 56b.

Pompey: *LGS*, pl. 62a; V. Poulsen, *Les Portraits romains* i (1962) No. 1, pls i–ii.

Attic portrait heads: *LGS*, pl. 59b—NM No. 320; Hekler, *ÖJh* xviii 1915 61. **242**

Relief of family: *LGS*, pl. 60; Bieber, *RM* xxxii 1917 130, fig. 8, pl. 2—the heads.

Bald heroic nude: Michalowski, op. cit., pls xiv–xix; Marcadé, op. cit., pl. lxxii; *LGS*, pls 57–8a.

Portraits in armour: Marcadé, op. cit. 329, pl. lxxv.

Half-length figures: M. Collignon, *Les statues funéraires dans l'art grec* (1911), figs 189–90; Keil, *ÖJh* xvi 1913 178, fig. 90, pl. iv; Benndorf, *ÖJh* i 1898 4, fig. 4, pl. 1.

THE GROWTH OF SCULPTURE IN ROME

Etruscan sculpture under Hellenistic influence: *LGS*, pls 93–101.

Terracotta pediment statues in Rome: British School at Rome, *Cat ... Conservatori* (1926), pls 121–2; Hel ii 1605—dating *c.* 100 B.C. or soon after.

'Arringatore': *Monumenta Artis Romanae* viii, T. Dohrn, *Der Arringatore* (1968); *LGS*, pl. **243** 97b.

Dioscurides: Marcadé, op. cit. 325, pls lxv–lxvi, lxviii; Fittschen, *RM* 77 1970, pls 74–6.

Ofellius: *BCH* v 1881, pl. xii; Marcadé, op. cit. 117.

Orpheus (now in Conservatori): Hel ii No. 1599; *LGS*, pl. 102b; D. Mustilli, *Il Museo Mussolini* (1939) No. 20, pl. xiii.

Flute-players: ibid. Nos 22–7, pl. ix; *LGS*, pl. 102a.

Wax masks: *Allard Pierson Bydragen* i, A. N. Zadok-Josephus Jitta, *Ancestral Portraiture in Rome* (1932) 22.

Page 244 Terracotta portrait heads: Richter, *Latomus* xlviii (1960).

Republican portraiture: B. Schweizer, *Die Bildniskunst der römischen. Republik* (1948); O. Vessberg, *Studien zur Kunstgeschichte der römischen. Republik* (1941). Cf. M. L. Vollenweider, *Gemmenportraits der römischen. Republik* (forthcoming)—will include copies on later seals.

Pasitelean school: Cf. p. 57; Bie, last chapter added in 2nd edn (1961).

Stephanus' Athlete (in Villa Albani): *SkGr* 150, fig. 144; *GrPl* 129 n. 9, pl. 36.3; BrBr 301; Hel i No. 1089—Lateran head of same type.

'Spinario': *Opus Nobile* 8, W. Fuchs, *Der Dornauszieher* (1968); Hel ii No. 1448, cf. No. 1785.

245 Resting Hermes: BrBr 282; *ScSc*, fig. 72.

Bronze head of Dionysus: BrBr 382; C. Waldstein and L. Shoobridge, *Herculaneum Past Present and Future* (1908), pl. v.

Bronze dancing girls: ibid., pl. iv; B. Maiuri, *Museo Nazionale di Napoli* (1957) 56–7 (illd).

'Piombino' Apollo: Ridgway, *AP* vii 43, pls 24–34; *Kou* 144, 152, figs 533–40—still dating to fifth century.

Archaistic marble statues: *Abhandlungen d. Bayer Akad.* xxx, H. Bulle, *Archaisiriende griechische Rundplastik* (1918); BrBr 350—Pompeii Artemis; *JHS* xxxii 1912 43, pl. 1— 'Chigi' Athena; *LGS*, pl. 81a—Metr. Mus. head.

246 Archaistic reliefs: *JdI Erganzungsheft* 20, W. Fuchs, *Die Vorbilder der Neuattischen Reliefs* (1959); Snyder, *RA* 1924 ii 37, pl. iii—satyrs on fourth-century stela; V. M. Strocka, *Piräusreliefs und Parthenosschild* (1969); *LGS*, pls 83—vase, 84–5—Maenads, 86a— Bacchic.

247 Busts of wife and husband (Marcus Gratidius if an inscription, now lost, belonged): Hel i No. 199.

Portraits of Caesar: Poulsen, op. cit. Nos 29–30, pls lxi–lxv—copies ascribed to Christian era.

248 Munich relief: Weichert, *Münchner Jahrbuch der bildenden Kunst* ii 1925 i, fig. on 3; A. Frova, *L'arte di Roma* (1961) 158, fig. 116.

Base with sea-monsters and census: *Monumenta Artis Romanae* vi, H. Kähler, *Seethiasos und Census* (1966); *LGS*, pl. 66; *ScR*, pls i–iii.

249 Laocoon: *Opus Nobile* 3, H. Sichtermann, *Laokoon* (1957); F. Magi, *Il ripristino del Laocoonte* (1960)—restoration; LH 262–3; *LGS*, pl. 67—father's head.

Sperlonga: G. Iacopi, *L'antro di Tiberio a Sperlonga* (1963); Lauter, *RM* 76 1969 162, pls 55–7, and Blanckenhagen, *AA* 1969 256—relation to Laocoon.

250 'Belvedere' torso: Hel i No. 265; BrBr 240; Carpenter, *Mem Am Ac* xviii 1941 84, pl. 26— identifying as Marsyas playing flute.

251 Bronze boxer: Hel iii No. 2272; Carpenter, *Mem Am Ac* 6 1927 133; LH 259–61; *LGS*, pl. 28.

'Pseudo-Seneca': *Por* i 58, figs 131–212—Naples bronze, figs 165–7; *LGS*, pl. 48.

CHAPTER XI: IMPERIAL CLASSICISM: AUGUSTUS TO NERO (23 B.C.–A.D. 68) [PAGES 252–266]

Troy metopes: F. W. Goethert and H. Schleif, *Der Athenatempel von Ilion* (1962) 23, pls **Page 253** 34–49; B. M. Holden, *Metopes of the Temple of Athena at Ilion* (1964); Hoepfner, *AM* 84 1969 165: Jucker, *AA* 1969 248.

Zoilus frieze: *Fasti Archaeologici* xvi 1961, pl. xvi. 254

Panels at Glanum: *Gallia Supplément* xxi, H. Rolland, *Le Mausolée de Glanum* (1969), pls 39–48; *AD* i 13–17.

Arch at Orange: *Gallia Supplément* xiv, R. Amy and others, *L'Arc d'Orange* (1962).

Frieze at Susa: B. M. Felletti Maj, *Atti della Pontificia Accademia, Rendiconti* xxxiii 1960–61 129.

Ara Pacis: G. Moretti, *Ara Pacis Augusti* (1948); Hel ii 673.

Altar of Vicomagistri, Conservatori: *ScR*, figs 33–4.

Camillus: *ScR*, fig. 62; Hel ii No. 1450. 256

Boy from Rhodes: Richter, *AJA* xix 1915 121, pls i–vi; G. Hafner, *Späthellenistische Bildnisplastik* (1954) 17, pl. 4.

Augustus of Prima Porta: *Monumenta Artis Romanae* i, H. Kähler, *Die Augustusstatue von Primaporta* (1959); Ingholt, *Archaeology* 22 1969 177, 304; Gross, *Nachrichten der Akademie der Wissenschaften Göttingen, phil. hist. Kl.* 1959. 8.7 143; Vermeule, *Berytus* xiii 1959 1— cuirass statues.

Head from Meroe: *Liverpool Annals of Art and Archaeology* iv, pls xii–xvi. 258

Livia: V. Poulsen, *Les portraits romains* i (1962) No. 39, pls lxiv–lxv—Ny Carlsberg head; W. H. Gross, *Iulia Augusta* (1962).

Agrippa: *Bull Metr Mus* x 1915 23, fig. 1; Hek 174.

Freedmen stela: Ashmole, *B.M. Quarterly* xx 1956 71.

Heads of mother and daughter: *Bull Metr Mus* x 1915 23, fig. 1. 259

Barracco boy's head: *ScR*, figs 215–16.

Equestrian statues: H. von Roques de Maumont, *Antike Reiterstandbilder* (1958).

Balbus equestrian statues: ibid. 79, figs 41*a*, *b*; Hek 152–3.

Viciria: Hek 205*a*.

Statues of Asia Minor women: K. Humann and C. Watzinger, *Magnesia am Maeander* (1904), figs 198–200.

Later Julio-Claudian emperors: L. Polacco, *Il volto di Tiberio* (1955); *JRS* xxix 1939, pl. **260** xv and *AA* 1938 738, fig. 51—Claudius from Leptis.

'Ludovisi' Antonia: *Opus Nobile* 4, H. von Heintze, *Juno Ludovisi* (1957); Hel iii No. 2341.

Agrippina: Poulsen, op. cit. No. 63, pl. cvii.

Plasma head: *ScR*, fig. 219; cf. Hek 212*b*—marble. 261

Heads of girls: Hek 210–11; *ScR*, fig. 221.

Head from Albania: Hekler, *ÖJh* xv 1912 68, figs 45–9, pls i–ii.

Princess, Ostia Museum: *ScR*, fig. 222; Calza, *Boll d'A* 1921–2 395; G. Traversari, *Aspetti formali della scultura neoclassica* (1968) 116, fig. 7.

Fundilius: Poulsen, op. cit. No. 77, pls cxxxv–cxxxvii.

Fundilia: ibid. No. 78, pls cxxxiv, cxxxviii–cxxxix.

Jucundus: Hek 200; B. Maiuri, *Museo Nazionale di Napoli* (1957) 71 (illd).

Apollo 'Belvedere': cf. p. 202; *ScSc*, fig. 786; Hel i No. 226—ascribing to second century on grounds of technique, ignoring possibility that this is a copy from an earlier Roman variant.

Page 262 'Narcissus': Maiuri, op. cit. 64 (illd); Bienkowski, *ÖJh* i 1898 189, pl. v—life-size; cf. *Winckelmannsfeste zu Berlin* 68, H. Winnefeld, *Hellenistische Silberreliefs* 19, pl. iii. 6–7 —terracottas.

263 Market woman: BrBr 395b, 730; *LGS*, pl. 68; Robinson, *Bull Metr Mus* iv 1909 201, 204.

Pastoral scenes: T. Schreiber, *Die hellenistischen Reliefbilder* (1894).

Prima Porta fresco (now in Terme): *AD* i 11, 60.

Stucco reliefs: *LGS*, pls 86b, 87b; *ScR*, pls xvi–xvii; Wadsworth, *Mem Am Ac* iv 1924 9, pls i–xlix; Bendinelli, *MA* xxxi 1927—Underground Basilica.

264 Munich pastoral: Sieveking, *Festschrift P. Arndt* (1925) 26.

'Campana' reliefs: *RM Erganzungsheft* 14, A. H. Borbein, *Campanareliefs: typologische und stilkritische Untersuchungen* (1968).

Mythological reliefs: *ScR*, pls xva—Perseus, xvb—Endymion, xivb—nymph and satyr child.

Grimani reliefs: Strocka, *AP* iv 87. pls 55–7.

265 Statues of animals: *K...Vatikan* ii; *Art and Archaeology* iii 1916 99, 153; Amelung, *RM* xxiii 1908 1, pls i–iii—peasant and cow.

Archaistic frieze: E. Galli, *Fiesole* 123, figs 109–19.

Jupiter Columns: *ScR*, figs 68–9; Arthur B. Cook, *Zeus* ii.1 (1925), 93, pl. iv.

Sepulchral altars: W. Altmann, *Römischen Grabaltäre der Kaiserzeit* (1905); *ScR*, fig. 39— Amemptus.

Sphinx from chair: Ny Carlsberg No. 41.

266 Head from temple of Isis, New Capitoline Museum (transferred from Conservatori): Bie figs 348–9; R. Delbrück, *Antike Porträts* (1912), pl. 28.

Table supports: G. M. A. Richter, *Ancient Furniture of the Greeks, Etruscans and Romans* (1926), figs 332–6.

CHAPTER XII: ROMAN EXPERIMENTS: VESPASIAN TO TRAJAN (A.D. 69–117) [PAGES 267–278]

267 Emperors' portraits: ed. M. Wegner, *Das römische Herrscherbild*, G. Daltrop, U. Hausmann and M. Wegner, *Die Flavier* (1966); Poulsen, *RM* 29 1914 44—Ny Carlsberg Vespasian.

Lady as Venus: Ny Carlsberg No. 541. **Page 268**

Ulpia Epigone (now in Vatican): *ScR*, pl. xxiii.

Victory of Brescia: Hölscher, *AP* x 67, pls 54–8.

Nile: Hel i No. 440, cf. iii No. 2403—mosaic; Bie, figs 407–9; A. Adriani, *Repertorio d'arte dell'Egitto greco-romano* A ii (1961), pls 41, 70; cf. Lugli, *Bull Comm* xlviii 1920 19, pl. ii—half-draped statue from Domitian's Villa.

Arch of Titus: *ScR*, figs 71–4, pl. xx. **269**

Pompeii sacrifice, Naples: K. Lehmann-Hartleben, *Trajanssäule* (1926), fig. 5. **270**

Haterii: Hel i 773 Nos 1071–7; Castagnoli, *Bull Comm* lxix 1941 59, pls i–iv—identifying some public buildings represented.

Finds from Domitian's Villa: Lugli, *Bull Comm* xlvii 1921, pls 61–75, and xlviii 1922 3. **271**

Forum of Nerva: P. H. von Blanckenhagen, *Flavische Architektur und ihre Dekoration untersucht am Nervaforum* (1940); *ScR*, fig. 84, pls xxix–xxx.

'Cancelleria' reliefs: F. Magi, *I relievi flavi del Palazzo della Cancelleria* (1945).

Domitia: E. Curtius and F. Adler, *Olympia* iii (1894), pl. lxxii.1.

Nerva: Ny Carlsberg No. 542.

Trajan: W. H. Gross, *Bildnisse Traians* (1940) Ny Carlsberg Trajan: ibid. 59, 78, pl. 1; **272** Poulsen, *RM* 29 1914 49, figs. 6–9, pls iii–iv.

Trajanic work on Arch of Constantine: *ScR*, figs 87–91; A. Giuliano, *Arco di Constantino* (1955)—pls.

'Thusnelda': *ScR*, fig. 118; Carpenter, *Mem Am Ac* xviii 1941 63, pls 21B, 22 A, C. **273**

Trajan's Column: L. Rossi, *Trajan's Column and the Dacian Wars* (1971); K. Lehmann-Hartleben, *Trajanssäule* (1926); *ScR*, figs 97–108, pls xxxvi–xxxvii.

Trajan's Trophy: F. B. Florescu, *Das Siegesdenkmal von Adamklissi* (1965). **276**

Philopappus: Santangelo, *ASAA* 1941–3 153—monument, 200—sculptures; C. C. **277** Vermeule, *Roman Imperial Art in Greece and Asia Minor* (1968) 80, fig. 26.

Arch of Benevento: *ScR*, figs 109–16, pls xxxviii–xli; C. Piéranges, *L'arc de Trajan à Benevento* (1943)—set of photographs; F. J. Haspel, *Der Trajansbogen in Benevent* (1966), cf. review by Lepper, *JRS* lix 1969 250.

Portraiture: G. Daltrop, *Die stadtrömischen Privatbildnisse trajanischer und hadrianischer Zeit* **278** (1958), but the bust of figs 9–10 may be a forgery.

Vestal: Hel iii No. 2303.

CHAPTER XIII: VIRTUOSITY: HADRIAN TO CARACALLA (A.D. 117–217) [PAGES 279–299]

THE REIGN OF HADRIAN: J. M. C. Toynbee, *The Hadrianic School* (1934). **279**

Portraits—of Hadrian: ed. M. Wegner, *Das römische Herrscherbild*, M. Wegner, *Hadrian* (1956);—of his empress: Carandini, *Vibia Sabina* (1969).

Cuirass statues: Vermeule, *Berytus*, xii 1959 1, pls iii–xxii, continued xv 1964 95, pls xviii–xxii, and xvi 1966 49, pls xii–xiii.

Page 280 Antinous: W. Clairmont, *Die Bildnisse des Antinous* (1966); Hek 250–53; *D* 202—Delphi.

281 Aphrodisian Sculpture: M. Squarciapino, *La Scuola di Afrodisia* (1943); Toynbee and Ward-Perkins, *Papers of the British School at Rome* xviii 1950 38, pl. xxiv.2—ornament; Picard and Macridy, *BCH* xlv 1921 455—influence on Macedonia.

282 Hunt medallions, Arch of Constantine: BrBr 555, 559, 560, 565; *AD* i 42–3; H. P. L'Orange and A. von Gerkan, *Der Spätantike Bildschmuck des Konstantinsbogen* (1939), figs 2–6.

Conservatori reliefs: *ScR*, figs 126–7.

Athenian heads: Hek 261; *ScR*, fig. 234; P. Graindor, *Marbres et textes antiques d'époque imperiale* (1922) 41, pl. iii.9.

283 Red satyr: Hel i No. 214, ii No. 1420—duplicates found in different parts of Hadrian's Villa.

Head of African: Paribeni, *Saggi...Beloch* (1910) 203, figs 4–5—Terme.

Old Fisherman: Louvre No. 1374, cf. Hel i No. 544, BrBr 164—Vatican.

Syracuse Venus: Cf. J. Charbonneaux, *La Sculpture grecque au Musée du Louvre* (1936), pl. 225—lower half of statue from Tripolitania, misdated as early Hellenistic.

284 Red supporting figures: Hel i No. 30. Cf. for placing, the Giants in the Athens Agora: Thompson, *Hesp* xix 1950 103, pls 61–71.

Spada reliefs: Hel ii 755 Nos 2000–2007; *Papers of British School at Rome* v 1910, pls xvii–xxi.

285 THE ANTONINE AGE: J. M. C. Toynbee, *Art of the Romans* (1965); P. G. Hamberg, *Studies in Roman Imperial Art* (1945).

Ephesus reliefs: C. C. Vermeule, *Roman Imperial Art in Greece and Asia Minor* (1968) 95, figs 34–52.

286 Hadrianeum: E. Nash, *Pictorial Dictionary of Ancient Rome* i (1961), figs 539–67; J. M. C. Toynbee, *The Hadrianic School* (1934), pls 34–5.

Herodes' group: E. Curtius and F. Adler, *Olympia* iii (1894), pls lxv–lxviii.

Vatican Column-base: *ScR*, figs 151–2.

Victory of Calvatone: *Winckelmannsfeste Berlin* 67, Schroder, *Victoria von Calvatone* (1907).

Marcus Aurelius on horse: Hek 266; K. Kluge and K. Lehmann-Hartleben, *Die antiken Grossbronzen* (1927) iii, pls xii, xxv.

Imperial portraits: ed. M. Wegner, *Das römische Herrscherbild*, M. Wegner, *Die Herrscherbildnisse in antoninischer Zeit* (1939).

287 Amorgos head, NM No. 325: Collignon, *BCH* xii 1889 40, pls x–xi.

Cosmetae: Graindor, *BCH* xxxix 1915 241, figs 5–32, pls xvi–xxvi, and xl 1916 74; Hek 258 etc.

288 Archaic sarcophagus at Samos: Kleemann, *Festschrift für F. Matz* (1961) 44, pls 12–15.

Belevi figure on couch: Keil, *ÖJh* xxix 1935 *Beiblatt* 135, figs 52–3.

289 Attic sarcophagi: BMC iii (1904) No. 2303; A. Giuliano, *Il Commercio dei sarcofagi attici* (1962)—distribution; Matz, *Gnomon* 31 1959 693—chronology.

Subjects of sarcophagi: F. Matz, *Die dionysischen Sarkophage* i–iii (1968–9); M. Wegner, *Die Musensarkophage* (1966).

'Casali' Sarcophagus: P. Arndt, *La Glyptothèque Ny Carlsberg* (1896) 213, pl. 152.   **Page 290**

Meleager sarcophagus: *Bull Metr Mus* xvii 1922 34.

'Asiatic' sarcophagi: H. Wiegartz, *Kleinasiatische Säulensarkophage* (1965); Vermeule, **291** *Berytus* xiii 1959 23—Providence; *ScR*, figs 181–2, pl. liv—Torre Nuova; *Sardis* v, C. R. Morey, *Roman and Christian Sculptures* i, *Sarcophagus of Claudia Antonia Sabina* (1924).

Melfi sarcophagus: *ScR*, pls xxxiv–xxxv, lv; Delbrück, *JdI* 28 1913 277.   **292**

Reliefs of Aurelius: I. S. Ryberg, *Panel Reliefs of Marcus Aurelius* (1967); R. B. Bandinelli, *Rome The Centre of Power* (1970), figs 357–9—heads on Arch of Constantine.

'Antonine Column': C. Caprino and others, *La Colonna di Marco Aurelio* (1955); *ScR*, figs **293** 163–75; G. Becatti, *La Colonna coclide istoriata* (1960).

Bust of Commodus: Wegner, op. cit. 265, pls 53–4; Hel ii No. 1486.   **294**

THE DYNASTY OF SEVERUS

Female head, Ny Carlsberg No. 717: P. Arndt and (publisher) Bruckmann, *Griechische und römische Porträts* 767–8.

Vestals: van Deman, *AJA* xii 1908 324, figs 1–17—segregating 7 statues demonstrably of **295** Vestals from the total of 13 found near their House.

Arch of Severus at Rome: R. Brilliant, *Mem Am Ac* xxix 1967; *ScR*, pls lx–lxii.

Arch of Argentarii: ed. E. Nash, Curtius-Nawrath, *Das antike Rom* (1944), pls 143–5.   **296**

Reliefs at Leptis: Ward-Perkins, *JRS* xxxviii 1948 72, pls vii–viii— ornament, 76, pls x–xi —friezes (now at Tripoli), and *Proceedings of British Academy* xxvii 1951 269, cf. Parlasca, *RM* 77 1970 123, pls 56–60—a head of Julia Domna.

Severan reliefs from Salonica: Rüsch, *JdI* 84 1969 148, figs 76–7, 89.

Pediment at Bath: J. M. C. Toynbee, *Art in Roman Britain* (1962) 161, pl. 96, and *Art in Britain under the Romans* (1964) 130, frontispiece and pls xxxvi–xxxii.

Riccardi sarcophagus: Rodenwaldt, *RM* xxxviii–xxxix 1923–4 10, figs 3–4; *ScR*, pl. lvi. **297**

Portraits of Emperors: A. M. McCann, *Mem Am Ac* xxx 1968, *Portraits of Septimius Severus*—89, 132, pls 'C', xxx—Nicosia; ed. M. Wegner, *Das römische Herrscherbild*, H. B. Wiggers and M. Wegner, *Caracalla bis Balbinus* (1971).

'Farnese' Heracles: see p. 207.

'Farnese Bull': Bie, fig. 529; *ScSc* 301, fig 172; Studniczka, *Zeitschrift für den bildender* **298** *Kunst* 1903 171—the Hellenistic group; Nagy, *RM* xl 1925 51, and Pfuhl xli 1926 227— mosaic adaptation of Hellenistic group.

Baalbek tanks: T. Weigand, *Baalbek* i (1921) 93, pls 105–14.   **299**

CHAPTER XIV: THE TRANSITION TO BYZANTINE ART: DECLINE OF THE PAGAN EMPIRE (A.D. 217–337) [PAGES 300–310]

'Ludovisi' sarcophagus: Hel iii No. 2354; *ScR*, fig. 200.   **300**

Page 301 Sidamara sarcophagus: G. Mendel, *Cat...Constantinople* i (1912) No. 112; *M. Piot* ix, pls xvii–xix.

302 Marriage sarcophagus, Ny Carlsberg No. 790. Cf. *JdI Erganzungsheft* xix, F. Matz, *Ein römisches Meisterwerk* (1958)–'Badminton' sarcophagus of *c.* 220–30 in Metr. Mus.

Portraits: B. M. Felletti Maj, *Iconografia romana imperiale* (1958).

303 Philip the Arab: Hel i No. 456.

Trajanus Decius: Floca, *Latomus* xxiv 353, pl. xxiv–Deva; cf. Hel ii No. 1320–Capitoline marble head.

Trebonianus: G. M. A. Richter, *Bronzes... Metr Mus* (1915) No. 350; R. Delbrück, *Bildnisse römischer Kaiser* (1914), pls 34–5.

Pupienus: *ScR*, fig. 242; ed. M. Wegner, *Das römische Herrscherbild*, H. B. Wiggers and M. Wegner, *Caracalla bis Balbinus* (1971), pls 76–7. Cf. for technique Fittschen, *JdI* 84 1969 197–heads supposedly of Gordian III, who reigned 237–244, aged 13–19.

Munich 'Maximin': *ScR*, pl. lxxvi; Delbrück, op. cit., pl. 52.

Old man on couch, Alexandria Museum: P. Graindor, *Bustes et statues-portraits d'Égypte romaine* (1937) 97, pl. xxxix.

304 Female head, Ny Carlsberg No. 753: Poulsen, *JRS* vi 1916 51, pl. viii.

Male heads from Greece: *Kongelige Danske Videnskabernes Selskab* 1913 No. 5, F. Poulsen, *Têtes et Bustes...Ny Carlsberg*–youth and boxer, Nos 469a and b, which L'Orange has ascribed (without explanation) to late Severan period.

Gallienus, Ny Carlsberg No. 768: *JRS* vi 1916, pl. x.

305 Doria-Pamphili statues: H. von Heintze, *AP* i 7, pls 1–18.

Probus and Carinus: *ScR*, pl. lxxvii; Delbrück, op. cit., pls 37–8.

'Diocletian', Ny Carlsberg No. 7716; H. P. L'Orange, *Studien zur Geschichte des spätantiken Porträts* (1933) 30, 35, fig. 66 and *RM* 44 1929 180, pl. 43, cf. pls 37–42–Doria-Pamphili head.

Constantius, Ny Carlsberg No. 774: L'Orange, op. cit. 30, 35 and–Berlin copy–figs 76, 78.

306 Arch of Galerius: C. C. Vermeule, *Roman Imperial Art in Greece and Asia Minor* (1968) 336, figs 171–6; K. P. Kinch, *L'arc de triomphe de Salonique* (1889).

307 Base in Forum: L'Orange, *RM* liii 1938 1, figs 1–7, pls 1–7; H. Kähler, *Das fuenfsaeulendenkmal fuer die Tetrarchen auf den Forum Romanum* (1964); *ScR*, pls lxv–lxvi.

Beginnings of Christian art: Klauser, *Jahrbuch für Antike und Christentum* i 1958 20.

Dumbarton Oaks sarcophagus; G. M. A. Hanfmann, *The Season Sarcophagus in Dumbarton Oaks* (1951).

Arch of Constantine: H. P. L'Orange and A. von Gerkan, *Der spätantike Bildschmuck des Konstantinsbogen* (1939); *ScR*, figs 201–8, pls lxvii–lxviii; A. Giuliano, *Arco di Constantino* (1955)–pls.

Constantine: *ScR*, pl. lxxx–Lateran statue; British School at Rome, *Cat... Conservatori* 5, pl. 1–marble fragments of colossus.

Bronze colossal head: ibid. 173, pl. 60; *ScR*, pl. lxxxi; Hel ii No. 1578–identifying as Constantine.

Edicts: *Codex Theodosianus* xiii Nos iv. 1–4.

APPENDIX I: DEITIES, THEIR ATTRIBUTES AND TYPES [PAGES 311–317]

Arthur B. Cook, *Zeus* (i–iii.2, 1914–40), offers material for a far more extensive list, **Page 311** especially if local or otherwise aberrant forms were to be included.

APPENDIX II: GREEK AND ROMAN DRESS [PAGES 318–321]

M. Bieber, *Griechische Kleidung* (1928); Sir J. E. Sandys, *Companion to Latin Studies* (2nd **318** edn 1921) 190; Mary G. Houston, *Ancient Greek, Roman and Byzantine Costume and Decoration* (2nd edn 1947).

INDEX

Plates are cited in italics. Lists of objects are arranged in approximate chronological order. No references are given to the Appendices.

sleeping Fury, 223; s. Hermaphrodite, 225; s. Eros, 235
smile, archaic, 82, 86, 112, 120; archaistic, 265
Smilis, 68
Smyrna, 229, 231
Socrates, 204, 208
Sofia Museum: stela, 117
Soidas, 128
Sophocles, 204, 218, *56b*
Sorrento, 196
Sosandra, 130
Spada Palace, Rome: reliefs, 284–5
Sparta, 39, 64, 68, 99–100, 104, 111–12, *19c*
Sperlonga, 249–50
sphinx, 83, 97, 265, *6c, 14a, 81d*
Spinario, 42, 57, 244–5, *72c*
stela, 22; *see also* Attic gravestones
Stephanus, 57, 244
Stockholm Museum: relief, 161
Strangford: kouros, 80, 116, *4c*; shield, 136
Stratonicus, 221
Strongylion, 164
stucco reliefs, 43, 263–4
Sunium *kouros*, 76
Suppliant, 150
Susa, arch at, 154
Syracuse: dedications by, 117–18; Museum, Venus, 283–4, *86a*

table support, 266, *81a*
Tanagra, 42
Taranto: goddess, 120; Zeus, 208; reliefs, 210
Tauriscus, 298
Tectaeus, 68
Tegea, 68, 194: Museum, fragments from temple, 193–5, *49a, 49b*
Telecles, 88
Telephanes, 98
Telephus frieze, 230–31, 235, *68c*
Tellus, 255, 285
temples, *see* Architectural sculpture
Tenea *kouros*, 80, *3c*
Teos, 227
Terme, National Museum of the, Rome: Ludovisi head, 120; Apollo, 129; peplos statue, 129, *28c*; Ludovisi Throne, 122, *24a, 24b, 25a*; Discobolus, 131, *28d, 29a*; bearded head, 151; Niobid, 155–6, *37b*; basalt boy, 169; Genetrix, 161–2, *39a*; Hygieia head, 183, *46c*; Ludovisi Ares, 195; Anzio girl, 219–20, *61b*; Ludovisi Gaul and wife, 222–3, *63b*; Dying Asiatic head, 223, *64a*; Fury, 223; bronze Ruler, 232, *69c*; Aphrodite, 241; bronze boxer, 251, *75b*; Ludovisi Juno, 260; stucco reliefs, 263; head of African, 283; Vestal, 278, *85d*; battle sarcophagus, 300
terracotta, 24, 41, 42–3, 60, 61, 66, 71, 72, 100, 138, 244, 264

Thasos, 29, 52, 75, 88, 96, 122, 171, *23b*
Themis from Rhamnus, 217
Theocles, 68
Theocosmus, 41, 42
Theodorus, 36, 46
Theophrastus, 217–18
Thera, 242
Thermon, 100
Theseum: frieze and metopes, 150; cult-statues, 162
Thespiae, 155
Thessaloniki, *see* Salonica
Thessaly, 54, 157, *38b*
Thrasyllus, 219
Thrasymedes, 180
Throne: of Amyclae, 94; Ludovisi and Boston, 52–3, 122, *24–25*; of Zeus at Olympia, 136–8, *Fig. 17*
Thusnelda, 273, *83b*
Thymilus, 191
Tiber: Apollo from, 129; personification, 268–9
Tiberius, 254, 257
Timarchides, 243
Timarchus, 216; *see also* Praxiteles, sons of
Timotheus, 180–81, 196, 200–201
Tisicrates, 215
Titus, Arch of, 267, 269–70
Tivoli, Hadrian's Villa near, 51
topaz, 30
Torlonia, Villa, Rome: Euthydemus, 223–4, *65a*
Torre Nuova, 291
Trajan, 272–8, *82d*
Trajanus Decius, 303
Tralles, 236, 298
Treasuries, 26, 103–4, 105–7, 110–11, *15a, 16, 17a, 19b*
Trebonianus, 303
Tripoli Museum: Claudius, 260, *80b*; frieze from Leptis, 296, *91b*
Triptolemus relief, 58
Trojan Horse, 164
Tropaeum Trajani, 276–7
Troy metopes, 253
Trysa, 175
Tübingen, bronze runner, 115
Tyche, 22, 215, 216, *59b, 60a*
Tyrannicides, 86, *114–16, 21b*
Twelve Gods, Altar of, 163

Uffizi Gallery, Florence: Heracles, 207; Marsyas group, 220–21, *62b, 62c*; satyr inviting to dance, 226, *60a*; Niobid group, 227, *66b*; Dionysus Narcissus, 262
Ulpia Epigone, 268
Urartu, 64

Varro, 44, 159
Varvakeion statuette, 135, *30a*

ILLUSTRATIONS

PLATE 1

a Dreros goddess
(Iraklion)

b 'Auxerre'
statuette (Louvre)

c 'Auxerre'
statuette, restored cast

d Mycenae relief
(Athens)

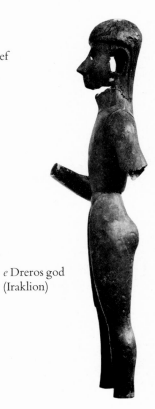

e Dreros god
(Iraklion)

PLATE 2

a Cleobis (Delphi)

b–d Kouros (New York)

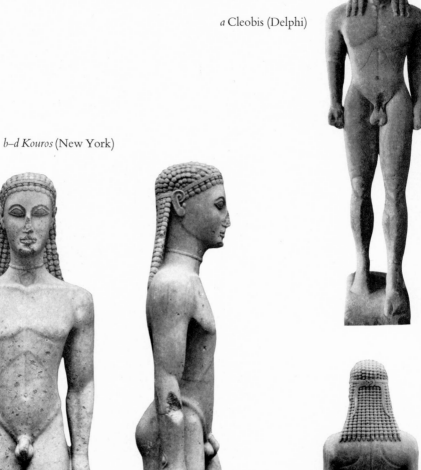

PLATE 3

Boeotian head (Athens)

b Boeotian *Kouros*
(British Museum)

c Tenea *Kouros* (Munich)

PLATE 4

a, b Piraeus *Kouros* Athens)

c 'Strangford' *Kouros*
(British Museum)

d 'Critian Boy' (Acropolis)

PLATE 5

a Three-headed monster (Acropolis)

b 'Moschophorus' (Acropolis)   *c* 'Rampin' horseman, casts

PLATE 6

a 'Blond Boy' (Acropolis)

b Head of Hera (Olympia)

c Naxian sphinx (Delphi)

PLATE 7

'Peplos' *Kore* (Acropolis)

PLATE 8

a Nike 'of Archermus' (Athens)

b Head of 'Peplos' *Kore* (Acropolis)

PLATE 9

a Kore 682 (Acropolis)

b Antenor's *Kore* (Acropolis)

PLATE 10

a Kore 674 (Acropolis)

b Euthydicus' *Kore* (Acropolis)

PLATE 11

b Kore 677 (Acropolis)

a Cheramyes' *Kore* (Louvre)

c Samian head (Istanbul)

PLATE 12

a Branchidae statue (British Museum)

b Ephesus fragment (British Museum)

c, d Ephesus fragments (British Museum)

PLATE 13

a Didyma fragment (Berlin)

b 'Harpy Tomb' (British Museum)

PLATE 14

a Xanthus sphinx (British Museum)

b, c Sele metopes (Paestum)

PLATE 15

a Sicyonian Treasury
metope (Delphi)

b Laconian stela (Berlin)

PLATE 16

a Siphnian Treasury
caryatid (Delphi)

b Siphnian Treasury
frieze (Delphi)

PLATE 17

a Siphnian Treasury frieze (Delphi)

b Boeotian stela
(Boston)

c Eretria group
(Chalcis)

PLATE 18

b Head of Aristion's stela (Athens)

a Stela of runner (Athens)

c 'Cat and dog' base
(Athens)

PLATE 19

Athletes on base (Athens)

Athenian Treasury metope (Delphi)

c 'Leonidas' (Sparta)

PLATE 20

a Aegina pedimental group (Munich)

b Aegina pedimental figure (Munich)

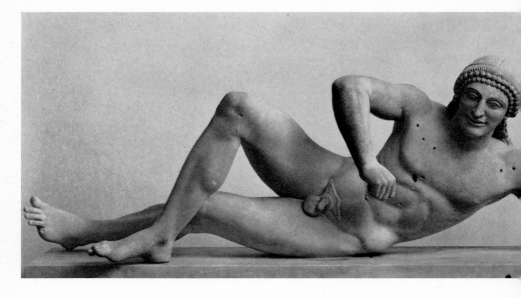

PLATE 21

a Bronze head (Athens)

b Tyrannicides, restored casts

c Alxenor's stela (Athens)

PLATE 22

a Head of Charioteer (Delphi)

c 'Esquiline' stela (Conservatori)

b Head of Taranto goddess (Berlin)

PLATE 23

a 'Leucothea' stela (Villa Albani)

b Thasos relief (Istanbul)

PLATE 24

a Flautist on 'Ludovisi Throne'
(Terme)

b Front of 'Ludovisi Throne'
(Terme)

PLATE 25

a Censer on 'Ludovisi Throne'
(Terme)

b Head on 'Throne' (Boston)

c Front of 'Throne' (Boston)

PLATE 26

a Metope (Olympia)

b Metope (Louvre and Olympia)

c, d Pedimental figures (Olympia)

PLATE 27

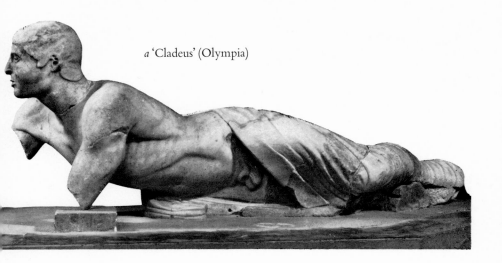

a 'Cladeus' (Olympia)

b 'Penelope' (Teheran)

c 'Chatsworth Head' (British Museum)

PLATE 28

a 'Choiseul-
Gouffier Apollo'
(British Museum)

b Artemisium 'Zeus' (Athens)

d Discobolus (Terme)

c Peplos statue
(Terme)

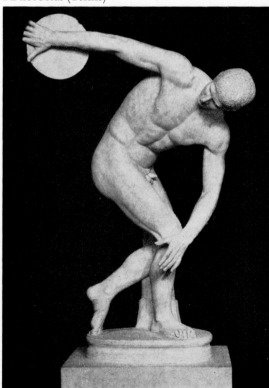

PLATE 29

a Head of 'Lancelotti' discobolus, cast

b Marsyas Group, restored casts

c 'Mourning' Athena (Athens)

PLATE 30

a 'Varvakeion' statuette
(Athens)

b Parthenon metope
(British Museum)

PLATE 31

a Parthenon metope
(British Museum)

b Parthenon frieze
(Acropolis)

PLATE 32

a Head 699
(Acropolis)

b Parthenon frieze, cast

PLATE 33

a Head on Parthenon frieze
(British Museum)

b 'Theseus' (British Museum)

PLATE 34

a 'Fates' (British Museum)

b 'Iris' (British Museum)

c 'Lemnian' Athena (Dresden)

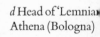

d Head of 'Lemnian' Athena (Bologna)

PLATE 35

a Head of Nike
(Agora)

b Bust of Pericles
(British Museum)

c Head of Amazon
(Conservatori)

d 'Doryphorus'
(Naples)

PLATE 36

a 'Diadumenus' (Athens)

b 'Diadumenus' head (Dresden)

d Boy victor
(Ashmolean)

c 'Doryphorus' bust (Naples)

PLATE 37

Niobid (Copenhagen)

b Niobid (Terme)

PLATE 38

a 'Giustiniani' stela (Berlin)

b Head of Thessalian stela (Athens)

c Athena (New Capitoline)

PLATE 39

a 'Genetrix' (Terme)

b Erechtheum caryatid (British Museum)

c Nike Temple frieze (British Museum)

d 'Satrap' sarcophagus (Istanbul)

PLATE 40

a Nike parapet (Acropolis)

b Hegeso's stela
(Cerameicus)

PLATE 41

a Maenad (Conservatori)

b Head from Argive Heraeum (Athens)

PLATE 42

Dexileus' stela (Cerameicus)

PLATE 43

a 'Idolino' (Florence)

b Paeonius' Nike, restored model

c Bassae frieze (British Museum)

PLATE 44

a Gjölbaschi frieze (Vien

b 'Nereid' (British Museum)

PLATE 45

a Epidaurus acroterion (Athens)

b 'Lycian' sarcophagus (Istanbul)

PLATE 46

b Eirene and Plutus (Munich)

a Male head (Fogg Museum)

d 'Hope' Hygieia (Los Angeles)

c Head of Hygieia (Terme)

PLATE 47

a Head of Hermes (Olympia)

b Head of Apollo (Dresden)

c Head of Hypnos (British Museum)

d Hypnos (Madrid)

PLATE 48

b Head of Aphrodite (Be

a 'Cnidian' Aphrodite (Vatican)

c 'Leconfield Head' (Petworth)

d 'Aberdeen Head' (British Museum)

PLATE 49

a Nike (Tegea)

b Head from pediment (Tegea)

enad (Dresden)

d Head of Heracles (British Museum)

PLATE 50

a Head of boxer (Olympia)

b Mourners (Istanbul)

PLATE 51

a 'Eubouleus' (Athens)

b Anticythera statue (Athens)

PLATE 52

a Artemisia and Mausolus (British Museum)

b Amazon frieze (British Museum)

PLATE 53

a Charioteer (British Museum)

b Charioteer (British Museum)

c Head of Alexander (Acropolis)

PLATE 54

a Demeter (British Museum)

b Kairos (Trogir)

PLATE 55

Ephesus column-base (British Museum)

PLATE 56

Delos 'Herculaneum Woman'
(Athens)

b Sophocles (Vatican)

PLATE 57

a 'Apoxyomenus' (Vatican)

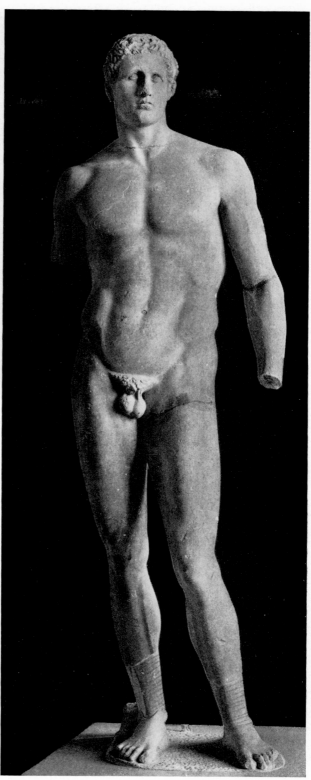

b Agias (Delphi)

PLATE 58

b Alexander on sarcophagus (Istanbul)

a 'Ilissus' stela (Athens)

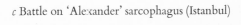
c Battle on 'Alexander' sarcophagus (Istanbul)

PLATE 59

Praying Boy (Berlin)

b Tyche of Antioch (Vatican)

c Tyche of Antioch (Budapest)

PLATE 60

a ? Tyche (Conservatori)

b 'Chios Head' (Boston)

c Head of Menander (Philadelphia)

d Demosthenes
(Vatican)

a Head of Demosthenes (Ashmolean)

b 'Anzio Girl' (Terme)

c Poet (Copenhagen)

PLATE 62

a Aphrodite
(Vatican)

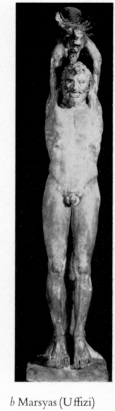

b Marsyas (Uffizi)

c Knifegrinder
(Uffizi)

PLATE 63

Dying Gaul (Capitoline)

Ludovisi' Gauls (Terme)

PLATE 64

a Dying Asiatic (Terme)

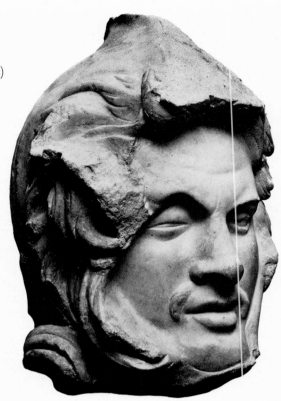

b Ptolemy IV (Boston)

c Arsinoe III (Boston)

PLATE 65

a Head of Euthydemus
(Rome: Villa Torlonia)

c Centaur (Capitoline)

b Dead Amazon (Naples)

PLATE 66

a Satyr (Uffizi)

b Niobe (Uffizi)

c 'South Slope Head' (Athens)

PLATE 67 (facing page
a, *b* Gigantomachy (Be

PLATE 67

PLATE 68

a Pergamon female head (Berlin)

b Head of Centaur (Conservatori)

c Telephus frieze (Berlin)

PLATE 69

a Erythrae woman
(British Museum)

b Magnesia woman (Istanbul)

c Head of Ruler (Terme)

PLATE 70

b Head of Artemis
(Athens)

a Boy boxer (Istanbul)

c 'Borghese Warrior' (Louvre)

PLATE 71

a Apotheosis of Homer (British Museum)

b, c Portraits from Delos (Athens)

PLATE 72

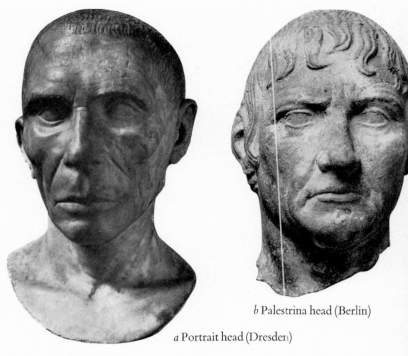

b Palestrina head (Berlin)

a Portrait head (Dresden)

c Boy pulling out thorn
(Capitoline)

PLATE 73

Seasons (Louvre)

Deities (Copenhagen)

c Laocoon's son (Vatican)

PLATE 74

PLATE 75

a Census (Louvre)

b Boxer (Terme)

PLATE 74 (facing page)
Married couple (Vatican)

Sea-deities (Munich)

PLATE 76

a Head of 'Pseudo-Seneca' (Naples)

b Battle (Glanum)

c Procession (Ara Pacis Museum)

PLATE 77

a Augustus (Vatican)

b Head of girl (New York)

PLATE 78

a Allegory (Ara Pacis Museum)

b Head of Livia (Copenhagen)

PLATE 79

a Freedmen's stela
(British Museum)

b Balbus on horseback
(Naples)

PLATE 80

a Viciria (Naples)

b Claudius
(Tripoli)

c Head of Agrippina
(Copenhagen)

d Fundilius
(Copenhagen)

PLATE 81

a Market woman (New York)

b Peasant and cow (Munich)

c Table-support
(Chicago)

d Head of sphinx
(Copenhagen)

PLATE 82

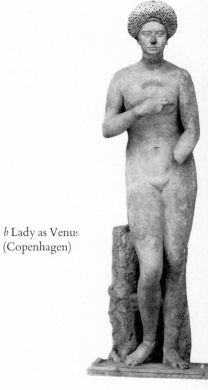

b Lady as Venus
(Copenhagen)

a Head of Vespasian (Copenhagen)

c Relief of tomb (Vatican)

d Trajan
(Copenhagen)

PLATE 83

a Head of Dacian (Berlin)

b 'Thusnelda'
(Loggia dei Lanzi

c Campaign scene (Trajan's Column)

PLATE 84

a Deities (Benevento)

b Antinous (Delphi)

d Aphrodisian
ornament (Istanbul)

c Head of Antinous (Louvre)

PLATE 85

a Hadrian's hunt (Arch of Constantine)

b Portrait head (Dresden)

(below)
Head of
African
Dresden)

d Vestal (Terme)

PLATE 86

b Bust of ?Verus (Copenhagen)

a Venus (Syracuse)

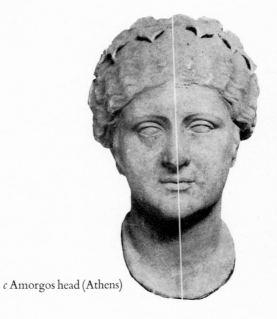

c Amorgos head (Athens)

PLATE 87

a Amazon sarcophagus (British Museum)

b 'Casali' sarcophagus (Copenhagen)

c Cupids
sarcophagus
(Providence)

PLATE 88

a Sarcophagus
(Melfi)

b Bounty
(Arch of Constantine)

PLATE 89

a Campaign scene (Antonine Column)

b Bust of Commodus (Conservatori)

c Portrait head (Copenhagen)

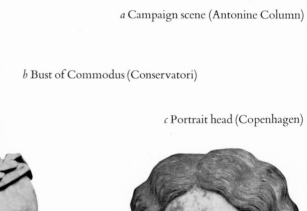

PLATE 90

a Fisherman (Louvre)

b Soldiers
(Arch of Severus)

PLATE 91

a Parthian captive (Arch of Severus)

b Leptis frieze (Tripoli)

PLATE 92

a 'Farnese Bull' (Naples)

b Sidamara sarcophagus (Istanbul)

PLATE 93

a Wedding (Copenhagen)

Bust of Philip
e Arab
atican)

c Portrait head
(Copenhagen)

PLATE 94

a Head of Youth
(Copenhagen)

b Head of Gallienus
(Copenhagen)

c Base of Tetrarch Column (Forum)

PLATE 95

a Head of ?Diocletian
(Copenhagen)

b Head of Constantius
(Copenhagen)

c Panel of Arch of Galerius (Salonica)

PLATE 96

a Frieze (Arch of Constantine)

b Head of Constantine (Conservatori)